I0762814

THE ENCYCLOPEDIA OF
ITALIAN FOOD

THE ENCYCLOPEDIA OF ITALIAN FOOD

OVER 400 CLASSIC RECIPES CELEBRATING ITALIAN TRADITIONS

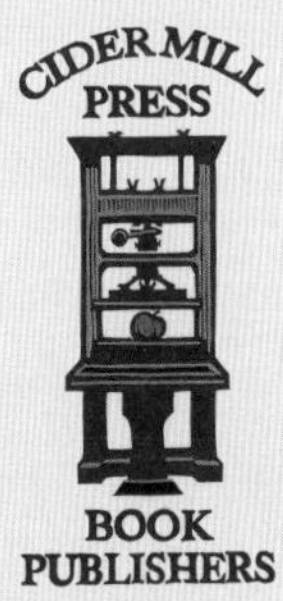

The Encyclopedia of Italian Food

 • Published by Cider Mill Press, an imprint of HarperCollins Focus LLC, 501 Nelson Place, Nashville, TN 37214 USA. • 13-Digit ISBN: 978-1-40035-514-3 • 10-Digit ISBN: 1-40035-514-1 • Books published by Cider Mill Press Book Publishers are available at special discounts for bulk purchases in the United States by corporations, institutions, and other organizations. For more information, please contact the publisher. • cidermillpress.com • HarperCollins Publishers, Macken House, 39/40 Mayor Street Upper, • Dublin 1, D01 C9W8, Ireland (https://www.harpercollins.com) • Typography: Hansief, Freight Sans, Freight Serif • Pages 29, 55, 79, 281, 286–287, 334, and 370–371 courtesy of Unsplash. All other images used under official license from Shutterstock. • Printed in Vietnam • 26 27 28 29 30 SEA 5 4 3 2 1 • First Edition

CONTENTS

INTRODUCTION

When asked what they think of Italian food, most people respond enthusiastically. Ask those same people what their favorite offering from the cuisine is, and many, maybe even an overwhelming majority, will offer up something like pizza, chicken Parmesan, penne alla vodka, or pasta primavera.

Purists will roll their eyes at these responses, but they do reflect a development that has been underway since large numbers of Italians begin to emigrate to the United States beginning in the early twentieth century: Italian food in America has developed into something else entirely, taking the cuisine increasingly toward the comforting, king-sized dishes that diners in the US tend to envision when "What about Italian?" comes up as dinner plans are being discussed.

This development, while no doubt delicious, does keep too many unaware of the emphasis on simplicity, freshness, and exceptional ingredients that drives the cuisine back in Italy, a trio so powerful that the country has come to be viewed as the world's culinary mecca by many of the food world's biggest superstars, who return year after year for inspiration.

This book takes its cue from them, focusing on Italian food as you would find it back in Italy, or in an especially authentic Italian restaurant. It seeks to celebrate Italian cuisine's unique ability to produce dishes that feel as fresh, vibrant, and contemporary as they would have centuries ago. To do this, recipes for those modern favorites mentioned above are pushed aside for the regional specialties at the heart of the cuisine.

This shift in focus reveals that what we refer to as "Italian" is actually much more nuanced, and difficult to frame with such a general term. Olive oil, for instance, which is closely identified with Italian cuisine the world over, is a staple only in Southern Italy and in specific regions of Central and Northern Italy, like Tuscany and Liguria. Other regional cuisines use different fats in cooking—traditionally lard, and occasionally butter. And while dried pasta is ubiquitous in the South and in parts of Central Italy, fresh egg pasta is the whole show in the North. Similarly, while rice is rarely utilized in Southern and Central Italy's cuisines, it is a staple in Northern Italy's cuisine. Traditional dishes in Southern Italy are largely vegetarian, while dishes in Northern and Central Italy tend to be more carnivorous.

In short, there is not one Italian cuisine, but many. This book showcases a good number of them, a richness and variety that leaves no doubt as to why Italian food has managed to conquer the world like no other cuisine. On each and every page, one will discover the reason it is able to supply such unprecedented satisfaction: every single dish tastes like home.

PASTA

Scialatielli

YIELD: 1½ LBS. / **ACTIVE TIME:** 30 MINUTES / **TOTAL TIME:** 1 HOUR

3¾ CUPS (450 G) FINELY GROUND DURUM WHEAT FLOUR, PLUS MORE AS NEEDED

⅞ CUP (200 ML) WHOLE MILK

1 LARGE EGG, LIGHTLY BEATEN

HANDFUL OF FRESH BASIL, FINELY CHOPPED

1 OZ. (30 G) PECORINO CHEESE, GRATED

2 TEASPOONS (10 G) EXTRA-VIRGIN OLIVE OIL

SALT, TO TASTE

1. Place the flour, milk, egg, basil, and pecorino in a large bowl and work the mixture until it starts to come together as a dough.
2. Add the olive oil and work the dough until it has been incorporated.
3. Transfer the dough to a flour-dusted work surface and knead it energetically until it is a smooth and homogeneous dough, about 10 minutes.
4. Cover the dough with plastic wrap and let it rest at room temperature for 30 minutes.
5. Divide the dough into two pieces. Cover one piece with plastic wrap and place the other piece on a flour-dusted work surface.
6. Roll the dough out into a rectangle that is about ⅕ inch thick. Sprinkle flour over the dough and, working from the long sides, roll up the dough from the edges so that they meet in the center.
7. Cut the dough into ⅖-inch-thick rings, unroll them, and dust them with flour. Let them dry until they are ready to be boiled.
8. Repeat Steps 6 and 7 with the other piece of dough.
9. To cook the scialatielli, bring water to a boil in a large saucepan. Add salt, let the water return to a boil, and add the scialatielli. Cook until they are al dente, about 5 minutes.

Cavatelli

YIELD: 1½ LBS. / **ACTIVE TIME:** 1 HOUR / **TOTAL TIME:** 1 HOUR AND 30 MINUTES

3¾ CUPS (450 G) FINELY GROUND DURUM WHEAT FLOUR, PLUS MORE AS NEEDED

1 (SCANT) CUP (225 ML) WATER, AT ROOM TEMPERATURE

PINCH OF TABLE SALT, PLUS MORE TO TASTE

1. Place all of the ingredients in a large bowl and work the mixture until it starts to come together as a dough.
2. Transfer the dough to a flour-dusted work surface and knead it energetically until it is a smooth and homogeneous dough, about 10 minutes.
3. Cover the dough with plastic wrap and let it rest at room temperature for 30 minutes.
4. Tear the dough into small pieces and form them into logs that are about ¼ inch thick. Cut the logs into 1-inch-long pieces.
5. Press down on one side of the cavatelli with the tips of your index and middle fingers, making a movement that first pushes it forward and then comes back, rolling the pasta so that it forms a hollow in the middle. Transfer the cavatelli to a flour-dusted baking sheet and let them dry.
6. To cook the cavatelli, bring water to a boil in a large saucepan. Add salt, let the water return to a boil, and add the cavatelli. Cook until they are al dente, about 8 minutes.

Fusilli al Ferro

YIELD: 1½ LBS. / **ACTIVE TIME:** 1 HOUR / **TOTAL TIME:** 1 HOUR AND 30 MINUTES

3¾ CUPS (450 G) FINELY GROUND DURUM WHEAT FLOUR, PLUS MORE AS NEEDED

1 (SCANT) CUP (225 ML) WATER, AT ROOM TEMPERATURE

PINCH OF TABLE SALT, PLUS MORE TO TASTE

1. Place all of the ingredients in a large bowl and work the mixture until it starts to come together as a dough.
2. Transfer the dough to a flour-dusted work surface and knead it energetically until it is a smooth and homogeneous dough, about 10 minutes.
3. Cover the dough with plastic wrap and let it rest at room temperature for 30 minutes.
4. Tear the dough into small pieces and form them into logs that are about ⅕ inch thick. Cut the logs into 3-inch-long pieces.
5. Coat a long, thin metal rod or a wooden skewer with flour. Working with one piece of pasta at a time, wrap it around the implement to form it into a spiral. Gently remove the fusilli from the implement, taking care not to undo the spiral. Transfer the fusilli to a flour-dusted baking sheet and let them dry.
6. To cook the fusilli, bring water to a boil in a large saucepan. Add salt, let the water return to a boil, and add the fusilli. Let them float to the surface and cook for another 3 minutes.

Lagane

YIELD: 1 LB. / **ACTIVE TIME:** 1 HOUR / **TOTAL TIME:** 5 HOURS

1¼ CUPS (150 G) FINELY GROUND DURUM WHEAT FLOUR, PLUS MORE AS NEEDED

1¼ CUPS (150 G) ALL-PURPOSE FLOUR

⅔ CUP (150 ML) WATER, AT ROOM TEMPERATURE

PINCH OF TABLE SALT, PLUS MORE TO TASTE

1. Place all of the ingredients in a large bowl and work the mixture until it starts to come together as a dough.
2. Transfer the dough to a flour-dusted work surface and knead it energetically until it is a smooth and homogeneous dough, about 10 minutes.
3. Cover the dough with plastic wrap and let it rest at room temperature for 30 minutes.
4. Divide the dough into two pieces. Cover one piece with plastic wrap and place the other piece on a flour-dusted work surface.
5. Roll the dough out into a ⅛-inch-thick sheet. Roll the dough up around the rolling pin, gently slide it off, and cut it into 1-inch-wide strips. Unroll the strips and place them on a flour-dusted baking sheet. Repeat with the remaining piece of dough.
6. Dust the lagane with flour, cover with kitchen towels, and let them rest for 2 to 3 hours before cooking.
7. To cook the lagane, bring water to a boil in a large saucepan. Add salt, let the water return to a boil, and add the lagane. Cook until they are al dente, about 5 minutes.

Busiate

YIELD: 1½ LBS. / **ACTIVE TIME:** 1 HOUR / **TOTAL TIME:** 1 HOUR AND 30 MINUTES

3¾ CUPS (450 G) FINELY GROUND DURUM WHEAT FLOUR, PLUS MORE AS NEEDED

1 (SCANT) CUP (225 ML) WATER, AT ROOM TEMPERATURE

PINCH OF TABLE SALT, PLUS MORE TO TASTE

1. Place all of the ingredients in a large bowl and work the mixture until it starts to come together as a dough.
2. Transfer the dough to a flour-dusted work surface and knead it energetically until it is a smooth and homogeneous dough, about 10 minutes.
3. Cover the dough with plastic wrap and let it rest at room temperature for 30 minutes.
4. Place the dough on a flour-dusted work surface, tear small pieces from it, and shape them into ¼-inch-thick logs. Cut the logs into 6-inch-long strands.
5. Coat a long, thin metal rod or a wooden skewer with flour. Working with one piece of pasta at a time, wrap it around the implement to form it into a long spiral. Gently remove the busiate from the implement, taking care not to undo the spiral. Transfer them to a flour-dusted baking sheet and let them dry.
6. To cook the busiate, bring water to a boil in a large saucepan. Add salt, let the water return to a boil, and add the busiate. Cook until they are al dente, 7 to 8 minutes.

Maccheroni al Ferretto

YIELD: 1½ LBS. / **ACTIVE TIME:** 1 HOUR / **TOTAL TIME:** 1 HOUR AND 30 MINUTES

3¾ CUPS (450 G) FINELY GROUND DURUM WHEAT FLOUR, PLUS MORE AS NEEDED

1 (SCANT) CUP (225 ML) WATER, AT ROOM TEMPERATURE

PINCH OF TABLE SALT, PLUS MORE TO TASTE

1. Place all of the ingredients in a large bowl and work the mixture until it starts to come together as a dough.
2. Transfer the dough to a flour-dusted work surface and knead it energetically until it is a smooth and homogeneous dough, about 10 minutes.
3. Cover the dough with plastic wrap and let it rest at room temperature for 30 minutes.
4. Tear the dough into small pieces and form them into logs that are about ⅓ inch thick. Cut the logs into 2-inch-long pieces.
5. Coat a long, thin metal rod or a wooden skewer with flour. Working with one piece of pasta at a time, press the implement into the center of the log, creating a hollow. Roll the implement back and forth until the pasta closes around it. Gently remove the maccheroni from the implement, taking care not to unfold it. Transfer the maccheroni to a flour-dusted baking sheet and let them dry.
6. To cook the maccheroni, bring water to a boil in a large saucepan. Add salt, let the water return to a boil, and add the maccheroni. Let them float to the surface and cook until al dente, about 5 minutes.

Sagne Ncannulate

YIELD: 1½ LBS. / **ACTIVE TIME:** 1 HOUR / **TOTAL TIME:** 3 HOURS AND 30 MINUTES

3¾ CUPS (450 G) FINELY GROUND DURUM WHEAT FLOUR, PLUS MORE AS NEEDED

1 (SCANT) CUP (225 ML) WATER, AT ROOM TEMPERATURE

2 PINCHES OF TABLE SALT, PLUS MORE TO TASTE

1. Place all of the ingredients in a large bowl and work the mixture until it starts to come together as a dough.
2. Transfer the dough to a flour-dusted work surface and knead it energetically until it is a smooth and homogeneous dough, about 10 minutes.
3. Cover the dough with plastic wrap and let it rest at room temperature for 15 minutes.
4. Place the dough on a flour-dusted work surface and roll into a ⅒-inch-thick sheet.
5. Cut the dough in half with a pasta wheel, and then cut it into 10-inch-long strips that are about ½ inch wide.
6. Dust the sagne with flour, pull the ends in opposite directions to twist them, and then bring the ends together so that the pasta has a horseshoe shape.
7. Place the sagne on a flour-dusted baking sheet and let them dry for 2 to 3 hours.
8. To cook the sagne, bring water to a boil in a large saucepan. Add salt, let the water return to a boil, and add the sagne. Cook until they are al dente, 7 to 8 minutes.

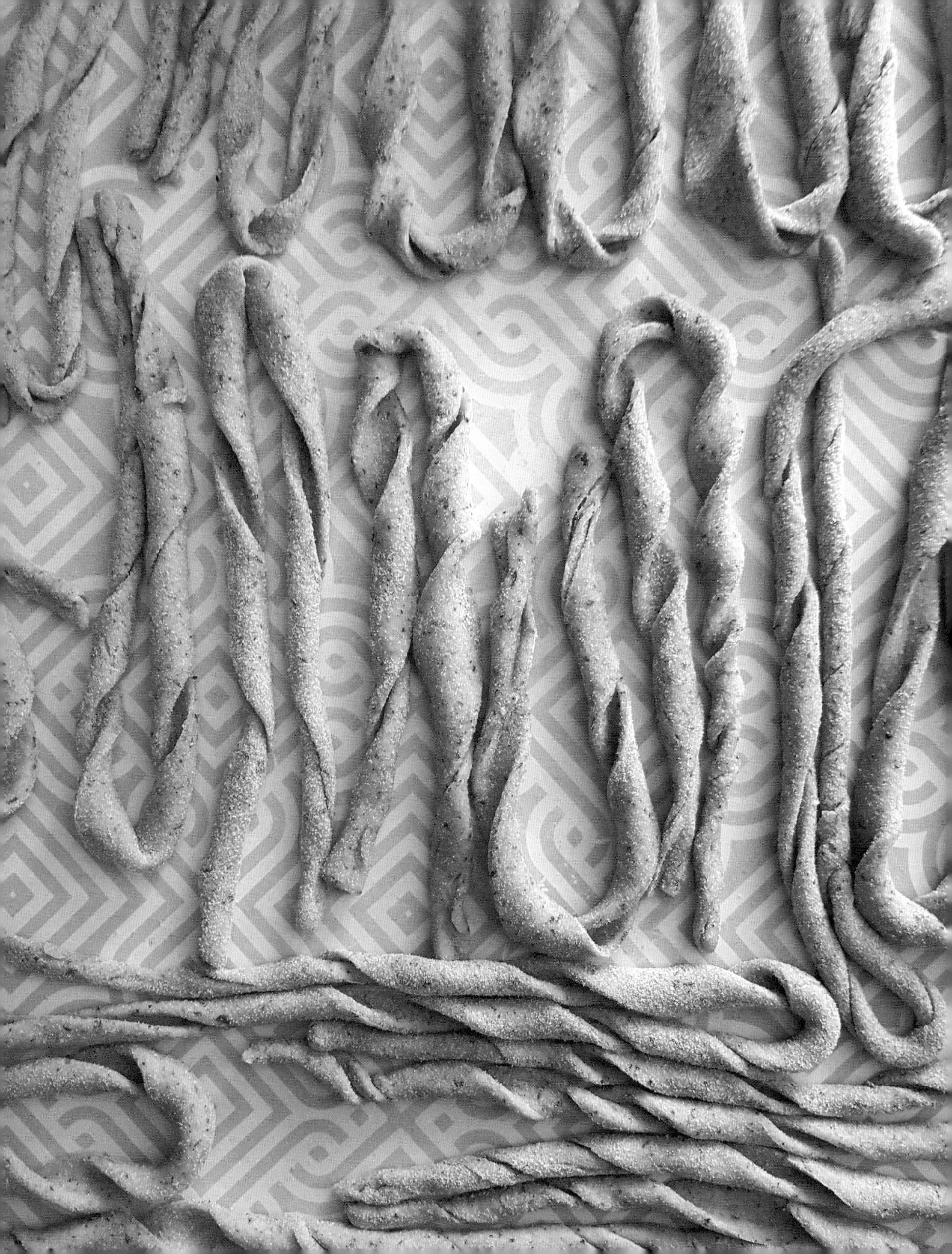

Fregola

YIELD: 1½ LBS. / **ACTIVE TIME:** 1 HOUR / **TOTAL TIME:** 1 HOUR AND 30 MINUTES

¾ TEASPOON (0.4 G) SAFFRON THREADS

1 CUP PLUS 2 TABLESPOONS (269 ML) LUKEWARM WATER (90°F)

3¾ CUPS (450 G) COARSE SEMOLINA FLOUR

1. Line a baking sheet with parchment paper. Place the saffron and water in a bowl and let the mixture steep for 30 minutes.
2. Place 2 tablespoons of flour and a tablespoon of saffron water in a terracotta dish or shallow ceramic bowl. Rub the moistened flour continuously against the bottom of the dish until it comes together in ⅙-inch balls. Transfer the fregola to the baking sheet.
3. Repeat Step 2 until all of the flour has been used up.
4. To cook the fregola, preheat the oven to 390°F. Place them in the oven and bake until they are lightly browned, about 20 minutes.

Spaghetti alla Nerano

YIELD: 4 SERVINGS / **ACTIVE TIME:** 15 MINUTES / **TOTAL TIME:** 30 MINUTES

½ CUP PLUS 3 TABLESPOONS EXTRA-VIRGIN OLIVE OIL

1½ LBS. ZUCCHINI, THINLY SLICED

SALT AND PEPPER, TO TASTE

14 OZ. SPAGHETTI

2 GARLIC CLOVES

7 OZ. PROVOLONE CHEESE, GRATED

2 OZ. PARMIGIANO REGGIANO CHEESE, GRATED

20 FRESH BASIL LEAVES

1. Place ½ cup of olive oil in a large, deep skillet and warm it to 350°F. Add the zucchini to the hot oil and fry until they are starting to brown, turning as necessary. Transfer the fried zucchini to a paper towel–lined plate to drain and season them with salt.
2. Bring water to a boil in a large saucepan. Add salt, let the water return to a full boil, and add the pasta. Cook until the pasta is very al dente. Reserve 1½ cups pasta water and drain the spaghetti.
3. Place the remaining olive oil in a large skillet and warm it over medium heat. Add the garlic, cook for 2 minutes, and then remove it from the pan.
4. Add the pasta to the garlic oil and toss to combine.
5. Add some of the pasta water and the cheeses and toss until well combined and the pasta is al dente.
6. Add the fried zucchini, half of the basil, and more pasta water if it is needed and gently toss to combine.
7. Stir in the remaining basil, season the dish with black pepper, and enjoy.

Culurgiones

YIELD: 40 CULURGIONES / **ACTIVE TIME:** 2 HOURS / **TOTAL TIME:** 24 HOURS

FOR THE FILLING

2 TABLESPOONS EXTRA-VIRGIN OLIVE OIL

2 GARLIC CLOVES, PEELED

SALT, TO TASTE

1½ LBS. POTATOES, PEELED

20 FRESH MINT LEAVES

1½ CUPS GRATED PECORINO CHEESE

FOR THE DOUGH

2 CUPS PLUS 1½ TABLESPOONS (250 G) FINELY GROUND DURUM WHEAT FLOUR, PLUS MORE AS NEEDED

1 CUP PLUS 1 TABLESPOON (127.5 G) ALL-PURPOSE FLOUR

⅔ CUP (160 ML) LUKEWARM WATER (90°F)

1 TABLESPOON (14 G) EXTRA-VIRGIN OLIVE OIL

¼ TEASPOON (1.5 G) TABLE SALT, PLUS MORE TO TASTE

1. The day before you are going to prepare the culurgiones, prepare the filling. Place the olive oil and garlic in an airtight container and let the mixture steep for 6 hours.
2. Bring water to a boil in a large saucepan. Add salt and the potatoes and cook until they are tender. Drain the potatoes, place them in a bowl, and mash until they are smooth. Add the mint and pecorino and stir to incorporate. Strain the olive oil into the filling and stir to incorporate. Chill the filling in the refrigerator overnight.
3. Remove the filling from the refrigerator and let it rest at room temperature.
4. To begin preparations for the dough, place all of the ingredients in a large bowl and work the mixture until it starts to come together as a dough.
5. Transfer the dough to a flour-dusted work surface and knead it energetically until it is a smooth and homogeneous dough, about 10 minutes.
6. Cover the dough with plastic wrap and let it rest at room temperature for 30 minutes.
7. Place the dough on a flour-dusted work surface and roll it into a ⅒-inch-thick sheet (you can also use a pasta maker to do this). Cut the dough into 5-inch rounds.
8. Form tablespoons of the filling into patties and place them in the center of the rounds. Fold the dough over the filling to form half-moons.
9. To seal the culurgiones and give them the correct shape, it's best to watch a video, of which there are many online. You want to fold in one end of each culurgiones, and then fold one side over the other, making pleats as you do to seal in the filling.
10. To cook the culurgiones, bring water to a boil in a large saucepan. Add salt, let the water return to a boil, and add the culurgiones. Cook for about 6 minutes.

Orecchiette

YIELD: 1½ LBS. / **ACTIVE TIME:** 1 HOUR / **TOTAL TIME:** 1 HOUR AND 30 MINUTES

3¾ CUPS (450 G) FINELY GROUND DURUM WHEAT FLOUR, PLUS MORE AS NEEDED

1 (SCANT) CUP (225 ML) WATER, AT ROOM TEMPERATURE

2 PINCHES OF TABLE SALT, PLUS MORE TO TASTE

1. Place all of the ingredients in a large bowl and work the mixture until it starts to come together as a dough.
2. Transfer the dough to a flour-dusted work surface and knead it energetically until it is a smooth and homogeneous dough, about 10 minutes.
3. Cover the dough with plastic wrap and let it rest at room temperature for 30 minutes.
4. Divide the dough into three pieces. Cover two pieces with plastic wrap and place the other on a flour-dusted work surface.
5. Shape the dough into a ⅖-inch-thick log and cut it into ⅖-inch-long pieces.
6. Using a knife with a smooth blade, shape the pieces into orecchiette by running the knife over their tops to drag them toward you. Use your thumb to turn the orecchiette over. Transfer them to flour-dusted baking sheets.
7. Repeat Steps 5 and 6 with the remaining pieces of dough.
8. To cook the orecchiette, bring water to a boil in a large saucepan. Add salt, let the water return to a full boil, and add the orecchiette. Cook until they are al dente, about 5 minutes.

Spaghetti alla Chitarra

YIELD: 1 LB. / **ACTIVE TIME:** 40 MINUTES / **TOTAL TIME:** 2 HOURS AND 30 MINUTES

3⅓ CUPS (400 G) SUPER-FINE SEMOLINA FLOUR, PLUS MORE AS NEEDED

4 EGGS

2 PINCHES OF TABLE SALT, PLUS MORE TO TASTE

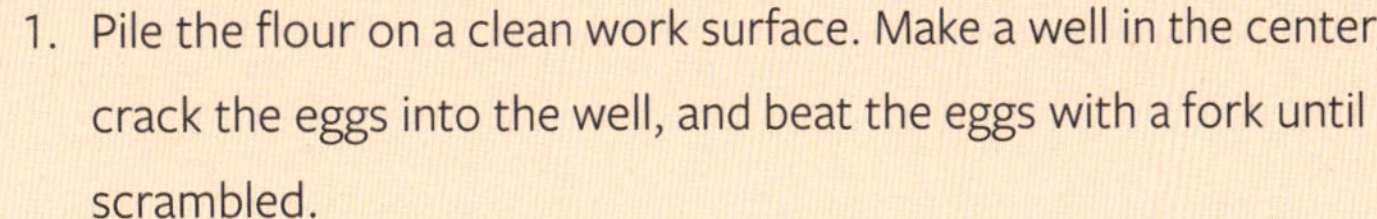

1. Pile the flour on a clean work surface. Make a well in the center, crack the eggs into the well, and beat the eggs with a fork until scrambled.
2. Incorporate the flour, a little at a time, until the dough starts to come together.
3. Check the dough to see if the consistency is right. Depending on a number of factors (size of the eggs, strength of the flour, and ambient humidity), you may need to incorporate 1 or 2 tablespoons of water, or more flour.
4. Work the dough until it is elastic and smooth, about 10 minutes.
5. Cover the dough with plastic wrap and let it rest for 30 minutes before rolling it out.
6. Place the dough on a flour-dusted work surface and divide it into six pieces. Roll out each piece of dough into a ⅖-inch-thick sheet that will fit your chitarra.
7. Let the dough dry, uncovered, for 30 minutes.
8. Turn the dough over and let the other side dry, uncovered, for 30 minutes.
9. Place a sheet of pasta on the chitarra and pass the rolling pin over the sheet to cut it. Dust the strands with flour, form them into nests, and let them dry.
10. To cook spaghetti alla chitarra, bring water to a boil in a large saucepan. Add salt, let the water return to a full boil, and add the pasta. Cook until it is al dente, about 5 minutes.

Malloreddus

YIELD: 1½ LBS. / **ACTIVE TIME:** 1 HOUR / **TOTAL TIME:** 3 HOURS

3¾ CUPS (450 G) FINELY GROUND DURUM WHEAT FLOUR, PLUS MORE AS NEEDED

1 (SCANT) CUP (225 ML) WATER, AT ROOM TEMPERATURE

PINCH OF TABLE SALT, PLUS MORE TO TASTE

1. Place all of the ingredients in a large bowl and work the mixture until it starts to come together as a dough.
2. Transfer the dough to a flour-dusted work surface and knead it energetically until it is a smooth and homogeneous dough, about 10 minutes.
3. Cover the dough with plastic wrap and let it rest at room temperature for 15 minutes.
4. Divide the dough into three pieces. Cover two pieces with plastic wrap and place the other on a flour-dusted work surface.
5. Shape the dough into a ⅖-inch-thick log and cut it into ⅖-inch-long pieces.
6. Roll the pieces over a gnocchi board or a fork while gently pressing down on them to shape the malloreddus. Place them on a flour-dusted baking sheet, cover with a kitchen towel, and let them rest for 1 hour.
7. Repeat Steps 5 and 6 with the remaining pieces of dough.
8. To cook the malloreddus, bring water to a boil in a large saucepan. Add salt, let the water return to a boil, and add the malloreddus. Let them rise to the surface and cook for 1 more minute.

Strangozzi

YIELD: 1 LB. / **ACTIVE TIME:** 30 MINUTES / **TOTAL TIME:** 1 HOUR

1¼ CUPS (150 G) FINELY GROUND DURUM WHEAT FLOUR, PLUS MORE AS NEEDED

1¼ CUPS (150 G) ALL-PURPOSE FLOUR

½ CUP PLUS 2 TABLESPOONS (150 ML) WATER, AT ROOM TEMPERATURE

PINCH OF TABLE SALT, PLUS MORE TO TASTE

1. Place all of the ingredients in a large bowl and work the mixture until it starts to come together as a dough.
2. Transfer the dough to a flour-dusted work surface and knead it energetically until it is a smooth and homogeneous dough, about 10 minutes.
3. Cover the dough with plastic wrap and let it rest at room temperature for 30 minutes.
4. Place the dough on a flour-dusted work surface and roll it into a ⅒-inch-thick sheet (you can also use a pasta maker to do this).
5. Roll the dough up around the rolling pin, gently slide it off, and cut it into ⅒-inch-wide strips. Unroll the strips and place them on a flour-dusted baking sheet.
6. To cook the strangozzi, bring water to a boil in a large saucepan. Add salt, let the water return to a boil, and add the strangozzi. Cook until they are al dente, 3 to 5 minutes.

Tonnarelli

YIELD: 1 LB. / **ACTIVE TIME:** 30 MINUTES / **TOTAL TIME:** 1 HOUR

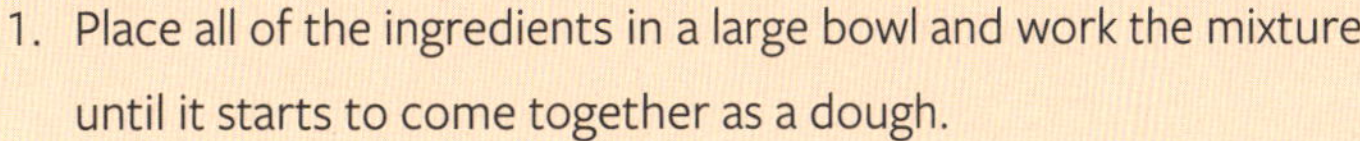

1¼ CUPS (150 G) FINELY GROUND DURUM WHEAT FLOUR, PLUS MORE AS NEEDED

1¼ CUPS (150 G) ALL-PURPOSE FLOUR

3 EGGS

2 PINCHES OF TABLE SALT, PLUS MORE TO TASTE

1. Place all of the ingredients in a large bowl and work the mixture until it starts to come together as a dough.
2. Transfer the dough to a flour-dusted work surface and knead it energetically until it is a smooth and homogeneous dough, about 10 minutes.
3. Cover the dough with plastic wrap and let it rest at room temperature for 30 minutes.
4. Place the dough on a flour-dusted work surface and roll it into a ⅒-inch-thick sheet (you can also use a pasta maker to do this).
5. Roll the dough up around the rolling pin, gently slide it off, and cut it into ⅒-inch-wide strips. Unroll the strips and place them on a flour-dusted baking sheet.
6. To cook the tonnarelli, bring water to a boil in a large saucepan. Add salt, let the water return to a boil, and add the tonnarelli. Cook until they are al dente, 3 to 5 minutes.

Ravioli

YIELD: ¾ LB. / **ACTIVE TIME:** 30 MINUTES / **TOTAL TIME:** 1 HOUR

2 CUPS (240 G) "00" FLOUR, PLUS MORE AS NEEDED

PINCH OF TABLE SALT, PLUS MORE TO TASTE

9 EGG YOLKS, BEATEN

2 TEASPOONS (10 G) EXTRA-VIRGIN OLIVE OIL

1 EGG

1 TABLESPOON (15 ML) WATER

1. Pile the flour on a clean work surface, add the salt, and whisk to combine. Make a well in the center of the flour, place the egg yolks and olive oil in the well, and beat with a fork until scrambled.
2. Incorporate the flour mixture, a little at a time, until the dough starts to come together.
3. Check the consistency of the dough. Depending on a number of factors (size of the egg yolks, strength of the flour, and ambient humidity), you may need to incorporate 1 to 2 tablespoons of water or flour.
4. Work the dough until it is elastic and smooth, about 10 minutes.
5. Cover the dough with plastic wrap and let it rest for 30 minutes.
6. Divide the dough into two pieces. Cover one piece with plastic wrap and place the other on a flour-dusted work surface. Roll the dough into a 1/10-inch-thick sheet (you can also use a pasta maker to do this). Repeat with the other piece of dough and cover one piece with plastic wrap.
7. If using a pastry wheel to cut the ravioli, distribute teaspoons of your desired filling over the sheet, leaving about 2½ inches between them.
8. If using a ravioli tray to cut the ravioli, lay the sheet of dough over the tray and place a teaspoon of your desired filling into each of the depressions.
9. Place the egg and water in a small bowl and beat until combined. Dip a pastry brush or a finger into the egg wash and lightly coat the edges of each ravioli with it.
10. Gently lay the other sheet of dough over the piece with the filling. Use a pastry wheel or a rolling pin to gently cut the ravioli. Remove the cut ravioli and place them on a flour-dusted baking sheet.
11. To cook the ravioli, bring water to a boil in a large saucepan. Add salt, let the water return to a boil, and add the ravioli. Cook until they are al dente, 2 to 4 minutes.

Gnocchi

YIELD: 8 SERVINGS / **ACTIVE TIME:** 1 HOUR / **TOTAL TIME:** 2 HOURS

2.2 LBS. (1 KG) STARCHY POTATOES, PEELED

2½ CUPS ALL-PURPOSE FLOUR, PLUS MORE AS NEEDED

1 MEDIUM EGG

SALT, TO TASTE

1. Place the potatoes in a large saucepan and cover them with cold water. Bring to a boil and cook until a knife inserted into the potatoes passes easily to their centers. Drain the potatoes.
2. Sift the flour onto a work surface, place the potatoes over it, and mash the potatoes.
3. Place the egg in a small bowl and season it with salt. Beat until scrambled and add it to the potato mixture. Work the mixture with your hands until it comes together as a soft, smooth dough. Be careful not to incorporate too much flour into the dough, otherwise the gnocchi will harden too much during cooking.
4. Cut the dough into several pieces and form them into long, ⅗-inch-thick logs. Cut them into 1-inch-long pieces.
5. Dust a fork or a gnocchi board with flour and roll the pieces of dough over it, gently pressing down to shape the gnocchi.
6. Place the gnocchi on a flour-dusted baking sheet.
7. To cook the gnocchi, bring water to a boil in a large saucepan. Add salt, let the water return to a boil, and add the gnocchi. Cook until they rise to the surface and remove them with a pasta fork.

Casonsei

YIELD: 4 SERVINGS / **ACTIVE TIME:** 1 HOUR / **TOTAL TIME:** 2 HOURS

1 TABLESPOON UNSALTED BUTTER

1 PEAR, PEELED, CORED, AND DICED

4½ OZ. SALAMI

3½ OZ. GROUND BEEF

1 TABLESPOON FRESHLY CHOPPED PARSLEY

½ GARLIC CLOVE, MINCED

ZEST OF ½ LEMON

1 OZ. GOLDEN RAISINS, SOAKED IN WARM WATER, DRAINED, AND MINCED

1 SMALL EGG

2 AMARETTI (SEE PAGE 378), FINELY CRUMBLED

1 CUP BREAD CRUMBS

1 CUP GRATED GRANA PADANO CHEESE

SALT AND PEPPER, TO TASTE

2 PINCHES OF CINNAMON

2 PINCHES OF FRESHLY GRATED NUTMEG

PASTA ALL'UOVO (SEE PAGE 34)

1. Place the butter in a large skillet and melt it over medium heat. Add the pear and cook, stirring, until it is browned, about 6 minutes. Remove the pan from heat and let the pear cool.
2. Place the salami in a food processor and blitz until it is a paste.
3. Place the salami in a large bowl and add all of the remaining ingredients, except for the pasta dough. Stir to combine, add the pear, and stir to incorporate. Set the filling aside.
4. Divide the dough into two pieces and cover one piece with plastic wrap. Run the other piece of dough through a pasta maker until it is ⅟₂₅ inch thick. Cut the dough into 2-inch rounds and cover them with a kitchen towel.
5. Knead the scraps into a ball and let it rest for 15 minutes before running it through the pasta maker until it is ⅟₂₅ inch thick and cutting it into 2-inch rounds.
6. Form tablespoons of the filling into balls and place one in the center of each round. Moisten the edge of the dough with water, fold the dough over the filling, and press down on the edge to seal the casonsei.
7. Place the casonsei seam side down and press your thumb in the center, making a slight depression and forming them into crescents.
8. Repeat Steps 5, 6, and 7 with the other piece of dough.
9. To cook the casonsei, bring water to a boil in a large saucepan. Add salt, let the water return to a boil, and add the casonsei. Cook them for 6 minutes.

Pici

YIELD: 1 LB. / **ACTIVE TIME:** 30 MINUTES / **TOTAL TIME:** 4 HOURS

3¾ CUPS (450 G) ALL-PURPOSE FLOUR, PLUS MORE AS NEEDED

1 CUP PLUS 2 TABLESPOONS (269 ML) LUKEWARM WATER (90°F)

PINCH OF TABLE SALT, PLUS MORE TO TASTE

2 TABLESPOONS (26 G) EXTRA-VIRGIN OLIVE OIL

SEMOLINA FLOUR, AS NEEDED

1. Place the all-purpose flour, water, and salt in a large bowl and work the mixture until it starts to come together as a dough. Add the olive oil and work the dough to incorporate it.
2. Transfer the dough to a work surface dusted with all-purpose flour and knead it energetically until it is a smooth and homogeneous dough, about 10 minutes.
3. Cover the dough with plastic wrap and let it rest at room temperature for 30 minutes.
4. Place the dough on a work surface dusted with all-purpose flour and roll it into a ⅖-inch-thick sheet. Roll the dough up around the rolling pin, gently slide it off, and cut it into ⅖-inch-wide strips.
5. Working with a few strands at a time, hold each end and pull in opposite directions to elongate the pici, taking care not to break them. Dust the pici with semolina, place them on a baking sheet, and let them dry for 3 hours.
6. To cook the pici, bring water to a boil in a large saucepan. Add salt, let the water return to a boil, and add the pici. Cook until they are al dente, 6 to 8 minutes.

Gnocchi di Grano Saraceno

YIELD: 4 SERVINGS / **ACTIVE TIME:** 40 MINUTES / **TOTAL TIME:** 1 HOUR

2¾ CUPS (330 G) ALL-PURPOSE FLOUR, PLUS MORE AS NEEDED

2 CUPS PLUS 1½ TABLESPOONS (250 G) BUCKWHEAT FLOUR

1 EGG YOLK

PINCH OF TABLE SALT, PLUS MORE TO TASTE

1 CUP PLUS 2 TABLESPOONS (269 ML) WATER, PLUS MORE AS NEEDED

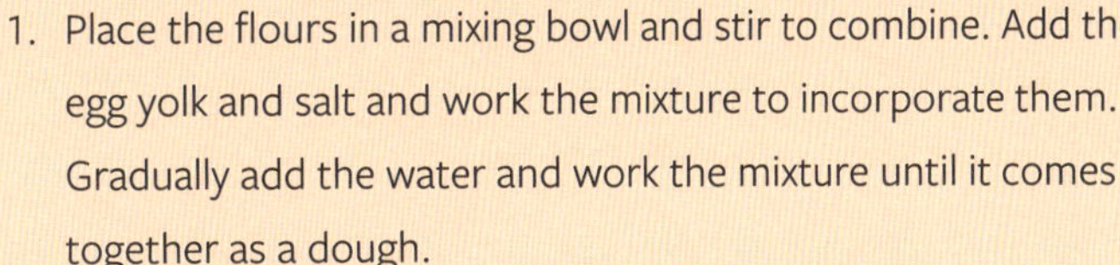

1. Place the flours in a mixing bowl and stir to combine. Add the egg yolk and salt and work the mixture to incorporate them. Gradually add the water and work the mixture until it comes together as a dough.
2. Place the dough on a flour-dusted work surface and knead it until it is smooth and not sticky, incorporating more water or flour as necessary. Form the dough into a loaf, cover it with plastic wrap, and chill it in the refrigerator for 1 hour.
3. Cut the dough into pieces and form them into long, ⅗-inch-thick logs. Cut them into 1-inch-long pieces.
4. Dust a fork or a gnocchi board with flour and roll the pieces of dough over it, gently pressing down to shape the gnocchi. Place the gnocchi on a flour-dusted baking sheet.
5. To cook the gnocchi, bring water to a boil in a large saucepan. Add salt, let the water return to a boil, and add the gnocchi. Cook until they rise to the surface and remove with a pasta fork.

Pasta All'uovo

YIELD: 1 LB. / **ACTIVE TIME:** 30 MINUTES / **TOTAL TIME:** 1 HOUR

3⅓ CUPS (400 G) ALL-PURPOSE FLOUR

4 MEDIUM EGGS

WATER, AS NEEDED

1. Pile the flour on a clean work surface. Make a well in the center, crack the eggs into the well, and beat the eggs with a fork until scrambled.
2. Incorporate the flour, a little at a time, until the dough starts to come together.
3. Check the dough to see if the consistency is right. Depending on a number of factors (size of the eggs, strength of the flour, and ambient humidity), you may need to incorporate 1 or 2 tablespoons of water or more flour.
4. Work the dough until it is elastic and smooth, about 10 minutes. Cover the dough with plastic wrap and let it rest for 30 minutes before rolling it out and cutting it into the desired format.

Spaghetti alla Puttanesca

YIELD: 4 SERVINGS / **ACTIVE TIME:** 10 MINUTES / **TOTAL TIME:** 25 MINUTES

1 LB. TOMATOES

¼ CUP EXTRA-VIRGIN OLIVE OIL

1 GARLIC CLOVE, CHOPPED

8 SALT-PACKED ANCHOVIES, RINSED AND CHOPPED

RED PEPPER FLAKES, TO TASTE

1 CUP PITTED BLACK OLIVES, CHOPPED

1 TABLESPOON SALT-PACKED CAPERS, SOAKED, DRAINED, DRIED, AND CHOPPED

2 TABLESPOONS FINELY CHOPPED FRESH ITALIAN PARSLEY

SALT, TO TASTE

14 OZ. SPAGHETTI

1. Bring water to a boil in a large saucepan. Add the tomatoes and boil them for 2 minutes. Drain the tomatoes and let them cool. When they are cool enough to handle, peel the tomatoes, remove the seeds, and chop the remaining flesh. Set the tomatoes aside.
2. Place the olive oil in a large skillet and warm it over medium-low heat. Add the garlic and cook for 2 minutes. Add the anchovies and red pepper flakes and cook for 1 minute.
3. Stir in the olives and capers and cook, stirring frequently, for 3 minutes.
4. Add the tomatoes and half of the parsley and cook, stirring occasionally, until the tomatoes start to break down, about 20 minutes.
5. Bring water to a boil in a large saucepan. Add salt, let the water return to a full boil, and add the pasta. Cook until the pasta is very al dente. Reserve ¼ cup of pasta water and drain the spaghetti.
6. Add the spaghetti and pasta water to the skillet, raise the heat to medium-high, and toss to combine. Cook until the pasta is al dente.
7. Stir in the remaining parsley and serve.

Pasta All'uovo Verde

YIELD: 4 SERVINGS / **ACTIVE TIME:** 30 MINUTES / **TOTAL TIME:** 1 HOUR

5½ OZ. (155 G) FRESH SPINACH, RINSED WELL

3⅓ CUPS (400 G) ALL-PURPOSE FLOUR, PLUS MORE AS NEEDED

3 EGGS

PINCH OF TABLE SALT

1. Place the spinach in a large skillet, add a little bit of water, and cover the pan. Steam the spinach over low heat until it has wilted, about 5 minutes. Remove the pan from heat and let the spinach cool completely.
2. Squeeze the spinach to remove any excess water and chop it fine or blitz it in a food processor until it is pureed. Set the spinach aside.
3. Pile the flour on a clean work surface. Make a well in the center, crack the eggs into the well, and beat the eggs with a fork until scrambled.
4. Incorporate the flour, a little at a time, until the dough starts to come together. Add the spinach and salt and work the mixture to incorporate them.
5. Check the dough to see if the consistency is right. Depending on a number of factors (size of the eggs, amount of water remaining in the spinach, strength of the flour, and ambient humidity), you may need to incorporate more flour.
6. Work the dough until it is elastic and smooth, about 10 minutes. Cover the dough with plastic wrap and let it rest for 30 minutes before rolling it out and cutting it into the desired format.

Spaghetti allo Scoglio

YIELD: 4 SERVINGS / **ACTIVE TIME:** 1 HOUR / **TOTAL TIME:** 2 HOURS

¼ CUP EXTRA-VIRGIN OLIVE OIL

2 GARLIC CLOVES

2 LBS. CLAMS, RINSED WELL

2 LBS. MUSSELS, RINSED WELL AND DEBEARDED

10 OZ. SQUID, CLEANED (SEE PAGE 140) AND CUT INTO RINGS

SALT, TO TASTE

1 CUP DRY WHITE WINE

1 CUP HALVED CHERRY TOMATOES

10 OZ. SHRIMP, DEVEINED

1 LB. SPAGHETTI

FRESH PARSLEY, FINELY CHOPPED, FOR GARNISH

1. Place half of the olive oil in a large skillet and warm it over medium heat. Add 1 garlic clove and cook, stirring occasionally, for 2 minutes.
2. Add the clams and mussels, raise the heat to medium-high, and cover the pan with a lid. Cook until the majority of the clams and mussels have opened, about 5 minutes.
3. Discard any clams and/or mussels that did not open. Remove the remaining clams and mussels from the pan, remove the meat from most of the shells, and set it aside. Leave the meat in some of the mussels and clams and reserve them for garnish. Strain any liquid in the pan and set it aside.
4. Add the remaining olive oil to the pan and warm it over medium heat. Add the remaining garlic clove and cook, stirring occasionally, for 2 minutes. Add the squid, season it lightly with salt, and cook for 2 minutes.
5. Add the wine and cook until it has evaporated. Remove the garlic clove, discard it, and add the tomatoes. Cook for 5 minutes.
6. Add the shrimp and cook until they turn pink, 2 to 3 minutes. Peel the shrimp, pressing down on their heads to release the juices. Reserve these juices.
7. Add the shrimp, their juices, mussels, and clams to the sauce, season it with salt, and remove the pan from heat.
8. Bring water to a boil in a large saucepan. Add salt, let the water return to a full boil, and add the pasta. Cook until the pasta is very al dente. Drain the spaghetti and add it to the skillet.
9. Cook the pasta and sauce over medium-high heat, tossing to combine and gradually adding the reserved liquid from cooking the mussels and clams.
10. When the pasta is al dente, garnish the dish with parsley and the reserved mussels and clams and enjoy.

Spaghetti d'o Puveriello

YIELD: 4 SERVINGS / **ACTIVE TIME:** 10 MINUTES / **TOTAL TIME:** 15 MINUTES

3½ OZ. LARD

4 EGGS

SALT AND PEPPER, TO TASTE

14 OZ. SPAGHETTI

¼ CUP GRATED PECORINO CHEESE

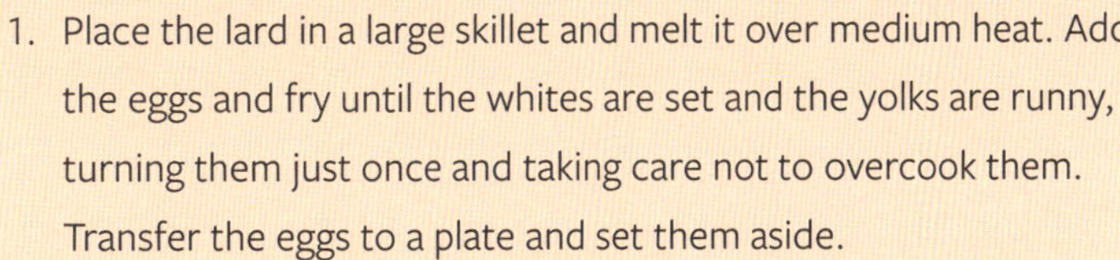

1. Place the lard in a large skillet and melt it over medium heat. Add the eggs and fry until the whites are set and the yolks are runny, turning them just once and taking care not to overcook them. Transfer the eggs to a plate and set them aside.
2. Bring water to a boil in a large saucepan. Add salt to the boiling water, let the water return to a full boil, and add the pasta. Cook until the pasta is very al dente. Reserve ½ cup pasta water and drain the spaghetti.
3. Add the pasta to the skillet and toss to combine.
4. Add the pasta water and toss to combine.
5. When the pasta is al dente, add the pecorino and eggs, season the dish generously with pepper, toss until combined, and enjoy.

Pasta e Piselli

YIELD: 4 SERVINGS / **ACTIVE TIME:** 10 MINUTES / **TOTAL TIME:** 25 MINUTES

2 TABLESPOONS EXTRA-VIRGIN OLIVE OIL

1 ONION, FINELY DICED

6 OZ. PANCETTA, DICED (OPTIONAL)

2 CUPS PEAS

2 CUPS WATER

SALT AND PEPPER, TO TASTE

9 OZ. PASTA (MACARONI OR BROKEN SPAGHETTI RECOMMENDED)

PARMESAN OR PECORINO CHEESE, GRATED, TO TASTE

1. Place the olive oil in a large skillet and warm it over medium heat. Add the onion and cook, stirring occasionally, until it has softened, about 5 minutes.
2. Add the pancetta (if desired), reduce the heat to medium-low, and cook until the fat starts to render, about 5 minutes.
3. Add the peas, raise the heat to medium, and cook, stirring occasionally, until they are tender, 3 to 5 minutes.
4. Add the water and bring to a boil. Add salt, let the water return to a full boil, and add the pasta. Cook until the pasta is al dente and has absorbed the water.
5. Season the dish with Parmesan and pepper and enjoy.

Pasta e Patate

YIELD: 4 SERVINGS / **ACTIVE TIME:** 15 MINUTES / **TOTAL TIME:** 1 HOUR

2 OZ. LARD, DICED

2 TABLESPOONS EXTRA-VIRGIN OLIVE OIL

½ MEDIUM WHITE ONION, FINELY DICED

1 LARGE CARROT, PEELED AND FINELY DICED

1 CELERY STALK, FINELY DICED

1 CUP DICED CHERRY TOMATOES

1⅓ LBS. POTATOES, PEELED AND DICED

2 CUPS VEGETABLE STOCK (SEE PAGE 447)

2 PARMESAN RINDS, EXTERIORS REMOVED

1½ CUPS WATER

6 OZ. SHORT-FORMAT PASTA (TUBETTI OR RUOTE)

SALT, TO TASTE

5 OZ. PROVOLA CHEESE, CUBED (OPTIONAL)

1. Place the lard and olive oil in a medium saucepan and warm the mixture over low heat. Add the onion, carrot, celery, and tomatoes and cook, stirring occasionally, until they have softened, about 6 minutes.
2. Add the potatoes and cook, stirring occasionally, for 6 minutes.
3. Add the stock, raise the heat to medium, and bring to a boil. Reduce the heat to low, cover the pan, and cook until the potatoes are tender, about 40 minutes, gently stirring occasionally.
4. Add the Parmesan rinds, water, and pasta, raise the heat to medium, and cook until the pasta is al dente. If there is too much liquid, raise the heat to reduce it to the desired amount.
5. Remove the Parmesan rinds, discard them, season the dish with salt, and remove the pan from heat.
6. Stir in the provola (if desired) and enjoy.

Calamarata

YIELD: 4 SERVINGS / **ACTIVE TIME:** 15 MINUTES / **TOTAL TIME:** 40 MINUTES

¼ CUP EXTRA-VIRGIN OLIVE OIL

1 GARLIC CLOVE

1 RED CHILE PEPPER, STEMMED, SEEDED, AND MINCED

10 OZ. SQUID, CLEANED (SEE PAGE 140) AND CUT INTO RINGS

½ CUP DRY WHITE WINE

2½ CUPS HALVED CHERRY TOMATOES

SALT, TO TASTE

14 OZ. MEZZI PACCHERI PASTA

FRESH PARSLEY, CHOPPED, FOR GARNISH

1. Place the olive oil in a large skillet and warm it over medium heat. Add the garlic and chile and cook, stirring occasionally, for 2 minutes.
2. Remove the garlic from the pan and discard it. Add the squid and cook for 2 minutes.
3. Add the wine and cook until it has evaporated. Add the tomatoes and cook, stirring occasionally, for 5 minutes.
4. Reduce the heat to low, cover the pan, and cook until the tomatoes have collapsed, about 20 minutes.
5. Bring water to a boil in a large saucepan. Add salt, let the water return to a full boil, and add the pasta. Cook until the pasta is very al dente.
6. Drain the pasta and add it to the skillet. Season the dish with salt, raise the heat to medium-high, and toss to combine. Cook until the pasta is al dente.
7. Garnish the dish with parsley and enjoy.

Pasta allo Scarpariello

YIELD: 4 SERVINGS / **ACTIVE TIME:** 10 MINUTES / **TOTAL TIME:** 20 MINUTES

¼ CUP EXTRA-VIRGIN OLIVE OIL

1 GARLIC CLOVE

½ MILD CHILE PEPPER, STEMMED, SEEDED, AND MINCED

1 LB. CHERRY TOMATOES, HALVED

SALT, TO TASTE

14 OZ. SPAGHETTI

LARGE HANDFUL OF FRESH BASIL

6 TABLESPOONS GRATED PECORINO CHEESE

6 TABLESPOONS GRATED PARMIGIANO REGGIANO CHEESE

1. Bring water to a boil in a large saucepan.
2. Place the olive oil in a large skillet and warm it over medium-low heat. Add the garlic and cook for 2 minutes. Add the chile and cook for 1 minute.
3. Add the tomatoes, raise the heat to medium, and cook, stirring occasionally, until the tomatoes start to collapse, about 10 minutes.
4. Add salt to the boiling water, let the water return to a full boil, and add the pasta. Cook until the pasta is very al dente. Reserve 2 cups of pasta water and drain the spaghetti.
5. Add the basil and some of the pasta water to the skillet, season the sauce with salt, and remove the garlic clove.
6. Add the pasta and more pasta water (if desired) and toss until combined and the pasta is al dente.
7. Turn off the heat, add the cheeses, and toss to combine. Serve immediately.

Pasta with Cannellini & Mussels

YIELD: 4 SERVINGS / **ACTIVE TIME:** 20 MINUTES / **TOTAL TIME:** 24 HOURS

SALT AND PEPPER, TO TASTE

¾ LB. DRIED CANNELLINI BEANS, SOAKED OVERNIGHT AND DRAINED

¼ CUP EXTRA-VIRGIN OLIVE OIL

2 GARLIC CLOVES

½ RED CHILE PEPPER, STEMMED, SEEDED, AND MINCED

2 LBS. MUSSELS, RINSED WELL AND DEBEARDED

8 CHERRY TOMATOES

¾ LB. MIXED SHORT-FORMAT PASTA

FRESH PARSLEY, CHOPPED, FOR GARNISH

1. Bring water to a boil in a large saucepan. Add salt and the beans and cook until they are tender, about 45 minutes. Drain the beans, reserving the cooking liquid. Strain the cooking liquid and set it and the beans aside.
2. Place half of the olive oil in a large skillet and warm it over medium heat. Add half of the garlic and chile and cook, stirring occasionally, for 2 minutes.
3. Add the mussels, raise the heat to medium-high, and cover the pan with a lid. Cook until the majority of the mussels have opened, about 5 minutes. Discard any mussels that did not open. Remove the remaining mussels from the pan, remove the meat from most of the shells, and set it aside. Leave the meat in some of the mussels and reserve them for garnish. Strain any liquid in the pan and set it aside.
4. Add the remaining olive oil to the pan and warm it over medium heat. Add the remaining garlic clove and chile and cook, stirring occasionally, for 2 minutes. Add the tomatoes and cook, stirring occasionally, for 5 minutes.
5. Add the beans, half of their cooking liquid, and half of the liquid reserved from cooking the mussels. Add the pasta, cover the pan, and cook until the pasta has absorbed most of the liquid, stirring occasionally.
6. Add the remaining cooking liquid from the mussels and some more of the cooking liquid from the beans. Cook until the pasta is al dente and the sauce is creamy.
7. Add the meat from the mussels, remove the pan from heat, and season the dish with salt and pepper.
8. Garnish the dish with parsley and the reserved mussels and enjoy.

Scialatielli All'amalfitana

YIELD: 4 SERVINGS / **ACTIVE TIME:** 40 MINUTES / **TOTAL TIME:** 1 HOUR AND 15 MINUTES

¼ CUP EXTRA-VIRGIN OLIVE OIL

1 GARLIC CLOVE, MINCED

5 MEDIUM TOMATOES, CHOPPED

HANDFUL OF FRESH BASIL

1 LB. MUSSELS, RINSED WELL AND DEBEARDED

½ LB. CLAMS, RINSED WELL

½ LB. SQUID, CLEANED (SEE PAGE 140) AND CHOPPED

½ LB. SHRIMP, SHELLS REMOVED, DEVEINED

SALT, TO TASTE

½ CUP DRY WHITE WINE

1 LB. SCIALATIELLI (SEE PAGE 10)

FRESH PARSLEY, CHOPPED, FOR GARNISH

1. Place the olive oil in a large skillet and warm it over medium-high heat. Add the garlic and cook for 1 minute.
2. Add the tomatoes and basil and cook, stirring occasionally, for 10 minutes.
3. Add the seafood, season the dish with salt, and cook until the majority of the clams and mussels have opened, about 5 minutes.
4. Remove the mussels and clams from the pan and set them aside. Discard any mussels and/or clams that did not open.
5. Add the wine, cook until it has evaporated, and remove the pan from heat.
6. Bring water to a boil in a large saucepan. Add salt, let the water return to a full boil, and add the pasta. Cook until the pasta is al dente.
7. While the pasta water is coming to a boil, remove the meat from two-thirds of the mussels and clams and reserve the remaining one-third for garnish.
8. Drain the pasta and add it to the sauce along with the mussels and clams. Cook over medium-high heat until everything is warmed through, tossing to combine.
9. Garnish the dish with parsley and the reserved mussels and clams and enjoy.

Pasta alla Genovese

YIELD: 4 SERVINGS / **ACTIVE TIME:** 40 MINUTES / **TOTAL TIME:** 5 HOURS

2½ LBS. BEEF

⅔ CUP EXTRA-VIRGIN OLIVE OIL

5 LBS. YELLOW OR WHITE ONIONS, SLICED THIN

SALT, TO TASTE

14 OZ. ZITI SPEZZATI OR RIGATONI

2 OZ. PECORINO CHEESE, GRATED

1. Leave one piece of beef as is and cut the rest of it into chunks.
2. Place some of the olive oil in a large saucepan and warm it over medium-high heat. Working in batches to avoid crowding the pan, add the beef and sear until it is browned all over, turning it as necessary. Add the remaining olive oil to the pan as necessary.
3. Place all of the beef in the pan and cover it with the onions. Reduce the heat to low, cover the pan, and cook, stirring occasionally, until the onions start to soften.
4. Uncover the pan and cook until the meat is tender but not yet falling apart, 2 to 3 hours.
5. Season the mixture with salt, remove the biggest piece of beef from the pan, and set it aside. Cover the pan and continue cooking the sauce until the onions have almost dissolved and the sauce becomes juicy, 1 to 2 hours.
6. Bring water to a boil in a large saucepan. Add salt, let the water return to a full boil, and add the pasta. Cook until the pasta is al dente.
7. Drain the pasta, place it in a serving dish, and add some of the sauce and half of the pecorino. Toss to combine and top with the remaining pecorino.
8. Pour the remaining sauce over the large piece of beef and serve it following the pasta dish.

Pasta al Forno Napoletana

YIELD: 6 SERVINGS / **ACTIVE TIME:** 40 MINUTES / **TOTAL TIME:** 1 HOUR AND 30 MINUTES

FOR THE MEATBALLS

½ LB. GROUND PORK

½ LB. GROUND BEEF

4 EGGS

½ LB. FRESH BREAD CRUMBS

1 CUP GRATED PECORINO OR PARMESAN CHEESE

SALT AND PEPPER, TO TASTE

EXTRA-VIRGIN OLIVE OIL, AS NEEDED

FOR THE PASTA

SALT, TO TASTE

1 LB. ZITI, MEZZE MANICHE, OR RIGATONI

1 LB. RICOTTA CHEESE

6 CUPS RAGÙ NAPOLETANO (SEE PAGE 91)

9 OZ. PROVOLA CHEESE, CUBED

3 HARD-BOILED EGGS, SLICED (OPTIONAL)

¼ LB. ITALIAN SALAMI, CHOPPED (OPTIONAL)

1 LB. FRESH MOZZARELLA CHEESE, DRAINED AND SHREDDED

1⅓ CUPS GRATED PECORINO OR PARMESAN CHEESE

1. To begin preparations for the meatballs, place all of the ingredients, except for the olive oil, in a mixing bowl and work the mixture until it is well combined. Form the mixture into small, walnut-sized meatballs.
2. Add olive oil to a large, deep skillet until it is about 1 inch deep and warm it over medium heat. Add the meatballs and cook until they are browned all over, turning them as necessary. Place the meatballs on paper towel–lined plates and let them drain.
3. Preheat the oven to 360°F. To begin preparations for the pasta, bring water to a boil in a large saucepan. Add salt, let the water return to a full boil, and add the pasta. Cook until the pasta is al dente. Drain the pasta and set it aside.
4. Place the ricotta and 1 cup of the ragù in a large mixing bowl and stir to combine. Add the mixture to the pasta along with 2 more cups of ragù and stir to combine.
5. Spread some ragù over the bottom of a 13 x 9–inch baking dish. Arrange half of the pasta, half of the provola, half of the meatballs, half of the eggs and salami (if desired), half of the mozzarella, and half of the pecorino in separate layers. Repeat the layering process with the remaining ingredients.
6. Place the dish in the oven and bake until the top is crispy, about 30 minutes.
7. Remove the dish from the oven and let it rest for 10 to 15 minutes before serving.

Lasagne alla Napoletana

YIELD: 6 SERVINGS / **ACTIVE TIME:** 1 HOUR / **TOTAL TIME:** 2 HOURS

FOR THE MEATBALLS

5½ OZ. GROUND BEEF

5½ OZ. GROUND PORK

2 EGGS

¼ LB. FRESH BREAD CRUMBS

2 OZ. PECORINO OR PARMESAN CHEESE, GRATED

SALT AND PEPPER, TO TASTE

EXTRA-VIRGIN OLIVE OIL, AS NEEDED

FOR THE LASAGNA

SALT, TO TASTE

1½ LBS. LASAGNA SHEETS

1 LB. RICOTTA CHEESE

4 CUPS RAGÙ NAPOLETANO (SEE PAGE 91), PLUS MORE FOR TOPPING

14 OZ. PROVOLA CHEESE, CUBED

3 HARD-BOILED EGGS, SLICED (OPTIONAL)

3 OZ. GRATED PECORINO OR PARMESAN CHEESE, PLUS MORE FOR TOPPING

1. To begin preparations for the meatballs, place all of the ingredients, except for the olive oil, in a mixing bowl and work the mixture until it is well combined. Form the mixture into small, walnut-sized meatballs.
2. Add olive oil to a large, deep skillet until it is about 1 inch deep and warm it over medium heat. Add the meatballs and cook until they are browned all over, turning them as necessary. Place the meatballs on paper towel–lined plates and let them drain.
3. Preheat the oven to 360°F. To begin preparations for the lasagna, bring water to a boil in a large saucepan. Add salt, let the water return to a full boil, and add a few of the lasagna sheets at a time to avoid overcrowding the pot. Cook until the lasagna sheets are al dente. Drain the lasagna sheets and set them on kitchen towels to dry.
4. Place the ricotta and 1 cup of the ragù in a large mixing bowl and stir to combine.
5. Spread some ragù over the bottom of a 13 x 9–inch baking dish. Arrange one-third of the lasagna sheets, one-third of the ricotta mixture, one-third of the provola, one-third of the meatballs, one-third of the eggs (if desired), and one-third of the pecorino in separate layers. Repeat the layering process two more times with the remaining ingredients.
6. Top the lasagna with additional ragù and pecorino, place it in the oven, and bake for 50 minutes.
7. Remove the lasagna from the oven and let it rest for 10 to 15 minutes before serving.

Pappardelle All'aquilana

YIELD: 4 SERVINGS / **ACTIVE TIME:** 20 MINUTES / **TOTAL TIME:** 50 MINUTES

1⅓ CUPS DRIED PORCINI MUSHROOMS

SALT, TO TASTE

¾ CUP PEAS

2 TABLESPOONS EXTRA-VIRGIN OLIVE OIL

½ ONION, DICED

⅔ CUP DICED ITALIAN COTTO OR PROSCIUTTO

1 SLICE OF GUANCIALE, SKINLESS AND DICED

1 ITALIAN SAUSAGE, CASING REMOVED AND CRUMBLED

1 LB. PAPPARDELLE

1½ TEASPOONS SAFFRON THREADS

½ CUP GRATED PECORINO CHEESE

1. Place the porcini mushrooms in a bowl, cover them with warm water, and let them soak for 30 minutes.
2. Drain the mushrooms, reserve the soaking liquid, and squeeze the mushrooms to remove as much moisture as possible. Chop the mushrooms and set them aside. Strain the soaking liquid and set it aside.
3. Bring water to a boil in a medium saucepan. Add salt and the peas and cook for 2 minutes. Drain the peas and set them aside.
4. Place the olive oil in a large skillet and warm it over medium heat. Add the onion, cotto, and guanciale and cook, stirring occasionally, until the onion has softened, about 5 minutes.
5. Add the sausage and cook, stirring occasionally, until it has browned, about 8 minutes.
6. Add the peas, mushrooms, and some of the reserved soaking liquid. Season the dish with salt, reduce the heat to low, and cook for 15 minutes.
7. Bring water to a boil in a large saucepan. Add salt, let the water return to a full boil, and add the pasta. Cook until the pasta is very al dente. Reserve ½ cup of pasta water, drain the pasta, and set it aside.
8. Place the saffron in the pasta water and let it steep for 10 minutes.
9. Add the pasta, saffron, and some of the saffron water to the skillet and toss until well combined. You want the sauce to be thick instead of soupy, and for the pasta to be al dente.
10. Stir in the pecorino and serve.

Pasta alla Mugnaia

YIELD: 4 SERVINGS / **ACTIVE TIME:** 40 MINUTES / **TOTAL TIME:** 2 HOURS

¼ CUP EXTRA-VIRGIN OLIVE OIL

1 GREEN BELL PEPPER, STEMMED, SEEDED, AND FINELY DICED

1 ONION, THINLY SLICED

½ CARROT, PEELED AND DICED

½ LB. PIECE OF BONE-IN BEEF OR PORK

SALT, TO TASTE

1 RED BELL PEPPER, STEMMED, SEEDED, AND FINELY DICED

1 EGGPLANT, CUBED

1 LB. WHOLE PEELED TOMATOES, PUREED

1 CUP WATER

1 LB. TAGLIATELLE OR FETTUCCINE

PECORINO CHEESE, GRATED, FOR GARNISH

1. Place the olive oil in a large skillet and warm it over medium heat. Add the green bell pepper, onion, and carrot and cook, stirring occasionally, until they have softened, about 5 minutes.
2. Season the beef with salt, add it to the pan, and sear it until it is browned all over, turning it as necessary.
3. Add the red bell pepper and eggplant and cook until they are browned.
4. Reduce the heat to low, add the tomatoes and water, and season the sauce with salt. Cover the pan and cook the sauce until the meat is tender, about 1 hour. Remove the sauce from heat and set it aside.
5. Bring water to a boil in a large saucepan. Add salt, let the water return to a full boil, and add the pasta. Cook until the pasta is al dente. Drain the pasta and place it in a serving dish.
6. Add the sauce to the pasta and toss to combine. Garnish the dish with pecorino and enjoy.

Bucatini with Asparagus & Sausage

YIELD: 4 SERVINGS / **ACTIVE TIME:** 30 MINUTES / **TOTAL TIME:** 50 MINUTES

10 OZ. FRESH ASPARAGUS, TRIMMED

SALT AND PEPPER, TO TASTE

¼ CUP EXTRA-VIRGIN OLIVE OIL

1 ONION, FINELY DICED

11 OZ. ITALIAN SAUSAGE, CASING REMOVED AND CRUMBLED

1 CUP WHITE WINE

1 LB. BUCATINI

⅔ CUP GRATED PECORINO CHEESE

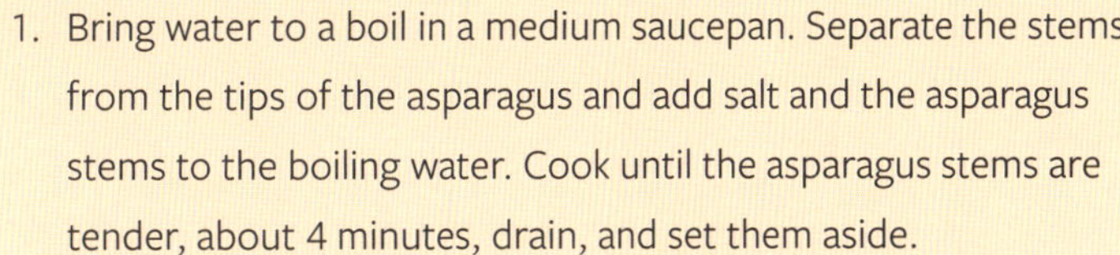

1. Bring water to a boil in a medium saucepan. Separate the stems from the tips of the asparagus and add salt and the asparagus stems to the boiling water. Cook until the asparagus stems are tender, about 4 minutes, drain, and set them aside.
2. Place 2 tablespoons of olive oil in a large skillet and warm it over medium heat. Add the onion and cook, stirring occasionally, until it has softened, about 5 minutes.
3. Add the sausage and cook, stirring occasionally, until it has browned, about 8 minutes.
4. Add the wine, reduce the heat to low, and cook for 15 minutes.
5. Place the remaining olive oil in a large skillet and warm it over medium heat. Add the asparagus tips and cook, stirring frequently, until they are tender, 3 to 4 minutes. Season the asparagus tips with salt and pepper, remove the pan from heat, and set the asparagus tips aside.
6. Bring water to a boil in a large saucepan. Chop the asparagus stems, add them to the sauce, and cook for 10 minutes.
7. Add salt to the boiling water, let the water return to a full boil, and add the pasta. Cook until the pasta is al dente. Drain the pasta, add it to the sauce, and toss to combine.
8. Top the dish with the asparagus tips and pecorino and enjoy.

Cavatelli alla Ventricina

YIELD: 4 SERVINGS / **ACTIVE TIME:** 10 MINUTES / **TOTAL TIME:** 50 MINUTES

3 TABLESPOONS EXTRA-VIRGIN OLIVE OIL

½ ONION, FINELY DICED

2 GARLIC CLOVES, HALVED

1 LB. PEELED TOMATOES, CRUSHED

SALT, TO TASTE

⅔ CUP CHOPPED VENTRICINA

1 LB. CAVATELLI (SEE PAGE 11)

HANDFUL OF FRESH BASIL, SHREDDED

2 OZ. PECORINO CHEESE, GRATED

1. Place the olive oil in a large skillet and warm it over medium heat. Add the onion and garlic and cook, stirring frequently, until the onion has softened, about 5 minutes.
2. Add the tomatoes, reduce the heat to low, and cook for 20 minutes.
3. Remove the garlic, season the sauce with salt, and stir in the ventricina. Cook for 20 minutes, stirring occasionally.
4. Bring water to a boil in a large saucepan. Add salt, let the water return to a full boil, and add the pasta. Cook until the pasta is al dente.
5. Drain the pasta and place it in a serving dish.
6. Stir the basil into the sauce. Top the pasta with the sauce and pecorino and serve.

Cavatelli al Sugo Vedovo

YIELD: 4 SERVINGS / **ACTIVE TIME:** 40 MINUTES / **TOTAL TIME:** 40 MINUTES

6 OZ. LARD, FINELY DICED

1 GARLIC CLOVE, HALVED

6 SPRIGS OF FRESH PARSLEY

2 LBS. TOMATOES, CHOPPED

SALT AND PEPPER, TO TASTE

1 LB. CAVATELLI (SEE PAGE 11)

HANDFUL OF FRESH BASIL

⅔ CUP GRATED PECORINO CHEESE

1. Place the lard in a large skillet and warm it over medium heat. Add the garlic and parsley and cook, stirring frequently, for 2 minutes.
2. Add the tomatoes and cook, stirring occasionally, until the tomatoes collapse, about 20 minutes.
3. Bring water to a boil in a large saucepan. Add salt, let the water return to a full boil, and add the pasta. Cook until the pasta is al dente.
4. Drain the pasta and place it in a serving dish.
5. Stir the basil into the sauce. Top the pasta with the sauce and pecorino, season it with salt and pepper, and serve.

Pasta al Pesto Calabrese

YIELD: 4 SERVINGS / **ACTIVE TIME:** 20 MINUTES / **TOTAL TIME:** 1 HOUR

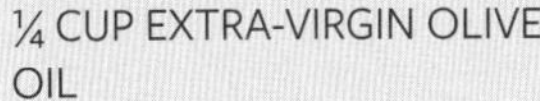

¼ CUP EXTRA-VIRGIN OLIVE OIL

1 RED ONION, FINELY DICED

2 RED BELL PEPPERS, STEMMED, SEEDED, AND SLICED THIN

5 OZ. WHOLE PEELED TOMATOES, CRUSHED

RED PEPPER FLAKES, TO TASTE

SALT, TO TASTE

½ CUP RICOTTA CHEESE

⅔ CUP GRATED CACIOCAVALLO OR PECORINO CHEESE

1 LB. PENNE OR DRIED FUSILLI

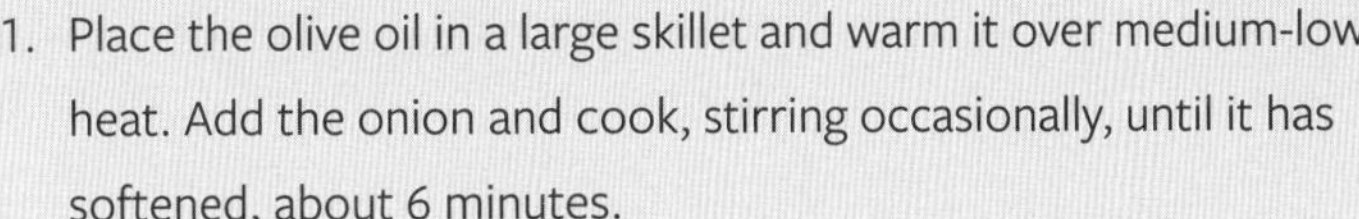

1. Place the olive oil in a large skillet and warm it over medium-low heat. Add the onion and cook, stirring occasionally, until it has softened, about 6 minutes.
2. Add the peppers, cover the pan, and cook, stirring occasionally, until they are tender, about 20 minutes.
3. Add the tomatoes and season the sauce with red pepper flakes and salt. Cover the pan and cook the sauce, stirring occasionally, for 20 minutes.
4. Stir in the ricotta and caciocavallo and use an immersion blender to puree the sauce until it is smooth.
5. Bring water to a boil in a large saucepan. Add salt, let the water return to a full boil, and add the pasta. Cook until the pasta is al dente.
6. Reserve 1 cup pasta water, drain the pasta, and stir it into the sauce.
7. Toss to combine, adding pasta water as needed to get the right consistency. Serve immediately.

Fusilli alla Molisana

YIELD: 4 SERVINGS / **ACTIVE TIME:** 30 MINUTES / **TOTAL TIME:** 3 HOURS

¼ CUP EXTRA-VIRGIN OLIVE OIL

1 ONION, FINELY DICED

1 CARROT, PEELED AND FINELY DICED

1 CELERY STALK, FINELY DICED

½ LB. LAMB, CHOPPED

½ LB. VEAL, CHOPPED

2 ITALIAN SAUSAGES, CASINGS REMOVED AND CRUMBLED

½ CUP WHITE WINE

2 LBS. WHOLE PEELED TOMATOES, CRUSHED

SALT, TO TASTE

1 LB. FUSILLI AL FERRO (SEE PAGE 12)

PECORINO CHEESE, GRATED, FOR GARNISH

1. Place the olive oil in a large saucepan and warm it over medium heat. Add the onion, carrot, and celery and cook, stirring occasionally, until the onion has softened, about 5 minutes.
2. Add the lamb, veal, and sausages and cook over medium-high heat until they are browned, 8 to 10 minutes.
3. Deglaze the pan with the white wine, scraping up any browned bits from the bottom. Cook until the wine has evaporated.
4. Add the tomatoes, season the sauce with salt, and reduce the heat to low. Cook until the meat starts falling apart, 2 to 3 hours.
5. Bring water to a boil in a large saucepan. Add salt, let the water return to a full boil, and add the pasta. Cook until the pasta is al dente, about 3 minutes after it rises to the surface.
6. Drain the pasta and stir it into the sauce. Garnish the dish with pecorino and serve.

Fusilli alla Silana

YIELD: 6 SERVINGS / **ACTIVE TIME:** 10 MINUTES / **TOTAL TIME:** 50 MINUTES

¼ CUP EXTRA-VIRGIN OLIVE OIL

1 SMALL ONION, FINELY DICED

2 OZ. GUANCIALE, SKINLESS AND CUT INTO STRIPS

5 OZ. SOPPRESSATA, SLICED

1 CHILE PEPPER, STEMMED, SEEDED, AND CHOPPED

1 OZ. COGNAC OR WHISKEY

1 LB. WHOLE PEELED TOMATOES, CRUSHED

SALT AND PEPPER, TO TASTE

1 LB. DRIED FUSILLI

7 OZ. CACIOCAVALLO CHEESE, CUBED

HANDFUL OF FRESH PARSLEY, CHOPPED

⅔ CUP GRATED PECORINO CHEESE

1. Place the olive oil in a large, deep skillet and warm it over medium heat. Add the onion, guanciale, soppressata, and chile and cook, stirring occasionally, until the guanciale's fat starts to render and the onion has softened, about 5 minutes.
2. Remove the pan from heat, add the cognac, and place the pan over medium-low heat. Cook until the cognac has evaporated.
3. Add the tomatoes and cook for 30 minutes, stirring occasionally.
4. Bring water to a boil in a large saucepan. Add salt, let the water return to a full boil, and add the pasta. Cook until the pasta is al dente.
5. Drain the pasta and stir it into the sauce.
6. Add the caciocavallo and parsley, cover the pan, and cook until the caciocavallo has melted.
7. Top the dish with the pecorino, season it with salt and pepper, and serve.

Maccheroni with Tomatoes & Sausage

YIELD: 4 SERVINGS / **ACTIVE TIME:** 15 MINUTES / **TOTAL TIME:** 1 HOUR AND 30 MINUTES

¼ CUP EXTRA-VIRGIN OLIVE OIL

1 RED ONION, FINELY DICED

4 ITALIAN SAUSAGES WITH FENNEL, CASINGS REMOVED AND CRUMBLED

1 LB. WHOLE PEELED TOMATOES, CRUSHED

1 MILD CHILE PEPPER, STEMMED, SEEDED, AND CHOPPED

SALT, TO TASTE

1 LB. MACCHERONI AL FERRETTO (SEE PAGE 16)

HANDFUL OF FRESH BASIL

⅔ CUP GRATED SMOKED AND AGED RICOTTA CHEESE

1. Place the olive oil in a large skillet and warm it over medium-low heat. Add the onion and cook, stirring occasionally, until it has softened, about 6 minutes.
2. Add the sausages and cook, stirring occasionally, until they are browned, 8 to 10 minutes.
3. Add the tomatoes and chile, season the sauce with salt, and reduce the heat to low. Cover the pan and cook the sauce until the flavor has developed to your liking, about 1 hour.
4. Bring water to a boil in a large saucepan. Add salt, let the water return to a full boil, and add the pasta. Cook until the pasta is al dente.
5. Drain the pasta and stir it into the sauce along with the basil. Toss to combine, top the dish with the smoked ricotta, and serve.

Maccheroni with ‘Nduja & Soppressata

YIELD: 4 SERVINGS / **ACTIVE TIME:** 20 MINUTES / **TOTAL TIME:** 24 HOURS

½ LB. DRIED CHICKPEAS, SOAKED OVERNIGHT

1 SPRIG OF FRESH ROSEMARY

1 GARLIC CLOVE

2 TABLESPOONS EXTRA-VIRGIN OLIVE OIL

1 RED ONION, FINELY DICED

¼ LB. SOPPRESSATA, FINELY DICED

1 LB. WHOLE PEELED TOMATOES, CRUSHED

2 TABLESPOONS ‘NDUJA

SALT, TO TASTE

1 LB. MACCHERONI AL FERRETTO (SEE PAGE 16)

⅔ CUP GRATED PECORINO CHEESE

1. Drain the chickpeas, place them in a large saucepan, and cover them with cold water. Add the rosemary and garlic, bring to a boil, and cook until the chickpeas are tender, about 45 minutes. Drain the chickpeas, reserve the cooking liquid, and set both aside.
2. Place the olive oil in a large, deep skillet and warm it over medium heat. Add the onion and soppressata and cook, stirring occasionally, until the onion has softened, about 5 minutes.
3. Add the tomatoes, reduce the heat to medium-low, and cook for 20 minutes, stirring occasionally.
4. Stir in the ‘nduja and cook for 20 minutes.
5. Place half of the chickpeas in a blender and puree until smooth. Add the puree and remaining chickpeas to the sauce, season it with salt, and stir to combine.
6. Bring water to a boil in a large saucepan. Add salt, let the water return to a full boil, and add the pasta. Cook until the pasta is al dente.
7. Drain the pasta and stir it into the sauce along with some of the reserved cooking liquid. Toss to combine, top the dish with the pecorino, and enjoy.

Maccheroni with 'Nduja & Ricotta

YIELD: 4 SERVINGS / **ACTIVE TIME:** 10 MINUTES / **TOTAL TIME:** 20 MINUTES

¼ CUP EXTRA-VIRGIN OLIVE OIL

1 RED ONION, FINELY DICED

1 SHALLOT, FINELY DICED

7 OZ. 'NDUJA, CHOPPED

11 OZ. RICOTTA CHEESE

3 OZ. PARMESAN CHEESE, GRATED

SALT, TO TASTE

1 LB. MACCHERONI AL FERRETTO (SEE PAGE 16)

1. Bring water to a boil in a large saucepan. Place the olive oil in a large, deep skillet and warm it over medium heat. Add the onion and shallot and cook, stirring occasionally, until they have softened, about 5 minutes.
2. Add the 'nduja and cook, stirring frequently, for 5 minutes.
3. Place the ricotta and Parmesan in a bowl and stir to combine.
4. Add salt to the boiling water, let the water return to a full boil, and add the pasta. Cook until the pasta is al dente. Add ½ cup of pasta water to the ricotta mixture and stir to incorporate.
5. Drain the pasta and stir it into the sauce along with the ricotta mixture. Toss quickly to combine and serve.

Spaghetti alla San Giuannin

YIELD: 4 SERVINGS / **ACTIVE TIME:** 30 MINUTES / **TOTAL TIME:** 30 MINUTES

¼ CUP EXTRA-VIRGIN OLIVE OIL

1 GARLIC CLOVE, HALVED

1 HOT CHILE PEPPER, STEMMED, SEEDED, AND MINCED

6 ANCHOVIES IN OLIVE OIL, DRAINED AND CHOPPED

19½ OZ. CHERRY TOMATOES, HALVED

SALT, TO TASTE

2 TABLESPOONS CAPERS IN BRINE, DRAINED AND RINSED

1 LB. SPAGHETTI

FRESH BASIL, SHREDDED, FOR GARNISH

PECORINO CHEESE, GRATED, FOR GARNISH

1. Place the olive oil in a large, deep skillet and warm it over medium heat. Add the garlic, chile, and anchovies and cook, stirring frequently, for 2 minutes.
2. Add the tomatoes, remove the garlic, and discard it. Season the tomatoes with salt and cook for 10 minutes.
3. Add the capers and a bit of water to the pan, reduce the heat to low, and let the sauce simmer gently.
4. Bring water to a boil in a large saucepan. Add salt, let the water return to a full boil, and add the pasta. Cook until the pasta is al dente.
5. Drain the pasta, add it to the sauce, and cook for 2 to 3 minutes, tossing to combine.
6. Garnish the dish with basil and pecorino and serve.

Pasta alla Ionica

YIELD: 4 SERVINGS / **ACTIVE TIME:** 30 MINUTES / **TOTAL TIME:** 50 MINUTES

4 TOMATOES

2 MEDIUM BELL PEPPERS

2 TABLESPOONS EXTRA-VIRGIN OLIVE OIL

2 GARLIC CLOVES, HALVED

¾ LB. GUANCIALE, SKIN REMOVED AND CUT INTO STRIPS

2 HANDFULS OF FRESH BASIL

SALT, TO TASTE

1 LB. MACCHERONI AL FERRETTO (SEE PAGE 16)

1 CUP GRATED PECORINO CHEESE

1. Bring water to a boil in a large saucepan and prepare an ice bath. Add the tomatoes and peppers, boil for 1 minute, and drain. Plunge them into the ice bath, drain them, and remove the skins.
2. Remove the stem and seeds from the peppers and discard them. Place the tomatoes and peppers in a food processor, puree until smooth, and set the mixture aside.
3. Place the olive oil in a large, deep skillet and warm it over medium-low heat. Add the garlic and cook, stirring frequently, for 2 minutes.
4. Add the guanciale and cook, stirring frequently, until its fat has rendered.
5. Add the tomato-and-pepper puree and cook for 20 minutes, stirring occasionally.
6. Remove the garlic and discard it. Add the basil, season the sauce with salt, and continue cooking it over low heat.
7. Bring water to a boil in a large saucepan. Add salt, let the water return to a full boil, and add the pasta. Cook until the pasta is al dente.
8. Drain the pasta, add it to the sauce, and toss to combine. Stir in the pecorino and serve.

‘Ndruppeche

YIELD: 4 SERVINGS / **ACTIVE TIME:** 30 MINUTES / **TOTAL TIME:** 1 HOUR AND 30 MINUTES

3 TABLESPOONS EXTRA-VIRGIN OLIVE OIL

1 GARLIC CLOVE, HALVED

5 OZ. GROUND BEEF

⅔ CUP DICED ITALIAN SALAMI

½ CUP DRY WHITE WINE

1 LB. WHOLE PEELED TOMATOES, LIGHTLY CRUSHED

2 BAY LEAVES

SALT, TO TASTE

1 LB. MACCHERONI AL FERRETTO (SEE PAGE 16) OR STROZZAPRETI

FRESH HORSERADISH, GRATED, FOR GARNISH

1. Place the olive oil in a large, deep skillet and warm it over medium heat. Add the garlic and cook, stirring frequently, for 2 minutes.
2. Add the beef and salami and cook, stirring occasionally, until the meat is browned, about 8 minutes.
3. Add the wine and cook until it has evaporated. Add the tomatoes and bay leaves, reduce the heat to low, partially cover the pan, and cook for 1 hour.
4. Bring water to a boil in a large saucepan. Add salt, let the water return to a full boil, and add the pasta. Cook until the pasta is al dente.
5. Remove the bay leaves from the sauce and discard them. Drain the pasta, stir it into the sauce, and toss to combine. Garnish the dish with horseradish and serve.

Pasta with Ragù, Horseradish & Bread Crumbs

YIELD: 4 SERVINGS / **ACTIVE TIME:** 30 MINUTES / **TOTAL TIME:** 1 HOUR AND 40 MINUTES

3 TABLESPOONS EXTRA-VIRGIN OLIVE OIL

1 ITALIAN SAUSAGE, CASING REMOVED AND CRUMBLED

6 OZ. LEAN PORK, CUBED

1 LB. WHOLE PEELED TOMATOES, LIGHTLY CRUSHED

¼ CUP BREAD CRUMBS

SALT, TO TASTE

1 LB. FUSILLI AL FERRO (SEE PAGE 12)

FRESH HORSERADISH, GRATED, FOR GARNISH

GRATED PECORINO CHEESE, FOR GARNISH

1. Place 2 tablespoons of olive oil in a large, deep skillet and warm it over medium heat. Add the sausage and pork and cook, stirring occasionally, until they are browned, about 8 minutes.
2. Add the tomatoes, reduce the heat to low, partially cover the pan, and cook for 1 hour.
3. Place the remaining olive oil in a small skillet and warm it over medium heat. Add the bread crumbs and cook, stirring occasionally, until they have browned. Remove the pan from heat and set it aside.
4. Bring water to a boil in a large saucepan. Add salt, let the water return to a full boil, and add the pasta. Cook until the pasta is al dente.
5. Drain the pasta, place it in a large serving dish, and add the sauce and bread crumbs. Toss to combine, garnish with horseradish and pecorino, and enjoy.

Pasta with Octopus Ragù

YIELD: 4 SERVINGS / **ACTIVE TIME:** 50 MINUTES / **TOTAL TIME:** 1 HOUR AND 20 MINUTES

2 LBS. FRESH OCTOPUS

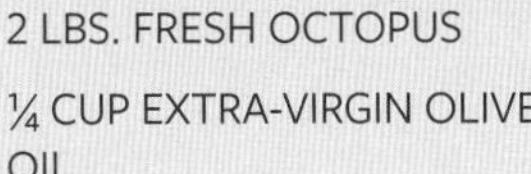

¼ CUP EXTRA-VIRGIN OLIVE OIL

1 GARLIC CLOVE

½ YELLOW ONION, FINELY DICED

⅓ HOT CHILE PEPPER, MINCED

½ CUP DRY WHITE WINE

2 LBS. PEELED TOMATOES, LIGHTLY CRUSHED

1 BAY LEAF

SALT, TO TASTE

1 LB. SCIALATIELLI (SEE PAGE 10)

FRESH PARSLEY, CHOPPED, FOR GARNISH

1. Rinse the octopus thoroughly under cold water and let it drain.
2. Cut the octopus into large pieces, leaving 4 tentacles whole.
3. Place the olive oil in a large, deep skillet and warm it over medium heat. Add the garlic, onion, and chile and cook, stirring frequently, for 5 minutes.
4. Add the octopus and cook, stirring frequently, until it is browned.
5. Add the white wine, raise the heat to medium-high, and cook until the wine has evaporated.
6. Remove the garlic and discard it. Add the tomatoes and bay leaf, reduce the heat to low, and season the sauce with salt. Cook until the sauce has thickened and the octopus is tender, 30 to 35 minutes.
7. Bring water to a boil in a large saucepan. Add salt, let the water return to a full boil, and add the pasta. Cook until the pasta is al dente.
8. Drain the pasta, add it to the sauce, and toss to combine.
9. To serve, top each portion with a long octopus tentacle and garnish with parsley.

Orecchiette alla Materana

YIELD: 4 SERVINGS / **ACTIVE TIME:** 30 MINUTES / **TOTAL TIME:** 1 HOUR AND 40 MINUTES

3 TABLESPOONS EXTRA-VIRGIN OLIVE OIL

¾ LB. LEAN LAMB, FINELY DICED

½ CUP DRY WHITE WINE

1½ LBS. WHOLE PEELED TOMATOES, LIGHTLY CRUSHED

SALT, TO TASTE

1 LB. ORECCHIETTE (SEE PAGE 22)

1⅔ CUPS DICED MOZZARELLA CHEESE

1⅔ CUPS GRATED PECORINO CHEESE

1. Place the olive oil in a large, deep skillet and warm it over medium heat. Add the lamb and cook, stirring occasionally, until it is browned, about 8 minutes.
2. Add the wine and cook until it has evaporated. Add the tomatoes, reduce the heat to low, partially cover the pan, and cook for 1 hour.
3. Bring water to a boil in a large saucepan. Add salt, let the water return to a full boil, and add the pasta. Cook until the pasta is very al dente.
4. Drain the pasta, place it in a large mixing bowl, and add the sauce. Stir to combine.
5. Preheat the oven to 360°F. Place one-third of the pasta in a layer on the bottom of a 13 x 9–inch baking pan and top it with a layer of the mozzarella and pecorino. Repeat the layering process two more times.
6. Place the dish in the oven and bake until the cheese is bubbling, 20 to 25 minutes.
7. Remove the dish from the oven and let it rest for 10 minutes before serving.

Orecchiette con Cime di Rapa

YIELD: 4 SERVINGS / **ACTIVE TIME:** 40 MINUTES / **TOTAL TIME:** 1 HOUR

SALT, TO TASTE

2.2 LBS. TURNIP GREENS, STEMMED AND RINSED WELL

¼ CUP EXTRA-VIRGIN OLIVE OIL, PLUS MORE AS NEEDED

2 GARLIC CLOVES, HALVED

1 HOT CHILE PEPPER, STEMMED, SEEDED, AND FINELY DICED

8 ANCHOVIES IN OLIVE OIL, DRAINED AND CHOPPED

¼ CUP BREAD CRUMBS

1 LB. ORECCHIETTE (SEE PAGE 22)

1. Bring salted water to a boil in a large saucepan. Add the turnip greens and cook until just tender, about 5 minutes. Drain the turnip greens and set them aside.
2. Place the olive oil in a large, deep skillet and warm it over medium heat. Add the garlic, chile, and anchovies and cook, stirring frequently, for 2 minutes. Remove the pan from heat and set it aside.
3. Lightly coat a small skillet with olive oil and warm it over medium heat. Add the bread crumbs and cook, stirring occasionally, until they are browned, about 5 minutes.
4. Bring water to a boil in a large saucepan. Add salt, let the water return to a full boil, and add the pasta. Cook until the pasta is al dente.
5. Add the turnip greens to the garlic mixture and cook over medium heat for 2 to 3 minutes, tossing to combine.
6. Drain the pasta, add it to the sauce, and toss to combine.
7. Top the dish with the toasted bread crumbs and serve.

Anelletti al Forno

YIELD: 4 SERVINGS / **ACTIVE TIME:** 1 HOUR / **TOTAL TIME:** 2 HOURS AND 30 MINUTES

1 CUP EXTRA-VIRGIN OLIVE OIL, PLUS MORE AS NEEDED

1 RED ONION, FINELY DICED

9 OZ. GROUND PORK

1 OZ. GROUND BEEF

1 CUP RED WINE

9 OZ. PEELED TOMATOES, LIGHTLY CRUSHED

9 OZ. PEAS

SALT AND PEPPER, TO TASTE

1 LARGE EGGPLANT, CUBED

1 LB. ANELLETTI

3½ OZ. CACIOCAVALLO CHEESE, CUBED

3 HARD-BOILED EGGS, SLICED

7 OZ. TOMINO OR PECORINO CHEESE, GRATED

2 TABLESPOONS BREAD CRUMBS

1. Place 2 tablespoons of olive oil in a large, deep skillet and warm it over medium-low heat. Add the onion and cook, stirring occasionally, until it has softened, about 6 minutes.
2. Add the pork and beef, raise the heat to medium-high, and cook, breaking the meat up with a wooden spoon, until it is browned, about 8 minutes.
3. Add the wine and cook until it has evaporated. Add the tomatoes and peas, season with salt and pepper, and reduce the heat to medium-low. Partially cover the pan and cook the sauce for about 40 minutes.
4. Place the eggplant in a colander and season it with salt. Fill a large saucepan with water and place it on top of the eggplant. Let the eggplant drain for 30 minutes.
5. Rinse the eggplant and squeeze it to remove as much water as possible. Place the eggplant on a kitchen towel and let it dry.
6. Place the remaining olive oil in a large skillet and warm it over medium-high heat. Add the eggplant and cook, stirring occasionally, until it is golden brown, 5 to 7 minutes. Transfer the eggplant to a paper towel–lined plate to drain.
7. Bring water to a boil in a large saucepan. Add salt, let the water return to a full boil, and add the pasta. Cook until the pasta is very al dente.
8. Drain the pasta and place it in a bowl. Add half of the sauce to the bowl and toss to combine. Preheat the oven to 360°F. Coat a 13 x 9–inch baking pan with olive oil and place half of the pasta on the bottom. Top the pasta with a layer consisting of half of the eggplant, one-third of the caciocavallo, one-third of the eggs, a few tablespoons of the sauce, and one-third of the tomino. Repeat this layering process and then top with a layer of the remaining caciocavallo and tomino, followed by the bread crumbs.
9. Place the anelletti al forno in the oven and bake until the cheese is melted and bubbling, about 35 minutes. Remove the anelletti al forno from the oven and let it rest for 10 minutes before serving.

Pasta con le Sarde

YIELD: 4 SERVINGS / **ACTIVE TIME:** 50 MINUTES / **TOTAL TIME:** 2 HOURS

1 LB. FRESH SARDINES

SALT AND PEPPER, TO TASTE

7 OZ. WILD FENNEL, RINSED WELL

PINCH OF SAFFRON THREADS

¼ CUP EXTRA-VIRGIN OLIVE OIL

1 LARGE WHITE ONION, FINELY DICED

5 ANCHOVIES IN OLIVE OIL, RINSED AND CHOPPED

3 TABLESPOONS RAISINS, SOAKED IN WARM WATER

3 TABLESPOONS BREAD CRUMBS

1 LB. BUCATINI

3 TABLESPOONS PINE NUTS

3 TABLESPOONS FINELY CHOPPED BLANCHED ALMONDS

1. Clean the sardines: scrub them, remove the heads, entrails, and spines, and open them completely. Rinse the sardines under running water and pat them dry with paper towels.
2. Bring water to a boil in a large saucepan. Add salt and the fennel and cook until the fennel is tender, about 10 minutes. Remove the fennel from the boiling water with a strainer or slotted spoon and set it aside. When the fennel has cooled slightly, chop it. Keep the water at a gentle boil.
3. Place the saffron in ½ cup water and let it steep.
4. Place the olive oil in a large skillet and warm it over medium heat. Add the onion and anchovies and cook, stirring occasionally, until the onion has softened and the anchovies have dissolved, about 5 minutes.
5. Add the saffron, saffron water, sardines, and fennel. Drain the raisins, squeeze them to remove any excess liquid, and add them to the pan. Cook until the sardines are cooked through and the sauce has thickened, about 10 minutes.
6. While the sauce is cooking, place the bread crumbs in a skillet and toast them over medium heat until they are browned, shaking the pan occasionally.
7. Add the pasta to the boiling water and cook until it is al dente.
8. Drain the pasta and add it to the sauce along with the bread crumbs, pine nuts, and almonds. Toss to combine, season with salt and pepper, remove the pan from heat, and let the dish sit for a few minutes before serving.

Pasta alla Norma

YIELD: 4 SERVINGS / **ACTIVE TIME:** 50 MINUTES / **TOTAL TIME:** 2 HOURS

2 LARGE EGGPLANTS, CUT INTO CHUNKS

¼ CUP COARSE SALT

2 LBS. TOMATOES

6 TABLESPOONS EXTRA-VIRGIN OLIVE OIL

1 GARLIC CLOVE, HALVED

SALT AND PEPPER, TO TASTE

1 LB. RIGATONI

¼ CUP GRATED RICOTTA SALATA CHEESE, FOR GARNISH

FRESH BASIL, SHREDDED, FOR GARNISH

1. Place the eggplants in a colander and season them with the coarse salt. Fill a large saucepan with water and place it on top of the eggplants. Let the eggplants drain for 1 hour.
2. Rinse the eggplants and squeeze them to remove as much water as possible. Place the eggplants on kitchen towels and let them dry.
3. Bring water to a boil in a large saucepan. Add the tomatoes and cook for 1 minute. Remove the tomatoes, peel them, and remove the seeds. Chop the remaining flesh and set them aside.
4. Place 2 tablespoons of olive oil in a medium saucepan and warm it over medium heat. Add the garlic and cook, stirring frequently, for 2 minutes.
5. Remove the garlic and discard it. Add the tomatoes, season with salt and pepper, and cook until the sauce starts to thicken, 20 to 30 minutes.
6. Place the remaining olive oil in a large skillet and warm it over medium-high heat. Add the eggplants and cook, stirring occasionally, until they are golden brown, 5 to 7 minutes. Transfer the eggplants to a paper towel–lined plate to drain.
7. Add the eggplants to the sauce and cook for a few minutes, stirring occasionally.
8. Bring water to a boil in a large saucepan. Add salt, let the water return to a full boil, and add the pasta. Cook until the pasta is very al dente.
9. Drain the pasta, add it to the sauce, and cook for 2 to 3 minutes, tossing to combine.
10. Garnish the dish with the ricotta salata and basil and serve.

Pasta with Sun-Dried Tomatoes

YIELD: 4 SERVINGS / **ACTIVE TIME:** 20 MINUTES / **TOTAL TIME:** 40 MINUTES

6 TABLESPOONS EXTRA-VIRGIN OLIVE OIL

1 GARLIC CLOVE, HALVED

12 SUN-DRIED TOMATOES IN OLIVE OIL, DRAINED AND CHOPPED

3 TABLESPOONS BREAD CRUMBS

SALT, TO TASTE

1 LB. SPAGHETTI

3 TABLESPOONS FRESHLY CHOPPED PARSLEY

PECORINO CHEESE, GRATED, FOR GARNISH

1. Place ¼ cup of olive oil in a large, deep skillet and warm it over medium heat. Add the garlic and cook, stirring frequently, for 2 minutes.
2. Remove the garlic and discard it. Add the tomatoes and cook for 5 minutes.
3. Place the remaining olive oil in a small skillet and warm it over medium heat. Add the bread crumbs and cook, stirring occasionally, until they are browned, about 5 minutes.
4. Bring water to a boil in a large saucepan. Add salt, let the water return to a full boil, and add the pasta. Cook until the pasta is very al dente.
5. Drain the pasta, add it to the sauce along with the parsley, and cook for 2 to 3 minutes, tossing to combine.
6. Garnish the dish with the bread crumbs and pecorino and serve.

Pasta 'Ncasciata

YIELD: 4 SERVINGS / **ACTIVE TIME:** 1 HOUR / **TOTAL TIME:** 2 HOURS AND 30 MINUTES

1 CUP EXTRA-VIRGIN OLIVE OIL, PLUS MORE AS NEEDED

1 WHITE ONION, FINELY DICED

6½ OZ. GROUND BEEF

6½ OZ. GROUND PORK

½ CUP DRY WHITE WINE

1½ LBS. PEELED TOMATOES, LIGHTLY CRUSHED

2 HANDFULS OF FRESH BASIL LEAVES

SALT AND PEPPER, TO TASTE

2 LARGE EGGPLANTS, CUT INTO ½-INCH-THICK SLICES

1 LB. SHORT-FORMAT PASTA

9 OZ. CACIOCAVALLO CHEESE, CUBED

1 CUP GRATED PECORINO CHEESE

1. Place 2 tablespoons of olive oil in a large, deep skillet and warm it over medium-low heat. Add the onion and cook, stirring occasionally, until it has softened, about 6 minutes.
2. Add the beef and pork, raise the heat to medium-high, and cook, breaking the meat up with a wooden spoon, until it is browned, about 8 minutes.
3. Add the wine and cook until it has evaporated. Add the tomatoes and basil, season with salt and pepper, and reduce the heat to medium-low. Partially cover the pan and cook the sauce for about 40 minutes.
4. Place the eggplants in a colander and season them with salt. Fill a large saucepan with water and place it on top of the eggplants. Let the eggplants drain for 30 minutes.
5. Rinse the eggplants and squeeze them to remove as much water as possible. Place the eggplants on kitchen towels and let them dry.
6. Place the remaining olive oil in a large skillet and warm it over medium-high heat. Add the eggplants and cook, stirring occasionally, until they are golden brown, 5 to 7 minutes. Transfer the eggplants to a paper towel–lined plate to drain.
7. Bring water to a boil in a large saucepan. Add salt, let the water return to a full boil, and add the pasta. Cook until the pasta is very al dente. Drain the pasta and place it in a bowl. Add half of the sauce to the bowl and toss to combine.
8. Preheat the oven to 360°F. Coat a 13 x 9–inch baking pan with olive oil and place half of the pasta on the bottom. Top the pasta with a layer consisting of half of the eggplant, one-third of the caciocavallo, a few tablespoons of sauce, and one-third of the pecorino. Repeat this layering process and then top with a layer of the remaining caciocavallo and pecorino. Place the 'ncasciata in the oven and bake until the cheese is melted and bubbling, about 20 minutes. Remove the 'ncasciata from the oven and let it rest for 10 minutes before serving.

Spaghetti all'Aragosta

YIELD: 4 SERVINGS / **ACTIVE TIME:** 30 MINUTES / **TOTAL TIME:** 1 HOUR

SALT, TO TASTE

2 MEDIUM LOBSTERS

¼ CUP EXTRA-VIRGIN OLIVE OIL

1 WHITE ONION, FINELY DICED

1 GARLIC CLOVE

1 LB. PEELED TOMATOES, LIGHTLY CRUSHED

1 LB. SPAGHETTI

FRESH PARSLEY, CHOPPED, FOR GARNISH

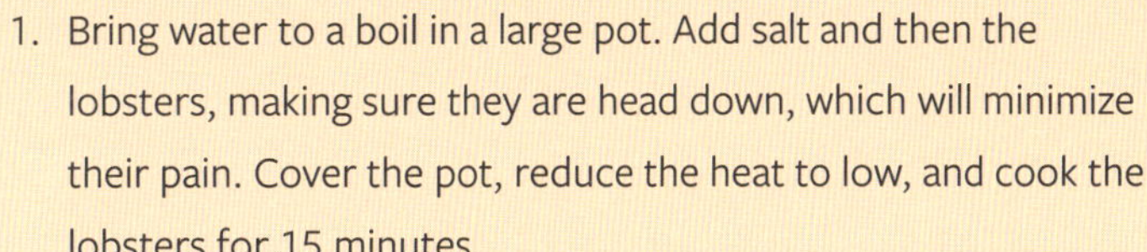

1. Bring water to a boil in a large pot. Add salt and then the lobsters, making sure they are head down, which will minimize their pain. Cover the pot, reduce the heat to low, and cook the lobsters for 15 minutes.
2. Drain the lobsters and let them cool. When they are cool enough to handle, extract the meat from the lobsters, chop it, and set it aside.
3. Place the olive oil in a large, deep skillet and warm it over medium heat. Add the onion and garlic and cook, stirring frequently, until the onion has softened, about 5 minutes.
4. Remove the garlic and discard it. Add the tomatoes, season with salt, and cook, stirring occasionally, for 20 minutes.
5. Bring water to a boil in a large saucepan. Add salt, let the water return to a full boil, and add the pasta. Cook until the pasta is very al dente.
6. Add the lobster to the sauce. Drain the pasta, add it to the sauce, and raise the heat to medium-high. Cook for 2 to 3 minutes, tossing to combine.
7. Garnish the dish with parsley and enjoy.

Busiate al Pesto alla Trapanese

YIELD: 4 SERVINGS / **ACTIVE TIME:** 30 MINUTES / **TOTAL TIME:** 45 MINUTES

½ LB. TOMATOES

⅓ CUP BLANCHED ALMONDS

2½ CUPS FRESH BASIL

1 GARLIC CLOVE

2 TABLESPOONS EXTRA-VIRGIN OLIVE OIL, PLUS MORE AS NEEDED

5 TABLESPOONS GRATED PECORINO CHEESE

SALT AND PEPPER, TO TASTE

RED PEPPER FLAKES, TO TASTE

1 LB. BUSIATE (SEE PAGE 15)

1. Bring water to a boil in a large saucepan. Cut a cross on the bottom of the tomatoes and add them to the boiling water. Cook for 2 minutes, remove the tomatoes with a slotted spoon, and peel them. Set the tomatoes aside. Keep the water at a boil.
2. Place the almonds, basil, and garlic in a blender and pulse until finely ground. Add the olive oil and puree until the mixture is a paste.
3. Add the tomatoes and 2 tablespoons of pecorino, season the mixture with salt, pepper, and red pepper flakes, and puree until the mixture is smooth and creamy, adding more olive oil if needed to get the desired texture.
4. Add salt to the boiling water, let the water return to a full boil, and add the pasta. Cook until the pasta is al dente.
5. Add a few tablespoons of pasta water to the sauce and stir to combine. Drain the pasta, place it in a bowl, and add the sauce. Toss to combine.
6. Top with the remaining pecorino and serve.

Pappardelle al Ragù di Cinghiale

YIELD: 4 SERVINGS / **ACTIVE TIME:** 10 MINUTES / **TOTAL TIME:** 20 MINUTES

RAGÙ DI CINGHIALE (SEE PAGE 451)

SALT, TO TASTE

14 OZ. PAPPARDELLE

1. Place the ragù in a large skillet and warm it over medium heat.
2. Bring water to a boil in a large saucepan. Add salt, let the water return to a full boil, and add the pasta. Cook the pasta until it is al dente. Reserve ½ cup pasta water and drain the pasta.
3. Add the pasta to the ragù. Add pasta water until the sauce has the desired consistency and cook, tossing to combine, for 2 to 3 minutes. Serve immediately.

Spaghetti alla Bottarga

YIELD: 4 SERVINGS / **ACTIVE TIME:** 10 MINUTES / **TOTAL TIME:** 30 MINUTES

SALT AND PEPPER, TO TASTE

1 LB. SPAGHETTI

¼ CUP EXTRA-VIRGIN OLIVE OIL

2 GARLIC CLOVES

3½ OZ. MULLET BOTTARGA, GRATED

¼ CUP FRESHLY CHOPPED PARSLEY

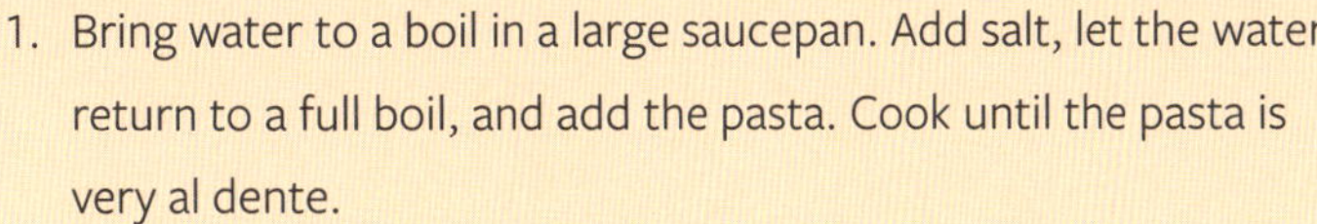

1. Bring water to a boil in a large saucepan. Add salt, let the water return to a full boil, and add the pasta. Cook until the pasta is very al dente.
2. Place the olive oil in a large skillet and warm it over medium heat. Add the garlic and cook, stirring frequently, for 2 minutes.
3. Add two-thirds of the bottarga and parsley, and a few tablespoons of the pasta water to the pan. Cook, gently stirring, for 2 minutes.
4. Reserve 1 cup of pasta water, drain the pasta, add it to the pan, and raise the heat to medium-high. Cook for 2 to 3 minutes, tossing to combine and adding pasta water as necessary to get the desired texture.
5. Top with the remaining bottarga and parsley, season with salt and pepper, and serve.

Malloreddus with Walnuts & Bread Crumbs

YIELD: 4 SERVINGS / **ACTIVE TIME:** 15 MINUTES / **TOTAL TIME:** 35 MINUTES

¼ CUP EXTRA-VIRGIN OLIVE OIL

1 GARLIC CLOVE, MINCED

5½ OZ. WALNUTS, GROUND

2 TABLESPOONS FRESHLY CHOPPED PARSLEY

1 CUP BREAD CRUMBS

SALT AND PEPPER, TO TASTE

1 LB. MALLOREDDUS (SEE PAGE 24)

1. Place the olive oil in a large skillet and warm it over medium-low heat. Add the garlic and cook for 2 minutes.
2. Add the walnuts and parsley and cook, stirring frequently, for 2 minutes. Remove the pan from heat and set it aside.
3. Place the bread crumbs in a small skillet and toast over low heat until they are browned, shaking the pan occasionally. Remove the pan from heat and set it aside.
4. Bring water to a boil in a large saucepan. Add salt, let the water return to a full boil, and add the pasta. Cook until the pasta is al dente.
5. Reserve 1 cup of pasta water, drain the pasta, and add it to the pan containing the walnut mixture. Stir in the bread crumbs, place the pan over medium-high heat, and cook for 2 to 3 minutes, tossing to combine and adding pasta water as needed to get the desired texture. Season with salt and pepper and serve immediately.

Fregola with Artichokes

YIELD: 4 SERVINGS / **ACTIVE TIME:** 40 MINUTES / **TOTAL TIME:** 1 HOUR

6 FRESH ARTICHOKE HEARTS, SLICED

JUICE OF ½ LEMON

¼ CUP EXTRA-VIRGIN OLIVE OIL

2 GARLIC CLOVES, MINCED

2 TABLESPOONS FRESHLY CHOPPED PARSLEY

3 CUPS VEGETABLE STOCK (SEE PAGE 447), WARM

¾ LB. FREGOLA (SEE PAGE 20)

SALT AND PEPPER, TO TASTE

½ CUP GRATED PECORINO CHEESE

1. Place the artichoke hearts and lemon juice in a bowl and cover with water.
2. Place the olive oil in a large, deep skillet and warm it over medium-low heat. Add the garlic and parsley and cook for 2 minutes.
3. Drain the artichoke hearts, add them to the pan, and cook for 3 minutes. Add half of the stock and cook, stirring occasionally, for about 15 minutes.
4. Add the Fregola and cook for 20 minutes, gradually incorporating the remaining stock and letting the Fregola absorb each addition, as you would with risotto.
5. Season the dish with salt and pepper, stir in the pecorino, and serve.

Malloreddus alla Campidanese

YIELD: 4 SERVINGS / **ACTIVE TIME:** 20 MINUTES / **TOTAL TIME:** 50 MINUTES

¼ CUP EXTRA-VIRGIN OLIVE OIL

1 ONION, FINELY DICED

11 OZ. ITALIAN SAUSAGE, CASING REMOVED AND CRUMBLED

1⅓ CUPS PEELED AND CRUSHED TOMATOES

SALT, TO TASTE

7 OZ. PECORINO CHEESE, GRATED

¼ CUP WATER

1 LB. MALLOREDDUS (SEE PAGE 24)

1. Place the olive oil in a large skillet and warm it over medium-low heat. Add the onion and cook until it has softened, about 5 minutes.
2. Add the sausage and cook, stirring frequently, until it has browned, about 8 minutes. Add the tomatoes, season with salt, and partially cover the pan. Cook for 30 minutes, stirring occasionally.
3. Place the pecorino and water in a bowl and whisk until the mixture is smooth and creamy.
4. Bring water to a boil in a large saucepan. Add salt, let the water return to a full boil, and add the pasta. Cook until the pasta is al dente.
5. Drain the pasta and add it to the sauce along with the pecorino cream. Raise the heat to medium-high and cook for 2 to 3 minutes, tossing to combine. Serve immediately.

Culurgiones al Pomodoro

YIELD: 4 SERVINGS / **ACTIVE TIME:** 10 MINUTES / **TOTAL TIME:** 20 MINUTES

2 CUPS SUGO AL BASILICO (SEE PAGE 447)

SALT, TO TASTE

1 LB. CULURGIONES (SEE PAGE 21)

½ CUP GRATED PECORINO CHEESE, FOR GARNISH

1. Place the tomato sauce in a medium saucepan and warm it over medium heat.
2. Bring water to a boil in a large saucepan. Add salt, let the water return to a full boil, and add the Culurgiones. Cook until they are al dente.
3. Drain the Culurgiones and add them to the sauce. Toss to combine, garnish with the pecorino, and serve.

Cicelievitati

YIELD: 4 SERVINGS / **ACTIVE TIME:** 1 HOUR / **TOTAL TIME:** 3 HOURS

4⅙ CUPS (500 G) ALL-PURPOSE FLOUR

1 PACKET (7 G) OF ACTIVE DRY YEAST

2 EGGS

2 PINCHES OF TABLE SALT, PLUS MORE TO TASTE

1 CUP (235 ML) WATER

SEMOLINA FLOUR, AS NEEDED

1. Place the flour, yeast, and eggs in the work bowl of a stand mixer fitted with the dough hook and work the mixture until combined. Add the salt, work the mixture until it has been incorporated, and then add the water, 1 tablespoon at a time. Work the mixture until it comes together as a dry dough.
2. Cover the work bowl with plastic wrap and let the dough rise until it has doubled in size, about 1½ hours.
3. Dust a work surface with semolina flour, place the dough on it, and tear off a small piece of the dough. Roll the small piece of dough into a 3-inch-long stick that is about the thickness of a ballpoint pen. Repeat with the remaining dough.
4. To cook the cicelievitati, bring water to a boil in a large saucepan. Add salt, let the water return to a full boil, and add the pasta. Cook until the pasta has the consistency of properly cooked gnocchi, light and slightly chewy, 3 to 5 minutes.

Fregola with Artichokes

SEE PAGE 74

Spaghetti alla Carbonara

YIELD: 4 SERVINGS / **ACTIVE TIME:** 20 MINUTES / **TOTAL TIME:** 25 MINUTES

6½ OZ. GUANCIALE, CUT INTO 1-INCH-LONG AND ¼-INCH-THICK STRIPS

5 EGG YOLKS

⅔ CUP GRATED PECORINO CHEESE

SALT AND PEPPER, TO TASTE

1 LB. SPAGHETTI

1. Place the guanciale in a large skillet and warm it over medium-low heat. Cook until the guanciale has rendered most of its fat and is lightly browned. Remove the guanciale from the pan and set it aside.
2. Place the egg yolks and pecorino in a large bowl and lightly beat to combine. Season the mixture with a generous amount of pepper and set it aside.
3. Bring water to a boil in a large saucepan. Add salt, let the water return to a full boil, and add the pasta. Cook the pasta until it is al dente.
4. Drain the pasta and add it to the bowl containing the egg-and-cheese mixture along with the guanciale. Toss to combine and serve immediately.

Vincisgrassi

YIELD: 6 SERVINGS / **ACTIVE TIME:** 20 MINUTES / **TOTAL TIME:** 1 HOUR

SALT, TO TASTE

10 LARGE LASAGNA SHEETS OR 40 SMALL ONES

RAGÙ RICCO (SEE PAGE 449)

1½ CUPS GRATED PARMESAN CHEESE

1. Preheat the oven to 350°F. If using dried lasagna sheets, bring water to a boil in a large saucepan. Add salt, let the water return to a full boil, and add the lasagna. Cook until it is al dente. Drain the pasta.
2. Spread some ragù over the bottom of a large baking dish. Place some lasagna on top, spread a thin layer of ragù on top, and top this with a generous sprinkle of Parmesan. Repeat until you have 10 layers.
3. Place the lasagna in the oven and bake until it is bubbling, about 30 minutes. Remove the lasagna from the oven and let it rest for 20 minutes before slicing and serving.

Spaghetti con Ricotta

YIELD: 4 SERVINGS / **ACTIVE TIME:** 10 MINUTES / **TOTAL TIME:** 20 MINUTES

SALT AND PEPPER, TO TASTE

1 LB. SPAGHETTI

1.1 LBS. RICOTTA CHEESE

1½ CUPS GRATED PECORINO CHEESE

1. Bring water to a boil in a large saucepan. Add salt, let the water return to a full boil, and add the pasta. Cook the pasta until it is al dente.
2. Place the ricotta and pecorino in a large bowl and add a few tablespoons of pasta water. Season with salt and pepper and whisk to combine.
3. Reserve 1 cup of pasta water, drain the pasta, and place it in the bowl.
4. Toss to combine, adding pasta water as needed to get the desired consistency. Serve immediately.

Pasta alla Gricia

YIELD: 4 SERVINGS / **ACTIVE TIME:** 20 MINUTES / **TOTAL TIME:** 25 MINUTES

½ LB. GUANCIALE, CUT IN 1-INCH-LONG AND ¼-INCH-WIDE STRIPS

SALT AND PEPPER, TO TASTE

14 OZ. RIGATONI

1 CUP GRATED PECORINO CHEESE, PLUS MORE FOR GARNISH

1. Place the guanciale in a large skillet and warm it over medium-low heat. Cook until the guanciale has rendered most of its fat and is lightly browned. Remove the guanciale from the pan with a slotted spoon and set it aside.
2. Bring water to a boil in a large saucepan. Add salt, let the water return to a full boil, and add the pasta. Cook the pasta until it is al dente. Reserve 1 cup of pasta water, drain the pasta, and set it aside.
3. Add a few tablespoons of pasta water to the skillet and place it over medium-high heat. Add the pasta and cook for 2 to 3 minutes, tossing to combine.
4. Season with a generous amount of pepper and remove the pan from heat.
5. Add the cheese and a few tablespoons of pasta water and toss to incorporate. Add the guanciale, toss to combine, garnish with additional pecorino, and serve.

Gnocchi alla Bava

YIELD: 4 SERVINGS / **ACTIVE TIME:** 20 MINUTES / **TOTAL TIME:** 30 MINUTES

1½ CUPS HEAVY CREAM

9 OZ. FONTINA CHEESE, CUBED

SALT AND PEPPER, TO TASTE

GNOCCHI DI GRANO SARACENO (SEE PAGE 33)

1. Place the cream in a small saucepan and warm it over low heat.
2. Add the fontina and let it melt very slowly over low heat.
3. Season the sauce with salt and pepper, remove the pan from heat, and cover it.
4. Bring water to a boil in a large saucepan. Add salt and the gnocchi, let the gnocchi rise to the surface, and cook for another minute once they do.
5. Drain the gnocchi and add them to the sauce. Toss to combine and serve immediately.

Strangozzi with Black Truffle

YIELD: 4 SERVINGS / **ACTIVE TIME:** 15 MINUTES / **TOTAL TIME:** 25 MINUTES

3½ OZ. BLACK TRUFFLES

5 TABLESPOONS EXTRA-VIRGIN OLIVE OIL

2 GARLIC CLOVES, HALVED

SALT, TO TASTE

STRANGOZZI (SEE PAGE 26)

1. Bring water to a boil in a large saucepan. Using a kitchen brush, remove any soil from the truffles. Cut them into small, thin flakes and set them aside.
2. Place the olive oil in a large skillet and warm it over medium-low heat. Add the garlic and cook, stirring frequently, for 2 minutes.
3. Remove the pan from heat, remove the garlic, and discard it. Stir the truffles into the infused oil and set it aside.
4. Add salt to the boiling water, let the water return to a full boil, and add the pasta. Cook the pasta until it is al dente.
5. Drain the pasta, add it to the truffle oil, and toss to combine. Serve immediately.

Penne all'Arrabbiata

YIELD: 4 SERVINGS / **ACTIVE TIME:** 20 MINUTES / **TOTAL TIME:** 30 MINUTES

¼ CUP EXTRA-VIRGIN OLIVE OIL

2 GARLIC CLOVES, HALVED

2 HOT CHILE PEPPERS, STEMMED, SEEDED, AND SLICED THIN

1.1 LBS. PEELED TOMATOES, LIGHTLY CRUSHED

SALT, TO TASTE

1 LB. PENNE RIGATE

HANDFUL OF FRESHLY CHOPPED PARSLEY

1 CUP GRATED PECORINO CHEESE, PLUS MORE FOR SERVING

1. Place the olive oil in a large skillet and warm it over low heat. Add the garlic and chiles and cook until the garlic is lightly browned.
2. Add the tomatoes, season with salt, raise the heat to medium, and cook, stirring occasionally, for 10 to 15 minutes.
3. Remove the garlic from the pan, reduce the heat to medium-low, and gently simmer the sauce.
4. Bring water to a boil in a large saucepan. Add salt, let the water return to a full boil, and add the pasta. Cook the pasta until it is al dente. Drain the pasta and place it in a bowl.
5. Add the sauce, parsley, and pecorino to the bowl and toss to combine. Serve immediately with additional pecorino.

Pasta Amatriciana

YIELD: 4 SERVINGS / **ACTIVE TIME:** 30 MINUTES / **TOTAL TIME:** 40 MINUTES

6 RIPE SAN MARZANO TOMATOES

1 TABLESPOON EXTRA-VIRGIN OLIVE OIL

4½ OZ. GUANCIALE, CUT INTO 1-INCH-LONG AND ¼-INCH-WIDE STRIPS

1 CHILE PEPPER

2 TABLESPOONS DRY WHITE WINE

SALT, TO TASTE

18 OZ. SPAGHETTI

1 CUP GRATED PECORINO CHEESE, PLUS MORE FOR SERVING

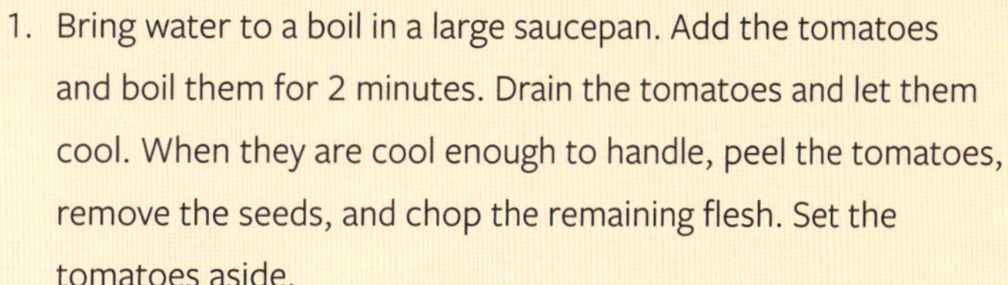

1. Bring water to a boil in a large saucepan. Add the tomatoes and boil them for 2 minutes. Drain the tomatoes and let them cool. When they are cool enough to handle, peel the tomatoes, remove the seeds, and chop the remaining flesh. Set the tomatoes aside.
2. Place the olive oil in a large cast-iron skillet and warm it over medium heat. Add the guanciale and chile and cook until the guanciale starts to render its fat. Raise the heat to medium-high and cook until the guanciale has browned.
3. Add the wine and cook until it has evaporated. Remove the guanciale from the pan with a slotted spoon. Set it aside.
4. Add the tomatoes to the pan, season with salt, and reduce the heat to medium. Cook for 2 minutes.
5. Remove the chile, return the guanciale to the pan, and gently simmer the sauce.
6. Bring water to a boil in a large saucepan. Add salt, let the water return to a full boil, and add the pasta. Cook the pasta until it is al dente. Drain the pasta and place it in a bowl.
7. Add the pecorino to the bowl and toss to combine. Add the sauce, toss to combine, and serve with additional pecorino.

Casonsei alla Bergamasca

YIELD: 4 SERVINGS / **ACTIVE TIME:** 30 MINUTES / **TOTAL TIME:** 30 MINUTES

3½ OZ. PANCETTA, CUT INTO STICKS (OPTIONAL)

SALT, TO TASTE

CASONSEI (SEE PAGE 31)

¼ CUP UNSALTED BUTTER

HANDFUL OF FRESH SAGE

3½ OZ. PARMESAN CHEESE, GRATED

1. Warm the oven to 200°F. Place the pancetta in a large skillet and cook it over medium heat until the fat renders, about 4 minutes. Remove the pancetta with a slotted spoon, place it in a crock, and place it in the oven to keep it warm.
2. Bring water to a boil in a large saucepan. Add salt and the Casonsei and cook until they float to the top and the meat is cooked through, about 4 minutes. Remove the Casonsei with a pasta fork and set them aside.
3. Place the butter in the skillet and melt it over medium heat. Add the sage and cook, stirring continually, for 2 minutes.
4. Add the Parmesan and some pasta water and stir until you have a creamy sauce.
5. Add the Casonsei and pancetta to the pan, toss to combine, and serve immediately.

Lasagne alla Bolognese

YIELD: 4 SERVINGS / **ACTIVE TIME:** 30 MINUTES / **TOTAL TIME:** 1 HOUR

PASTA ALL'UOVO VERDE (SEE PAGE 36)

ALL-PURPOSE FLOUR, AS NEEDED

SALT, TO TASTE

BESCIAMELLA (SEE PAGE 452)

RAGÙ RICCO (SEE PAGE 449)

7 OZ. PARMESAN CHEESE, GRATED

2 TABLESPOONS UNSALTED BUTTER, CHOPPED

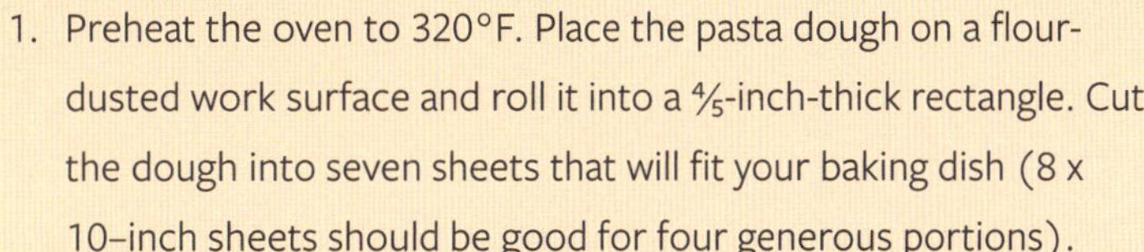

1. Preheat the oven to 320°F. Place the pasta dough on a flour-dusted work surface and roll it into a 4/5-inch-thick rectangle. Cut the dough into seven sheets that will fit your baking dish (8 x 10–inch sheets should be good for four generous portions).
2. Bring water to a boil in a large saucepan. Add salt, let the water return to a full boil, and add the pasta. Cook until the pasta has just softened.
3. Drain the pasta and place it on a kitchen towel to dry.
4. Spread a thin layer of béchamel over the baking dish. Top with a sheet of pasta, cover the pasta with a layer of béchamel, spread a layer of the ragù over the béchamel, and finish with a generous sprinkle of the Parmesan. Repeat until all of the pasta sheets have been used up. Top the last pasta sheet with bèchamel, ragù, the butter, and the remaining Parmesan.
5. Place the lasagna in the oven and bake until the cheese has melted and the top is golden brown, about 30 minutes.
6. Remove the lasagna from the oven and let it rest for 20 minutes before slicing and serving.

Spaghetti with Garlic Oil & Chiles

YIELD: 4 SERVINGS / **ACTIVE TIME:** 10 MINUTES / **TOTAL TIME:** 20 MINUTES

6 TABLESPOONS EXTRA-VIRGIN OLIVE OIL

2 GARLIC CLOVES, HALVED

2 HOT CHILE PEPPERS, STEMMED, SEEDED, AND MINCED

SALT, TO TASTE

1 LB. SPAGHETTI

HANDFUL OF FRESH PARSLEY, CHOPPED

1. Bring water to a boil in a large saucepan.
2. Place the olive oil in a large skillet and warm it over low heat. Add the garlic and chiles and cook until the garlic is lightly browned. Then remove the garlic from the pan and set it aside.
3. Add salt to the boiling water, let it return to a full boil, and add the pasta. Cook until the pasta is al dente.
4. Drain the pasta and add it to the skillet along with the parsley. Raise the heat to medium-high and cook for 2 to 3 minutes, tossing to combine. Serve immediately.

Pansoti alla Genovese

YIELD: 4 SERVINGS / **ACTIVE TIME:** 1 HOUR / **TOTAL TIME:** 1 HOUR AND 30 MINUTES

2.2 LBS. PREBUGGIÙN (SEE NOTE BELOW)

1 EGG

3½ OZ. LIGURIAN PRESCINSÊUA OR RICOTTA CHEESE

3½ OZ. PARMESAN CHEESE, GRATED

1 TABLESPOON FINELY CHOPPED FRESH MARJORAM

PINCH OF FRESHLY GRATED NUTMEG

SALT AND PEPPER, TO TASTE

RAVIOLI (SEE PAGE 28), CUT AND UNFILLED

ALL-PURPOSE FLOUR, AS NEEDED

SALSA DI NOCI (SEE PAGE 453)

1. Place the prebuggiùn, egg, cheeses, marjoram, and nutmeg in a bowl, season with salt and pepper, and stir until well combined. Set the filling aside.
2. Place a spoonful of the filling in the center of each Ravioli square and moisten the edges of the square with water. Fold one corner of the square over the filling, creating a triangle. Press down on the edges to seal the pansoti. Join the two ends of the base of the triangle together and gently press to seal.
3. Place the pansoti on flour-dusted baking sheets and dust them with flour.
4. Bring water to a boil in a large saucepan. Place the sauce in a large saucepan and warm it over medium-low heat.
5. Add salt to the boiling water and let the water return to a full boil. Add the pansoti to the boiling water and cook for about 8 minutes.
6. Drain the pasta and place it in a large serving bowl. Add the sauce, toss to combine, and serve immediately.

Note: Prebuggiùn is a bouquet of wild leafy green vegetables such as borage, nettle, chard, dandelion, wild fennel, wild radicchio, wild poppy leaves, horseradish leaves, wild arugula, Pimpinella, and/or chicory. In the absence of these wild greens, use baby spinach, small leaves of chard, arugula, and whatever other small leafy greens you prefer.

Pasta with Bread Crumbs & Cayenne

YIELD: 4 SERVINGS / **ACTIVE TIME:** 15 MINUTES / **TOTAL TIME:** 25 MINUTES

¼ CUP EXTRA-VIRGIN OLIVE OIL

3 GARLIC CLOVES, HALVED

CAYENNE PEPPER, TO TASTE

7 OZ. STALE BREAD, CRUSTLESS AND CRUMBLED

SALT, TO TASTE

1 LB. SPAGHETTI

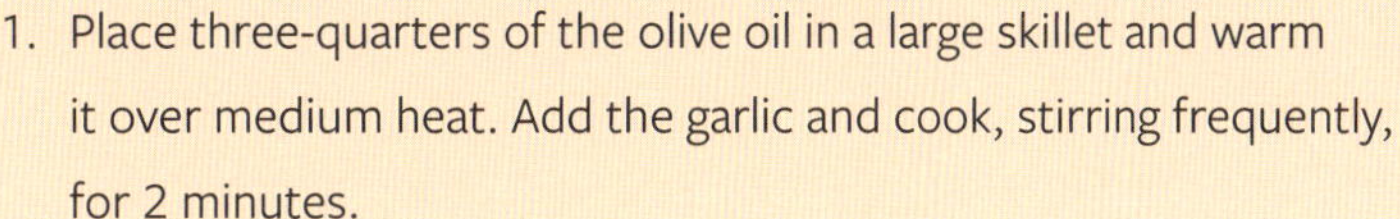

1. Place three-quarters of the olive oil in a large skillet and warm it over medium heat. Add the garlic and cook, stirring frequently, for 2 minutes.

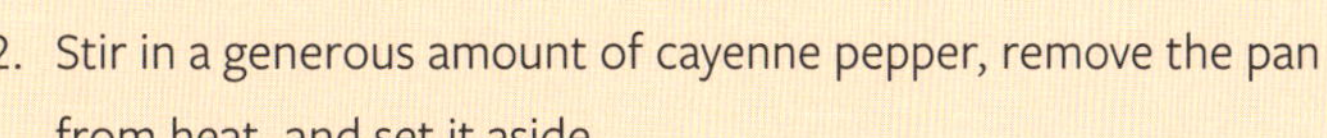

2. Stir in a generous amount of cayenne pepper, remove the pan from heat, and set it aside.
3. Place the remaining olive oil in a large skillet and warm it over medium heat. Add the bread crumbs and cook, stirring, until they are browned.
4. Bring water to a boil in a large saucepan. Add salt, let the water return to a full boil, and add the pasta. Cook until the pasta is al dente.
5. Drain the pasta and place it in a serving dish. Add the infused oil and bread crumbs, quickly toss to combine, and serve.

Pasta alla Norcina

YIELD: 4 SERVINGS / **ACTIVE TIME:** 20 MINUTES / **TOTAL TIME:** 35 MINUTES

3 TABLESPOONS EXTRA-VIRGIN OLIVE OIL

½ ONION, THINLY SLICED

1 GARLIC CLOVE, HALVED

11 OZ. ITALIAN SAUSAGE, CASING REMOVED AND CRUMBLED

½ CUP WHITE WINE

SALT AND PEPPER, TO TASTE

1 LB. PENNE

7 OZ. RICOTTA CHEESE

½ CUP GRATED PARMESAN CHEESE

TRUFFLES, SHAVED, FOR GARNISH

1. Bring water to a boil in a large saucepan. Place the olive oil in a large skillet and warm it over medium-high heat. Add the onion and garlic and cook, stirring frequently, until the onion is translucent, about 3 minutes.
2. Add the sausage and cook, stirring occasionally, until it starts to brown.
3. Deglaze the pan with the wine and cook until it has evaporated. Add salt, let the water return to a full boil, and add the pasta. Cook the pasta until it is al dente. Reserve 1 cup pasta water and drain the pasta.
4. Add the ricotta and a few tablespoons of pasta water to the skillet and stir to combine.
5. Add the Parmesan and pasta, season with salt and pepper, and cook for 2 to 3 minutes, tossing to combine.
6. Garnish the dish with shaved truffles and serve.

Cacio e Pepe

YIELD: 4 SERVINGS / **ACTIVE TIME:** 20 MINUTES / **TOTAL TIME:** 25 MINUTES

2 TABLESPOONS BLACK PEPPERCORNS

SALT, TO TASTE

1 LB. TONNARELLI OR SPAGHETTI

3 CUPS GRATED PECORINO CHEESE, PLUS MORE FOR SERVING

1. Use a spice grinder or mortar and pestle to coarsely grind the peppercorns. Set them aside.
2. Bring water to a boil in a large saucepan. Add salt, let the water return to a full boil, and add the pasta. Cook the pasta until it is very al dente. Reserve 1 cup of pasta water, drain the pasta, and set it aside.
3. Place 1 tablespoon of the ground pepper in a large skillet and toast it over medium heat for 1 minute. Add a few tablespoons of pasta water and stir to incorporate.
4. Place the pecorino and a few tablespoons of pasta water in a bowl and stir to combine. Set the mixture aside.
5. Add the pasta to the skillet, raise the heat to medium-high, and cook for 2 to 3 minutes, tossing to combine.
6. Pour the pasta into the bowl with the pecorino cream and toss to combine, adding more pasta water if needed to get the desired consistency.
7. Serve with the remaining ground pepper and additional pecorino on the side.

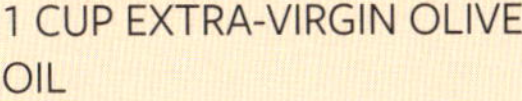

Pasta al Ragù Napoletano

YIELD: 6 SERVINGS / **ACTIVE TIME:** 1 HOUR / **TOTAL TIME:** 7 TO 8 HOURS

1 CUP EXTRA-VIRGIN OLIVE OIL

2 YELLOW ONIONS, FINELY DICED

3 (1 LB.) PIECES OF STEW BEEF

6 PORK RIBS

1 CUP RED WINE

1 TABLESPOON TOMATO PASTE

4 LBS. WHOLE PEELED TOMATOES, LIGHTLY CRUSHED

SALT, TO TASTE

1½ LBS. ZITI OR RIGATONI

2 OZ. PECORINO OR PARMESAN CHEESE, GRATED

HANDFUL OF FRESH BASIL

1. Place the olive oil in a large saucepan and warm it over medium heat. Add the onions, beef, and pork ribs and cook until the onions have caramelized and the meat is browned all over, about 1½ hours. You will need to stay close to the pan, turning the meat as needed and increasing or decreasing the heat accordingly.
2. Add the wine and cook until it has nearly evaporated. Remove the meat from the pan and set it aside.
3. Reduce the heat to low, add the tomato paste, and cook, stirring occasionally, for 2 minutes.
4. Add the tomatoes, season with salt, partially cover the pan, and cook, stirring every 15 minutes, for 3 hours.
5. Return the meat to the pan and cook the sauce until it changes from bright red to a deep maroon and the flavor develops to your liking, 3 to 4 hours.
6. Bring water to a boil in a large saucepan. Add salt, let the water return to a full boil, and add the pasta. Cook until the pasta is al dente.
7. Drain the pasta, place it in a serving dish, and add some of the sauce and the smaller pieces of meat along with half of the pecorino and the basil. Toss to combine and top with the remaining pecorino.
8. Serve the larger pieces of meat and remaining sauce following the pasta.

Lagane e Ceci

YIELD: 4 SERVINGS / **ACTIVE TIME:** 15 MINUTES / **TOTAL TIME:** 24 HOURS

14 OZ. DRIED CHICKPEAS, SOAKED OVERNIGHT

1 SPRIG OF FRESH ROSEMARY

3 GARLIC CLOVES, HALVED

2 TABLESPOONS EXTRA-VIRGIN OLIVE OIL

11 OZ. WHOLE PEELED TOMATOES, LIGHTLY CRUSHED

2 BAY LEAVES

RED PEPPER FLAKES, TO TASTE

SALT, TO TASTE

1 LB. LAGANE (SEE PAGE 14) OR DRIED PAPPARDELLE OR FETTUCCINE

1. Drain the chickpeas, place them in a large saucepan, and cover them with cold water. Add the rosemary and 1 garlic clove, bring to a boil, and cook until the chickpeas are tender, about 45 minutes. Drain the chickpeas, reserve the cooking liquid, and set both aside.
2. Place the olive oil in a large skillet and warm it over medium heat. Add the remaining garlic and cook, stirring frequently, for 2 minutes.
3. Add the tomatoes and bay leaves and cook, stirring occasionally, until the tomatoes have collapsed, about 20 minutes.
4. Remove the garlic and discard it. Season the sauce with red pepper flakes and salt and stir in the chickpeas. Reduce the heat to low and cook the sauce for 20 minutes.
5. Bring water to a boil in a large saucepan. Add salt, let the water return to a full boil, and add the pasta. Cook until the pasta is al dente.
6. Reserve 1 cup pasta water, drain the pasta, and stir it into the sauce.
7. Toss to combine, adding pasta water as needed to get the right consistency. Serve immediately.

Spaghetti All'assassina

YIELD: 4 SERVINGS / **ACTIVE TIME:** 30 MINUTES / **TOTAL TIME:** 50 MINUTES

¼ CUP EXTRA-VIRGIN OLIVE OIL, PLUS MORE TO TASTE

3 GARLIC CLOVES

HOT CHILE PEPPERS, STEMMED, SEEDED, AND MINCED, TO TASTE

19½ OZ. WHOLE PEELED TOMATOES, CHOPPED

SALT, TO TASTE

1 LB. SPAGHETTI

2 TABLESPOONS TOMATO PASTE

1. Place the olive oil in a large, deep skillet and warm it over medium heat. Add the garlic and chiles and cook, stirring frequently, for 2 minutes.
2. Remove the garlic and discard it. Add the tomatoes, season them with salt, and cook for 10 minutes.
3. Bring water to a boil in a large saucepan. Add salt, let the water return to a full boil, and add the pasta. Cook for half of the typical cooking time, 4 to 5 minutes.
4. Using a pasta fork, remove the spaghetti from the boiling water and place it in the tomato sauce.
5. Raise the heat to medium-high and stir in the tomato paste and more olive oil.
6. Stir in the spaghetti, making sure not to break the strands, and cook until it sticks to the pan and is slightly charred.
7. Turn the spaghetti over and cook until it is slightly charred all over. Serve immediately.

Pasta C'anciova e Muddica Atturrata

YIELD: 4 SERVINGS / **ACTIVE TIME:** 20 MINUTES / **TOTAL TIME:** 45 MINUTES

5 TABLESPOONS EXTRA-VIRGIN OLIVE OIL

1 CUP BREAD CRUMBS

SALT AND PEPPER, TO TASTE

½ ONION, FINELY DICED

2 GARLIC CLOVES

8 ANCHOVIES IN OLIVE OIL, DRAINED AND CHOPPED

⅓ CUP RAISINS, SOAKED IN WARM WATER

⅓ CUP PINE NUTS

1 CUP TOMATO PASTE

1 CUP WARM WATER

1 LB. LINGUINE

1. Place 1 tablespoon of olive oil in a small skillet and warm it over medium heat. Add the bread crumbs, season them with salt, and cook, stirring occasionally, until they have browned, about 4 minutes. Remove the pan from heat and set it aside.
2. Place the remaining olive oil in a large skillet and warm it over medium heat. Add the onion, garlic, and anchovies and cook, stirring occasionally, until the onion has softened and the anchovies have dissolved, about 5 minutes.
3. Drain the raisins, squeeze them to remove any excess liquid, and add them to the skillet along with the pine nuts. Cook for 5 minutes.
4. Combine the tomato paste and water and stir the mixture into the pan. Raise the heat to medium-high and cook until the sauce has thickened, 5 to 10 minutes.
5. Bring water to a boil in a large saucepan. Add salt, let the water return to a full boil, and add the pasta. Cook until the pasta is al dente.
6. Drain the pasta and add it to the sauce along with the bread crumbs. Toss to combine, season with salt and pepper, and serve.

ENTREES WITH MEAT

Falsomagro

YIELD: 6 SERVINGS / **ACTIVE TIME:** 40 MINUTES / **TOTAL TIME:** 2 HOURS

1½ LBS. LEAN BEEF, IN 1 LARGE AND THIN SLICE

5 OZ. GROUND BEEF

2 TABLESPOONS GRATED PECORINO CHEESE

¼ CUP BREAD CRUMBS

SALT AND PEPPER, TO TASTE

1 OZ. GUANCIALE, CUT INTO STRIPS

2 OZ. CACIOCAVALLO CHEESE, CUT INTO STRIPS

2 OZ. MORTADELLA, CUT INTO STRIPS

3 HARD-BOILED EGGS, CHOPPED

½ CUP EXTRA-VIRGIN OLIVE OIL

1 CARROT, PEELED AND FINELY CHOPPED

1 CELERY STALK, FINELY DICED

1 ONION, FINELY DICED

¼ CUP RED WINE

1½ LBS. WHOLE PEELED TOMATOES, CRUSHED

1 TABLESPOON TOMATO PASTE

1. Beat the slice of beef with a meat tenderizer to ensure that it is uniformly thick.
2. Place the ground beef, pecorino, and bread crumbs in a large bowl and stir to combine. Season the mixture with salt and pepper and then spread it over the slice of beef, leaving a ½-inch border around the edge.
3. Layer the guanciale, caciocavallo, and mortadella on top and then place the hard-boiled eggs in the center. Roll up the slice of beef, starting from a short side, and secure it with kitchen twine.
4. Place ¼ cup of olive oil in a large skillet and warm it over medium heat. Add the slice of beef and sear it until it is browned all over, turning it as necessary. Remove the pan from heat and set it aside.
5. Place the remaining olive oil in a Dutch oven and warm it over medium heat. Add the carrot, celery, and onion and cook, stirring occasionally, until the vegetables have softened, about 5 minutes.
6. Add the seared beef to the pot and cook for about 5 minutes. Add the red wine and cook until it has almost evaporated, scraping up any browned bits from the bottom of the pot.
7. Stir in the tomatoes and tomato paste, season the dish with salt and pepper, and reduce the heat to low. Cover the pan and cook, stirring occasionally, until the beef is tender, about 1 hour.
8. Cut the twine off of the beef and let it rest for 5 minutes before slicing and serving.

Polpette al Sugo

YIELD: 6 SERVINGS / **ACTIVE TIME:** 30 MINUTES / **TOTAL TIME:** 1 HOUR

¾ LB. GROUND BEEF

¾ LB. GROUND PORK

4 EGGS

4 LARGE SLICES OF DAY-OLD BREAD, SOAKED IN WATER FOR 10 MINUTES AND SQUEEZED DRY

1½ CUPS GRATED PECORINO OR PARMESAN CHEESE

1 GARLIC CLOVE, MINCED

2 TABLESPOONS FINELY CHOPPED FRESH PARSLEY

SALT AND PEPPER, TO TASTE

SUGO AL BASILICO (SEE PAGE 447)

CRUSTY BREAD, FOR SERVING

1. Place all of the ingredients, except for the sauce and crusty bread, in a large bowl and work the mixture until well combined. Form the mixture into balls (each should weigh approximately 2 oz.) and set them aside.
2. Place the sauce in a large, deep skillet and warm it over low heat.
3. Add the meatballs, cover the pan, and cook for 10 minutes.
4. Shake the pan a few times to coat the meatballs in the sauce, cover the pan again, and cook for another 5 minutes.
5. Gently turn the meatballs over, raise the heat to medium, and cook until the meatballs are cooked through, 10 to 15 minutes. Serve immediately with crusty bread.

Arrosticini

YIELD: 4 SERVINGS / **ACTIVE TIME:** 20 MINUTES / **TOTAL TIME:** 30 MINUTES

2 LBS. BONELESS LEG LAMB, TRIMMED AND CUT INTO ½-INCH CUBES

SALT AND PEPPER, TO TASTE

1 TABLESPOON EXTRA-VIRGIN OLIVE OIL

1. Thread the lamb onto skewers and season it with salt and pepper. Place the olive oil in a large cast-iron skillet and warm it over high heat.
2. Add the skewers to the pan and cook until they are seared all over and just medium-rare (the interior temperature should be 125°F), turning them as necessary.
3. Remove the skewers from the pan and let them rest for 2 minutes before serving.

Braciole Napoletane

YIELD: 6 SERVINGS / **ACTIVE TIME:** 20 MINUTES / **TOTAL TIME:** 40 MINUTES

8 THIN SLICES OF LEAN BEEF (5 OZ. EACH)

SALT AND PEPPER, TO TASTE

4 GARLIC CLOVES, 2 MINCED AND 2 HALVED

6 TABLESPOONS RAISINS, CHOPPED

¼ CUP PINE NUTS, CHOPPED

3 TABLESPOONS CHOPPED FRESH PARSLEY

1 CUP GRATED PECORINO CHEESE

3 TABLESPOONS EXTRA-VIRGIN OLIVE OIL

1 CUP RED WINE

SUGO AL BASILICO (SEE PAGE 447)

1. Beat the slices of beef with a meat tenderizer to ensure that they are of a uniform thickness. Season them with salt and pepper and set them aside.
2. Place the minced garlic, raisins, pine nuts, and parsley in a bowl and stir to combine. Evenly distribute the mixture and the pecorino over the slices of beef.
3. Starting from a short side, roll up the slices of beef and then secure them with skewers or large toothpicks.
4. Place the olive oil in a large skillet and warm it over medium heat. Add the remaining garlic and cook for 1 minute. Add the slices of stuffed beef and sear until they are browned all over, turning them as necessary.
5. Remove the garlic from the pan and add the red wine. Cook until it has nearly evaporated, about 5 minutes.
6. Add the sauce, stir to combine, and cover the pan. Reduce the heat to low and cook until the slices of stuffed beef are just cooked through, 10 to 15 minutes. Serve immediately.

Pollo allo Zafferano

YIELD: 4 SERVINGS / **ACTIVE TIME:** 20 MINUTES / **TOTAL TIME:** 1 HOUR

4 LB. WHOLE CHICKEN, BROKEN DOWN

SALT, TO TASTE

4 TABLESPOONS UNSALTED BUTTER

3 TABLESPOONS EXTRA-VIRGIN OLIVE OIL

½ CUP WHITE WINE

¼ CUP COGNAC OR BRANDY

1 CUP BEEF STOCK (SEE PAGE 446)

1 CUP LIGHT CREAM

1 TABLESPOON SAFFRON THREADS

2 TABLESPOONS CHOPPED FRESH PARSLEY

3 TABLESPOONS ALL-PURPOSE FLOUR

1. Trim the fattiest parts from the chicken, season it with salt, and set it aside. Place the butter and olive oil in a large skillet and warm the mixture over medium-high heat. Add the chicken, skin side down, and sear until it is browned on both sides, turning it as necessary.
2. Deglaze the pan with the wine and cognac, scraping up any browned bits from the bottom of the pan. Cook until the liquid has nearly evaporated. Add two-thirds of the stock, reduce the heat to medium-low, and cover the pan. Cook for 20 minutes.
3. Uncover the pan, raise the heat to medium-high, and cook for 5 to 10 minutes. Remove the chicken from the pan, transfer it to a plate, and cover loosely with aluminum foil to keep it warm.
4. Add the remaining stock, the cream, saffron, parsley, and flour, season the mixture with salt, and cook, stirring continually, until the flavor of the sauce has developed to your liking.
5. To serve, ladle the sauce over the chicken and enjoy.

Pollo alla Pizzaiola

YIELD: 4 SERVINGS / **ACTIVE TIME:** 20 MINUTES / **TOTAL TIME:** 1 HOUR

4 LARGE BONE-IN, SKIN-ON CHICKEN THIGHS

SALT AND PEPPER, TO TASTE

¼ CUP EXTRA-VIRGIN OLIVE OIL

2 GARLIC CLOVES, MINCED

⅔ CUP WHITE WINE

1½ LBS. WHOLE PEELED TOMATOES, CRUSHED

½ CUP PITTED BLACK OLIVES, SLICED

2 TABLESPOONS CAPERS, RINSED IF PACKED IN SALT OR DRAINED IF PACKED IN BRINE

6 OZ. FRESH MOZZARELLA CHEESE, DRAINED AND SLICED

DRIED OREGANO, TO TASTE

1. Trim the fattiest parts from the chicken, season it with salt and pepper, and set it aside.
2. Place the olive oil in a large skillet and warm it over low heat. Add the garlic and cook until it starts to brown, about 2 minutes. Add the chicken, skin side down, raise the heat to medium-high, and sear until it is browned all over, turning it as necessary.
3. Add the wine and cook until it has nearly evaporated. Add the tomatoes, reduce the heat to low, and cover the pan. Cook until the chicken is tender, about 30 minutes.
4. Add the olives and capers, season the dish with salt and pepper, and cook, uncovered, until the sauce has thickened, about 10 minutes.
5. Add the mozzarella, season the dish with oregano, and cover the pan. Cook until the mozzarella has melted, about 5 minutes, and serve immediately.

Pampanella Molisana

YIELD: 4 SERVINGS / **ACTIVE TIME:** 15 MINUTES / **TOTAL TIME:** 2 HOURS AND 20 MINUTES

2 TABLESPOONS CHILI POWDER

2 TABLESPOONS SWEET PAPRIKA

4 GARLIC CLOVES, MINCED

SALT, TO TASTE

2 LBS. PORK TENDERLOIN

2 TABLESPOONS WHITE WINE VINEGAR

1. Preheat the oven to 350°F. Place the chili powder, paprika, and garlic in a bowl, season the mixture with salt, and stir to combine.
2. Cut the pork every ½ inch, taking care not to cut all the way through so that the tenderloin remains together. Rub the seasoning blend over every part of the pork, place it in a roasting pan, and cover it with aluminum foil.
3. Place the pan in the oven and roast the pork for 2 hours.
4. Remove the pork from the oven, drizzle the vinegar over it, and return the pork to the oven, uncovered. Roast until it is nicely browned, about 10 minutes.
5. Remove the pork from the oven and let it rest for a few minutes before serving.

Il Cif e Ciaf

YIELD: 5 SERVINGS / **ACTIVE TIME:** 20 MINUTES / **TOTAL TIME:** 1 HOUR AND 40 MINUTES

½ CUP EXTRA-VIRGIN OLIVE OIL

1 SPRIG OF FRESH ROSEMARY

3 BAY LEAVES

2½ LBS. ASSORTED CUTS OF PORK (BACON, RIBS, LEAN CUTS, ETC.)

1 CUP DRY WHITE WINE

SALT AND PEPPER, TO TASTE

10 GARLIC CLOVES, PEELED

5 DRIED SWEET PEPPERS, STEMMED, SEEDED, AND TORN

CRUSTY BREAD, TOASTED, FOR SERVING

1. Place the olive oil in a large cast-iron skillet and warm it over medium-high heat. Add the rosemary and bay leaves and cook for 1 minute.
2. Add the pork to the pan and sear until it is browned all over, turning it as necessary.
3. Deglaze the pan with the wine, scraping up any browned bits from the bottom. Cook until the wine has evaporated, cover the pan, and reduce the heat to low. Cook, stirring occasionally, for 30 minutes.
4. Remove the bay leaves and discard them. Season the dish with salt and pepper and check to see if the pork is sticking to the pan. If it is, add 1 cup water, cover the pan, and cook for another 30 minutes.
5. Preheat the oven to 390°F. Add the garlic and peppers, transfer the pan to the oven, and braise the pork until it is very tender, about 20 minutes.
6. Remove the pan from the oven and serve with toasted bread.

Lamb al Forno

YIELD: 4 SERVINGS / **ACTIVE TIME:** 20 MINUTES / **TOTAL TIME:** 1 HOUR AND 30 MINUTES

2½ LBS. LAMB, CUBED

6 TABLESPOONS EXTRA-VIRGIN OLIVE OIL

SALT AND PEPPER, TO TASTE

2 SPRIGS OF FRESH ROSEMARY

⅔ CUP DRY WHITE WINE

3 GARLIC CLOVES, MINCED

2½ LBS. POTATOES, PEELED AND CHOPPED

1. Preheat the oven to 390°F. Pat the lamb dry with paper towels. Coat a large, deep baking dish with half of the olive oil and arrange the lamb in it in a single layer.
2. Season the lamb with salt and pepper, add the rosemary, wine, and garlic, and toss to combine.
3. Place the dish in the oven and roast for 30 minutes.
4. Place the potatoes and remaining olive oil in a bowl, season with salt and pepper, and toss to combine.
5. Remove the dish from the oven, add the potatoes, and toss to combine. Place the dish back in the oven and roast until the potatoes are tender and golden brown, 40 to 50 minutes, stirring occasionally.
6. Remove the dish from the oven and let the lamb cool slightly before serving.

Pork with Peppers

YIELD: 4 SERVINGS / **ACTIVE TIME:** 20 MINUTES / **TOTAL TIME:** 1 HOUR

2 CUPS WHITE VINEGAR

5 BELL PEPPERS, STEMMED, SEEDED, AND CUT INTO STRIPS

2 TABLESPOONS EXTRA-VIRGIN OLIVE OIL

2 GARLIC CLOVES

8 PORK CHOPS

4 BAY LEAVES

2 WHOLE CLOVES

SALT AND PEPPER, TO TASTE

1. Place the vinegar in a medium saucepan and bring to a boil. Add the peppers and cook for 5 minutes. Drain the peppers and set them aside.
2. Place the olive oil in a large skillet and warm it over low heat. Add the garlic and cook for about 2 minutes.
3. Raise the heat to medium, add the pork chops, bay leaves, and cloves, and sear the pork chops until they are browned on both sides, turning them as necessary.
4. Add the peppers and 1 cup water, season the dish with salt and pepper, and cook until the pork chops are cooked through (the interior is 145°F). Serve immediately.

Lamb Cacio e Ova

YIELD: 4 SERVINGS / **ACTIVE TIME:** 20 MINUTES / **TOTAL TIME:** 1 HOUR AND 20 MINUTES

¼ CUP EXTRA-VIRGIN OLIVE OIL

1 YELLOW ONION, SLICED THIN

5 JUNIPER BERRIES

2 LBS. BONELESS OF LEG LAMB, TRIMMED AND CUT INTO 1-INCH CUBES

SALT AND PEPPER, TO TASTE

1 SPRIG OF FRESH ROSEMARY

1 SPRIG OF FRESH THYME

1 BAY LEAF

½ CUP WHITE WINE

7 EGGS

2 CUPS GRATED PECORINO CHEESE

1. Place the olive oil in a large skillet and warm it over medium heat. Add the onion and juniper berries and cook, stirring occasionally, until the onion has softened, about 5 minutes.
2. Season the lamb with salt and pepper and add it to the pan along with the rosemary, thyme, and bay leaf. Sear until the lamb is browned, turning it as necessary.
3. Add the wine, scraping up any browned bits from the bottom of the pan. Cook until the wine has nearly evaporated and then add enough water to cover the lamb. Cover the pan and braise the lamb until it is tender, about 40 minutes.
4. Uncover the pan and let the sauce reduce. Remove the rosemary, thyme, and bay leaf and discard the herbs. Reduce the heat to low.
5. Place the eggs in a bowl, whisk until scrambled, and then whisk in the pecorino. Add the egg mixture to the lamb and cook until it has set, 3 to 4 minutes. Serve immediately.

Lamb alla Gallurese

YIELD: 5 SERVINGS / **ACTIVE TIME:** 20 MINUTES / **TOTAL TIME:** 1 HOUR AND 20 MINUTES

7 TABLESPOONS UNSALTED BUTTER

3 LBS. BONELESS LEG OF LAMB, TRIMMED AND CUT INTO 2-INCH CUBES

SALT AND PEPPER, TO TASTE

2 GARLIC CLOVES

2 JUNIPER BERRIES

2 SPRIGS OF FRESH ROSEMARY

2 SPRIGS OF FRESH THYME

4 BAY LEAVES

6 POTATOES, PEELED AND CUBED

½ CUP PITTED GREEN OLIVES

1. Place the butter in a large skillet and melt it over medium heat. Season the lamb with salt and pepper and add it to the pan along with the garlic and juniper berries. Sear the lamb until it is browned all over, turning it as necessary.
2. Add the rosemary, thyme, bay leaves, and potatoes, season the dish with salt and pepper, and cook, stirring occasionally, for 5 minutes.
3. Add water until the lamb is covered and bring to a simmer. Reduce the heat to medium-low, cover the pan, and cook for 30 minutes.
4. Remove the rosemary, thyme, and bay leaves and discard them. Add the olives and cook until the lamb and potatoes are tender, about 20 minutes, stirring occasionally. Serve immediately.

Fagioli con le Cotiche

YIELD: 4 SERVINGS / **ACTIVE TIME:** 40 MINUTES / **TOTAL TIME:** 24 HOURS

14 OZ. DRIED WHITE BEANS, SOAKED OVERNIGHT AND DRAINED

SALT AND PEPPER, TO TASTE

6 OZ. PORK RIND

2 OZ. PROSCIUTTO FAT, CHOPPED

1 WHITE ONION, FINELY DICED

1 GARLIC CLOVE, MINCED

1.1 LBS. WHOLE PEELED TOMATOES, CRUSHED

HANDFUL OF FRESH PARSLEY, CHOPPED

SLICES OF BREAD, TOASTED, FOR SERVING

1. Place the beans in a large pot, cover them with cold water, and bring to a boil. Reduce the heat and simmer the beans until they are tender, 45 minutes to 1 hour, seasoning them with salt halfway through. Drain the beans and set them aside.
2. Bring salted water to a boil in a large saucepan. Remove the fat from the pork rind, place it in the boiling water, and boil it for 5 minutes.
3. Drain the pork rind and cut it into short and thin strips.
4. Bring unsalted water to a boil in a large saucepan. Add the pork rind and cook until it is tender, about 1 hour. Drain the pork rind and set it aside.
5. Place the prosciutto fat in a Dutch oven and warm it over low heat until it has rendered. Add the onion and garlic and cook, stirring occasionally, until they start to brown, about 5 minutes.
6. Add the tomatoes and cook, stirring occasionally, for 15 minutes.
7. Add the beans and pork rind, season with salt and pepper, and cook for 45 minutes, adding water as necessary if the dish starts to look dry.
8. Stir in the parsley and cook for 1 minute. Serve with toasted bread and enjoy.

Note: The pork rind used in this dish is not the American junk food, but a product that some butchers and specialty Italian groceries will have on hand. As difficult as it may be to track down, it is absolutely essential to this dish, as evidenced by the name: "beans with pork rind."

Lamb a Cutturiedde

YIELD: 5 SERVINGS / **ACTIVE TIME:** 30 MINUTES / **TOTAL TIME:** 5 HOURS

2½ LBS. BONELESS LEG OF LAMB OR MUTTON, TRIMMED AND CUT INTO ½-INCH CUBES

1 CUP RED WINE VINEGAR

4 BAY LEAVES

6 TABLESPOONS EXTRA-VIRGIN OLIVE OIL

1 YELLOW ONION, FINELY DICED

1 CELERY STALK, FINELY DICED

1 CARROT, PEELED AND FINELY DICED

1 LB. TOMATOES, CHOPPED

1 LB. POTATOES, PEELED AND DICED

3½ OZ. LAMPASCIONI OR BABY ONIONS, CLEANED AND LEFT WHOLE

7 OZ. CHICORY OR COLLARD GREENS, RINSED WELL

SALT AND PEPPER, TO TASTE

1 CUP GRATED PECORINO CHEESE, FOR GARNISH

1. Place the lamb, vinegar, and bay leaves in a bowl, add water until the lamb is covered, and let it marinate for 2 hours.
2. Place the olive oil in a Dutch oven and warm it over medium heat. Add the onion, celery, and carrot and cook, stirring occasionally, until they have softened, about 5 minutes.
3. Add the tomatoes and cook, stirring occasionally, for about 5 minutes. Add the potatoes, lampascioni, greens, and enough water to cover the vegetables, season with salt and pepper, and bring to a boil.
4. Drain the lamb and add it to the pot along with the bay leaves. Add water until the lamb is covered and bring to a simmer.
5. Reduce the heat to low, cover the pot, and cook until the lamb is tender, about 2 hours.
6. Remove the lid, remove the lamb from the pot, and raise the heat to high. Cook until the liquid has reduced.
7. To serve, ladle the sauce and vegetables over the lamb, top with the pecorino, and enjoy.

Trippa alla Romana

YIELD: 4 SERVINGS / **ACTIVE TIME:** 30 MINUTES / **TOTAL TIME:** 2 HOURS

1 LB. READY-TO-COOK TRIPE

2 TABLESPOONS EXTRA-VIRGIN OLIVE OIL

½ CARROT, PEELED AND FINELY DICED

½ CELERY STALK, FINELY DICED

½ ONION, FINELY DICED

1 GARLIC CLOVE, MINCED

1 TEASPOON CHOPPED FRESH MINT, PLUS MORE FOR GARNISH

3 WHOLE CLOVES

½ CUP DRY WHITE WINE

1 (HEAPING) CUP GRATED PECORINO CHEESE

14 OZ. WHOLE PEELED TOMATOES, CRUSHED

1 TABLESPOON TOMATO PASTE

SALT, TO TASTE

RED PEPPER FLAKES, TO TASTE

CRUSTY BREAD, FOR SERVING

1. Bring water to a boil in a large saucepan. Cut the tripe into 2-inch-long strips, rinse them under cold water, and add them to the boiling water. Boil for about 10 minutes. Drain the tripe and set it aside.
2. Place the olive oil in a large, deep skillet and warm it over medium heat. Add the carrot, celery, onion, and garlic and cook, stirring occasionally, until they have softened, about 5 minutes.
3. Add the tripe and cook until it has browned, about 5 minutes.
4. Add the mint, cloves, and wine and cook until the wine has evaporated. Stir in half of the pecorino cheese and cook until it has melted.
5. Add the tomatoes and tomato paste, season with salt and red pepper flakes, and cook for about 30 minutes, stirring occasionally.
6. Garnish the dish with the remaining pecorino cheese and additional mint and serve with crusty bread.

Stracotto alla Fiorentina

YIELD: 4 SERVINGS / **ACTIVE TIME:** 30 MINUTES / **TOTAL TIME:** 4 HOURS

¼ CUP EXTRA-VIRGIN OLIVE OIL

1 ONION, CHOPPED

1 GARLIC CLOVE

1 SPRIG OF FRESH ROSEMARY

2 LBS. POT ROAST

2 CELERY STALKS, CHOPPED

3 CARROTS, PEELED AND CHOPPED

2 CUPS CHIANTI

5 TOMATOES, CHOPPED

SALT AND PEPPER, TO TASTE

MASHED POTATOES, FOR SERVING

1. Place the olive oil in a Dutch oven and warm it over medium heat. Add the onion, garlic, and rosemary and cook, stirring frequently, until the onion is translucent, about 3 minutes.
2. Add the pot roast and sear until it is browned all over, turning it as necessary.
3. Add the celery and carrots and cook, stirring occasionally, for 15 minutes.
4. Deglaze the pot with the wine, scraping up any browned bits from the bottom. Cover the pot and cook for 30 minutes, turning the pot roast often.
5. Add the tomatoes and 1 cup of water, season with salt and pepper, and bring to a boil.
6. Reduce the heat to low, cover the pot, and cook until the pot roast is very tender, 2 or 3 hours, turning the pot roast occasionally and adding more water as needed.
7. Remove the pot roast and let it rest for 10 minutes. Transfer the broth and vegetables to a food processor and blitz until smooth. Set the sauce aside.
8. Slice the pot roast and serve with the sauce and mashed potatoes.

Chicken Cacciatore

YIELD: 4 SERVINGS / **ACTIVE TIME:** 30 MINUTES / **TOTAL TIME:** 1 HOUR AND 30 MINUTES

¼ CUP EXTRA-VIRGIN OLIVE OIL

1 CARROT, PEELED AND FINELY DICED

1 CELERY STALK, FINELY DICED

1 ONION, FINELY DICED

6 GARLIC CLOVES

2 SPRIGS OF FRESH ROSEMARY

3 LBS. CHICKEN THIGHS AND WINGS

SALT, TO TASTE

RED PEPPER FLAKES, TO TASTE

⅔ CUP RED WINE

14 OZ. WHOLE PEELED TOMATOES, CRUSHED

2 BAY LEAVES

1 (HEAPING) CUP PITTED BLACK OLIVES (OPTIONAL)

CRUSTY BREAD OR SPAGHETTI, FOR SERVING

1. Place the olive oil in a large, deep skillet and warm it over medium heat. Add the carrot, celery, onion, garlic, and rosemary and cook, stirring occasionally, until they have softened, about 5 minutes.
2. Add the chicken, season with salt and red pepper flakes, and sear the chicken until it is browned all over.
3. Add the wine and cook until it has evaporated. Remove the garlic and rosemary and discard them. Add the tomatoes, bay leaves, and olives (if desired), season with salt and red pepper flakes, and cover the pan. Reduce the heat to low and cook until the chicken is tender, about 45 minutes, turning it occasionally.
4. Serve with crusty bread and enjoy.

Saltimbocca alla Romana

YIELD: 4 SERVINGS / **ACTIVE TIME:** 20 MINUTES / **TOTAL TIME:** 40 MINUTES

8 MEDIUM VEAL CUTLETS

4 SLICES OF PROSCIUTTO, HALVED

8 FRESH SAGE LEAVES

½ CUP ALL-PURPOSE FLOUR

¼ CUP UNSALTED BUTTER

BLACK PEPPER, TO TASTE

⅔ CUP DRY WHITE WINE

2 TABLESPOONS WATER

CARCIOFI ALLA GIUDIA (SEE PAGE 246), FOR SERVING

CRUSTY BREAD, FOR SERVING

1. Beat the veal cutlets with a meat tenderizer to make them thinner. Place a piece of prosciutto over each cutlet and place a sage leaf in the middle of the prosciutto. Secure the prosciutto and sage with a toothpick, but do not roll the slice up.
2. Place the flour in a shallow bowl and dredge the bottom of the cutlets in it until coated. Place two-thirds of the butter in a large skillet and melt it over low heat until it starts to brown.
3. Raise the heat to high and add the veal, floured side down. Season with pepper and cook until the bottoms of the cutlets are golden.
4. Add the wine and cook until it has evaporated. Cover the pan with a lid and cook for 1 minute.
5. Remove the veal from the pan, place it on a plate, and tent it with aluminum foil.
6. Place the water and remaining butter in the pan and cook over medium heat, scraping up any browned bits from the bottom of the pan, until the sauce thickens.
7. Pour the sauce over the veal and serve with Carciofi alla Giudia and crusty bread.

Rifreddo

YIELD: 4 SERVINGS / **ACTIVE TIME:** 30 MINUTES / **TOTAL TIME:** 1 HOUR AND 30 MINUTES

11 OZ. GROUND PORK

11 OZ. GROUND CHICKEN OR VEAL

6 OZ. MORTADELLA, FINELY DICED

1½ CUPS GRATED PARMESAN CHEESE

2 LARGE EGGS

SALT AND PEPPER, TO TASTE

11 OZ. TUNA IN OLIVE OIL, DRAINED

1 (HEAPING) CUP PITTED GREEN OLIVES, FINELY DICED

2 TABLESPOONS CAPERS PACKED IN BRINE, DRAINED, SQUEEZED, AND MINCED, PLUS MORE FOR GARNISH

3 TABLESPOONS EXTRA-VIRGIN OLIVE OIL, PLUS MORE FOR GARNISH

JUICE OF ½ LEMON

1. Place the ground meats, mortadella, Parmesan, and eggs in a bowl, season with salt and pepper, and stir until well combined. Spread the mixture over a clean kitchen towel. Roll it up and tie the ends closed with kitchen twine.
2. Bring water to a boil in a large saucepan. Add the rifreddo and boil until it is cooked through, about 1 hour.
3. While the rifreddo is boiling, place the tuna, olives, capers, olive oil, and lemon juice in a bowl and stir until well combined. Store the sauce in the refrigerator.
4. Remove the rifreddo from the boiling water. Unwrap it from the kitchen towel and let it cool completely.
5. Slice the rifreddo and drizzle the sauce over the top. Garnish with additional capers and olive oil and serve.

Braciola Rifatta Toscana

YIELD: 4 SERVINGS / **ACTIVE TIME:** 20 MINUTES / **TOTAL TIME:** 40 MINUTES

3 EGGS

SALT, TO TASTE

1 CUP BREAD CRUMBS

1 CUP EXTRA-VIRGIN OLIVE OIL

8 BEEF STEAKS, SLICED THIN

SUGO AL BASILICO (SEE PAGE 447)

FRESH PARSLEY, CHOPPED, FOR GARNISH

1. Place the eggs and a pinch of salt in a shallow bowl and beat until scrambled. Place the bread crumbs in a separate bowl.
2. Place the olive oil in a large skillet and warm it over medium heat.
3. Dredge the steaks in the egg and then in the bread crumbs until they are completely coated. Place them in the skillet and cook until they are browned on both sides, 3 to 5 minutes, turning them over once. .
4. Transfer the steaks to a paper towel–lined plate to drain.
5. Place the tomato sauce in a large skillet and warm it over medium heat. Place the steaks in the sauce, reduce the heat to medium-low, and cook until the steaks are cooked through, about 10 minutes.
6. Garnish with parsley and serve.

Rabbit in Potacchio

YIELD: 4 SERVINGS / **ACTIVE TIME:** 20 MINUTES / **TOTAL TIME:** 1 HOUR AND 15 MINUTES

1 SPRIG OF FRESH ROSEMARY

6 FRESH SAGE LEAVES

8 GARLIC CLOVES, HALVED

½ FRESH CHILE PEPPER, CHOPPED

¼ CUP EXTRA-VIRGIN OLIVE OIL

⅔ CUP DRY WHITE WINE

1 RABBIT, CHOPPED INTO LARGE PIECES

8 CHERRY TOMATOES, HALVED

SALT AND PEPPER, TO TASTE

1. Place the rosemary, sage, garlic, chile, olive oil, and wine in a Dutch oven.
2. Place the rabbit and tomatoes on top of the aromatics, season with salt and pepper, and cover the pot. Cook over low heat for about 50 minutes, turning the rabbit and tomatoes over halfway through.
3. Uncover the pot, raise the heat to medium, and cook until the sauce has reduced. Serve immediately.

Wild Boar Cacciatore

YIELD: 4 SERVINGS / **ACTIVE TIME:** 30 MINUTES / **TOTAL TIME:** 15 HOURS

FOR THE MARINADE

4 CUPS RED WINE

1 GARLIC CLOVE

2 SPRIGS OF FRESH ROSEMARY

1 SPRIG OF FRESH THYME

1 SPRIG OF FRESH MARJORAM

2 BAY LEAVES

5 FRESH SAGE LEAVES

5 JUNIPER BERRIES

FOR THE CACCIATORE

2 LBS. WILD BOAR TENDERLOIN

2 TABLESPOONS LARD

3 GARLIC CLOVES

½ ONION, SLICED THIN

½ CELERY STALK, FINELY DICED

½ CARROT, PEELED AND FINELY DICED

2 BAY LEAVES

SALT, TO TASTE

RED PEPPER FLAKES, TO TASTE

1 CUP DRY WHITE WINE

¼ CUP TOMATO PASTE

2 CUPS BEEF STOCK (SEE PAGE 446), PLUS MORE AS NEEDED

1. To prepare the marinade, place all of the ingredients in a large bowl and stir to combine.
2. To begin preparations for the cacciatore, add the boar to the marinade and let it marinate in the refrigerator for 12 hours.
3. Drain the boar and chop it into small pieces. Place the lard in a large, deep skillet and melt it over medium heat. Add the boar, garlic, onion, celery, carrot, and bay leaves and cook, stirring occasionally, until the boar is browned all over, about 10 minutes.
4. Season with salt and red pepper flakes and add the wine. Cook until the wine has evaporated.
5. Add the tomato paste and stock, reduce the heat to low, and cover the pan. Cook for 2 hours, stirring occasionally and adding more stock as needed if the dish starts to look dry.
6. Remove the bay leaves and discard them. Cook the cacciatore for another 30 minutes and serve immediately.

Peposo alla Fornacina

YIELD: 4 SERVINGS / **ACTIVE TIME:** 30 MINUTES / **TOTAL TIME:** 4 HOURS

- 2 LBS. STEW BEEF, CUT INTO BIG CHUNKS
- 8 GARLIC CLOVES
- 3 CUPS CHIANTI
- 1 TABLESPOON TOMATO PASTE
- 2 TABLESPOONS BLACK PEPPERCORNS
- SALT AND PEPPER, TO TASTE
- CANNELLINI BEANS, COOKED, FOR SERVING
- CRUSTY BREAD, FOR SERVING

1. Place all of the ingredients, except for the beans and bread, in a Dutch oven and add water until the beef is covered. Stir to combine and bring to a simmer.
2. Cover the pot, reduce the heat to low, and cook until the beef is very tender, about 3 hours, stirring occasionally.
3. Uncover the pot, raise the heat, and cook until the sauce has reduced.
4. Season with pepper and serve with white beans and crusty bread.

Pasticciata alla Pesarese

YIELD: 4 SERVINGS / **ACTIVE TIME:** 40 MINUTES / **TOTAL TIME:** 3 HOURS AND 30 MINUTES

¼ CUP EXTRA-VIRGIN OLIVE OIL

1 CARROT, PEELED AND CHOPPED

1 CELERY STALK, COARSELY CHOPPED

1 ONION, CHOPPED

2 GARLIC CLOVES

2 WHOLE CLOVES

1 LB. VEAL TOP ROUND

1 CUP RED WINE

SALT AND PEPPER, TO TASTE

1½ CUPS WHOLE PEELED TOMATOES, CRUSHED

CRUSTY BREAD, FOR SERVING

1. Place the olive oil in a Dutch oven and warm it over medium heat. Add the carrot, celery, onion, garlic, and cloves and cook, stirring frequently, until the onion is translucent, about 3 minutes.
2. Add the veal and sear until it is browned all over, turning it as necessary.
3. Deglaze the pot with the wine, scraping up any browned bits from the bottom. Cover the pot and cook for 30 minutes, turning the veal often.
4. Add 1 cup of hot water, season with salt and pepper, and bring to a boil.
5. Reduce the heat to low, cover the pot, and cook until the veal is very tender, about 1 hour, adding more water as needed.
6. Remove the veal and vegetables from the pan. Cut the veal into ¼-inch-thick slices. Set the vegetables aside.
7. Add the tomatoes to the pot and return the veal to the pot. Season with salt and pepper, cover the pot, and cook over low heat until the flavor has developed to your liking, about 1 hour.
8. Serve with the vegetables and crusty bread.

Pajata

YIELD: 4 SERVINGS / **ACTIVE TIME:** 40 MINUTES / **TOTAL TIME:** 2 HOURS

2 LBS. VEAL PAJATA

¼ CUP EXTRA-VIRGIN OLIVE OIL

1 CARROT, PEELED AND FINELY DICED

1 CELERY STALK, FINELY DICED

1 ONION, FINELY DICED

1 CUP DRY WHITE WINE

14 OZ. WHOLE PEELED TOMATOES, GENTLY CRUSHED BY HAND

HANDFUL OF FRESH PARSLEY, CHOPPED

SALT AND PEPPER, TO TASTE

FRESH OREGANO, CHOPPED, TO TASTE

1. Rinse the pajata under cold water for a few minutes and cut it into 8-inch-long pieces. Knot the ends of each piece together, forming them into rings.
2. Place the olive oil in a Dutch oven and warm it over medium heat. Add the carrot, celery, and onion and cook, stirring frequently, until the onion is translucent, about 3 minutes.
3. Add the pajata and sear until it is browned on both sides, turning it over once.
4. Add the wine and cook until it has evaporated. Add the tomatoes and parsley, season with salt, pepper, and oregano, and cook for 15 minutes.
5. Add 1 cup of hot water, cover the pot, and cook for 1 hour, stirring occasionally and adding more hot water as needed.
6. Uncover the pot, raise the heat to medium, and cook until the sauce has reduced. Serve immediately.

Cotoletta alla Milanese

YIELD: 4 SERVINGS / **ACTIVE TIME:** 15 MINUTES / **TOTAL TIME:** 30 MINUTES

2 EGGS

SALT, TO TASTE

BREAD CRUMBS, AS NEEDED

4 VEAL CHOPS (EACH ABOUT 1 INCH THICK)

7 OZ. UNSALTED BUTTER

LEMON WEDGES, FOR SERVING

1. Place the eggs and 2 pinches of salt in a shallow bowl and whisk to scramble the eggs.
2. Place bread crumbs in a separate shallow bowl. Dredge the veal chops in the eggs and then in the bread crumbs until they are completely coated.
3. Place the butter in a large skillet and melt it over medium heat. Add the veal and cook until it is browned on both sides and the interior temperature is 125°F.
4. Transfer the veal to a paper towel–lined plate and let it drain. Serve with lemon wedges.

Lamb alla Scottadito

YIELD: 4 SERVINGS / **ACTIVE TIME:** 10 MINUTES / **TOTAL TIME:** 40 MINUTES

8 LAMB CHOPS

½ CUP EXTRA-VIRGIN OLIVE OIL

2 GARLIC CLOVES

1 TEASPOON CHOPPED FRESH ROSEMARY

SALT AND PEPPER, TO TASTE

BRUSCHETTA (SEE PAGE 237), FOR SERVING

1. Pat the lamb dry with paper towels and set it aside. Place the olive oil, garlic, and rosemary in a bowl and stir to combine. Add the lamb to the marinade and let it marinate at room temperature for 30 minutes.
2. Warm a large cast-iron skillet over high heat. Place the lamb in the skillet and cook until it is browned on both sides and medium-rare (the interior is 125°F), turning it over just once.
3. Transfer the lamb to a serving platter, tent it with aluminum foil, and let it rest for 3 minutes.
4. Season the lamb with salt and pepper and serve with Bruschetta.

Timballo di Riso alla Lucana

YIELD: 4 SERVINGS / **ACTIVE TIME:** 40 MINUTES / **TOTAL TIME:** 1 HOUR AND 30 MINUTES

FOR THE MEATBALLS

2½ OZ. DAY-OLD BREAD, CHOPPED

2 TABLESPOONS WATER

6 OZ. GROUND VEAL

1 EGG

½ GARLIC CLOVE, MINCED

1 TABLESPOON FINELY CHOPPED FRESH PARSLEY

2 TABLESPOONS GRATED PECORINO CHEESE

SALT, TO TASTE

2 TABLESPOONS EXTRA-VIRGIN OLIVE OIL

FOR THE TIMBALLO

3 TABLESPOONS EXTRA-VIRGIN OLIVE OIL

3½ OZ. CHICKEN LIVER, CUBED

6 OZ. ITALIAN SAUSAGE, CASING REMOVED AND CRUMBLED

SALT AND PEPPER, TO TASTE

1 LB. ARBORIO RICE

BUTTER, AS NEEDED

BREAD CRUMBS, AS NEEDED

2 HARD-BOILED EGGS, DICED

6 OZ. PROVOLONE CHEESE, SLICED THIN

¼ CUP GRATED PECORINO CHEESE, PLUS MORE FOR TOPPING

1. To begin preparations for the meatballs, place the bread and water in a bowl and let the bread soak for 15 minutes.
2. Drain the bread, squeeze it to remove as much liquid as possible, and place it in a large mixing bowl. Add the veal, egg, garlic, parsley, and pecorino, season the mixture with salt, and work the mixture until it is well combined. Form the mixture into 1 oz. balls.
3. Place the olive oil in a large, deep skillet and warm it over medium heat. Add the meatballs and cook them until they are browned all over, turning them as necessary. Transfer the cooked meatballs to a paper towel–lined plate to drain.
4. To begin preparations for the timballo, place the olive oil in a large skillet and warm it over medium heat. Add the chicken liver and sausage and cook until they are browned all over, about 8 minutes, stirring occasionally.
5. Preheat the oven to 390°F. Bring water to a boil in a large saucepan. Add salt, let the water return to a full boil, and add the rice. Cook until the rice is tender, about 15 minutes.
6. Coat a 13 x 9–inch baking pan with butter and bread crumbs. Drain the rice and spread half of it over the bottom of the baking dish. Cover the rice with the meatballs, sausage, chicken liver, eggs, provolone, and pecorino and season with pepper. Cover with the remaining rice and sprinkle pecorino generously over the top.
7. Place the timballo in the oven and bake for 20 minutes.
8. Remove the timballo from the oven and let it rest for 10 minutes before serving.

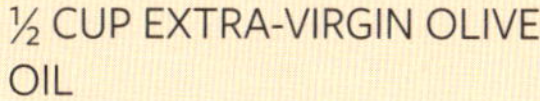

Lamb with Black Truffles

YIELD: 4 SERVINGS / **ACTIVE TIME:** 20 MINUTES / **TOTAL TIME:** 1 HOUR AND 30 MINUTES

½ CUP EXTRA-VIRGIN OLIVE OIL

3 GARLIC CLOVES

2 SPRIGS OF FRESH ROSEMARY

3 LBS. LAMB, CUBED

⅔ CUP DRY WHITE WINE

2 TABLESPOONS CAPERS IN SALT, SOAKED, RINSED, AND DRAINED

2 TABLESPOONS WHITE VINEGAR

2 OZ. NORCIA BLACK TRUFFLES

JUICE OF ¼ LEMON

SALT AND PEPPER, TO TASTE

1. Place half of the olive oil in a large, deep skillet and warm it over medium heat. Add 2 garlic cloves and the rosemary and cook, stirring continually, for 2 minutes.
2. Add the lamb and sear until it is browned all over, turning it as needed.
3. Add the wine and cook until it has evaporated. Cover the pan, reduce the heat to low, and cook for 20 minutes.
4. Using a mortar and pestle, grind the remaining garlic, the capers, and vinegar into a paste.
5. Stir the paste into the pan, cover, and cook until the lamb is tender, about 30 minutes.
6. Uncover the pan, raise the heat to medium, and cook until the sauce has reduced.
7. Using a mortar and pestle, grind the truffles, lemon juice, and remaining olive oil until combined. Season the truffle oil with salt and pepper.
8. To serve, divide the lamb and sauce among serving dishes and top each portion with truffle oil.

Veal Tonnato

YIELD: 6 SERVINGS / **ACTIVE TIME:** 30 MINUTES / **TOTAL TIME:** 16 HOURS

FOR THE VEAL

2.1 LB. PIECE OF VEAL TOP ROUND

3 CUPS DRY WHITE WINE

5 GARLIC CLOVES, HALVED

2 BAY LEAVES

1 CARROT, PEELED AND CHOPPED

1 ONION, CHOPPED

1 CELERY STALK, CHOPPED

6 CUPS WATER

SALT, TO TASTE

FOR THE SALSA TONNATA

9 OZ. TUNA IN OLIVE OIL, DRAINED

3 HARD-BOILED EGG YOLKS

4 ANCHOVIES IN OLIVE OIL, DRAINED

3½ TABLESPOONS CAPERS PACKED IN BRINE, RINSED WELL AND SQUEEZED DRY

1 TABLESPOON WHITE WINE VINEGAR

1 TABLESPOON FRESH LEMON JUICE

¼ CUP EXTRA-VIRGIN OLIVE OIL

1. Tie the veal with kitchen twine and place it in a Dutch oven with the wine, garlic, bay leaves, carrot, onion, and celery. Cover the Dutch oven and let the veal marinate in the refrigerator for 12 hours.
2. Drain the veal, reserving the liquid. Strain the liquid and return it to the Dutch oven with the veal.
3. Add the water, season with salt, and place the Dutch oven over medium heat. Bring to a simmer. Reduce the heat to low, cover the Dutch oven, and cook until the veal is tender, about 1 hour, turning it occasionally.
4. Drain the veal, reserving two ladles of broth for the sauce. Let the veal cool to room temperature. Place the veal in the refrigerator and chill it for 2 hours.
5. To begin preparations for the salsa tonnata, place the tuna, egg yolks, anchovies, capers, vinegar, and lemon juice in a blender and puree until smooth.
6. With the blender running, slowly stream in the olive oil until it has emulsified. Slowly stream in the reserved broth until the sauce is creamy.
7. Cut the veal into thin slices and serve it alongside the sauce.

Brasato al Barolo

YIELD: 6 SERVINGS / **ACTIVE TIME:** 40 MINUTES / **TOTAL TIME:** 16 HOURS

2.6 LBS. BONELESS BEEF SHOULDER

2 CUPS BAROLO

1 LARGE WHITE ONION, CHOPPED

1 CELERY STALK, CHOPPED

2 LARGE CARROTS, PEELED AND CHOPPED

2 BAY LEAVES

2 GARLIC CLOVES

2 TABLESPOONS UNSALTED BUTTER

2 TABLESPOONS EXTRA-VIRGIN OLIVE OIL

SALT AND PEPPER, TO TASTE

1 TABLESPOON ALL-PURPOSE FLOUR

1. Tie the beef with kitchen twine, place it in a roasting pan, and add the Barolo, onion, celery, carrots, bay leaves, and garlic. Cover the pan with plastic wrap and let the beef marinate in the refrigerator for 12 hours.
2. Drain the beef, reserving the marinade and vegetables. Pat the beef dry with paper towels.
3. Place the butter and olive oil in a Dutch oven and warm the mixture over medium heat. Add the beef and sear until it is browned all over, turning it as needed.
4. Remove the beef from the pot and set it aside. Add the reserved vegetables and cook, stirring occasionally, until they start to brown, about 5 minutes.
5. Return the beef to the pot and cover the dish with the reserved marinade. Bring to a boil, reduce the heat to low, and cover the pot. Cook until the beef is very tender, 3 to 4 hours. Turn the beef occasionally as it cooks, and season it with salt and pepper halfway through cooking.
6. Remove the beef from the pot and let it cool completely before slicing.
7. Place the Dutch oven over high heat and stir in the flour. Cook until the cooking liquid has thickened slightly.
8. Serve the brasato with the cooking liquid and vegetables.

Arrosto Morto

YIELD: 8 SERVINGS / **ACTIVE TIME:** 30 MINUTES / **TOTAL TIME:** 3 HOURS

2.2 LB. VEAL OR PORK TENDERLOIN

2 SPRIGS OF FRESH ROSEMARY

2 SPRIGS OF FRESH SAGE

2 TABLESPOONS UNSALTED BUTTER

3 TABLESPOONS EXTRA-VIRGIN OLIVE OIL

1 CUP DRY WHITE WINE

2 GARLIC CLOVES

1 ONION, CHOPPED

1 LARGE CARROT, PEELED AND CHOPPED

1 CELERY STALK, CHOPPED

SALT AND PEPPER, TO TASTE

BEEF STOCK (SEE PAGE 446), AS NEEDED

1. Tie the tenderloin with kitchen twine. Stick the herbs under the twine so that they are in contact with the tenderloin.
2. Place the butter and olive oil in a Dutch oven and warm the mixture over medium-high heat. Add the tenderloin and sear until it is browned all over, turning it as needed and basting it with the pan juices. Use two spoons to turn the tenderloin, as you want to avoid piercing it.
3. Add the wine and cook until it has evaporated, turning the tenderloin frequently. Reduce the heat to low, add the garlic, onion, carrot, and celery, season with salt and pepper, and cook for 10 minutes.
4. Add a few ladles of stock and cook until the tenderloin is cooked through, about 2 hours, turning it occasionally and adding more stock as needed. The stock should not cover the meat entirely, instead it should be added in small amounts, as the aim is making a roast and not a stew.
5. Remove the tenderloin from the pot and let it cool completely.
6. Taste the cooking liquid and strain it. Taste and adjust the seasoning as necessary. Slice the tenderloin and serve it, reheated or cold, with its cooking liquid.

Bollito Misto alla Piemontese

YIELD: 8 SERVINGS / **ACTIVE TIME:** 30 MINUTES / **TOTAL TIME:** 6 HOURS

3 (1 LB.) PIECES OF ASSORTED CUTS OF BEEF

SALT, TO TASTE

4 CARROTS, PEELED AND CUT INTO BIG PIECES

3 ONIONS, CUT INTO BIG PIECES

4 CELERY STALKS, CUT INTO BIG PIECES

2 SPRIGS OF FRESH PARSLEY

4 GARLIC CLOVES

10 BLACK PEPPERCORNS

1 WHOLE CAPON, CLEANED

1 COTECHINO

BAGNET VERT (SEE PAGE 452), FOR SERVING

SALSA RUBRA, FOR SERVING

SALSA AL CREN (SEE PAGE 454), FOR SERVING

1. Tie the beef with kitchen twine and set it aside. Bring water to a boil in a stockpot. Add salt and half of the carrots, onions, and celery and cook for 15 minutes.
2. Add the beef and half of the parsley, garlic, and peppercorns. Boil for 15 minutes. Reduce the heat to medium-low, cover the pot, and cook until the beef is very tender and falling apart, 2 to 3 hours, occasionally skimming any impurities that rise to the surface.
3. Place the pieces of beef in a serving dish and cover them with aluminum foil to keep warm.
4. While the beef is cooking, bring water to a boil in a large saucepan. Add salt, the chicken, and the remaining vegetables, peppercorns, and parsley and cook until the chicken is cooked through, about 1½ hours.
5. Bring water to a boil in another large saucepan. Add the cotechino and cook for 1 hour.
6. Slice the beef and cotechino. Place the chicken in the center of a very large serving platter and surround it with the beef and cotechino. Serve with the sauces and enjoy.

Ànara col Pién

YIELD: 6 SERVINGS / **ACTIVE TIME:** 40 MINUTES / **TOTAL TIME:** 3 HOURS

2 DAY-OLD ROLLS

½ CUP WHOLE MILK

1 WHOLE DUCK

1 ITALIAN SAUSAGE, CASING REMOVED AND CRUMBLED

1 GARLIC CLOVE, MINCED

HANDFUL OF FRESH PARSLEY, CHOPPED

1 EGG, BEATEN

⅔ CUP GRATED GRANA PADANO CHEESE

½ CUP EXTRA-VIRGIN OLIVE OIL

SALT AND PEPPER, TO TASTE

1 CELERY STALK, CHOPPED

1 ONION, CHOPPED

1 CARROT, PEELED AND CHOPPED

1 SPRIG OF FRESH ROSEMARY

2 BAY LEAVES

½ CUP DRY WHITE WINE

1. Place the rolls and milk in a bowl and let the rolls soak. Remove the duck's innards, finely chop them, and place them in a bowl.
2. Add the softened rolls to the chopped innards and stir to combine. Add the sausage, garlic, parsley, egg, Grana Padano, and half of the olive oil, season with salt and pepper, and work the mixture with your hands until combined.
3. Preheat the oven to 390°F. Stuff the duck with the mixture and tie it closed with kitchen twine. Season the duck's skin with salt. Place the remaining olive oil in a Dutch oven and warm it over medium heat. Add the duck, celery, onion, carrot, rosemary, and bay leaves and sear the duck until it is browned all over, turning it as needed.
4. Add the wine and cook until it has evaporated. Cover the Dutch oven and place it in the oven. Braise the duck until it is cooked through, about 2 hours, basting the duck frequently.
5. Remove the duck from the oven, slice it, and serve.

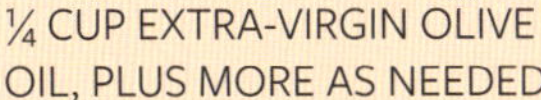

Cappone Ripieno

YIELD: 10 SERVINGS / **ACTIVE TIME:** 40 MINUTES / **TOTAL TIME:** 3 HOURS

¼ CUP EXTRA-VIRGIN OLIVE OIL, PLUS MORE AS NEEDED

4 LB. WHOLE CAPON

7 OZ. GROUND VEAL

7 OZ. ITALIAN SAUSAGE, CASING REMOVED AND CRUMBLED

1½ CUPS FRESH BREAD CRUMBS, SOAKED IN WATER FOR 10 MINUTES AND SQUEEZED DRY

1 CUP GRATED PARMESAN CHEESE

2 EGGS

1 WHITE ONION, FINELY CHOPPED

1 GARLIC CLOVE, MINCED

HANDFUL OF FRESH PARSLEY, FINELY CHOPPED

HANDFUL OF FRESH SAGE, FINELY CHOPPED

1 TEASPOON FINELY CHOPPED FRESH ROSEMARY

FRESH GRATED NUTMEG, TO TASTE

SALT AND PEPPER, TO TASTE

1 CUP DRY WHITE WINE

1 CUP BEEF STOCK (SEE PAGE 446)

1. Preheat the oven to 355°F and coat a baking dish with olive oil. Remove the capon's innards and rinse out the cavity.
2. Place the veal, sausage, bread crumbs, Parmesan, eggs, onion, garlic, parsley, sage, rosemary, and olive oil in a large bowl, season with nutmeg, salt, and pepper, and work the mixture with your hands until well combined.
3. Stuff the capon with the mixture and tie it closed with kitchen twine. Season the capon with salt, place it in the baking dish, and place it in the oven.
4. Combine the wine and stock in a bowl. Roast the capon until it is cooked through, about 2 hours, basting it with the wine mixture frequently and turning it occasionally, making sure not to pierce the flesh when you do.
5. Remove the capon from the oven, slice, and serve.

Ossobuco alla Milanese

YIELD: 4 SERVINGS / **ACTIVE TIME:** 30 MINUTES / **TOTAL TIME:** 1 HOUR

4 VEAL SHANKS (EACH ABOUT 9 OZ.)

ALL-PURPOSE FLOUR, AS NEEDED

¼ CUP EXTRA-VIRGIN OLIVE OIL

2 TABLESPOONS UNSALTED BUTTER

1 LARGE WHITE ONION

½ CUP DRY WHITE WINE

2 CUPS BEEF STOCK (SEE PAGE 446)

HANDFUL OF FRESH PARSLEY, FINELY CHOPPED

ZEST OF 1 LEMON

1 GARLIC CLOVE, MINCED

RISOTTO ALLA MILANESE (SEE PAGE 173), FOR SERVING

1. Clean any residual fragments of bones from the veal shanks. Cut away the connective tissue surrounding the meat with scissors.
2. Rinse the veal and pat it dry with paper towels. Place flour in a shallow bowl and dredge the veal in it until completely coated.
3. Place the olive oil and butter in a large, deep skillet and warm the mixture over medium heat. Add the onion and cook, stirring occasionally, until it has softened, about 5 minutes.
4. Add the shanks and sear until they are browned all over, turning them as necessary.
5. Add the wine and cook until it has evaporated. Add the stock, cover the pan, and reduce the heat to low. Cook until the veal is very tender, about 40 minutes.
6. Place the parsley, lemon zest, and garlic in a bowl and stir to combine.
7. Stir the parsley mixture, which is known as gremolata, into the pan and serve the veal and liquid over the risotto.

ENTREES WITH SEAFOOD

Peperoni Ripieni di Tonno

YIELD: 8 SERVINGS / **ACTIVE TIME:** 20 MINUTES / **TOTAL TIME:** 2 HOURS AND 20 MINUTES

1⅓ LBS. STALE BREAD, SOAKED IN WATER AND SQUEEZED DRY

1 LB. TUNA IN OLIVE OIL, DRAINED

14 ANCHOVIES IN OLIVE OIL, DRAINED AND CHOPPED

⅔ CUP PITTED GREEK OLIVES, CHOPPED

3 TABLESPOONS CAPERS IN SALT, SOAKED, DRAINED, AND SQUEEZED DRY

2 GARLIC CLOVES, MINCED

3 TABLESPOONS FINELY CHOPPED FRESH PARSLEY

½ CUP EXTRA-VIRGIN OLIVE OIL, PLUS MORE TO TASTE

SALT AND PEPPER, TO TASTE

8 RED OR YELLOW BELL PEPPERS

1. Preheat the oven to 350°F. Place all of the ingredients, except for the peppers, in a bowl and stir until well combined.
2. Cut off the top of the peppers and set the tops aside. Remove the seeds and ribs from the peppers, taking care not to break the peppers.
3. Stuff the peppers with the filling and place the pepper tops back on top. Place the peppers in a baking dish, on their sides so that they sit end to end, lightly season them with salt, and drizzle olive oil over them.
4. Place the peppers in the oven and bake until they start to look slightly charred, about 1 hour, turning them over halfway through.
5. Remove the peppers from the oven and let them cool completely.
6. Chill the peppers in the refrigerator for 1 hour before serving.

Mussels Zafferano

YIELD: 4 SERVINGS / **ACTIVE TIME:** 20 MINUTES / **TOTAL TIME:** 40 MINUTES

7 TABLESPOONS EXTRA-VIRGIN OLIVE OIL

½ ONION, CHOPPED

1 BAY LEAF

4½ LBS. MUSSELS, RINSED WELL AND DEBEARDED

1 TABLESPOON SAFFRON THREADS

1 TEASPOON CORNSTARCH (OPTIONAL)

SALT, TO TASTE

FRESH PARSLEY, FINELY CHOPPED, FOR GARNISH

1. Place 2 tablespoons of olive oil in a Dutch oven and warm it over medium heat. Add the onion and bay leaf and cook, stirring occasionally, until the onion has softened, about 5 minutes.
2. Add the mussels, cover the pot, and cook until the majority of the mussels have opened, 5 to 7 minutes. Discard any mussels that did not open. Strain the mussels through a fine-mesh sieve, reserving any liquid.
3. Place the reserved liquid in a large saucepan and bring it to a boil. Add the saffron and remaining olive oil and whisk until the mixture has emulsified. If desired, add the cornstarch to thicken the emulsion.
4. Season the emulsion with salt, drizzle it over the mussels, garnish with parsley, and enjoy.

Calamari Ripieni

YIELD: 4 SERVINGS / **ACTIVE TIME:** 30 MINUTES / **TOTAL TIME:** 1 HOUR

½ CUP EXTRA-VIRGIN OLIVE OIL

8 SQUID, CLEANED (SEE PAGE 140)

⅔ CUP PITTED BLACK OLIVES, MINCED

1 TABLESPOON CAPERS IN BRINE, DRAINED AND RINSED

10 ANCHOVIES IN OLIVE OIL, DRAINED AND CHOPPED

3 GARLIC CLOVES, FINELY MINCED

2 TABLESPOONS FINELY CHOPPED FRESH PARSLEY, PLUS MORE FOR TOPPING

⅔ CUP BREAD CRUMBS, PLUS MORE FOR TOPPING

SALT AND PEPPER, TO TASTE

1. Preheat the oven to 390°F. Place 2 tablespoons of olive oil in a large skillet and warm it over medium-low heat. Dice the squid tentacles, pat them dry, and add them to the pan. Cook, stirring frequently, until they are cooked through, about 2 minutes. Remove the tentacles from the pan and place them in a bowl.
2. Add 2 tablespoons of olive oil, the olives, capers, anchovies, garlic, parsley, and bread crumbs to the bowl, season the mixture with salt and pepper, and stir to combine.
3. Place the mixture on the strips of squid, roll them up, and secure them with toothpicks.
4. Coat a baking dish with some of the remaining olive oil. Place the squid in the dish, season with salt, top with additional parsley and bread crumbs, and drizzle the remaining olive oil over the top.
5. Place the squid in the oven and bake until they just start to brown, 15 to 20 minutes. Take care not to overcook the squid, as they will harden.
6. Remove the squid from the oven and serve immediately.

Cuttlefish with Peas

YIELD: 4 SERVINGS / **ACTIVE TIME:** 30 MINUTES / **TOTAL TIME:** 1 HOUR AND 10 MINUTES

2 LBS. SQUID

¼ CUP EXTRA-VIRGIN OLIVE OIL

1 WHITE ONION, FINELY DICED

1 CUP VEGETABLE STOCK (SEE PAGE 447)

SALT AND PEPPER, TO TASTE

¼ CUP WHITE WINE

1 LB. PEAS

1 LB. WHOLE PEELED TOMATOES, CRUSHED BY HAND

2 TABLESPOONS CHOPPED FRESH PARSLEY

1. To clean the squid, find the bone and make a transversal cut to eliminate it. Remove the internal organs of the squid and the ink sac (if present). Separate the head from the body and remove the innards of the head. Remove the tentacles and the beak that is positioned in the center of the tentacles. Make a small incision on the back and remove the skin. Remove the eyes, rinse the squid, and cut the body into wide strips. Set the strips and tentacles aside.
2. Place the olive oil in a large skillet and warm it over low heat. Add the onion and cook, stirring occasionally, until it has softened, about 6 minutes.
3. Add half of the stock and the squid, season with salt and pepper, and raise the heat to medium. Cook until the liquid has evaporated.
4. Add the wine and cook until it has evaporated.
5. Add the peas, tomatoes, and remaining stock, cover the pan, and reduce the heat to low. Cook for 15 minutes.
6. Stir in the parsley and serve.

Swordfish Involtini

YIELD: 4 SERVINGS / **ACTIVE TIME:** 30 MINUTES / **TOTAL TIME:** 1 HOUR

FOR THE SWORDFISH

7 TABLESPOONS EXTRA-VIRGIN OLIVE OIL

1 CUP BREAD CRUMBS

1 GARLIC CLOVE, MINCED

2 TABLESPOONS RAISINS

2 TABLESPOONS PINE NUTS

3 TABLESPOONS GRATED PECORINO CHEESE

2 TABLESPOONS CHOPPED FRESH PARSLEY

JUICE OF ½ LEMON

SALT AND PEPPER, TO TASTE

12 LONG, THIN SLICES OF SWORDFISH

8 BAY LEAVES

1 LEMON, CUT INTO 8 SLICES

FOR THE SALMORIGLIO SAUCE

½ CUP EXTRA-VIRGIN OLIVE OIL

½ CUP HOT WATER

1 TABLESPOON CHOPPED FRESH PARSLEY

1 GARLIC CLOVE, MINCED

JUICE OF ½ LEMON

DRIED OREGANO, TO TASTE

SALT AND PEPPER, TO TASTE

1. Preheat the oven to 390°F. To begin preparations for the swordish, place 2 tablespoons of olive oil in a large skillet and warm it over medium-high heat. Add two-thirds of the bread crumbs and cook, stirring occasionally, until they are golden brown, 5 to 7 minutes.
2. Transfer the toasted bread crumbs to a bowl, add the garlic, raisins, pine nuts, pecorino, parsley, lemon juice, and 3 tablespoons of olive oil, and stir to combine. Season the mixture with salt and pepper.
3. Top the slices of swordfish with the bread crumb mixture, roll them up, and thread the rolls, bay leaves, and lemon slices onto skewers, portioning three rolls to each skewer and alternating between the rolls, bay leaves, and lemon slices.
4. Place the skewers in a baking dish, drizzle the remaining olive oil over them, and sprinkle the remaining bread crumbs on top.
5. Place the baking dish in the oven and bake until the swordfish is just golden brown, about 20 minutes.
6. To begin preparations for the salmoriglio sauce, place all of the ingredients in a small bowl and stir until well combined.
7. Remove the swordfish from the oven and serve it alongside the salmoriglio sauce.

Sarde a Beccaficu

YIELD: 4 SERVINGS / **ACTIVE TIME:** 20 MINUTES / **TOTAL TIME:** 1 HOUR

7 TABLESPOONS EXTRA-VIRGIN OLIVE OIL, PLUS MORE AS NEEDED

1 CUP BREAD CRUMBS

JUICE OF ½ ORANGE

½ CUP RAISINS

⅓ CUP PINE NUTS

7 ANCHOVIES IN OLIVE OIL, DRAINED AND CHOPPED

2 TABLESPOONS CHOPPED FRESH PARSLEY

1 GARLIC CLOVE, MINCED

1 TABLESPOON SUGAR

SALT AND PEPPER, TO TASTE

2 LBS. FRESH SARDINES, CLEANED, DEBONED, AND RINSED

4 BAY LEAVES

½ ORANGE, SLICED

1. Preheat the oven to 350°F and coat a baking dish with olive oil. Place 2 tablespoons of olive oil in a large skillet and warm it over medium-high heat. Add the bread crumbs and cook, stirring occasionally, until they are golden brown, 5 to 7 minutes.
2. Set 2 tablespoons of the toasted bread crumbs aside and place the rest in a bowl. Add the orange juice, raisins, pine nuts, anchovies, parsley, garlic, sugar, and 2 tablespoons of olive oil and stir to combine. Season the mixture with salt and pepper.
3. Top the sardines with the bread crumb mixture, roll them up from head to tail, and arrange them in the baking dish, packing them together tightly so that they do not open.
4. Arrange the bay leaves and orange slices between the sardines, drizzle the remaining olive oil over the dish, and sprinkle the reserved bread crumbs on top.
5. Place the baking dish in the oven and bake until the sardines are cooked through and starting to brown, 10 to 15 minutes.
6. Remove the sardines from the oven and enjoy.

Stockfish alla Messinese

YIELD: 4 SERVINGS / **ACTIVE TIME:** 30 MINUTES / **TOTAL TIME:** 2 HOURS

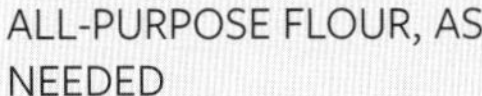

ALL-PURPOSE FLOUR, AS NEEDED

2 LBS. STOCKFISH (DRIED COD), SOAKED, CLEANED, AND CHOPPED

6 TABLESPOONS EXTRA-VIRGIN OLIVE OIL

1 ONION, SLICED THIN

1 LB. WHOLE PEELED TOMATOES, CRUSHED

⅔ CUP PITTED OLIVES

6 TABLESPOONS CAPERS IN SALT, SOAKED, DRAINED, AND SQUEEZED DRY

1 CELERY STALK WITH ITS LEAVES, SLICED THIN

2 LBS. POTATOES, PEELED AND CHOPPED

SALT, TO TASTE

RED PEPPER FLAKES, TO TASTE

CRUSTY BREAD, FOR SERVING

1. Place flour in a shallow bowl and dredge the stockfish in it until the stockfish is completely coated.
2. Place 2 tablespoons of olive oil in a large skillet and warm it over medium heat. Working in batches to avoid crowding the pan, add the stockfish and fry until it is golden brown, about 5 minutes, turning it as necessary. Transfer the fried stockfish to a paper towel–lined plate and let it drain.
3. Place the remaining olive oil in a large saucepan and warm it over medium heat. Add the onion and cook, stirring occasionally, until it has softened, about 5 minutes.
4. Add the tomatoes, olives, capers, and celery, reduce the heat to low, and cover the pan. Cook for 15 minutes.
5. Add the stockfish and enough water so that the mixture is covered. Cover the pan and cook for 30 minutes.
6. Add the potatoes and more water if there doesn't seem to be enough liquid. Season the dish with salt and red pepper flakes, cover the pan, and cook until the potatoes are tender, 30 to 40 minutes.
7. Serve with crusty bread and enjoy.

Stockfish all'Anconetana

YIELD: 4 SERVINGS / **ACTIVE TIME:** 40 MINUTES / **TOTAL TIME:** 4 HOURS AND 40 MINUTES

2 CUPS EXTRA-VIRGIN OLIVE OIL, PLUS MORE AS NEEDED

2 LBS. STOCKFISH, SOAKED, CLEANED, AND CHOPPED

2 CELERY STALKS, FINELY DICED

3 CARROTS, PEELED AND FINELY DICED

1 ONION, FINELY DICED

2 OZ. CAPERS IN SALT, SOAKED, RINSED, AND SQUEEZED DRY

5 ANCHOVIES IN SALT, RINSED, PATTED DRY, AND CHOPPED

2 TEASPOONS CHOPPED FRESH ROSEMARY

2 LBS. POTATOES, PEELED AND CUT INTO WEDGES

2 LBS. TOMATOES, CUT INTO WEDGES

1 (HEAPING) CUP PITTED BLACK OLIVES

1 CHILE PEPPER, STEMMED, SEEDED, AND MINCED

¾ CUP VERDICCHIO

SALT AND PEPPER, TO TASTE

1. Preheat the oven to 280°F. Coat a large, deep baking dish with olive oil and arrange the stockfish in it in a single layer.
2. Place the celery, carrots, onion, capers, anchovies, and rosemary in a bowl and stir to combine. Pour half of the mixture over the stockfish, season with salt, and toss to combine.
3. Drizzle the olive oil over the mixture and top with the potatoes. Top the potatoes with the other half of the vegetable mixture and then distribute the tomatoes and olives over the top.
4. Add the chile, season with salt and pepper, and add the wine. Add water until the mixture is covered and place it in the oven.
5. Bake for about 2 hours. Remove the dish from the oven and let it rest for 2 to 3 hours before serving.

Ciuppin

YIELD: 6 SERVINGS / **ACTIVE TIME:** 1 HOUR / **TOTAL TIME:** 1 HOUR AND 30 MINUTES

5 TABLESPOONS EXTRA-VIRGIN OLIVE OIL

1 ONION, FINELY DICED

1 CARROT, PEELED AND FINELY DICED

1 CELERY STALK, PEELED AND FINELY DICED

2 GARLIC CLOVES, MINCED

3 LBS. MIXED SEAFOOD

½ CUP DRY WHITE WINE

1 LB. TOMATOES, PEELED AND CRUSHED

SALT AND PEPPER, TO TASTE

HANDFUL OF FRESH PARSLEY, FINELY CHOPPED

CRUSTY BREAD, TOASTED, FOR SERVING

1. Place the olive oil in a Dutch oven and warm it over medium heat. Add the onion, carrot, celery, and garlic and cook, stirring frequently, until the onion is translucent, about 3 minutes.
2. Add the octopus or cuttlefish (if using) and wine and cook until the wine has evaporated.
3. Add the tomatoes, mash them with a wooden spoon, and cover the pot. Cook for 20 minutes.
4. Bring water to a boil in a large saucepan. Add salt and the biggest fish. After a few minutes, add the second biggest, and so on. Cook the fish until they are cooked through, about 10 minutes for the medium and small fish, and 15 to 20 minutes for the larger fish.
5. Drain the fish, reserve the broth, and remove the heads, skin, and all of the bones.
6. Add the fish to the Dutch oven and break it up with a wooden spoon. Stir in two to three ladles of the reserved broth and the parsley. Cook for 3 minutes.
7. Season the ciuppin with salt and pepper and serve with crusty bread.

Mullet alla Livornese

YIELD: 4 SERVINGS / **ACTIVE TIME:** 20 MINUTES / **TOTAL TIME:** 40 MINUTES

2 LBS. RED MULLET, CLEANED AND DESCALED

2 GARLIC CLOVES, MINCED

HANDFUL OF FRESH PARSLEY, CHOPPED

¼ CUP EXTRA-VIRGIN OLIVE OIL, PLUS MORE TO TASTE

2 LBS. TOMATOES, PEELED, SEEDED, AND CHOPPED

SALT AND PEPPER, TO TASTE

CRUSTY BREAD, FOR SERVING

1. Rinse the fish under cold water and set it aside. Place the garlic and parsley in a small bowl and stir to combine. Place the olive oil in a large, deep skillet and warm it over low heat. Add the garlic mixture and cook until the garlic is lightly browned, about 2 minutes.
2. Add the tomatoes, season with salt, and cook for 15 minutes, stirring frequently.
3. Set the fish on top of the tomatoes, drizzle olive oil over it, and season with salt and pepper.
4. Cook the fish for 5 minutes per side, shaking the pan regularly to prevent the fish from sticking. Serve immediately with crusty bread.

Mullet alla Genovese

YIELD: 4 SERVINGS / **ACTIVE TIME:** 30 MINUTES / **TOTAL TIME:** 1 HOUR

4 WHOLE MULLET

¼ CUP EXTRA-VIRGIN OLIVE OIL

1 SMALL ONION, FINELY DICED

HANDFUL OF FRESH PARSLEY, CHOPPED

1 TABLESPOON FENNEL SEEDS

2 ANCHOVIES IN OLIVE OIL, DRAINED AND CHOPPED

2 OZ. DRIED PORCINI MUSHROOMS, SOAKED, DRAINED, AND SQUEEZED DRY

1 LB. WHOLE PEELED TOMATOES, CRUSHED

SALT, TO TASTE

1. Clean the fish, removing the innards and most of the scales. Rinse the fish and pat it dry. Chill it in the refrigerator.
2. Place the olive oil in a large, deep skillet and warm it over medium heat. Add the onion, parsley, fennel seeds, anchovies, and mushrooms and cook, stirring occasionally, for 5 minutes.
3. Add the tomatoes, season with salt, and reduce the heat to low. Cook, stirring occasionally, for 20 minutes.
4. Add the fish and cook until it is flaky and opaque, 15 to 20 minutes.
5. Season with salt and serve immediately.

Trout alla Piemontese

YIELD: 4 SERVINGS / **ACTIVE TIME:** 30 MINUTES / **TOTAL TIME:** 1 HOUR

4 TROUT

¼ CUP EXTRA-VIRGIN OLIVE OIL

1 ONION, FINELY DICED

½ CARROT, PEELED AND FINELY DICED

1 CELERY STALK, FINELY DICED

1 GARLIC CLOVE, MINCED

1 TEASPOON FINELY CHOPPED FRESH ROSEMARY

HANDFUL OF FRESH SAGE, FINELY CHOPPED

3 OZ. RAISINS, SOAKED IN WARM WATER, DRAINED, AND SQUEEZED DRY

1½ CUPS VEGETABLE STOCK (SEE PAGE 447)

¼ CUP WHITE WINE VINEGAR

ZEST OF 1 LEMON

SALT, TO TASTE

1. Clean the trout, removing the innards and most of the scales. Rinse the fish and pat it dry. Chill it in the refrigerator.
2. Place the olive oil in a large, deep skillet and warm it over medium heat. Add the onion, carrot, celery, garlic, rosemary, and sage and cook, stirring occasionally, for 5 minutes.
3. Add the raisins, stock, vinegar, and lemon zest, place the fish on top, and season with salt. Cover the pan and reduce the heat to low.
4. Cook until the fish is flaky and opaque, 15 to 20 minutes.
5. Remove the fish from the pan. Remove the skin and bones, taking care not to break the fillets. Serve the fish with the sauce.

Tiella Barese

YIELD: 4 SERVINGS / **ACTIVE TIME:** 50 MINUTES / **TOTAL TIME:** 2 HOURS

7 TABLESPOONS EXTRA-VIRGIN OLIVE OIL

2 LBS. MUSSELS, RINSED WELL AND DEBEARDED

3 ONIONS, SLICED THIN

6 POTATOES, PEELED AND SLICED THIN

1 LB. CHERRY TOMATOES, QUARTERED

1 GARLIC CLOVE, MINCED

6 TABLESPOONS FINELY CHOPPED FRESH PARSLEY

SALT AND PEPPER, TO TASTE

¾ LB. ARBORIO RICE

3½ OZ. GRATED PECORINO CHEESE

3 TABLESPOONS BREAD CRUMBS

1. Place 3 tablespoons of olive oil in a deep pot and warm it over medium heat. Add the mussels, cover the pot, and cook until the majority of the mussels have opened, about 5 minutes. Discard any mussels that did not open. Strain the remaining mussels, reserving the liquid. Strain the liquid and set it aside.
2. Split the mussels in half, reserving the halves containing the meat. Set them aside.
3. Coat a Dutch oven with 2 tablespoons of olive oil and cover the bottom of the pot with the onions. Arrange half of the potatoes, half of the tomatoes, the garlic, and half of the parsley in layers on top, and season the dish with salt and pepper.
4. Add the mussels, making sure their openings are facing upward.
5. Cover the mussels with the rice, making sure that it fills both the mussels and the empty spaces in the dish. Season the dish with salt and pepper and drizzle the remaining olive oil and the reserved liquid over the dish.
6. Arrange the remaining potatoes and tomatoes on top in layers. Top with the remaining parsley, season the dish with salt and pepper, and sprinkle the pecorino and bread crumbs over the top.
7. Pour water into the pot until the rice is covered, making sure the liquid does not reach the top layer.
8. Preheat the oven to 360°F. Cover the pot and bring it to a boil over medium heat. Place the pot in the oven and bake for 40 minutes. Uncover the pot and bake for another 20 minutes so that the top becomes crunchy.
9. Remove the tiella Barese from the oven and serve.

Couscous alla Trapanese

YIELD: 4 SERVINGS / **ACTIVE TIME:** 1 HOUR / **TOTAL TIME:** 1 HOUR AND 30 MINUTES

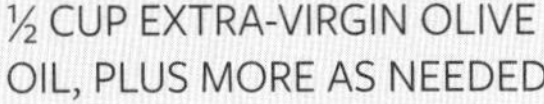

½ CUP EXTRA-VIRGIN OLIVE OIL, PLUS MORE AS NEEDED

1 WHITE ONION, FINELY DICED

2 GARLIC CLOVES, MINCED

¾ CUP ALMONDS, FINELY CHOPPED

1 BUNCH OF FRESH PARSLEY, CHOPPED

2 TABLESPOONS TOMATO PASTE

2 LBS. WHITING FILLETS, CUT INTO LARGE PIECES

SALT, TO TASTE

10 OZ. COUSCOUS

7 OZ. LANGOUSTINES

7 OZ. CLAMS, RINSED WELL

11 OZ. GURNARD FILLETS

1. Place half of the olive oil in a large, deep skillet and warm it over medium-low heat. Add the onion, garlic, almonds, and parsley and cook, stirring occasionally, until the onion has softened, about 6 minutes.
2. Add the tomato paste and cook, stirring continually, for 3 minutes.
3. Add the whiting, cover it with water, and season with salt. Raise the heat to medium and cook the fish for 30 minutes.
4. Strain the broth into a bowl and set it aside. Use the solids for another preparation if desired.
5. Cook the couscous according to the package instructions. You want the grains to be separated, and not at all sticky. If they are clumping together, add some olive oil.
6. Place the couscous in a serving bowl, add the broth, and let the mixture sit for 15 minutes.
7. Place the remaining olive oil in a large skillet and warm it over medium heat. Add the langoustines and cook until they are cooked through, about 3 minutes, turning them as necessary. Remove the langoustines from the pan and set them aside.
8. Add the clams, cover the pan, and cook until the majority of them have opened, about 5 minutes. Discard any clams that did not open. Remove the clams from the pan and set them aside.
9. Place the gurnard in the pan and cook until it is just cooked through, 6 to 8 minutes, turning it over just once.
10. Top the couscous with the langoustines, clams, and gurnard and enjoy.

PLANT-BASED ENTREES

Eggplant Parmigiana alla Napoletana

YIELD: 4 SERVINGS / **ACTIVE TIME:** 1 HOUR / **TOTAL TIME:** 2 HOURS AND 30 MINUTES

4 LARGE EGGPLANTS

SALT (FINE AND COARSE), TO TASTE

EXTRA-VIRGIN OLIVE OIL, AS NEEDED

4 EGGS

ALL-PURPOSE FLOUR, AS NEEDED

3½ CUPS SUGO AL BASILICO (SEE PAGE 447)

9 OZ. FRESH MOZZARELLA CHEESE, DRAINED AND SLICED

2 HANDFULS OF FRESH BASIL

1 CUP GRATED PARMESAN CHEESE, PLUS MORE FOR TOPPING

1. Slice the eggplants thin lengthwise; if you have a mandoline available, use it on a rather thick setting. Layer the sliced eggplants in a colander, seasoning each layer with coarse salt. Fill a large saucepan with water and place it on top of the eggplants. Let the eggplants drain for 1 hour.
2. Rinse the eggplants and squeeze them to remove as much water as possible. Place the eggplants on paper towels and let them dry.
3. Preheat the oven to 375°F. Add olive oil to a narrow, deep, heavy-bottomed saucepan with high edges until it is about 2 inches deep and warm it to 350°F.
4. Place the eggs in a bowl, season them lightly with fine salt, and whisk until scrambled. Place flour in a shallow bowl and dredge the eggplants in the flour and then the egg until they are completely coated.
5. Gently slip the eggplants into the hot oil and fry until they are golden brown, working in batches to avoid crowding the pot. Transfer the fried eggplants to a paper towel–lined plate to drain.
6. Cover the bottom of a 13 x 9–inch baking dish with some of the tomato sauce. Arrange the eggplants, mozzarella, basil, Parmesan, and tomato sauce in individual layers in the dish, continuing the layering process until everything has been used up.
7. Top the dish with additional Parmesan, place it in the oven, and bake until the cheese and sauce start to bubble, about 25 minutes.
8. Remove the parmigiana from the oven and let it rest for at least 30 minutes before slicing and serving.

Frittata di Zucchine

YIELD: 4 SERVINGS / **ACTIVE TIME:** 20 MINUTES / **TOTAL TIME:** 30 MINUTES

6 TABLESPOONS EXTRA-VIRGIN OLIVE OIL

2 LARGE ONIONS, SLICED THIN

1⅓ LBS. ZUCCHINI, TRIMMED AND CHOPPED

5 EGGS

SALT AND PEPPER, TO TASTE

3½ OZ. PECORINO OR PARMESAN CHEESE, GRATED

3 TABLESPOONS BREAD CRUMBS

1 TABLESPOON CHOPPED FRESH PARSLEY

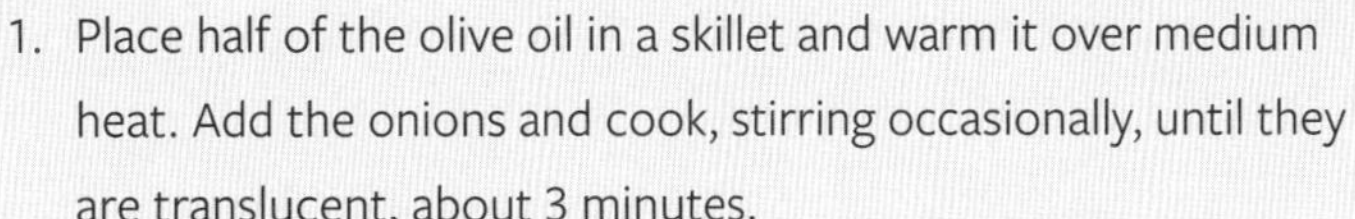

1. Place half of the olive oil in a skillet and warm it over medium heat. Add the onions and cook, stirring occasionally, until they are translucent, about 3 minutes.
2. Add the zucchini and cook, stirring occasionally, until it is tender, about 10 minutes. Remove the pan from heat and let the mixture cool.
3. Place the eggs in a bowl, season them with salt and pepper, and whisk until scrambled. Add the pecorino, bread crumbs, and parsley and whisk to combine.
4. Add the cooled vegetable mixture and fold to incorporate.
5. Place the remaining olive oil in a large skillet and warm it over medium-low heat. Add the egg mixture, cover the pan, and cook until the bottom is set, 5 to 8 minutes.
6. Gently lift the frittata on one side and check to see if it is golden brown. When it is, use a large plate to invert the pan and flip the frittata over. Cook until the frittata is browned on the other side, 3 to 4 minutes. Serve immediately.

Eggplant Parmigiana alla Palermitana

YIELD: 4 SERVINGS / **ACTIVE TIME:** 1 HOUR / **TOTAL TIME:** 3 HOURS AND 30 MINUTES

4 LARGE EGGPLANTS

COARSE SALT, TO TASTE

EXTRA-VIRGIN OLIVE OIL, AS NEEDED

3½ CUPS SUGO AL BASILICO (SEE PAGE 447)

2 HANDFULS OF FRESH BASIL

1 CUP GRATED PECORINO OR CACIOCAVALLO CHEESE

1. Slice the eggplants thin lengthwise; if you have a mandoline available, use it on a rather thick setting. Layer the sliced eggplants in a colander, seasoning each layer with coarse salt. Fill a large saucepan with water and place it on top of the eggplants. Let the eggplants drain for 1 hour.
2. Rinse the eggplants and squeeze them to remove as much water as possible. Place the eggplants on kitchen towels and let them dry.
3. Add olive oil to a narrow, deep, heavy-bottomed saucepan with high edges until it is about 2 inches deep and warm it to 350°F.
4. Gently slip the eggplants into the hot oil and fry until they are golden brown, working in batches to avoid crowding the pot. Place the fried eggplants on a paper towel–lined plate to drain.
5. Cover the bottom of a 13 x 9–inch baking pan with some of the tomato sauce. Arrange some of the eggplants, sauce, basil, and pecorino in individual layers in the dish, continuing the layering process until everything has been used up.
6. Place the parmigiana in the refrigerator and chill it for 2 to 3 hours before serving.

Eggplant Parmigiana alla Catanese

YIELD: 4 SERVINGS / **ACTIVE TIME:** 1 HOUR / **TOTAL TIME:** 2 HOURS AND 30 MINUTES

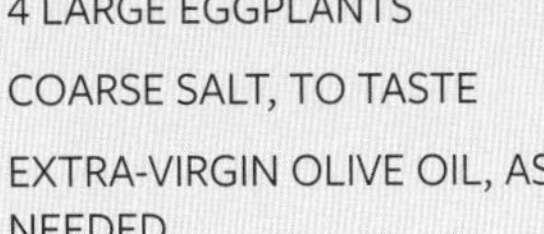

4 LARGE EGGPLANTS

COARSE SALT, TO TASTE

EXTRA-VIRGIN OLIVE OIL, AS NEEDED

3½ CUPS SUGO AL BASILICO (SEE PAGE 447)

2 HANDFULS OF FRESH BASIL

3 HARD-BOILED EGGS, SLICED

½ LB. FRESH MOZZARELLA CHEESE, DRAINED AND SLICED

7 OZ. HAM OR MORTADELLA, SLICED

1 CUP GRATED PECORINO OR CACIOCAVALLO CHEESE

1. Slice the eggplants thin lengthwise; if you have a mandoline available, use it on a rather thick setting. Layer the sliced eggplants in a colander, seasoning each layer with coarse salt. Fill a large saucepan with water and place it on top of the eggplants. Let the eggplants drain for 1 hour.
2. Rinse the eggplants and squeeze them to remove as much water as possible. Place the eggplants on kitchen towels and let them dry.
3. Preheat the oven to 375°F. Add olive oil to a narrow, deep, heavy-bottomed saucepan with high edges until it is about 2 inches deep and warm it to 350°F.
4. Gently slip the eggplants into the hot oil and fry until they are golden brown, working in batches to avoid crowding the pot. Place the fried eggplants on a paper towel–lined plate to drain.
5. Cover the bottom of a 13 x 9–inch baking pan with some of the tomato sauce. Arrange some of the eggplants, sauce, basil, eggs, mozzarella, ham, and pecorino in individual layers in the dish, continuing the layering process until everything has been used up.
6. Place the parmigiana in the oven and bake until the cheese is melted and bubbling, 25 to 30 minutes.
7. Remove the parmigiana from the oven and let it rest for 30 minutes before serving.

Rafanata

YIELD: 4 SERVINGS / **ACTIVE TIME:** 10 MINUTES / **TOTAL TIME:** 45 MINUTES

SALT AND PEPPER, TO TASTE

11 OZ. POTATOES, PEELED AND CHOPPED

5 EGGS

3½ OZ. PECORINO CHEESE, GRATED

3½ OZ. FRESH HORSERADISH, GRATED

3 TABLESPOONS EXTRA-VIRGIN OLIVE OIL

1. Bring salted water to a boil in a large saucepan. Add the potatoes and boil until they are tender, 15 to 20 minutes. Drain the potatoes and place them in a bowl.
2. Mash the potatoes until they are smooth and let them cool completely.
3. Place the eggs in a bowl, season them with salt and pepper, and stir to combine.
4. Add the mashed potatoes, pecorino, and horseradish and stir until the mixture is combined.
5. Place the olive oil in a large skillet and warm it over medium-high heat. Add the potato-and-egg mixture and spread it into an even layer. Cook until you see the bottom and edge of the frittata detach from the pan.
6. Using a large plate, invert the pan and flip the frittata over. Cook until the frittata is browned on the other side and cooked through, 5 to 8 minutes. Serve immediately.

Affunniatella Molisana

YIELD: 4 SERVINGS / **ACTIVE TIME:** 10 MINUTES / **TOTAL TIME:** 30 MINUTES

¼ CUP EXTRA-VIRGIN OLIVE OIL

1 ONION, FINELY DICED

13 OZ. SWEET ITALIAN PEPPERS, STEMMED, SEEDED, AND CUT INTO STRIPS

½ CHILE PEPPER, STEMMED, SEEDED, AND MINCED

1 TABLESPOON CHOPPED FRESH PARSLEY

3 TOMATOES, CHOPPED

SALT, TO TASTE

4 EGGS, LIGHTLY BEATEN

⅔ CUP GRATED PECORINO CHEESE

1. Place the olive oil in a large skillet and warm it over medium heat. Add the onion and cook, stirring occasionally, until it has softened, about 5 minutes.
2. Add the sweet peppers and cook, stirring occasionally, until they have softened, about 5 minutes.
3. Add the chile, parsley, and tomatoes, season with salt, and reduce the heat to low. Cook until the sauce has thickened, 15 to 20 minutes.
4. Add the eggs and scramble until they are almost set.
5. Sprinkle the pecorino over the eggs and cook until it has melted. Serve immediately.

Fried Eggs & Peppers alla Cosentina

YIELD: 4 SERVINGS / **ACTIVE TIME:** 15 MINUTES / **TOTAL TIME:** 30 MINUTES

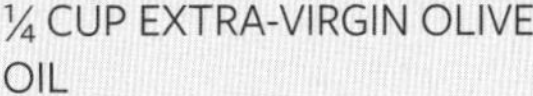

¼ CUP EXTRA-VIRGIN OLIVE OIL

2 GARLIC CLOVES

5 ANCHOVIES IN OLIVE OIL, DRAINED AND CHOPPED

RED PEPPER FLAKES OR 'NDUJA, TO TASTE

8 CHERRY TOMATOES, HALVED

1 RED BELL PEPPER, STEMMED, SEEDED, AND SLICED

1 YELLOW BELL PEPPER, STEMMED, SEEDED, AND SLICED

SALT, TO TASTE

8 EGGS, BEATEN

⅔ CUP GRATED PECORINO CHEESE

DRIED OREGANO, TO TASTE

SOURDOUGH BREAD, TOASTED OR GRILLED, FOR SERVING

1. Place the olive oil in a large skillet and warm it over medium-low heat. Add the garlic, anchovies, and red pepper flakes and cook for 2 minutes.
2. Add the tomatoes and cook, stirring occasionally, until they have softened.
3. Add the bell peppers, season the dish with salt, and raise the heat to medium. Cover the pan and cook for about 30 minutes, stirring occasionally and adding water if the dish starts to look dry.
4. Add the eggs and scramble them until they are almost set.
5. Sprinkle the pecorino over the eggs and cook until it has melted. Season the dish with oregano and salt and serve immediately with slices of sourdough bread.

Frittata Pasquale

YIELD: 4 SERVINGS / **ACTIVE TIME:** 30 MINUTES / **TOTAL TIME:** 1 HOUR

5 OZ. LEAFY GREEN VEGETABLES (CHICORY, DANDELION GREENS, BEET GREENS, COLLARD GREENS)

3 OZ. ASPARAGUS

2 HANDFULS OF MIXED FRESH HERBS (ROSEMARY, PARSLEY, SAGE, MARJORAM, CHIVES, AND/OR MINT RECOMMENDED)

6 TABLESPOONS EXTRA-VIRGIN OLIVE OIL

1 GARLIC CLOVE

SALT AND PEPPER, TO TASTE

8 EGGS

2 TABLESPOONS GRATED PARMESAN CHEESE

2 TABLESPOONS WHOLE MILK

1. Carefully rinse the leafy greens, asparagus, and herbs. Remove any woody stems, tough ends, or damaged leaves and discard. Chop the vegetables and herbs and set them aside.
2. Place half of the olive oil in a large skillet and warm it over low heat. Add the garlic and cook until it is lightly browned, about 2 minutes.
3. Add the asparagus and cook, stirring occasionally, until it has softened, about 5 minutes.
4. Add the leafy greens, herbs, and a few tablespoons of water, season with salt and pepper, and cover the pan. Cook, stirring occasionally, for 15 minutes.
5. Place the eggs, Parmesan, and milk in a large bowl and whisk to combine. Remove the pan from heat and let the vegetables and herbs cool. Pour the mixture into the egg mixture and stir to combine.
6. Place the remaining olive oil in a large skillet and warm it over medium heat.
7. Add the vegetable-and-egg mixture to the pan, reduce the heat to medium-low, and cover the pan.
8. Cook the frittata until the bottom is browned and sides are set. Place a plate over the frittata and invert the pan so the frittata falls on the plate. Place the frittata back in the pan and cook until it is browned on that side.
9. Remove the frittata from the pan and serve immediately.

Pitta di Patate

YIELD: 6 SERVINGS / **ACTIVE TIME:** 40 MINUTES / **TOTAL TIME:** 1 HOUR AND 30 MINUTES

¼ CUP EXTRA-VIRGIN OLIVE OIL

3 LARGE YELLOW OR RED ONIONS, SLICED THIN

1 LB. WHOLE PEELED TOMATOES, CRUSHED

½ CUP PITTED BLACK OLIVES, CHOPPED

1 TABLESPOON CAPERS IN BRINE, RINSED AND DRAINED

4 FRESH MINT LEAVES, FINELY CHOPPED

SALT AND PEPPER, TO TASTE

DRIED OREGANO, TO TASTE

2½ LBS. POTATOES

2 EGGS

1 CUP GRATED PECORINO CHEESE

3½ TABLESPOONS WHOLE MILK

BUTTER, AS NEEDED

¼ CUP BREAD CRUMBS

1. Place half of the olive oil in a large skillet and warm it over medium-low heat. Add the onions and cook, stirring occasionally, until they have softened, about 6 minutes.
2. Add the tomatoes and cook, stirring occasionally, until the mixture has thickened.
3. Stir in the olives, capers, and mint, season the mixture with salt and oregano, and cook for about 2 minutes. Remove the pan from heat and let the mixture cool.
4. Bring salted water to a boil in a large pot. Add the potatoes and boil until they are tender, about 40 minutes.
5. Preheat the oven to 390°F. Drain the potatoes and run them under cold water. Peel the potatoes, mash them, and season them with salt and pepper.
6. Add the remaining olive oil, the eggs, pecorino, and milk and stir to combine.
7. Coat a deep baking dish with butter. Sprinkle half of the bread crumbs over the bottom and then spread half of the potato mixture on top. Top with the tomato mixture, spread the remaining potato mixture over the top, and sprinkle the remaining bread crumbs over it.
8. Place the baking dish in the oven and bake for 35 minutes.
9. Set the oven's broiler to high and place the baking dish directly below it. Broil until the top is golden brown. Turn off the broiler and let the dish cool in the oven, which will allow it to become firmer when you serve it.

Scarola Mbuttunat

YIELD: 4 SERVINGS / **ACTIVE TIME:** 30 MINUTES / **TOTAL TIME:** 1 HOUR

SALT, TO TASTE

4 SMALL HEADS OF ESCAROLE

5 TABLESPOONS EXTRA-VIRGIN OLIVE OIL, PLUS MORE FOR TOPPING

1 GARLIC CLOVE, MINCED

RED PEPPER FLAKES, TO TASTE

5 ANCHOVIES IN OLIVE OIL, DRAINED AND CHOPPED

½ CUP PITTED BLACK OLIVES, CHOPPED

½ CUP PITTED GREEN OLIVES, CHOPPED

2 TABLESPOONS CAPERS, RINSED IF PACKED IN SALT OR DRAINED IF PACKED IN BRINE

½ CUP RAISINS, SOAKED IN WARM WATER FOR 10 MINUTES, DRAINED, AND SQUEEZED DRY

3 TABLESPOONS PINE NUTS

2 TABLESPOONS CHOPPED WALNUTS

2 TABLESPOONS CHOPPED FRESH PARSLEY

2 OZ. PECORINO CHEESE, SHAVED

½ CUP BREAD CRUMBS, PLUS MORE FOR TOPPING

1. Preheat the oven to 480°F. Bring salted water to a boil in a large saucepan. Remove and discard the core and outer leaves from the heads of escarole and rinse the heads under cold water. Tie the heads of escarole tightly with kitchen twine, place them in the boiling water, and boil for 2 minutes. Drain the escarole and let it cool.
2. Place the olive oil in a large skillet and warm it over medium heat. Add the garlic and red pepper flakes and cook for 1 minute. Add the anchovies, olives, capers, raisins, pine nuts, walnuts, and parsley, season with salt, and cook for 5 minutes.
3. Add the pecorino and bread crumbs and cook for 2 minutes.
4. Gently open the heads of escarole and fill them with the olive mixture. Tie the stuffed escarole closed with kitchen twine and place it in a baking dish. Drizzle olive oil over the stuffed escarole and sprinkle bread crumbs on top. Place the stuffed escarole in the oven and roast until it is golden brown, about 20 minutes.
5. Remove the stuffed escarole from the oven and let it cool slightly before serving.

Pizza di Scarola

YIELD: 6 SERVINGS / **ACTIVE TIME:** 40 MINUTES / **TOTAL TIME:** 4 HOURS

FOR THE DOUGH

1 SACHET OF ACTIVE DRY YEAST

2 CUPS LUKEWARM WATER (90°F)

1 TABLESPOON SUGAR

6⅔ CUPS ALL-PURPOSE FLOUR, PLUS MORE AS NEEDED

2 TABLESPOONS EXTRA-VIRGIN OLIVE OIL, PLUS MORE AS NEEDED

1 TABLESPOON TABLE SALT

FOR THE FILLING

5 TABLESPOONS EXTRA-VIRGIN OLIVE OIL

1 GARLIC CLOVE, MINCED

3 ANCHOVIES IN OLIVE OIL

RED PEPPER FLAKES, TO TASTE

1 LARGE HEAD OF ESCAROLE, RINSED WELL AND CHOPPED

½ CUP PITTED BLACK OLIVES

2 TABLESPOONS CAPERS, RINSED IF PACKED IN SALT OR DRAINED IF PACKED IN BRINE

SALT, TO TASTE

1. To begin preparations for the dough, place the yeast, water, and sugar in a large bowl, gently stir to combine, and let the mixture sit until it starts to foam, about 10 minutes. Add the flour and work the mixture until it just comes together as a dough. Add the olive oil and salt and knead the dough until it is smooth and elastic.
2. Shape the dough into a round, place it in a clean bowl, and cover it with plastic wrap. Let the dough rest at room temperature until it has almost doubled in size, about 3 hours.
3. To begin preparations for the filling, place the olive oil in a large skillet and warm it over medium-low heat. Add the garlic and anchovies, season with red pepper flakes, and cook for 2 minutes.
4. Add the escarole, cover the pan with a lid, and cook until the escarole has wilted, about 15 minutes.
5. Add the olives and capers, lightly season the mixture with salt, and cook for 5 more minutes. Remove the pan from heat and let the filling cool.
6. Preheat the oven to 430°F. Place the dough on a flour-dusted work surface and divide it into two pieces, one larger than the other. Roll out the larger piece into a ¼-inch-thick, 10-inch round.
7. Coat a 9-inch pie plate with olive oil and place the 10-inch round over it. Place the filling on top of the dough, roll out the remaining piece of dough, and place it on top of the filling. Fold the bottom crust down over the top crust and press down on the seam to seal. Brush the top crust with olive oil and place the scarola in the oven.
8. Bake until the scarola is golden brown, about 30 minutes. Remove it from the oven and enjoy it warm or at room temperature.

Friarielli e Salsiccia

YIELD: 4 SERVINGS / **ACTIVE TIME:** 30 MINUTES / **TOTAL TIME:** 1 HOUR

SALT, TO TASTE

2 LBS. TURNIP GREENS, RINSED WELL, WOODY STEMS REMOVED

6 TABLESPOONS EXTRA-VIRGIN OLIVE OIL

4 GARLIC CLOVES, HALVED

1 CHILE PEPPER, STEMMED, SEEDED, AND CHOPPED

8 ITALIAN SAUSAGES

1. Bring salted water to a boil in a large saucepan. Add the turnip greens and cook until just tender, about 5 minutes. Drain the turnip greens and set them aside.
2. Place 5 tablespoons of olive oil in a large skillet and warm it over medium-low heat. Add the garlic and chile and cook for 2 minutes. Remove the pan from heat and season the mixture with salt.
3. Place the remaining olive oil in a large skillet and warm it over medium heat. Poke holes in the sausages, place them in the pan, and cook until they are browned all over and nearly cooked through, about 10 minutes.
4. Stir in the garlic mixture and turnip greens and cook until the sausages are completely cooked through, 3 to 4 minutes. Serve immediately.

Risotto alla Pilota

YIELD: 4 SERVINGS / **ACTIVE TIME:** 30 MINUTES / **TOTAL TIME:** 50 MINUTES

4 CUPS WATER

SALT, TO TASTE

14 OZ. VIALONE NANO RICE

3½ OZ. UNSALTED BUTTER

6 OZ. SALAMELLA MANTOVANA OR OTHER ITALIAN SAUSAGE, CASING REMOVED AND CRUMBLED

1 CUP GRATED GRANA PADANO CHEESE

1. Place the water in a medium saucepan and bring to a boil. Add salt and the rice, ideally making the rice descend from a sheet of paper shaped into a funnel. The tip of the funnel should be ½ inch above the water.
2. When the rice starts simmering, shake the saucepan and cook over high heat for about 12 minutes.
3. Remove the pan from heat, cover it, and let the rice rest for about 15 minutes.
4. While the rice is resting, place the butter in a large skillet and melt it over medium heat. Add the sausage and cook, stirring occasionally, until it is browned and cooked through, about 10 minutes.
5. Top the rice with the Grana Padano and sausage. Toss to combine and serve immediately.

Pizza di Scarola

SEE PAGE 164

Gattò di Patate

YIELD: 6 SERVINGS / **ACTIVE TIME:** 40 MINUTES / **TOTAL TIME:** 1 HOUR AND 30 MINUTES

SALT AND PEPPER, TO TASTE

2½ LBS. POTATOES

2 TABLESPOONS EXTRA-VIRGIN OLIVE OIL

2 EGGS

⅔ CUP GRATED PARMESAN CHEESE

3½ TABLESPOONS WHOLE MILK

BUTTER, AS NEEDED

¼ CUP BREAD CRUMBS

7 OZ. SMOKED PROVOLA OR SMOKED SCAMORZA CHEESE, DICED

3½ OZ. SALAMI, CHOPPED

3½ OZ. HAM, DICED

1. Preheat the oven to 390°F. Bring salted water to a boil in a large pot. Add the potatoes and boil until they are tender, about 40 minutes.
2. Drain the potatoes and run them under cold water. Peel the potatoes, mash them, and season them with salt and pepper. Add the olive oil, eggs, Parmesan, and milk and stir to combine.
3. Coat a deep baking dish with butter. Sprinkle half of the bread crumbs over the bottom and then spread half of the potato mixture on top.
4. Top with the provola, salami, and ham, spread the remaining potato mixture over the top, and sprinkle the remaining bread crumbs over it. Place the baking dish in the oven and bake for 35 minutes.
5. Set the oven's broiler to high and place the baking dish directly below it. Broil until the top is golden brown. Turn off the broiler and let the gattò cool in the oven, which will allow it to become firmer when you serve it.

Pallotte Cace e Ove

YIELD: 20 PALLOTTE / **ACTIVE TIME:** 30 MINUTES / **TOTAL TIME:** 1 HOUR

2 CUPS GRATED GRANA PADANO CHEESE

2 CUPS GRATED PARMESAN CHEESE

1 CUP GRATED PECORINO CHEESE

1 CUP DRAINED RICOTTA CHEESE

5 EGGS

1 CUP FRESH BREAD CRUMBS, PLUS MORE AS NEEDED

EXTRA-VIRGIN OLIVE OIL, AS NEEDED

SUGO AI PEPERONI (SEE PAGE 448)

CRUSTY BREAD, FOR SERVING

1. Place all of the cheeses in a large bowl and stir to combine. Incorporate the eggs one at a time and then add the bread crumbs. Gently stir until the mixture holds together enough to keep its shape during the cooking process. If necessary, incorporate more bread crumbs.
2. Add olive oil to a narrow, deep, heavy-bottomed saucepan with high edges until it is about 2 inches deep and warm it to 350°F. Form the cheese mixture into ovals (each should weigh approximately 2 oz.) and gently slip them into the hot oil. Fry the pallotte until they are crispy and golden brown, turning as necessary.
3. Remove the pallotte from the hot oil and transfer them to a paper towel–lined plate to drain.
4. Place the sauce in a large skillet and warm it over low heat. Add the pallotte and cook them for 10 minutes. Serve immediately with crusty bread.

Polpette di Eggplant

YIELD: 4 SERVINGS / **ACTIVE TIME:** 30 MINUTES / **TOTAL TIME:** 1 HOUR

SALT AND PEPPER, TO TASTE

4 LARGE EGGPLANTS, TRIMMED AND CUT INTO STRIPS

2 SLICES OF STALE BREAD, BRIEFLY SOAKED IN WATER AND SQUEEZED DRY

2 EGGS

2 TABLESPOONS FINELY CHOPPED FRESH PARSLEY

1 GARLIC CLOVE, MINCED

1 TABLESPOON BREAD CRUMBS

½ CUP GRATED PECORINO CHEESE

EXTRA-VIRGIN OLIVE OIL, AS NEEDED

1. Bring salted water to a boil in a large saucepan. Add the eggplants and cook until they soften slightly, about 5 minutes. Drain the eggplants and let them cool.
2. Squeeze the eggplants to remove any excess water and place them in a large bowl. Add the stale bread, eggs, parsley, garlic, bread crumbs, and pecorino, season the mixture with salt and pepper, and stir to combine.
3. Add olive oil to a narrow, deep, heavy-bottomed saucepan with high edges until it is about 2 inches deep and warm it to 350°F. Form the eggplant mixture into ovals (each should weigh approximately 2 oz.) and gently slip them into the hot oil. Fry the polpettes until they are crispy and golden brown, turning as necessary.
4. Remove the polpettes from the hot oil and transfer them to a paper towel–lined plate to drain. Serve once all of the polpettes have drained and cooled slightly.

Polenta Concia alla Valdostana

YIELD: 4 SERVINGS / **ACTIVE TIME:** 15 MINUTES / **TOTAL TIME:** 1 HOUR AND 15 MINUTES

6 CUPS WATER, PLUS MORE AS NEEDED

1 (SCANT) TABLESPOON COARSE SEA SALT

2 CUPS POLENTA

¼ CUP UNSALTED BUTTER

¾ LB. FONTINA CHEESE, CUBED

1. Place the water and salt in a large saucepan and bring to a boil.
2. While whisking continually, slowly stream in the polenta. Reduce the heat to low and cook, stirring frequently, until the polenta is thick and creamy, about 1 hour. If the polenta thickens too quickly, add water as necessary.
3. Stir the butter into the polenta.
4. Remove the polenta from heat, add the cheese, and stir until it has almost melted. Serve immediately.

Polenta al Sugo di Salsiccia

YIELD: 6 SERVINGS / **ACTIVE TIME:** 30 MINUTES / **TOTAL TIME:** 2 HOURS

7 OZ. EXTRA-VIRGIN OLIVE OIL

½ ONION, FINELY DICED

1½ LBS. LUGANEGA-STYLE ITALIAN SAUSAGE, CUT INTO LARGE CHUNKS

½ CUP DRY WHITE WINE

2 LBS. WHOLE PEELED TOMATOES, CRUSHED

3 BAY LEAVES

8 CUPS WATER, PLUS MORE AS NEEDED

1 (SCANT) TABLESPOON COARSE SEA SALT

3 CUPS POLENTA

2 CUPS GRATED PARMESAN CHEESE

1. Place one-quarter of the olive oil in a large skillet and warm it over medium-high heat. Add the onion and cook, stirring occasionally, until it has softened, about 5 minutes.
2. Add the sausage and cook, stirring occasionally, until it is browned all over.
3. Add the wine and cook until it has evaporated. Add the tomatoes and bay leaves, reduce the heat to medium, and cook, stirring occasionally, until the sauce has thickened, about 30 minutes.
4. Place the water and salt in a large saucepan and bring to a boil.
5. While whisking continually, slowly stream in the polenta. Reduce the heat to low and cook, stirring frequently, until the polenta is thick and creamy, about 1 hour. If the polenta thickens too quickly, add water as necessary.
6. Remove the polenta from heat, add the remaining olive oil and half of the Parmesan, and stir until the Parmesan has almost melted.
7. Ladle the polenta into serving bowls and let it rest for 5 minutes. Top it with the sauce and remaining Parmesan and serve immediately.

Risotto alla Piemontese

YIELD: 4 SERVINGS / **ACTIVE TIME:** 30 MINUTES / **TOTAL TIME:** 30 MINUTES

4 CUPS VEGETABLE STOCK (SEE PAGE 447)

¼ CUP UNSALTED BUTTER

1 SMALL ONION, FINELY DICED

11 OZ. CARNAROLI RICE

½ CUP DRY WHITE WINE

SALT AND PEPPER, TO TASTE

½ CUP GRATED PARMESAN CHEESE

1. Place the stock in a saucepan and bring it to a simmer. Turn off the heat under the stock but leave it on the burner.
2. Place half of the butter in a large, deep skillet and melt it over medium heat. Add the onion and cook, stirring occasionally, until it has softened, about 5 minutes.
3. Add the rice and cook until it gives off a nutty aroma, about 2 minutes. Add the wine and cook, stirring continually, until the rice absorbs it.
4. Add a few ladles of warm stock to cover the rice and cook, stirring frequently, until the rice absorbs it. Continue adding stock until the rice is al dente and the dish is creamy.
5. Season the risotto with salt and pepper and remove the pan from heat. Stir the Parmesan and remaining butter into the risotto and serve immediately.

Risotto alla Milanese

YIELD: 4 SERVINGS / **ACTIVE TIME:** 30 MINUTES / **TOTAL TIME:** 1 HOUR AND 30 MINUTES

6 CUPS BEEF STOCK (SEE PAGE 446)

PINCH OF SAFFRON THREADS

¼ CUP UNSALTED BUTTER

2 TABLESPOONS ROASTED VEAL BONE MARROW

1 SMALL ONION, FINELY DICED

11 OZ. CARNAROLI RICE

SALT, TO TASTE

½ CUP GRATED PARMESAN CHEESE

1. Place the stock in a saucepan and bring it to a simmer. Turn off the heat under the stock but leave it on the burner. Remove 1 cup of stock, place it in a bowl, and add the saffron. Let the saffron steep for 1 hour.
2. Place two-thirds of the butter in a large, deep skillet and melt it over medium heat. Add the bone marrow and onion and cook, stirring occasionally, until it has softened, about 5 minutes.
3. Add the rice and cook until it gives off a nutty aroma, about 2 minutes.
4. Add the saffron and the stock it soaked in, season the risotto with salt, and stir to combine.
5. Continue adding stock until the rice is al dente and the dish is creamy.
6. Remove the pan from heat, stir the Parmesan and remaining butter into the risotto, season with salt, and serve immediately.

Polenta Taragna

YIELD: 4 SERVINGS / **ACTIVE TIME:** 15 MINUTES / **TOTAL TIME:** 1 HOUR AND 15 MINUTES

8 CUPS WATER, PLUS MORE AS NEEDED

1 (SCANT) TABLESPOON COARSE SEA SALT

1¾ CUPS BUCKWHEAT FLOUR

1 (SCANT) CUP POLENTA

¼ CUP UNSALTED BUTTER

5 FRESH SAGE LEAVES

1 GARLIC CLOVE

11 OZ. SEMISOFT CHEESE (SUCH AS ALPINE BRANZI OR EMMENTAL), CUBED

1. Place the water and salt in a large saucepan and bring to a boil.
2. While whisking continually, slowly stream in the flour and polenta. Reduce the heat to low and cook, stirring continually, until the polenta is thick and creamy, about 1 hour. If the polenta thickens too quickly, add water as necessary.
3. Place the butter in a large skillet and melt it over medium heat. Add the sage and garlic and cook, stirring continually, for 1 minute.
4. Remove the garlic and discard it. Stir the sage and butter into the polenta.
5. Remove the polenta from heat, add the cheese, and stir until it has almost melted. Serve immediately.

Risi e Bisi

YIELD: 4 SERVINGS / **ACTIVE TIME:** 40 MINUTES / **TOTAL TIME:** 1 HOUR

4 CUPS VEGETABLE STOCK (SEE PAGE 447)

¼ CUP UNSALTED BUTTER

½ SMALL ONION, FINELY DICED

1 LB. PEAS

3½ OZ. PANCETTA, DICED (OPTIONAL)

SALT AND PEPPER, TO TASTE

½ CUP DRY WHITE WINE

HANDFUL OF FRESH PARSLEY, FINELY CHOPPED

11 OZ. CARNAROLI OR VIALONE NANO RICE

½ CUP GRATED PARMESAN CHEESE

1. Place the stock in a saucepan and bring it to a simmer. Turn off the heat under the stock but leave it on the burner.
2. Place half of the butter in a large, deep skillet and melt it over medium heat. Add the onion and cook, stirring occasionally, until it starts to brown, about 8 minutes.
3. Add the peas and pancetta (if desired), season with salt and pepper, and add the wine, parsley, and ½ cup of warm stock. Cook, stirring continually, until the peas are tender and the pancetta is browned, 6 to 8 minutes. Remove the pan from heat.
4. Place the rice in a dry skillet and toast over medium heat until it gives off a nutty aroma, about 2 minutes.
5. Add half of the pea mixture, add a few ladles of warm stock to cover the rice, and cook, stirring frequently, until the rice absorbs the stock. Continue adding stock until the rice is al dente and the dish is creamy.
6. Season the dish with salt and pepper and stir in the remaining pea mixture, the remaining butter, and the Parmesan. Stir until the cheese has melted and add more stock if a soupy risi e bisi is desired. Serve immediately.

Risotto ai Funghi e Taleggio

YIELD: 4 SERVINGS / **ACTIVE TIME:** 40 MINUTES / **TOTAL TIME:** 40 MINUTES

4 CUPS VEGETABLE STOCK (SEE PAGE 447)

¼ CUP UNSALTED BUTTER

½ SMALL ONION, FINELY DICED

1 LB. MUSHROOMS, CLEANED AND CHOPPED

HANDFUL OF FRESH PARSLEY, FINELY CHOPPED

11 OZ. VIALONE NANO RICE

½ CUP DRY WHITE WINE

SALT AND PEPPER, TO TASTE

6 OZ. TALEGGIO CHEESE, CUBED

1. Place the stock in a saucepan and bring it to a simmer. Turn off the heat under the stock but leave it on the burner.
2. Place half of the butter in a large, deep skillet and melt it over medium heat. Add the onion and cook, stirring occasionally, until it starts to brown, about 8 minutes.
3. Add the mushrooms and parsley and cook until the mushrooms release their liquid, about 8 minutes.
4. Add the rice and cook until it gives off a nutty aroma, about 2 minutes. Add the wine and cook, stirring continually, until the rice absorbs it.
5. Season with salt and pepper, add a few ladles of warm stock to cover the rice, and cook, stirring frequently, until the rice absorbs it. Continue adding stock until the rice is al dente and the dish is creamy.
6. Season the risotto with salt and pepper and remove the pan from heat. Add the taleggio and remaining butter to the risotto and stir until the cheese has melted. Serve immediately.

Risotto al Radicchio Rosso

YIELD: 4 SERVINGS / **ACTIVE TIME:** 50 MINUTES / **TOTAL TIME:** 50 MINUTES

4 CUPS VEGETABLE STOCK (SEE PAGE 447)

6 TABLESPOONS UNSALTED BUTTER

1 SMALL ONION, FINELY DICED

11 OZ. RADICCHIO ROSSO, FINELY DICED

SALT AND PEPPER, TO TASTE

11 OZ. VIALONE NANO RICE

½ CUP RED WINE

2 OZ. PARMESAN CHEESE, GRATED

1. Place the stock in a saucepan and bring it to a simmer. Turn off the heat under the stock but leave it on the burner.
2. Place two-thirds of the butter in a large, deep skillet and melt it over medium heat. Add the onion and cook, stirring occasionally, until it has softened, about 5 minutes.
3. Add the radicchio and a ladle of warm stock, season with salt and pepper, and cook until the radicchio has softened and the stock has evaporated, about 10 minutes.
4. Add the rice and cook until it gives off a nutty aroma, about 2 minutes.
5. Add the wine and cook, stirring continually, until the rice absorbs it.
6. Add a few ladles of warm stock to cover the rice and cook, stirring frequently, until the rice absorbs it. Continue adding stock until the rice is al dente and the dish is creamy.
7. Season the risotto with salt and pepper and remove the pan from heat. Stir the Parmesan and remaining butter into the risotto and serve immediately.

Frittata di Carciofi

YIELD: 4 SERVINGS / **ACTIVE TIME:** 30 MINUTES / **TOTAL TIME:** 1 HOUR

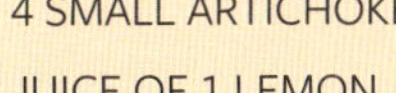

4 SMALL ARTICHOKES

JUICE OF 1 LEMON

6 TABLESPOONS EXTRA-VIRGIN OLIVE OIL

2 TO 3 DRIED PORCINI MUSHROOMS, SOAKED IN WARM WATER

½ ONION, FINELY DICED

2 OZ. STALE BREAD, CRUSTS REMOVED

2 TABLESPOONS WHOLE MILK

5 EGGS

½ CUP GRATED PARMESAN CHEESE

¼ TEASPOON DRIED MARJORAM

½ GARLIC CLOVE, FINELY CHOPPED

SALT AND PEPPER, TO TASTE

1. Clean the artichokes, removing the tough leaves and thorns. Trim and peel the stems, place the artichokes in a bowl, and cover them with water. Stir in the lemon juice and set the artichokes aside.
2. Place half of the olive oil in a large skillet and warm it over medium heat. Drain the mushrooms and squeeze them to remove any excess liquid. Add them and the onion to the pan and cook, stirring occasionally, until they start to brown, about 8 minutes.
3. Cut the artichokes into thin wedges and add them to the pan. Cook, stirring occasionally, until they have softened, adding water if the pan starts to look dry. Remove the pan from heat and let the mixture cool.
4. Place the bread and milk in a bowl and let the mixture soak. Place the eggs, Parmesan, marjoram, and garlic in a large bowl and whisk to combine.
5. Add the vegetable mixture. Squeeze the bread, add it to the egg mixture, season with salt and pepper, and whisk to combine.
6. Place the remaining olive oil in a large, shallow skillet and warm it over medium heat. Pour the egg mixture into the pan and shake the skillet to evenly distribute the mixture. Cook until the bottom of the frittata is set and starting to brown.
7. Place a large plate over the skillet and invert the frittata onto the plate. Place the frittata back in the pan and cook until it is completely cooked through.
8. Remove the frittata from the pan and let it cool to room temperature before serving.

Parmigiana di Gobbi

YIELD: 4 SERVINGS / **ACTIVE TIME:** 40 MINUTES / **TOTAL TIME:** 2 HOURS

4 LBS. CARDOONS

JUICE OF ½ LEMON

SALT, TO TASTE

3 EGGS

1 CUP ALL-PURPOSE FLOUR

EXTRA-VIRGIN OLIVE OIL, AS NEEDED

SUGO CON SOFFRITTO (SEE PAGE 448)

2 CUPS GRATED PARMESAN CHEESE

1 LB. FRESH MOZZARELLA CHEESE, DRAINED AND CUBED

1. Remove the flower buds from the cardoons and cut the stems into 3-inch-long pieces. While working with the cardoons, place the cut pieces in a bowl of water and stir in the lemon juice to prevent them from blackening.
2. Bring water to a boil in a large saucepan. Add salt and the cardoons and boil until they are tender. Cooking times will vary based on the quality of your cardoons. Drain the cardoons and let them cool. When they are cool enough to handle, squeeze them to remove any excess water.
3. Place the eggs in a bowl, add a pinch of salt, and beat until scrambled. Place the flour in a shallow bowl.
4. Add olive oil to a narrow, deep, heavy-bottomed saucepan with high edges until it is about 2 inches deep and warm it to 350°F.
5. Dredge the cardoons in the flour and then in the beaten eggs until they are completely coated. Working in batches to avoid crowding the pot, gently slip them into the hot oil and fry until they are golden brown.
6. Remove the fried cardoons and place them on a paper towel–lined plate to drain and cool. Preheat the oven to 350°F.
7. Spread some tomato sauce over the bottom of a large baking dish. Top with half of the cardoons, sprinkle one-third of the Parmesan on top, and arrange one-third of the mozzarella on top of the Parmesan. Spread a thin layer of tomato sauce over the cheeses. Repeat this layering process and then top the dish with the remaining Parmesan and mozzarella.
8. Place the dish in the oven and bake until the top looks crunchy, about 40 minutes. Remove the parmigiana from the oven and let it rest for 15 minutes before slicing and serving.

Torta Pasqualina

YIELD: 6 SERVINGS / **ACTIVE TIME:** 1 HOUR / **TOTAL TIME:** 3 HOURS

FOR THE CRUST

5 CUPS ALL-PURPOSE FLOUR, PLUS MORE AS NEEDED

1½ CUPS WATER

2 TABLESPOONS EXTRA-VIRGIN OLIVE OIL, PLUS MORE AS NEEDED

PINCH OF TABLE SALT

FOR THE FILLING

2 TABLESPOONS EXTRA-VIRGIN OLIVE OIL

½ ONION, FINELY DICED

1 LB. CHARD, HARD STEMS REMOVED, RINSED WELL AND CHOPPED

1 LB. FRESH SPINACH, RINSED WELL AND CHOPPED

10 EGGS

1 CUP GRATED PARMESAN CHEESE

⅔ CUP GRATED PECORINO CHEESE

HANDFUL OF FRESH MARJORAM, FINELY CHOPPED

2 PINCHES OF FRESHLY GRATED NUTMEG

SALT AND PEPPER, TO TASTE

1 LB. RICOTTA CHEESE, DRAINED IN THE REFRIGERATOR FOR 1 HOUR

1 TABLESPOON CORNSTARCH

1. To begin preparations for the crust, place all of the ingredients in a large bowl and work the mixture until it starts to come together as a dough. Transfer the dough to a flour-dusted work surface and knead it until it is smooth and elastic.
2. Divide the dough into six pieces, form them into rounds, and wrap each one with plastic wrap. Chill the dough in the refrigerator for 1 hour.
3. To begin preparations for the filling, place the olive oil in a large skillet and warm it over medium heat. Add the onion, chard, and spinach and cook, stirring occasionally, until the onion has softened and the greens have wilted, 5 to 7 minutes.
4. Remove the vegetables from the pan and let them cool. When they are cool enough to handle, squeeze them to remove any excess liquid and finely chop them.
5. Place the mixture in a large bowl, add 2 of the eggs, two-thirds of the Parmesan, the pecorino, the marjoram, and 1 pinch of nutmeg. Season with salt and pepper and stir until well combined. Set the mixture aside.
6. Place the ricotta, 2 of the eggs, the cornstarch, the remaining Parmesan, and the remaining nutmeg in a separate bowl, season with salt, and stir until the mixture is smooth and creamy.
7. Preheat the oven to 355°F. Place the pieces of dough on a flour-dusted work surface and roll them into very thin 12-inch rounds.
8. Coat a round 10-inch cake pan with olive oil and place a round over the bottom. Spread 1 tablespoon of olive oil over the dough and cover with another round, making sure that there are no air bubbles between the disks and that they adhere perfectly to each other. Repeat with 2 more rounds, reserving the last 2 for the top of the pie.

9. Top the fourth round with the vegetable mixture. Top with the ricotta mixture and level it with a spatula.
10. Make six hollows in the ricotta filling, leaving equal space between each one, and crack the remaining eggs into them.
11. Top the filling with another round and spread 1 tablespoon of olive oil over it. Top with the last round and spread olive oil over it.
12. Place the pie in the oven and bake for about 50 minutes.
13. Remove the pie from the oven and let it cool slightly. Serve warm or at room temperature.

Erbazzone

YIELD: 6 SERVINGS / **ACTIVE TIME:** 40 MINUTES / **TOTAL TIME:** 1 HOUR AND 30 MINUTES

FOR THE CRUST

2½ CUPS ALL-PURPOSE FLOUR, PLUS MORE AS NEEDED

¼ CUP LARD

½ TEASPOON TABLE SALT

7 TABLESPOONS LUKEWARM WATER (90°F), PLUS MORE AS NEEDED

FOR THE FILLING

¼ CUP LARD, PLUS MORE AS NEEDED

1 GARLIC CLOVE, FINELY DICED

2 SPRING ONIONS, TRIMMED AND FINELY DICED

2 LBS. CHARD LEAVES, HARD STEMS REMOVED, RINSED WELL AND CHOPPED

1 LB. FRESH SPINACH, RINSED WELL AND CHOPPED

2 CUPS GRATED PARMESAN CHEESE

SALT AND PEPPER, TO TASTE

1. To begin preparations for the crust, place all of the ingredients in a large bowl and work the mixture until it starts to come together as a firm dough. Add 1 to 2 tablespoons of water if the dough appears too dry.
2. Transfer the dough to a flour-dusted work surface and knead it until it is smooth and elastic. Divide the dough into two pieces, form them into rounds, and wrap each one with plastic wrap. Let the dough rest for 30 minutes.
3. To begin preparations for the filling, place the lard in a large skillet and melt it over medium heat. Add the garlic and spring onions and cook, stirring frequently, until they have softened, about 5 minutes.
4. Add the chard and spinach and cook until they have wilted and all of the liquid they release has evaporated, about 15 minutes.
5. Remove the vegetables from the pan and let them cool. When they are cool enough to handle, squeeze them to remove excess liquid and finely chop them.
6. Place the mixture in a large bowl, add the Parmesan, season with salt and pepper, and stir until well combined. Set the mixture aside.
7. Preheat the oven to 390°F. Place the pieces of dough on a flour-dusted work surface and roll them into 14-inch rounds.
8. Coat a round 12-inch cake pan with lard and place a round over the bottom. Spread the vegetable mixture over the dough, making sure it is level.
9. Top with the remaining round, trying to make it wrinkly. Prick the top crust with a fork. Place the pie in the oven and bake for 25 minutes.
10. Remove the pie from the oven, brush it with lard, and return it to the oven. Bake until the top is lightly browned, 5 to 10 minutes.
11. Remove the pie from the oven and let it cool slightly before slicing and serving.

Pomodori Ripieni di Riso

YIELD: 4 SERVINGS / **ACTIVE TIME:** 30 MINUTES / **TOTAL TIME:** 2 HOURS AND 30 MINUTES

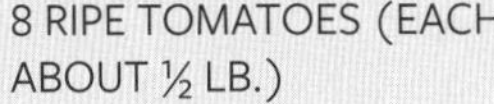

8 RIPE TOMATOES (EACH ABOUT ½ LB.)

HANDFUL OF FRESH PARSLEY, CHOPPED

HANDFUL OF FRESH MINT, CHOPPED

3 TABLESPOONS EXTRA-VIRGIN OLIVE OIL, PLUS MORE AS NEEDED

1 GARLIC CLOVE, MINCED

½ LB. CARNAROLI OR ARBORIO RICE

5 OZ. WHOLE PEELED TOMATOES, CRUSHED

SALT AND PEPPER, TO TASTE

1. Rinse the ripe tomatoes, cut off the tops, and reserve the tops. Extract the pulp and juice from the tomatoes and put them aside. Place the hollowed-out tomatoes, upside down, on a plate to drain.
2. Remove the white parts from the tomato pulp, place them in a food processor, and blitz until pureed. Place the puree in a bowl, add the parsley, mint, and olive oil, and stir to combine.
3. Stir in the garlic, rice, crushed tomatoes, and remaining tomato pulp and juice. Season the mixture with salt and pepper and toss to combine.
4. Cover the bowl with plastic wrap, place it in the refrigerator, and chill for 1 hour.
5. Preheat the oven to 350°F. Coat a deep baking dish with olive oil. Arrange the hollowed-out tomatoes, right side up, in the dish and fill each tomato with the rice mixture. Do not fill the tomatoes to the top, as the rice will expand during cooking.
6. Place the tops back on the tomatoes. Season them with salt and pepper and drizzle olive oil over the top.
7. Place the stuffed tomatoes in the oven and bake until the tops look slightly charred and their skins start to wrinkle.
8. Remove the stuffed tomatoes from the oven and let them cool. Serve them lukewarm or cold.

SOUPS & STEWS

Minestra Maritata

YIELD: 6 SERVINGS / **ACTIVE TIME:** 1 HOUR / **TOTAL TIME:** 5 HOURS

FOR THE BROTH

2 CELERY STALKS, EACH CUT INTO 2 TO 3 PIECES

2 CARROTS, PEELED AND HALVED

1 ONION, HALVED

HANDFUL OF SPRIGS OF FRESH PARSLEY, SPRIGS OF FRESH THYME, AND BAY LEAVES, TIED TOGETHER WITH KITCHEN TWINE

½ WHOLE CHICKEN

1 LB. PORK RIBS

1 LB. STEW BEEF

3 ITALIAN SAUSAGES

SALT, TO TASTE

FOR THE VEGETABLES

SALT, TO TASTE

1 LB. ESCAROLE OR LETTUCE, TRIMMED AND RINSED WELL

1 LB. CABBAGE, CHOPPED

1 LB. CHARD OR CHICORY, TRIMMED AND RINSED WELL

1 LB. COLLARD GREENS, TRIMMED AND RINSED WELL

½ CUP LARD, WHIPPED (OPTIONAL)

EXTRA-VIRGIN OLIVE OIL, FOR TOPPING

PARMESAN CHEESE, GRATED, FOR GARNISH

CRUSTY BREAD, FOR SERVING

1. To begin preparations for the broth, place all of the ingredients, except for the salt, in a stockpot and cover with cold water. Bring to a boil, reduce the heat to low, and gently simmer the broth until the flavor has developed to your liking, 3 to 4 hours, frequently skimming off any foam that rises to the surface.
2. Season the broth with salt, strain it, and reserve the solids. Chill the broth in the refrigerator until the layer of fat has solidified. Remove the layer of fat, discard it, and strain the broth through a fine-mesh sieve. Place the broth in a large saucepan and set it aside.
3. Remove the meat from the chicken and ribs and dice it. Dice the stew beef and sausages and then set all of the meat aside.
4. To begin preparations for the vegetables, bring water to a boil in a large saucepan and prepare an ice bath. Add salt to the boiling water and then add the vegetables one at a time. Boil the vegetables for 2 minutes, remove them from the boiling water, and plunge them into the ice bath.
5. Chop the blanched vegetables and add them to the broth along with the meat. Add the lard (if desired) and simmer until the flavor has developed to your liking, 30 to 40 minutes.
6. Season the dish with salt and drizzle some olive oil over the top. Garnish with Parmesan, serve with crusty bread, and enjoy.

Lentil & Chestnut Soup

YIELD: 4 SERVINGS / **ACTIVE TIME:** 1 HOUR / **TOTAL TIME:** 3 HOURS

2 CUPS FRESH CHESTNUTS

SALT, TO TASTE

1⅓ CUPS DARK ITALIAN LENTILS, PICKED OVER

2 GARLIC CLOVES

12 SPRIGS OF FRESH PARSLEY

2 BAY LEAVES

1 TABLESPOON EXTRA-VIRGIN OLIVE OIL, PLUS MORE FOR GARNISH

4 SLICES OF CRUSTY BREAD, TOASTED

PECORINO CHEESE, GRATED, FOR GARNISH

1. Place the chestnuts in a bowl, cover them with cold water, and let them soak for 2 to 3 minutes.
2. Bring water to a boil in a large saucepan. Make a long, shallow incision on the back of each chestnut and add them to the boiling water along with salt. Cook the chestnuts for 4 minutes and then drain them.
3. Warm a large skillet over medium-high heat. Add the chestnuts and cook until they start to pop open. Remove the chestnuts from the pan and peel them.
4. Bring water to a boil in a large saucepan. Add the chestnuts and cook until they are tender, 35 to 40 minutes. Drain the chestnuts and set them aside.
5. Place the lentils, garlic, parsley, and bay leaves in a saucepan, cover the lentils with cold water, and bring to a boil. Cook for 15 minutes, season the lentils with salt, and continue cooking them until they are tender, another 15 minutes or so.
6. Remove the garlic, parsley, and bay leaves and discard them. Add the chestnuts and olive oil and cook until the chestnuts are warmed through.
7. Place a slice of bread in each of the serving bowls and ladle the soup over the top. Garnish with pecorino and additional olive oil and enjoy.

Virtù Teramane

YIELD: 4 SERVINGS / **ACTIVE TIME:** 1 HOUR AND 30 MINUTES / **TOTAL TIME:** 24 HOURS

SALT, TO TASTE

3 CUPS FRESH SPINACH

1 SMALL ZUCCHINI, CHOPPED

1 HEAD OF ENDIVE, CHOPPED

1 CARROT, PEELED AND CHOPPED

1 CELERY STALK, CHOPPED

¾ CUP DRIED CHICKPEAS, SOAKED OVERNIGHT AND DRAINED

¾ CUP LENTILS

1 (SCANT) CUP DRIED FAVA BEANS, SOAKED OVERNIGHT AND DRAINED

⅔ CUP DRIED SPLIT PEAS

2 OZ. LARD, CHOPPED

1 ONION, FINELY DICED

1 GARLIC CLOVE

5 OZ. PANCETTA, CUBED

1 TEASPOON CHOPPED FRESH PARSLEY

2 TOMATOES, CHOPPED

8 CUPS CHICKEN STOCK OR BEEF STOCK (SEE PAGE 446)

½ LB. SHORT-FORMAT PASTA (MIX DRIED SEMOLINA PASTA AND HOMEMADE EGG PASTA RECOMMENDED)

PECORINO CHEESE, GRATED, FOR GARNISH

1. Bring water to a boil in a large saucepan. Add salt and the spinach, zucchini, endive, carrot, and celery and cook for 5 minutes. Drain the vegetables and let them cool. When they are cool enough to handle, squeeze them to remove as much water as possible and set them aside.
2. Place the chickpeas, lentils, beans, and split peas in separate saucepans, cover them with water, and cook until they just start to soften—the cook times will differ for each legume. Drain the legumes and set them aside.
3. Place the lard in a large saucepan and warm it over medium heat. Add the onion, garlic, and pancetta and cook, stirring frequently, until the pancetta's fat starts to render.
4. Remove the garlic from the pan and discard it. Add the parsley and tomatoes and cook, stirring occasionally, until the tomatoes start to collapse, about 15 minutes.
5. Add the stock and cooked vegetables to the pan and cook for 10 minutes.
6. Add the pasta and legumes and cook until they are tender, about 30 minutes.
7. Ladle the soup into warmed bowls, garnish each portion with pecorino, and enjoy.

Scurdijata

YIELD: 4 SERVINGS / **ACTIVE TIME:** 20 MINUTES / **TOTAL TIME:** 30 MINUTES

6 TABLESPOONS EXTRA-VIRGIN OLIVE OIL

1 LB. STALE BREAD, CHOPPED

2 GARLIC CLOVES

½ HOT CHILE PEPPER, MINCED

1½ LBS. COOKED CHICKPEAS OR PEAS

2 LBS. COOKED LEAFY VEGETABLES (CHICORY, BEET GREENS, TURNIP GREENS, AND/OR BROCCOLI RABE RECOMMENDED)

SALT AND PEPPER, TO TASTE

1. Place the olive oil and bread in a large skillet and cook over medium heat, stirring occasionally, until it is golden brown. Remove the bread with a slotted spoon and place it on a paper towel–lined plate to drain.
2. Add the garlic and chile to the pan and cook, stirring frequently, for 2 minutes.
3. Remove the garlic and chile and discard them. Add the chickpeas and vegetables, season with salt and pepper, and cook, stirring vigorously and mashing the chickpeas slightly, for 10 minutes.
4. Stir in the fried bread and serve warm or cold.

Riso e Verza

YIELD: 4 SERVINGS / **ACTIVE TIME:** 30 MINUTES / **TOTAL TIME:** 1 HOUR

2 TABLESPOONS EXTRA-VIRGIN OLIVE OIL

1 SMALL ONION, FINELY DICED

½ CARROT, PEELED AND FINELY DICED

½ CELERY STALK, FINELY DICED

1 SMALL HEAD OF SAVOY CABBAGE, SLICED VERY THIN

1 CUP VIALONE NANO RICE, RINSED WELL

SALT, TO TASTE

HOT WATER, AS NEEDED

⅔ CUP GRATED PECORINO CHEESE

1. Place the olive oil in a large skillet and warm it over medium heat. Add the onion, carrot, and celery and cook, stirring occasionally, until the onion has softened, about 5 minutes.
2. Add the cabbage, reduce the heat to medium-low, and cover the pan. Cook the cabbage until it is tender, 10 to 15 minutes.
3. Add the rice, season the dish with salt, and add a few ladles of hot water. Cook, stirring frequently and adding hot water as necessary, until the rice is al dente, 15 to 20 minutes.
4. Remove the pan from heat and let it rest for a few minutes.
5. Stir in the pecorino and serve.

Licurdia

YIELD: 6 SERVINGS / **ACTIVE TIME:** 30 MINUTES / **TOTAL TIME:** 3 HOURS

¼ CUP EXTRA-VIRGIN OLIVE OIL

2 LBS. RED ONIONS, SLICED THIN

SALT, TO TASTE

1 LB. POTATOES, PEELED AND GRATED

4 CUPS WATER

6 SLICES OF CRUSTY BREAD, TOASTED

6 OZ. CACIOCAVALLO CHEESE, CUBED

RED PEPPER FLAKES, TO TASTE

PECORINO CHEESE, GRATED, FOR GARNISH

1. Place the olive oil in a large skillet and warm it over low heat. Add the onions, season them with salt, and cover the pan. Cook, stirring occasionally, until the onions are very tender, about 30 minutes, taking care not to let them brown.
2. Add the potatoes and water, partially cover the pan, and cook until the broth is very creamy, about 2 hours.
3. Place a slice of the bread in each serving bowl and top with the caciocavallo, soup, and red pepper flakes. Garnish each portion with pecorino and serve.

Polpette di Ricotta in Brodo

YIELD: 4 SERVINGS / **ACTIVE TIME:** 40 MINUTES / **TOTAL TIME:** 1 HOUR

1½ CUPS RICOTTA CHEESE (MADE FROM SHEEP'S MILK PREFERRED), DRAINED

¼ CUP GRATED PARMESAN CHEESE

⅔ CUP BREAD CRUMBS

2 HANDFULS OF FRESH PARSLEY, FINELY CHOPPED

1 EGG

SALT AND PEPPER, TO TASTE

6 CUPS VEGETABLE STOCK (SEE PAGE 447)

1. Place all of the ingredients, except for the stock, in a mixing bowl and stir until well combined. Place the mixture in the refrigerator and chill for 30 minutes.
2. Place the stock in a medium saucepan and bring it to a boil.
3. Form the mixture into 1 oz. balls and slip them into the broth. Cook the ricotta balls for 10 minutes.
4. Ladle the soup into warmed bowls and enjoy.

Egg & Asparagus Soup

YIELD: 4 SERVINGS / **ACTIVE TIME:** 30 MINUTES / **TOTAL TIME:** 45 MINUTES

8 CUPS WATER

1 LB. ASPARAGUS, TRIMMED

SALT, TO TASTE

2 EGGS

2 EGG WHITES

¼ CUP GRATED PECORINO OR PARMESAN CHEESE

¼ CUP EXTRA-VIRGIN OLIVE OIL

1. Place the water in a large saucepan and bring it to a boil. Separate the asparagus into stems and tips. Chop the stems and set the tips aside.
2. Add salt and the asparagus stems to the water and boil for 5 minutes. Add the tips to the boiling water and boil until they are just tender.
3. Place the eggs, egg whites, pecorino, and olive oil in a bowl and whisk to combine.
4. Stir the mixture into the broth and serve immediately.

Zuppa Gallurese

YIELD: 4 SERVINGS / **ACTIVE TIME:** 20 MINUTES / **TOTAL TIME:** 1 HOUR

6 CUPS BEEF STOCK (SEE PAGE 446)

7 OZ. PECORINO CHEESE, GRATED

3 TABLESPOONS CHOPPED FRESH PARSLEY

1 TEASPOON CHOPPED MIXED HERBS

¼ TEASPOON CINNAMON

¼ TEASPOON FRESHLY GRATED NUTMEG

2 LBS. DAY-OLD BREAD, SLICED THIN

1 LB. CACIOCAVALLO CHEESE, SLICED THIN

1. Place the stock in a saucepan and warm it over medium heat. Place the pecorino, parsley, herbs, cinnamon, and nutmeg in a bowl and stir to combine.
2. Preheat the oven to 350°F. Layer some of the bread on the bottom of a 13 x 9–inch baking pan. Top with some of the caciocavallo and the pecorino mixture and prick the cheese with a fork. Continue the layering process until all of these ingredients have been used up.
3. Pour the stock over the dish, place it in the oven, and bake until the gallurese is golden brown, about 30 minutes.
4. Remove the gallurese from the oven and let it rest for 20 minutes before serving.

Pappa al Pomodoro

YIELD: 4 SERVINGS / **ACTIVE TIME:** 10 MINUTES / **TOTAL TIME:** 1 HOUR

¾ OZ. DAY-OLD CRUSTY BREAD, SLICED AND LIGHTLY TOASTED

2 GARLIC CLOVES, HALVED

¼ CUP EXTRA-VIRGIN OLIVE OIL

2 LBS. WHOLE PEELED TOMATOES, CRUSHED BY HAND

4 CUPS VEGETABLE STOCK (SEE PAGE 447)

1 TEASPOON SUGAR

SALT AND PEPPER, TO TASTE

2 HANDFULS OF FRESH BASIL, TORN, FOR GARNISH

1. Rub the slices of bread with the garlic. Place half of the olive oil in a large pot and arrange the slices of bread on the bottom.
2. Pour the tomatoes and stock over the bread. Add the sugar, season with salt and pepper, and gently stir. Cover the pot and cook the soup over low heat, stirring occasionally, until the bread becomes pulpy, about 50 minutes.
3. Taste the soup and adjust the seasoning as necessary. Ladle the soup into warmed bowls, drizzle the remaining olive oil over each portion, garnish with the fresh basil, and serve.

Imbrecciata Umbra

YIELD: 6 SERVINGS / **ACTIVE TIME:** 20 MINUTES / **TOTAL TIME:** 24 HOURS

1 CUP DRIED CHICKPEAS, SOAKED OVERNIGHT AND DRAINED

1 CUP DRIED CANNELLINI OR BORLOTTI BEANS, SOAKED OVERNIGHT AND DRAINED

1 CUP DRIED FAVA BEANS, SOAKED OVERNIGHT AND DRAINED

SALT AND PEPPER, TO TASTE

¾ CUP LENTILS

1 CUP BARLEY

¼ CUP LARD, FINELY DICED

3 TABLESPOONS EXTRA-VIRGIN OLIVE OIL, PLUS MORE FOR GARNISH

2 SMALL ONIONS, FINELY DICED

2 GARLIC CLOVES, MINCED

2 CELERY STALKS, FINELY DICED

2 CARROTS, PEELED AND FINELY DICED

12 CUPS WATER

1 CUP WHOLE PEELED TOMATOES, CRUSHED BY HAND

1 CUP CORN

1. Place the chickpeas and beans in a large pot, cover them with cold water, and bring to a boil. Reduce the heat and simmer the chickpeas and beans until they are tender, 1 to 1½ hours, seasoning them with salt halfway through. Drain the legumes and set them aside.
2. Place the lentils in a saucepan and cover them with water. Bring to a boil, reduce the heat so that the water simmers, and cook until the lentils are tender, 15 to 20 minutes. Drain the lentils and set them aside.
3. Place the barley in a bowl, cover it with boiling water, and cover the bowl with a kitchen towel. Let the barley sit until it has absorbed the water and become tender, 25 to 30 minutes. Set the barley aside.
4. Place the lard in a medium saucepan and warm it over medium heat. When most of the lard has melted, remove any parts that did not melt.
5. Add the olive oil and warm it. Add the onions, garlic, celery, and carrots and cook, stirring occasionally, until they are tender, about 10 minutes.
6. Add the water and tomatoes and cook until the water has reduced by half.
7. Either strain the broth to remove the vegetables or puree the broth with an immersion blender.
8. Add the chickpeas, beans, corn, lentils, and barley, season the soup with salt and pepper, and cook until everything is warmed through and the flavor has developed to your liking, 10 to 15 minutes.
9. Ladle the soup into warmed bowls, drizzle olive oil over each portion, and serve.

Acquacotta della Transumanza

YIELD: 4 SERVINGS / **ACTIVE TIME:** 20 MINUTES / **TOTAL TIME:** 1 HOUR AND 20 MINUTES

3 TABLESPOONS EXTRA-VIRGIN OLIVE OIL

8 WHITE ONIONS, FINELY DICED

4 CELERY STALKS, PEELED AND CHOPPED

2 CARROTS, PEELED AND CHOPPED

4 POTATOES, PEELED AND CHOPPED

3 CUPS LEAFY GREEN VEGETABLES, CHOPPED

1 CUP WHITE WINE

SALT, TO TASTE

RED PEPPER FLAKES, TO TASTE

4 EGGS

4 SLICES OF DAY-OLD OR TOASTED BREAD, FOR SERVING

¼ CUP GRATED PECORINO CHEESE, FOR GARNISH

1. Place the olive oil in a large saucepan and warm it over medium heat. Add the onions and cook, stirring occasionally, until they have softened, about 5 minutes.
2. Add the celery, carrots, potatoes, and leafy greens, raise the heat to medium-high, and cook, stirring occasionally, for 5 minutes.
3. Deglaze the pan with the wine, scraping up any browned bits from the bottom. Cook for 5 minutes.
4. Add enough water to cover the vegetables, season with salt and red pepper flakes, and reduce the heat to medium-low. Cover the pan with a lid and simmer the vegetables until they are tender, about 50 minutes.
5. Stir in the eggs and cook until they are set.
6. To serve, divide the bread among serving bowls, ladle the acquacotta over each one, and garnish with the pecorino.

Stracciatella alla Romana

YIELD: 4 SERVINGS / **ACTIVE TIME:** 10 MINUTES / **TOTAL TIME:** 20 MINUTES

4 EGGS

¼ CUP GRATED PECORINO CHEESE

6 CUPS BEEF STOCK (SEE PAGE 446)

SALT AND PEPPER, TO TASTE

FRESHLY GRATED NUTMEG, TO TASTE

1. Place the eggs and pecorino in a bowl and whisk until well combined.
2. Place the stock in a medium saucepan and warm it over medium heat. When it is almost boiling, pour the egg-and-cheese mixture into the stock, whisking vigorously. You want to make sure that the egg sets in thin strands, avoiding the formation of lumps.
3. Season the soup with salt, pepper, and nutmeg and cook for 2 minutes.
4. Ladle the soup into warmed bowls and enjoy.

Brodetto all'Abruzzese

YIELD: 6 SERVINGS / **ACTIVE TIME:** 1 HOUR / **TOTAL TIME:** 3 HOURS

5 OZ. CLAMS

SALT, TO TASTE

5 OZ. MUSSELS, RINSED WELL AND DEBEARDED

2 TABLESPOONS EXTRA-VIRGIN OLIVE OIL

2 GARLIC CLOVES

1 CUP WHITE WINE VINEGAR

4 CUPS WHOLE PEELED TOMATOES, CRUSHED

1 CHILE PEPPER, STEMMED, SEEDED, AND MINCED

11 OZ. SQUID, CLEANED (SEE PAGE 140) AND SLICED INTO RINGS

1½ LBS. MONKFISH FILLETS, CUT INTO 2 TO 3 PIECES

1½ LBS. TURBOT FILLETS, CUT INTO 2 TO 3 PIECES

1 LB. COD FILLETS, CUT INTO 2 TO 3 PIECES

5 OZ. SOLE FILLETS, CUT INTO 2 TO 3 PIECES

4 LANGOUSTINES

4 MANTIS SHRIMP OR OTHER LARGE SHRIMP, LEGS AND ANTENNAE REMOVED, DEVEINED

1 BUNCH OF FRESH PARSLEY, CHOPPED

1 BUNCH OF FRESH BASIL, CHOPPED

CRUSTY BREAD, TOASTED, FOR SERVING

1. Place the clams in a large bowl, cover them with cold water, and stir in 4 handfuls of salt. Let them soak for 2 hours to remove the sand.
2. Drain the clams, place them in a pot, and add the mussels. Cover the pot and cook them over high heat until the majority of the clams and mussels have opened, about 5 minutes. Transfer them to a plate and set them aside. Strain the cooking liquid and set it aside. Discard any clams and mussels that did not open.
3. Place the olive oil in a large saucepan and warm it over medium heat. Add the garlic and cook, stirring occasionally, for 2 minutes. Add the vinegar and cook until it has evaporated. Add the tomatoes and chile, season the sauce with salt, and cook for about 20 minutes.
4. Add the squid and monkfish and cook for 10 minutes. Add the turbot and cod, top with the sole, langoustines, and shrimp, cover the pan, and reduce the heat to medium-low. Cook for 10 minutes, gently shaking the pan occasionally.
5. Turn off the heat, taste the broth, and adjust the seasoning as necessary.
6. Top the dish with the mussels, clams, reserved liquid, parsley, and basil, serve with toasted bread, and enjoy.

Tuscan Kale Soup

YIELD: 4 SERVINGS / **ACTIVE TIME:** 20 MINUTES / **TOTAL TIME:** 24 HOURS

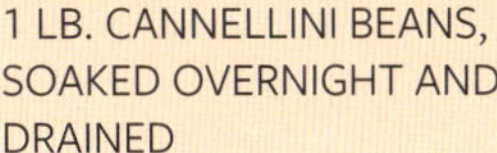

1 LB. CANNELLINI BEANS, SOAKED OVERNIGHT AND DRAINED

SALT, TO TASTE

¼ CUP EXTRA-VIRGIN OLIVE OIL

1 WHITE ONION, SLICED

1 CARROT, PEELED AND SLICED

1 CELERY STALK, SLICED

1 LB. TUSCAN KALE, TOUGH STEMS REMOVED, LEAVES HALVED

2 POTATOES, PEELED AND DICED

1 BAY LEAF

4 CUPS VEGETABLE STOCK (SEE PAGE 447)

1 CUP WHOLE PEELED TOMATOES, CRUSHED BY HAND

CRUSTY BREAD, SLICED AND TOASTED, FOR SERVING

1. Place the beans in a large pot, cover them with cold water, and bring to a boil. Reduce the heat and simmer the beans until they are tender, 45 minutes to 1 hour, seasoning them with salt halfway through. Drain the beans and set them aside.
2. Place the olive oil in a medium saucepan and warm it over medium heat. Add the onion, carrot, and celery and cook, stirring occasionally, until they have softened, about 6 minutes.
3. Stir in the kale, potatoes, and bay leaf and then add the stock and tomatoes. Season with salt, cover the pan, and cook until the potatoes and carrot are tender, 15 to 20 minutes.
4. Remove the bay leaf and discard it. Add the beans, season with salt, and simmer the soup for 10 minutes.
5. Ladle the soup into warmed bowls, serve with crusty bread, and enjoy.

Tuscan Leek Soup

YIELD: 4 SERVINGS / **ACTIVE TIME:** 20 MINUTES / **TOTAL TIME:** 1 HOUR

¼ CUP EXTRA-VIRGIN OLIVE OIL

2 LBS. LEEKS, WHITE PARTS ONLY, RINSED WELL AND SLICED

2 TABLESPOONS ALL-PURPOSE FLOUR

4 CUPS VEGETABLE STOCK (SEE PAGE 447)

SALT, TO TASTE

8 SLICES OF DAY-OLD CRUSTY BREAD

3 TABLESPOONS PINE NUTS, FOR GARNISH

3½ OZ. PARMESAN CHEESE, GRATED, FOR GARNISH

1. Place the olive oil in a medium saucepan and warm it over low heat. Add the leeks and cook, stirring occasionally, until they are tender, about 10 minutes. If the leeks start sticking to the pan, add a few tablespoons of water.
2. Add the flour and stir until it has been incorporated. Add the stock, season with salt, and cook until the leeks have almost dissolved.
3. Divide the bread among serving bowls and ladle the soup over it. Garnish each portion with the pine nuts and Parmesan and serve.

Seupa à la Vapelenentse

YIELD: 4 SERVINGS / **ACTIVE TIME:** 25 MINUTES / **TOTAL TIME:** 1 HOUR

6 CUPS BEEF STOCK (SEE PAGE 446)

4 LARGE SAVOY CABBAGE LEAVES, FINELY CHOPPED

11 TABLESPOONS UNSALTED BUTTER, PLUS MORE AS NEEDED

1 LB. DAY-OLD CRUSTY BREAD, SLICED

14 OZ. FONTINA CHEESE, GRATED

⅓ TEASPOON CINNAMON

1. Preheat the oven to 390°F. Place the stock in a medium saucepan and bring to a boil. Add the cabbage and cook until the cabbage is tender. Remove the pan from heat and set it aside.
2. Coat a baking dish with high edges with butter and cover the bottom with one-third of the bread, making sure not to leave any empty spaces.
3. Cover the bread with one-third of the fontina. Repeat until you have three layers of bread and cheese.
4. Pour the stock over the dish, pricking the layers of bread and cheese with a fork several times to make sure the stock is evenly distributed.
5. Place the butter in a saucepan and melt it over medium heat. Sprinkle the cinnamon over the butter and then drizzle the mixture over the dish.
6. Place the dish in the oven and bake until it is golden brown, about 40 minutes.
7. Remove the dish from the oven and let it rest for 10 minutes before serving.

Ribollita Toscana

YIELD: 6 SERVINGS / **ACTIVE TIME:** 30 MINUTES / **TOTAL TIME:** 24 HOURS

2 LBS. DRIED CANNELLINI BEANS, SOAKED OVERNIGHT AND DRAINED

SALT AND PEPPER, TO TASTE

¼ CUP EXTRA-VIRGIN OLIVE OIL, PLUS MORE FOR GARNISH

2 SMALL WHITE ONIONS, SLICED

3 CARROTS, PEELED AND SLICED

2 CELERY STALKS, SLICED

2 SPRIGS OF FRESH ROSEMARY

2 LBS. MIXED LEAFY GREEN VEGETABLES (TUSCAN KALE, SAVOY CABBAGE, AND COLLARD GREENS RECOMMENDED), TOUGH STEMS REMOVED, CHOPPED

4 MEDIUM POTATOES, PEELED AND DICED

6 CUPS VEGETABLE STOCK (SEE PAGE 447)

1 CUP WHOLE PEELED TOMATOES, CRUSHED BY HAND

8 THICK SLICES OF DAY-OLD CRUSTY BREAD

1. Place the beans in a large pot, cover them with cold water, and bring to a boil. Reduce the heat and simmer the beans until they are tender, 45 minutes to 1 hour, seasoning them with salt halfway through. Drain the beans and set them aside.
2. Place the olive oil in a medium saucepan and warm it over medium heat. Add the onions, carrots, celery, and rosemary and cook, stirring occasionally, until they have softened, about 6 minutes.
3. Add the leafy greens and potatoes and then add the stock and tomatoes. Season the soup with salt and pepper, cover the pan, and cook until the potatoes and carrots are tender, 15 to 20 minutes.
4. Place half of the beans in a bowl and mash them. Remove the rosemary and discard it. Add the beans, season the soup with salt and pepper, and cook for 10 minutes.
5. Arrange half of the bread in a Dutch oven and cover it with half of the soup. Top with the remaining bread and ladle the remaining soup over it.
6. Cover the pot and let the ribollita rest at room temperature for 1 hour.
7. Place the pot on the stove and cook the ribollita over medium heat until it is hot, about 10 minutes.
8. Ladle the ribollita into warmed bowls, drizzle olive oil over each portion, and serve.

Barzoffia Ciociara

YIELD: 6 SERVINGS / **ACTIVE TIME:** 30 MINUTES / **TOTAL TIME:** 1 HOUR AND 15 MINUTES

4 ARTICHOKES

JUICE OF 1 LEMON

¼ CUP EXTRA-VIRGIN OLIVE OIL

1 ONION, SLICED

2 CHARD LEAVES, CHOPPED

5 ROMAINE LETTUCE LEAVES, CHOPPED

2½ CUPS GREEN PEAS

2½ CUPS FAVA BEANS

6 CUPS BOILING WATER

SALT AND PEPPER, TO TASTE

4 EGGS

8 SLICES OF DAY-OLD CRUSTY BREAD

¼ CUP GRATED PECORINO CHEESE, FOR GARNISH

1. To trim the artichokes, cut the stems, leaving just 1 inch attached to the flower. Remove the outer leaves and trim the hearts, removing the pointy ends and the beards. Cut the artichokes into thin wedges, place them in a bowl, and cover them with cold water. Add the lemon juice and set the artichokes aside.
2. Place the olive oil in a large saucepan and warm it over medium heat. Add the onion and cook, stirring occasionally, until it is translucent, about 3 minutes.
3. Add the chard, lettuce, peas, and beans. Drain the artichokes and add them along with the water. Season with salt and pepper, cover the pan, and bring the soup to a simmer.
4. Reduce the heat to low and gently simmer the soup until the artichokes, beans, and chard are tender.
5. Gently slide the eggs into the soup and poach until the whites are set, 4 to 5 minutes.
6. Remove the eggs with a slotted spoon and set them aside.
7. Divide the bread among serving bowls and ladle the soup over it. Top each portion with a poached egg and some pecorino and serve.

Canederli in Brodo

YIELD: 4 SERVINGS / **ACTIVE TIME:** 40 MINUTES / **TOTAL TIME:** 1 HOUR

2 TABLESPOONS UNSALTED BUTTER

¼ ONION, FINELY DICED

5½ OZ. SPECK, FAT REMOVED, FINELY DICED

9 OZ. DAY-OLD BREAD, CRUSTS REMOVED, CUBED

1 CUP WHOLE MILK

2 TABLESPOONS FINELY CHOPPED FRESH PARSLEY

2 TABLESPOONS FINELY CHOPPED FRESH CHIVES

2 EGGS, LIGHTLY BEATEN

SALT AND PEPPER, TO TASTE

ALL-PURPOSE FLOUR, AS NEEDED

6 CUPS BEEF STOCK (SEE PAGE 446)

1. Place the butter in a saucepan and melt it over medium heat. Add the onion and cook, stirring occasionally, until it is translucent, about 3 minutes.
2. Add the speck and cook, stirring occasionally, until it starts to brown, about 5 minutes.
3. Place the bread and speck mixture in a mixing bowl and stir to combine. Add the milk, parsley, half of the chives, and the eggs, season lightly with salt and pepper, and work the mixture until it is well combined. Cover the bowl and chill it in the refrigerator for 30 minutes.
4. Remove the mixture from the refrigerator and check the consistency. If it feels too loose to shape into balls, incorporate a little bit of flour until it has the desired consistency.
5. Form the mixture into 2-inch balls, trying not to make them too compact.
6. Place the stock in a medium saucepan and bring it to a boil. Add the canederli, reduce the heat, and simmer until the canederli are cooked through, about 15 minutes. Sprinkle the remaining chives over the top and serve immediately.

Caciucco

YIELD: 4 SERVINGS / **ACTIVE TIME:** 40 MINUTES / **TOTAL TIME:** 2 HOURS

1 CUP EXTRA-VIRGIN OLIVE OIL

2 GARLIC CLOVES, HALVED

1 CHILE PEPPER, STEMMED, SEEDED, AND CHOPPED

HANDFUL OF FRESH SAGE

1 LB. OCTOPUS, CLEANED AND DICED

1 LB. SQUID AND CUTTLEFISH, CLEANED (SEE PAGE 140) AND SLICED

1 CUP RED WINE

1 LB. TOMATOES, PEELED, SEEDED, AND CHOPPED

1 ONION, CHOPPED

1 CELERY STALK, CHOPPED

1 TABLESPOON TOMATO PASTE

2 CUPS WATER

SALT, TO TASTE

11 OZ. PRAWNS, SHELLED AND DEVEINED

11 OZ. MORAY EEL, CONGER, OR SWORDFISH

9 OZ. SCORPION FISH, GURNARD, WEEVER, OR ANY INEXPENSIVE SMALL WHOLE FISH

BRUSCHETTA (SEE PAGE 237), FOR SERVING

1. Place half of the olive oil in a large saucepan and warm it over low heat. Add half of the garlic, the chile, and sage and cook, stirring frequently, for 3 minutes.
2. Add the octopus and cook for about 20 minutes.
3. Add the squid and cuttlefish and cook for another 5 minutes. Add the wine and tomatoes and cook over low heat for 10 minutes.
4. Place the remaining olive oil in another large saucepan and warm it over low heat. Add the onion, celery, and remaining garlic and cook, stirring occasionally, for 3 minutes.
5. Add the fish soup from the other pan, stir in the tomato paste and water, and season the soup with salt. Raise the heat to medium-high and bring the soup to a boil.
6. Reduce the heat and simmer for 20 minutes. Add the prawns, eel, and scorpion fish and simmer for another 10 minutes.
7. Strain the soup, return the broth to the saucepan, and cook until it thickens.
8. Remove the bones from the scorpion fish. Return all of the seafood and vegetables to the soup, cook until warmed through, and serve with Bruschetta.

Zuppa alla Pavese

YIELD: 4 SERVINGS / **ACTIVE TIME:** 10 MINUTES / **TOTAL TIME:** 20 MINUTES

4 CUPS BEEF STOCK (SEE PAGE 446)

¼ CUP UNSALTED BUTTER

8 SLICES OF DAY-OLD CRUSTY BREAD

⅔ CUP GRATED PARMESAN CHEESE

SALT AND PEPPER, TO TASTE

4 TO 6 EGGS

1. Place the stock in a medium saucepan and bring to a boil. Place the butter in a large skillet and melt it over low heat. Add the bread and cook until it is browned on both sides, 4 to 6 minutes.
2. Divide the bread among serving bowls and sprinkle half of the Parmesan over the top. Season with salt and pepper and crack an egg over the top, taking care not to break the yolk.
3. Ladle a cup of the warm stock into each bowl, making sure not to let it hit the egg yolk.
4. Sprinkle the remaining Parmesan over each portion and serve immediately.

Vegetable Minestrone

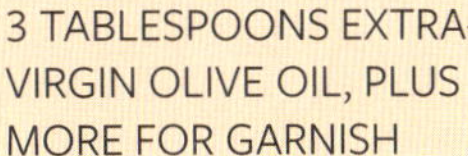

YIELD: 4 SERVINGS / **ACTIVE TIME:** 40 MINUTES / **TOTAL TIME:** 24 HOURS

3 TABLESPOONS EXTRA-VIRGIN OLIVE OIL, PLUS MORE FOR GARNISH

½ ONION, FINELY DICED

½ CELERY STALK, FINELY DICED

1½ CARROTS, PEELED AND FINELY DICED

1 POTATO, PEELED AND DICED

7 OZ. GREEN BEANS, TRIMMED AND CHOPPED

6 OZ. DRIED BORLOTTI BEANS, SOAKED OVERNIGHT AND DRAINED

2 TO 3 PARMESAN RINDS

6 CUPS WATER, PLUS MORE AS NEEDED

SALT, TO TASTE

6 OZ. PEAS

½ LARGE ZUCCHINI, FINELY DICED

3½ OZ. CHARD LEAVES, CHOPPED

½ CUP WHOLE PEELED TOMATOES, CRUSHED BY HAND

PARMESAN CHEESE, GRATED, FOR GARNISH

1. Place the olive oil in a large pot and warm it over medium heat. Add the onion, celery, and carrots and cook, stirring occasionally, until they have softened, about 5 minutes.
2. Add the potato, green beans, borlotti beans, Parmesan rinds, and water, season with salt, and cook for 1 hour.
3. Add the peas, zucchini, chard, and tomatoes and cook until the borlotti beans are tender, about 1 hour. If the dish starts to look too dry, add more water as necessary.
4. Season with salt, remove the Parmesan rinds, and discard them. Garnish the soup with Parmesan and additional olive oil and serve.

Jota Triestina

YIELD: 4 SERVINGS / **ACTIVE TIME:** 40 MINUTES / **TOTAL TIME:** 24 HOURS

2 CUPS BLACK-EYED PEAS, SOAKED OVERNIGHT AND DRAINED

6 CUPS VEGETABLE STOCK (SEE PAGE 447)

2 BAY LEAVES

¼ CUP LARD

4 GARLIC CLOVES, LIGHTLY CRUSHED

1½ LBS. SAUERKRAUT

SALT AND PEPPER, TO TASTE

2 SMOKED CRAGNO SAUSAGES, CHOPPED

4 POTATOES, CUBED

3 TABLESPOONS EXTRA-VIRGIN OLIVE OIL

2 TABLESPOONS ALL-PURPOSE FLOUR

1. Place the peas, stock, and bay leaves in a large pot and bring to a boil. Reduce the heat and simmer until the peas are tender, about 1 hour.
2. Place the lard in a large saucepan and melt it over medium heat. Add the garlic and cook, stirring occasionally, until it is browned, 2 to 3 minutes.
3. Remove the garlic and discard it. Add the sauerkraut and cover it with warm water. Season with salt and pepper, reduce the heat to low, and cook for 30 minutes. Remove the pan from heat and set it aside.
4. Add the sausages to the peas and cook until the sausages are cooked through, about 15 minutes.
5. Add the potatoes to the peas and cook until they are tender, about 20 minutes.
6. Remove half of the peas and potatoes from the pot and mash them. Return them to the pot, add the sauerkraut, and stir to combine.
7. Place the olive oil in a skillet and warm it over medium heat. Add the flour, whisking continually, and cook until it turns golden brown.
8. Stir the flour mixture into the soup, season it with salt and pepper, and serve.

APPETIZERS & SIDES

Scagliuòzzi

YIELD: 4 SERVINGS / **ACTIVE TIME:** 40 MINUTES / **TOTAL TIME:** 2 HOURS

9 OZ. INSTANT POLENTA

4 CUPS WATER

1 TEASPOON KOSHER SALT, PLUS MORE FOR TOPPING

EXTRA-VIRGIN OLIVE OIL, AS NEEDED

1. Line a loaf pan with parchment paper. Place the polenta, water, and salt in a saucepan and cook over medium heat, stirring frequently, until the polenta is thick and creamy, 10 to 15 minutes.
2. Transfer the polenta to the loaf pan and let it cool completely.
3. Turn the polenta out onto a cutting board and cut it into ½-inch-thick slices. Cut each slice in half diagonally, forming 2 triangles.
4. Add olive oil to a narrow, deep, heavy-bottomed saucepan until it is about 2 inches deep and warm it to 350°F. Gently slip the polenta triangles into the hot oil and fry until they are a light golden brown, turning as necessary.
5. Remove the fried polenta from the hot oil, transfer them to a paper towel–lined plate to drain, and season them with salt. Serve once the fried polenta have drained and cooled slightly.

Rustico Napoletano

YIELD: 15 TO 20 RUSTICI / **ACTIVE TIME:** 30 MINUTES / **TOTAL TIME:** 1 HOUR AND 15 MINUTES

2 CUPS RICOTTA CHEESE

5 EGGS

SALT AND PEPPER, TO TASTE

10½ OZ. BUFFALO MOZZARELLA CHEESE, CUBED AND DRAINED IN THE REFRIGERATOR FOR 2 HOURS

10½ OZ. SMOKED PROVOLA CHEESE, CUBED

6 OZ. ITALIAN SALAMI, CHOPPED

1 CUP PLUS 1 TABLESPOON GRATED PARMESAN CHEESE

PASTA FROLLA AL LARDO (SEE PAGE 457), AT ROOM TEMPERATURE

1 EGG YOLK, BEATEN

1. Preheat the oven to 350°F and coat two muffin tins with nonstick cooking spray. Place the ricotta in a mixing bowl, add the eggs, and season the mixture with salt and pepper. Whisk to combine, add the mozzarella, provola, salami, and Parmesan, and stir until well combined.
2. Beat the frolla with a rolling pin to soften it and roll it out until it is about ¼ inch thick. Using a pastry cutter or mason jar, cut the dough into rounds that are large enough to cover the wells of the muffin tins.
3. Place the rounds in the muffin tins and fill them with a generous spoonful of the cheese mixture.
4. Roll the remaining dough into a slightly thinner sheet and cut it into rounds that are large enough to use as lids for the rustici. Place them over the filling, fold the bottom layers over them, and gently press down on the seams to seal the rustici.
5. Brush the rustici with the egg yolk and place them in the oven. Cook until the rustici are golden brown, which will depend on the depth of the wells in the muffin tins. For deeper molds, bake for approximately 40 minutes. For shallower molds, bake for approximately 25 minutes. Also, do not worry if the lids of the rustici come off, as they will be reattached as the rustici cool.
6. Remove the rustici from the oven and let them cool for 5 minutes. Place a large heatproof tray over each of the muffin tins and invert the muffin tins, making sure the rustici do not come out of the tins quite yet. Let the rustici cool until they are slightly warm before removing them from the tins and enjoying.

Rustico Napoletano

SEE PAGE 217

Mozzarella in Carrozza

YIELD: 6 SERVINGS / **ACTIVE TIME:** 20 MINUTES / **TOTAL TIME:** 2 HOURS AND 40 MINUTES

1 LB. FRESH MOZZARELLA CHEESE (BUFALA IS PREFERRED)

8 SLICES OF SANDWICH BREAD, CRUSTS REMOVED

3 EGGS

SALT AND PEPPER, TO TASTE

2 CUPS BREAD CRUMBS

EXTRA-VIRGIN OLIVE OIL, AS NEEDED

1. Cut the mozzarella into ½-inch-thick slices and place them in a colander. Set the colander in a bowl and let the mozzarella drain in the refrigerator for 2 hours.
2. Top four of the slices of bread with the mozzarella, making sure it is distributed evenly. Cover the cheese with the remaining slices of bread.
3. Place the eggs in a bowl, season them with salt and pepper, and beat them lightly. Place the bread crumbs in a separate bowl and then dredge the sandwiches in the eggs and then in the bread crumbs until they are coated. Set the breaded sandwiches aside.
4. Add olive oil to a narrow, deep, heavy-bottomed saucepan with high edges until it is about 2 inches deep and warm it to 350°F. Working with one sandwich at a time, slip it into the hot oil and fry until golden brown, turning as necessary.
5. Remove the sandwich from the hot oil, transfer it to a paper towel–lined plate to drain, and season it with salt. Serve once all of the sandwiches have drained and cooled slightly.

Panelle

YIELD: 8 SERVINGS / **ACTIVE TIME:** 40 MINUTES / **TOTAL TIME:** 1 HOUR AND 30 MINUTES

5½ (SCANT) CUPS CHICKPEA FLOUR

6 CUPS WATER

1½ TEASPOONS KOSHER SALT

BLACK PEPPER, TO TASTE

2 TABLESPOONS CHOPPED FRESH PARSLEY

EXTRA-VIRGIN OLIVE OIL, AS NEEDED

1. Place the chickpea flour in a saucepan and gradually add the water, whisking to prevent lumps from forming. Stir in the salt, season the mixture with pepper, and cook over low heat, stirring continually, until the mixture starts to pull away from the side of the pan, 30 to 40 minutes.
2. Stir in the parsley and remove the pan from heat.
3. Coat a baking dish with olive oil, spoon the mixture into it, and level the surface with a rubber spatula. You want the mixture to be about ½ inch thick. Let the mixture cool completely.
4. Cut the mixture into squares. Add olive oil to a narrow, deep, heavy-bottomed saucepan with high edges until it is about 2 inches deep and warm it to 350°F. Gently slip the squares into the hot oil and fry until they are crispy and brown, turning as necessary.
5. Remove the panelle from the hot oil and transfer them to a paper towel–lined plate to drain. Serve once the panelle have drained and cooled slightly.

Crocchè

YIELD: 20 CROCCHÈ / **ACTIVE TIME:** 40 MINUTES / **TOTAL TIME:** 24 HOURS

SALT AND PEPPER, TO TASTE

2 LBS. POTATOES, PEELED AND CHOPPED

4 EGGS, SEPARATED

½ CUP GRATED PARMESAN CHEESE

2 HANDFULS OF FRESH PARSLEY, FINELY CHOPPED

1⅓ CUPS MOZZARELLA CHEESE, CUT INTO STRIPS AND DRAINED IN THE REFRIGERATOR FOR 1 HOUR

2 CUPS BREAD CRUMBS

EXTRA-VIRGIN OLIVE OIL, AS NEEDED

1. Bring salted water to a boil in a large saucepan. Add the potatoes and boil until they are tender, 15 to 20 minutes. Drain the potatoes and place them in a bowl.
2. Mash the potatoes until they are smooth. Add the egg yolks, Parmesan, and parsley to the potatoes, season the mixture with salt and pepper, and knead the mixture until it feels smooth and well combined.
3. Line two baking sheets with parchment paper. To shape the crocchè, take a dollop of the potato mixture, place it in the palm of your hand, and flatten it. Place a piece of mozzarella in the center, form the mixture over the cheese, and then shape it into a 2-inch-long cylinder. Repeat until all of the potato mixture has been used.
4. Place the egg whites in a bowl, add a pinch of salt, and beat the egg whites slightly. Place the bread crumbs in a separate bowl and then dredge the crocchè in the egg whites and then in the bread crumbs until they are coated. Place the crocchè on the baking sheets, cover them with kitchen towels, and let them chill in the refrigerator overnight.
5. Remove the crocchè from the refrigerator and let them warm up at room temperature for 20 minutes.
6. Add olive oil to a narrow, deep, heavy-bottomed saucepan with high edges until it is about 2 inches deep and warm it to 350°F. Working in batches of 2 or 3, slip the crocchè into the hot oil and fry until they are golden brown, turning as necessary.
7. Remove the crocchè from the hot oil and transfer them to a paper towel–lined plate to drain. Serve once all of the crocchè have drained and cooled slightly.

Cozze Fritte

YIELD: 4 SERVINGS / **ACTIVE TIME:** 20 MINUTES / **TOTAL TIME:** 40 MINUTES

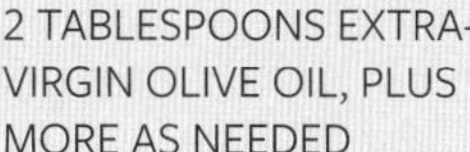

2 TABLESPOONS EXTRA-VIRGIN OLIVE OIL, PLUS MORE AS NEEDED

2 LBS. MUSSELS, RINSED WELL AND DEBEARDED

½ LB. DAY-OLD BREAD

2 EGGS

2 TABLESPOONS BREAD CRUMBS, PLUS MORE AS NEEDED

⅔ CUP GRATED PECORINO CHEESE

1 TABLESPOON CHOPPED FRESH PARSLEY

1 GARLIC CLOVE, MINCED

SALT AND PEPPER, TO TASTE

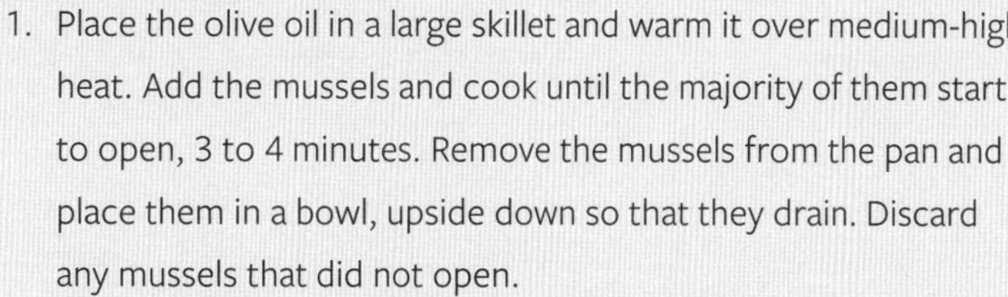

1. Place the olive oil in a large skillet and warm it over medium-high heat. Add the mussels and cook until the majority of them start to open, 3 to 4 minutes. Remove the mussels from the pan and place them in a bowl, upside down so that they drain. Discard any mussels that did not open.
2. Strain the liquid from the mussels into a clean bowl, add the bread, and let it soak until it softens.
3. Squeeze the bread dry and place it in a bowl. Add the eggs, bread crumbs, pecorino, parsley, and garlic, season the mixture with salt and pepper, and stir until the mixture is well combined. Add more bread crumbs if the consistency of the mixture is too soft.
4. Form the mixture into ovals that are roughly the size of the mussels.
5. Remove the piece of shell not containing the meat from each of the mussels. Top the mussels with the bread mixture.
6. Add olive oil to a narrow, deep, heavy-bottomed saucepan with high edges until it is about 2 inches deep and warm it to 350°F. Working in batches to avoid crowding the pot, gently slip the mussels into the hot oil and fry until they are cooked through and golden brown, turning as necessary.
7. Remove the mussels from the hot oil and transfer them to a paper towel–lined plate to drain. Serve once all of the mussels have drained and cooled slightly.

Calamari Fritti

YIELD: 4 SERVINGS / **ACTIVE TIME:** 30 MINUTES / **TOTAL TIME:** 50 MINUTES

2 LBS. SQUID, CLEANED (SEE PAGE 140)

3 CUPS ALL-PURPOSE FLOUR

EXTRA-VIRGIN OLIVE OIL, AS NEEDED

SALT, TO TASTE

LEMON WEDGES, FOR SERVING

1. Cut the squid into 1-inch-wide rings. Place the flour in a shallow bowl, add the squid, and toss them until completely coated. Place the squid in a fine-mesh sieve and gently shake to remove any excess flour.
2. Add olive oil to a narrow, deep, heavy-bottomed saucepan with high edges until it is about 2 inches deep and warm it to 350°F. Working in batches to avoid crowding the pot, slip the squid into the hot oil and fry until they are cooked through and golden brown, turning as necessary.
3. Remove the calamari from the hot oil, transfer them to a paper towel–lined plate to drain, and season them with salt. Serve with lemon wedges once all of the calamari have drained and cooled slightly.

Cipollina Catanese

YIELD: 8 CIPOLLINE / **ACTIVE TIME:** 30 MINUTES / **TOTAL TIME:** 1 HOUR

¼ CUP EXTRA-VIRGIN OLIVE OIL

2 LARGE WHITE OR RED ONIONS, SLICED VERY THIN

1 CUP CRUSHED TOMATOES

SALT AND PEPPER, TO TASTE

2 SHEETS OF FROZEN PUFF PASTRY, THAWED

8 THIN SLICES OF HAM

3 OZ. PROVOLA CHEESE OR MOZZARELLA CHEESE, CUT INTO STRIPS AND DRAINED IN THE REFRIGERATOR FOR 2 HOURS

1 EGG, BEATEN

1. Preheat the oven to 370°F and line a baking sheet with parchment paper. Place the olive oil in a large skillet and warm it over low heat. Add the onions and cook, stirring occasionally, until they have softened and slightly caramelized, 10 to 15 minutes.
2. Stir in the tomatoes, season the mixture with salt and pepper, and remove the pan from heat.
3. Cut each sheet of puff pastry into four squares.
4. Place a slice of ham on each square and top it with the tomato sauce and cheese. Bring the four corners of the squares to the center and press down on the seams to seal them. Brush the cipolline with the egg and place them on the baking sheet.
5. Place the cipolline in the oven and bake until they are golden brown, about 15 minutes.
6. Remove the cipolline from the oven and let them cool slightly before serving.

Insalata di Arance e Finocchio

YIELD: 4 SERVINGS / **ACTIVE TIME:** 15 MINUTES / **TOTAL TIME:** 30 MINUTES

6 ORANGES

1 SMALL ONION, SLICED THIN

1 SMALL FENNEL BULB, TRIMMED AND SLICED THIN

½ CUP PITTED BLACK OLIVES

¼ CUP EXTRA-VIRGIN OLIVE OIL

SALT AND PEPPER, TO TASTE

1. Peel the oranges and, using a sharp knife, remove the white pith. Slice the oranges thin and set them aside.
2. Arrange the onion and fennel on a serving platter and top with the oranges and olives.
3. Drizzle the olive oil over the salad and season it with salt and pepper.
4. Let the salad marinate for about 15 minutes before serving.

Puntarelle alla Romana

YIELD: 4 SERVINGS / **ACTIVE TIME:** 20 MINUTES / **TOTAL TIME:** 20 MINUTES

½ GARLIC CLOVE, MINCED

4 ANCHOVIES PACKED IN SALT, RINSED AND DRAINED

¼ CUP EXTRA-VIRGIN OLIVE OIL

1 TABLESPOON WHITE WINE VINEGAR

1 HEAD OF PUNTARELLE

1. Using a mortar and pestle, work the garlic, anchovies, olive oil, and vinegar until combined. Set the mixture aside.
2. To trim the puntarelle, remove the outer leaves and cut them into long strips. There is a specific tool for cutting puntarelle, but you can achieve decent results with a sharp knife.
3. Place the puntarelle in a bowl, add some cold water, and toss until they curl up.
4. Drain the puntarelle, add the vinaigrette, and toss to combine. Serve immediately.

Panzanella alla Toscana

YIELD: 4 SERVINGS / **ACTIVE TIME:** 15 MINUTES / **TOTAL TIME:** 1 HOUR AND 15 MINUTES

3 TABLESPOONS WHITE WINE VINEGAR

2 CUPS WATER

1 LB. DAY-OLD CRUSTY BREAD, SLICED

SALT AND PEPPER, TO TASTE

EXTRA-VIRGIN OLIVE OIL, TO TASTE

2 RIPE ROMA TOMATOES, FINELY DICED

1 CUCUMBER, SLICED

1 LARGE RED OR WHITE ONION, FINELY DICED

2 HANDFULS OF FRESH BASIL LEAVES, TORN

1. Place the vinegar and water in a bowl and stir to combine. Dip the bread in the mixture until it has softened.
2. Squeeze the bread to remove any excess moisture and tear it into large pieces.
3. Place the bread in a bowl, season it with salt and olive oil, and add the tomatoes. Toss until the bread has turned red.
4. Add the cucumber, onion, and basil, season the salad with salt and pepper, and drizzle olive oil over the top.
5. Cover the bowl with plastic wrap and chill it in the refrigerator for at least 1 hour before serving.

Panzerotti

YIELD: 6 TO 8 PANZEROTTI / **ACTIVE TIME:** 1 HOUR / **TOTAL TIME:** 3 HOURS

FOR THE DOUGH

1½ PACKETS OF ACTIVE DRY YEAST

1 TEASPOON SUGAR

⅞ CUP LUKEWARM WATER (90°F)

7 TABLESPOONS WHOLE MILK

1¾ CUPS FINELY GROUND SEMOLINA FLOUR

2½ (SCANT) CUPS BREAD OR "00" FLOUR, PLUS MORE AS NEEDED

2 TABLESPOONS EXTRA-VIRGIN OLIVE OIL

2 TEASPOONS TABLE SALT

FOR THE FILLING

1 (HEAPING) CUP WHOLE PEELED TOMATOES, CRUSHED BY HAND

1 TABLESPOON EXTRA-VIRGIN OLIVE OIL

DRIED OREGANO, TO TASTE

SALT AND PEPPER, TO TASTE

4½ OZ. MOZZARELLA OR SCAMORZA CHEESE, CUBED

2 TABLESPOONS GRATED PECORINO CHEESE

EXTRA-VIRGIN OLIVE OIL, AS NEEDED

1. To begin preparations for the dough, place the yeast, sugar, and water in a large bowl, gently stir to combine, and let the mixture sit until it starts to foam, about 10 minutes.
2. Add the milk and flours and work the mixture until it just comes together as a dough. Add the olive oil and salt and knead the dough until it is smooth and elastic.
3. Shape the dough into a round, place it in a clean bowl, and cover it with plastic wrap. Let the dough rest at room temperature until it has almost doubled in size, about 1½ hours.
4. Place the dough on a flour-dusted work surface and divide it into six pieces. Shape the pieces into rounds, cover them with a kitchen towel, and let them rest for 45 minutes. Roll each round into a 16-inch disk and set them aside.
5. To begin preparations for the filling, place the tomatoes and olive oil in a bowl, season the mixture with oregano, salt, and pepper, and stir to combine.
6. Place 2 tablespoons of the tomato mixture, 2 tablespoons mozzarella, and 1 teaspoon pecorino in the center of each round and then fold the round over itself. Press down on the edges to seal the rounds, first with your fingers and then with a fork.
7. Add olive oil to a large skillet until it is about 1 inch deep and warm it to 350°F. Working with one panzerotto at a time, add them to the hot oil and fry until they are golden brown, turning as necessary, making sure to spoon hot oil over the tops of the panzerotti as they cook to prevent them from exploding.
8. Remove the panzerotti from the hot oil and transfer them to a paper towel–lined plate to drain. Serve once all of the panzerotti have drained and cooled slightly.

Peperonata alla Salentina

YIELD: 4 SERVINGS / **ACTIVE TIME:** 20 MINUTES / **TOTAL TIME:** 1 HOUR

6 TABLESPOONS EXTRA-VIRGIN OLIVE OIL

1 LARGE ONION, FINELY DICED

1 GARLIC CLOVE, MINCED

1 HOT CHILE PEPPER, STEM AND SEEDS REMOVED, MINCED

4 LARGE BELL PEPPERS, STEMMED, SEEDED, AND CHOPPED INTO LARGE PIECES

¼ CUP PITTED OLIVES

3 TOMATOES, SEEDED AND CHOPPED

DRIED OREGANO, TO TASTE

SALT, TO TASTE

1. Place the olive oil in a large skillet and warm it over medium-low heat. Add the onion and cook, stirring occasionally, until it has softened, about 6 minutes.
2. Add the garlic and chile and cook for 1 minute.
3. Add the bell peppers and olives, raise the heat to medium, and cook, stirring frequently, until the peppers start to brown, about 8 minutes.
4. Add the tomatoes, season the mixture with oregano and salt, and reduce the heat to low. Cover the pan and cook until the peppers are soft and nicely browned, stirring occasionally and adding water if the dish starts to look too dry, about 20 minutes. Serve immediately.

Insalata di Rinforzo

YIELD: 6 SERVINGS / **ACTIVE TIME:** 15 MINUTES / **TOTAL TIME:** 30 MINUTES

SALT, TO TASTE

1 HEAD OF CAULIFLOWER, CUT INTO FLORETS

8 ANCHOVIES IN OLIVE OIL, DRAINED

½ CUP CAPERS IN SALT, SOAKED, DRAINED, AND SQUEEZED DRY

¾ CUP GREEN OLIVES, PITTED

½ CUP MIXED PICKLES, DRAINED

3½ OZ. PAPACCELLE (STUFFED PEPPERS IN OIL), HALVED

5 TABLESPOONS EXTRA-VIRGIN OLIVE OIL

3 TABLESPOONS RED WINE VINEGAR

1. Bring salted water to a boil in a large saucepan. Add the cauliflower and cook until it is al dente, about 10 minutes. Drain the cauliflower and let it cool completely.
2. Arrange the cooled cauliflower in a serving dish and top with the anchovies, capers, olives, pickles, and papaccelle.
3. Place the olive oil, vinegar, and a pinch of salt in a bowl and whisk until the mixture has emulsified. Pour the dressing over the salad and enjoy.

Arancini

YIELD: 10 ARANCINI / **ACTIVE TIME:** 1 HOUR / **TOTAL TIME:** 1 HOUR AND 30 MINUTES

RAGÙ NAPOLETANO (SEE PAGE 91)

⅔ CUP PEAS

5⅓ CUPS WATER

1½ TEASPOONS SAFFRON THREADS

1 CHICKEN BOUILLON CUBE

1⅔ TEASPOONS KOSHER SALT, PLUS MORE TO TASTE

4 TABLESPOONS UNSALTED BUTTER

2½ CUPS RISOTTO RICE (CARNAROLI, VIALONE, ROMA, OR ORIGINARIO PREFERRED)

2 EGGS

2 CUPS ALL-PURPOSE FLOUR

2 CUPS BREAD CRUMBS

EXTRA-VIRGIN OLIVE OIL, AS NEEDED

1. Place the ragù and peas in a medium saucepan, cover the pan, and cook over low heat until the peas are tender. Remove the pan from heat and let the mixture cool.
2. Place the water, saffron, bouillon cube, salt, and butter in a medium saucepan and bring to a boil. Stir in the rice and wait for the water to start boiling again. Reduce the heat to low and cook, stirring frequently, until the rice has absorbed all of the water and is al dente, 15 to 20 minutes. Pour the rice immediately into a large baking dish and spread it into an even layer so that it will cool quickly.
3. Take a handful of rice, place it in the palm of your hand, and flatten it. The portion of rice should weigh about 4½ oz. Place about 1 oz. of the ragù mixture in the center of the rice and form the rice into a cone or ball around it. Repeat with the remaining rice and ragù mixture.
4. Place the eggs in a bowl, season them with salt, and beat them lightly. Place the flour and bread crumbs in separate bowls and then dredge the arancini in the flour, then in the eggs, and then in the bread crumbs until they are coated. Set the breaded arancini aside.
5. Add olive oil to a narrow, deep, heavy-bottomed saucepan with high edges until it is about 2 inches deep and warm it to 350°F. Working with two to three arancini at a time, slip them into the hot oil and fry until golden brown, turning as necessary.
6. Remove the arancini from the hot oil and transfer them to a paper towel–lined plate to drain. Serve once all of the arancini have drained and cooled slightly.

Cialledda

YIELD: 4 SERVINGS / **ACTIVE TIME:** 20 MINUTES / **TOTAL TIME:** 1 HOUR AND 20 MINUTES

1 SMALL RED ONION, SLICED THIN

2 TABLESPOONS WHITE BALSAMIC VINEGAR

SALT, TO TASTE

1 LB. DAY-OLD BREAD, CHOPPED

4 TOMATOES, CUT INTO WEDGES

1 CUCUMBER, FINELY DICED

1 CELERY STALK, SLICED THIN

HANDFUL OF FRESH BASIL, CHOPPED

2 TABLESPOONS CAPERS, DRAINED

¼ CUP EXTRA-VIRGIN OLIVE OIL

DRIED OREGANO, TO TASTE

1. Place the onion and vinegar in a bowl, season the mixture with salt, and let it sit for 1 hour.
2. Place the bread in a bowl, gently squeeze the tomatoes over it, and then add the tomatoes. Add the remaining ingredients, season the mixture with salt, and toss to combine.
3. Cover the bowl with plastic wrap and let the salad rest for 1 hour.
4. Drain the onion and rinse it. Add it to the salad, gently toss to incorporate, and enjoy.

Insalata di Patate e Fagiolini

YIELD: 4 SERVINGS / **ACTIVE TIME:** 15 MINUTES / **TOTAL TIME:** 40 MINUTES

SALT, TO TASTE

4 LARGE POTATOES, SCRUBBED

1½ LBS. GREEN BEANS

1½ CUPS CHERRY TOMATOES, HALVED

FRESH BASIL, CHOPPED, TO TASTE

FRESH OREGANO, CHOPPED, TO TASTE

¼ CUP EXTRA-VIRGIN OLIVE OIL

1. Bring salted water to a boil in a large saucepan. Add the potatoes and boil until they are tender, about 30 minutes. Remove the potatoes from the boiling water and let them cool.
2. Add the green beans and boil until they are tender, about 5 minutes. Drain the green beans and let them cool.
3. When the potatoes and green beans are cool enough to handle, peel the potatoes, chop them, and place them in a bowl. Chop the green beans and add them to the bowl.
4. Add the tomatoes, basil, oregano, and olive oil to the bowl, toss to combine, and either serve the salad immediately or store it in the refrigerator and serve chilled.

Patate al Forno alla Siciliana

YIELD: 4 SERVINGS / **ACTIVE TIME:** 25 MINUTES / **TOTAL TIME:** 1 HOUR AND 15 MINUTES

2 LBS. POTATOES, PEELED AND CHOPPED

¼ CUP EXTRA-VIRGIN OLIVE OIL

SALT AND PEPPER, TO TASTE

1 RED ONION, SLICED

1⅓ CUPS CHERRY TOMATOES, HALVED

½ CUP PITTED BLACK OLIVES

HANDFUL OF FRESH SAGE, CHOPPED

1 SPRIG OF FRESH ROSEMARY

3 BAY LEAVES

1. Preheat the oven to 390°F and line a baking dish with parchment paper. Rinse the potatoes and pat them dry. Place them in a large bowl with the olive oil, season them with salt and pepper, and toss to coat.
2. Add the remaining ingredients and toss to combine.
3. Place the mixture in the baking dish, place it in the oven, and roast until the potatoes are crispy, golden brown, and tender, about 50 minutes.
4. Remove the dish from the oven, remove the rosemary and bay leaves, and discard them. Stir the mixture so that the cooking juices are incorporated and serve immediately.

Rape 'Nfucate

YIELD: 6 SERVINGS / **ACTIVE TIME:** 20 MINUTES / **TOTAL TIME:** 1 HOUR AND 20 MINUTES

6 TABLESPOONS EXTRA-VIRGIN OLIVE OIL

2 GARLIC CLOVES, MINCED

1 CHILE PEPPER, STEMMED, SEEDED, AND MINCED

4½ LBS. TURNIP GREENS, RINSED WELL, FIBROUS STEMS REMOVED

½ CUP WATER

COARSE SEA SALT, TO TASTE

½ CUP DRY WHITE WINE

1. Place the olive oil in a large skillet and warm it over medium-low heat. Add the garlic and chile and cook for 2 minutes.
2. Add the turnip greens and water, season with salt, and cover the pan. Cook for 20 minutes.
3. Taste and adjust the seasoning as necessary. Add the wine, cover the pan again, and cook until the turnip greens are very tender, about 30 minutes. Serve immediately.

Zucchine alla Scapece

YIELD: 6 SERVINGS / **ACTIVE TIME:** 40 MINUTES / **TOTAL TIME:** 4 HOURS

2 LBS. ZUCCHINI, TRIMMED AND CUT INTO ¼-INCH-THICK SLICES

SALT, TO TASTE

4 CUPS EXTRA-VIRGIN OLIVE OIL

1 CUP WHITE WINE VINEGAR

HANDFUL OF FRESH MINT, CHOPPED

4 GARLIC CLOVES, MINCED

1. Season the zucchini with salt and let them sit until they look slightly shriveled. Or do as an Italian grandmother would, skip the salt, and let the zucchini dry in the sun for a couple of hours.
2. Place the olive oil in a deep skillet and warm it over medium-high heat. Working in small batches, gently slip the zucchini into the hot oil and fry until they are golden brown, turning as necessary. Transfer the fried zucchini to a paper towel–lined plate to drain and, if you chose to dry them in the sun, season them with salt.
3. Place the vinegar and mint in a bowl and stir to combine.
4. Arrange the zucchini in a layer in a serving dish and top with some of the garlic and some of the dressing. Repeat until all of the zucchini, garlic, and dressing have been used and let the dish rest for a few hours before serving.

Insalata Caprese

YIELD: 4 SERVINGS / **ACTIVE TIME:** 15 MINUTES / **TOTAL TIME:** 15 MINUTES

5 TOMATOES, CUT INTO ½-INCH-THICK SLICES

SALT AND PEPPER, TO TASTE

2 BALLS OF FRESH MOZZARELLA CHEESE, CUT INTO ½-INCH-THICK SLICES

HANDFUL OF FRESH BASIL LEAVES

2 TABLESPOONS EXTRA-VIRGIN OLIVE OIL

DRIED OREGANO, TO TASTE

1. Season the tomatoes with salt and let them rest.
2. Pat the mozzarella dry with paper towels. Arrange the mozzarella, tomatoes, and basil on a platter, alternating between them.
3. Drizzle the olive oil over the salad, season it with oregano and pepper, and enjoy.

Caponata

YIELD: 4 SERVINGS / **ACTIVE TIME:** 30 MINUTES / **TOTAL TIME:** 4 HOURS

2 LBS. EGGPLANTS, SLICED

SALT (COARSE AND FINE), TO TASTE

10 TABLESPOONS EXTRA-VIRGIN OLIVE OIL

2 RED BELL PEPPERS, STEMMED, SEEDED, AND DICED

3 CELERY STALKS, SLICED

2 SMALL RED ONIONS, SLICED THIN

3½ TABLESPOONS PINE NUTS

¾ CUP PITTED GREEN OLIVES

½ CUP CAPERS IN SALT, SOAKED IN WATER FOR 20 MINUTES AND DRAINED

6 CHERRY TOMATOES, HALVED

¼ CUP SUGAR

½ CUP WHITE WINE VINEGAR

HANDFUL OF FRESH BASIL, CHOPPED

1. Place the eggplants in a large colander and cover them with coarse salt. Place a saucepan filled with water on top of the eggplants and let them sit for 1 hour.
2. Rinse the eggplants and let them drain. Pat them dry and chop them into cubes.
3. Place half of the olive oil in a large skillet and warm it over medium-high heat. Add the eggplants and cook until they are golden brown, about 8 minutes, turning them as necessary. Transfer the eggplants to a paper towel–lined plate to drain.
4. Place the peppers in the skillet and cook, stirring occasionally, until they are starting to char, about 12 minutes. Transfer them to the paper towel–lined plate.
5. Place the remaining olive oil in a large saucepan and warm it over low heat. Add the celery and onions and cook, stirring occasionally, until they have softened, about 6 minutes.
6. Add the pine nuts, olives, and capers, raise the heat to medium, and cook, stirring occasionally, for 5 minutes.
7. Turn off the heat, stir in the tomatoes, eggplants, and peppers, and season the mixture with fine salt. Combine the sugar and vinegar and add the mixture to the pan. Set the heat to medium and cook until the vinegar mixture has evaporated, about 5 minutes.
8. Add the basil leaves, transfer the caponata to a serving dish, and let it cool.
9. Store the caponata in the refrigerator for a few hours before serving.

Fried Zucchini Blossoms

YIELD: 12 SERVINGS / **ACTIVE TIME:** 30 MINUTES / **TOTAL TIME:** 50 MINUTES

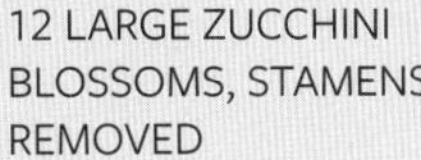

12 LARGE ZUCCHINI BLOSSOMS, STAMENS REMOVED

1 BALL OF FRESH MOZZARELLA CHEESE, CUT INTO STRIPS AND DRAINED

12 ANCHOVIES IN OLIVE OIL, DRAINED

1⅓ CUPS ALL-PURPOSE FLOUR

1 TEASPOON SUGAR

2 PINCHES OF KOSHER SALT

⅞ CUP SPARKLING WATER, ICE-COLD

EXTRA-VIRGIN OLIVE OIL, AS NEEDED

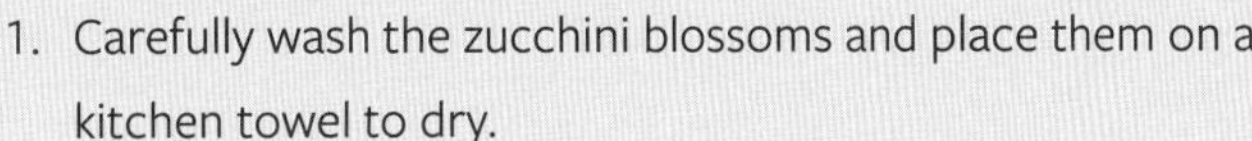

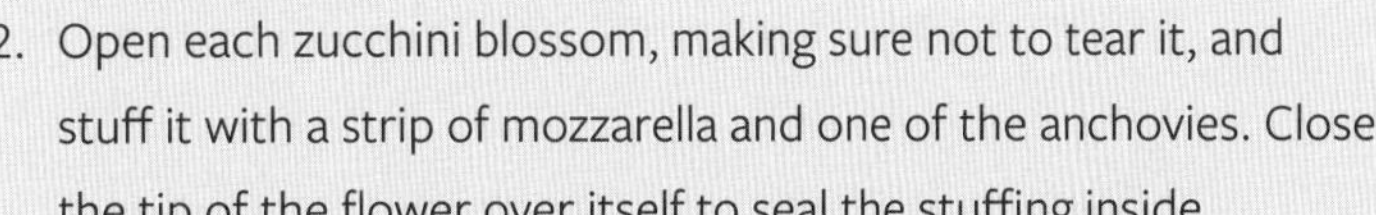

1. Carefully wash the zucchini blossoms and place them on a kitchen towel to dry.
2. Open each zucchini blossom, making sure not to tear it, and stuff it with a strip of mozzarella and one of the anchovies. Close the tip of the flower over itself to seal the stuffing inside.
3. Place the flour, sugar, and salt in a bowl. While whisking, gradually add the sparkling water until the mixture comes together as a smooth batter.
4. Add olive oil to a narrow, deep, and heavy-bottomed saucepan with high edges until it is about 2 inches deep and warm it to 350°F.
5. Dredge the zucchini blossoms, one at a time, in the batter until they are completely coated.
6. Working in batches to avoid crowding the pot, gently slip the stuffed zucchini blossoms into the hot oil and fry until they are golden brown, turning them over once.
7. Transfer the zucchini blossoms to a paper towel–lined plate to drain and cool before serving.

Olive All'ascolana

YIELD: 60 PIECES / **ACTIVE TIME:** 30 MINUTES / **TOTAL TIME:** 50 MINUTES

2 TABLESPOONS EXTRA-VIRGIN OLIVE OIL, PLUS MORE AS NEEDED

1 ONION, FINELY DICED

1 CARROT, PEELED AND FINELY DICED

3 GARLIC CLOVES

3½ OZ. BONELESS, SKINLESS CHICKEN BREAST, CHOPPED

3½ OZ. PORK, CHOPPED

3½ OZ. VEAL, CHOPPED

½ CUP DRY WHITE WINE

1 TEASPOON BLACK PEPPER

1 TEASPOON FRESHLY GRATED NUTMEG

SALT, TO TASTE

1½ CUPS PLUS 2 TABLESPOONS BREAD CRUMBS

2 TABLESPOONS GRATED PARMESAN CHEESE

2 LBS. LARGE GREEN OLIVES

ZEST OF 1 LEMON

2 EGGS, LIGHTLY BEATEN

1 CUP ALL-PURPOSE FLOUR

1. Place the olive oil in a large skillet and warm it over medium-low heat. Add the onion, carrot, and garlic and cook, stirring frequently, until the onion has softened, about 6 minutes.
2. Add the meat and cook, stirring occasionally, until it has browned on all sides, about 5 minutes.
3. Deglaze the pan with the wine, scraping up any browned bits from the bottom. Cook until the wine has evaporated. Stir in the pepper and nutmeg, season with salt, and cover the pan. Cook until the meat is cooked through, 10 to 15 minutes. Remove the pan from heat and let the mixture cool.
4. Remove the garlic and discard it. Strain the mixture, add it to a blender along with 2 tablespoons of bread crumbs and the Parmesan, and puree until the mixture is a smooth paste.
5. To pit the olives, cut the flesh away from the pit and into a spiral. This will make it easy to wrap the olives around the filling.
6. Place the pitted olives in a bowl of water and add the lemon zest. When all of the olives have been pitted, form the meat into olive-shaped nuggets and wrap the olives around them. It is OK to leave some of the filling exposed, as it will help the breading adhere.
7. Place the eggs, flour, and remaining bread crumbs in separate bowls. Dredge the stuffed olives in the flour, then in the eggs, and finally in the bread crumbs until they are completely coated.
8. Add olive oil to a narrow, deep, and heavy-bottomed saucepan with high edges until it is about 2 inches deep and warm it to 350°F. Working in batches to avoid crowding the pot, gently slip the stuffed olives into the hot oil and fry until they are golden brown, turning as necessary.
9. Transfer the fried olives to a paper towel–lined plate to drain and cool before serving.

Baccalà Fritto

YIELD: 6 SERVINGS / **ACTIVE TIME:** 30 MINUTES / **TOTAL TIME:** 24 HOURS

1 LB. DRIED COD

2¾ CUPS ALL-PURPOSE FLOUR

SALT, TO TASTE

1⅓ CUPS SPARKLING WATER, ICE COLD

EXTRA-VIRGIN OLIVE OIL, AS NEEDED

1. Carefully rinse the dried cod, handling it very delicately.
2. Place the cod in a large bowl, cover it with cold water, and chill it in the refrigerator for 24 hours, changing the water every 8 hours.
3. Drain the cod and set it aside.
4. Place the flour and 2 pinches of salt in a bowl. While whisking, gradually add the sparkling water until the mixture comes together as a smooth batter.
5. Hold each cod fillet by the tail, remove the skin, and cut it into large chunks.
6. Add olive oil to a narrow, deep, and heavy-bottomed saucepan with high edges until it is about 2 inches deep and warm it to 350°F.
7. Dredge the cod in the batter until it is completely coated.
8. Working in batches to avoid crowding the pot, gently slip the cod into the hot oil and fry until they are golden brown, turning them over once.
9. Transfer the fried cod to a paper towel–lined plate to drain and cool. Season them with salt and serve.

Bruschetta

YIELD: 4 SERVINGS / **ACTIVE TIME:** 10 MINUTES / **TOTAL TIME:** 15 MINUTES

8 SLICES OF CRUSTY BREAD

2 GARLIC CLOVES, HALVED

EXTRA-VIRGIN OLIVE OIL, FOR GARNISH

SALT, TO TASTE

1. Toast both sides of the bread on the grill, or in a grill pan on the stove.
2. Remove the toasted bread from the cooking surface and rub both sides with the garlic.
3. Place the bread on a serving plate, drizzle olive oil generously over it, and season with salt. Serve immediately.

Frittelle di Broccolo Romanesco

YIELD: 15 FRITTERS / **ACTIVE TIME:** 30 MINUTES / **TOTAL TIME:** 1 HOUR

2 LBS. ROMANESCO BROCCOLI

SALT, TO TASTE

2¾ CUPS ALL-PURPOSE FLOUR

1⅓ CUPS SPARKLING WATER, ICE-COLD

EXTRA-VIRGIN OLIVE OIL, AS NEEDED

1. Rinse the broccoli and cut it into florets. Cut the florets that are especially large in half.
2. Bring water to a boil in a large saucepan. Add salt and the broccoli and cook until it is just tender. Drain the broccoli and let it cool.
3. Place the flour and two pinches of salt in a bowl. While whisking, gradually add the sparkling water until the mixture comes together as a smooth batter.
4. Add olive oil to a narrow, deep, and heavy-bottomed saucepan with high edges until it is about 2 inches deep and warm it to 350°F.
5. Dredge the broccoli in the batter until it is completely coated.
6. Working in batches of 2 or 3 to avoid crowding the pot, gently slip the broccoli into the hot oil and fry until it is golden brown, turning it over once.
7. Transfer the fried broccoli to a paper towel–lined plate to drain and cool before serving.

Panzanella Romana

YIELD: 4 SERVINGS / **ACTIVE TIME:** 10 MINUTES / **TOTAL TIME:** 10 MINUTES

8 SLICES OF DAY-OLD CRUSTY BREAD

4 LARGE, EXTRA-RIPE TOMATOES

2 HANDFULS OF FRESH BASIL, FOR TOPPING

EXTRA-VIRGIN OLIVE OIL, FOR TOPPING

SALT, TO TASTE

1. Quickly dip the bread in a bowl of cold water and arrange it on a serving plate.
2. Coarsely chop the tomatoes, distribute them over the bread, and press down on them with a fork, making sure their juices moisten the bread.
3. Top the bread with the basil, drizzle olive oil over it, and season with salt. Serve immediately.

Supplì al Telefono

YIELD: 20 CROQUETTES / **ACTIVE TIME:** 30 MINUTES / **TOTAL TIME:** 1 HOUR

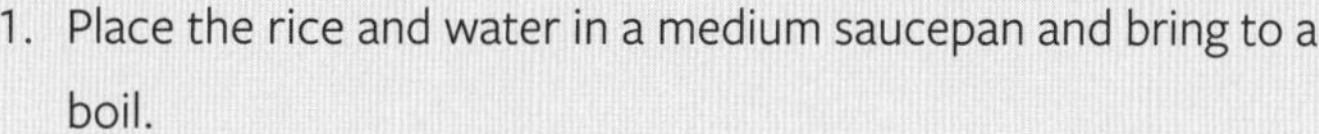

2 LBS. RISOTTO RICE, RINSED AND DRAINED

6 CUPS WATER

6 CUPS WHOLE PEELED TOMATOES, MASHED

3 HANDFULS OF FRESH BASIL, TORN

SALT, TO TASTE

7 OZ. PECORINO CHEESE, GRATED

4 BALLS OF FRESH MOZZARELLA CHEESE, CUT INTO STRIPS AND DRAINED IN THE REFRIGERATOR FOR 1 HOUR

6 EGGS, LIGHTLY BEATEN

1½ CUPS ALL-PURPOSE FLOUR

2 CUPS BREAD CRUMBS

EXTRA-VIRGIN OLIVE OIL, AS NEEDED

1. Place the rice and water in a medium saucepan and bring to a boil.
2. Add the tomatoes and basil, reduce the heat to low, and season with salt. Cook, stirring frequently, until the rice is al dente, 15 to 20 minutes. Pour the rice immediately onto a large rimmed baking sheet. Add the pecorino, gently stir to combine, and spread the rice mixture into an even layer so that it will cool quickly.
3. When the rice is cool enough to handle, take a handful, place it in the palm of your hand, and flatten it. The portion of rice should weigh about 3½ oz. Place a strip of mozzarella in the center and form the rice into a ball around it. Repeat with the remaining rice and mozzarella.
4. Place the eggs in a bowl, season them with salt, and beat them lightly. Place the flour and bread crumbs in separate bowls and then dredge the supplì in the flour, then in the eggs, and then in the bread crumbs until they are coated. Set the breaded supplì aside.
5. Add olive oil to a narrow, deep, and heavy-bottomed saucepan with high edges until it is about 2 inches deep and warm it to 350°F. Working with batches of 2 to 3 supplì at a time, slip them into the hot oil and fry until golden brown, turning as necessary.
6. Remove the supplì from the hot oil and transfer them to a paper towel–lined plate to drain and cool slightly before serving.

Pomodori Ripieni di Tonno

YIELD: 4 SERVINGS / **ACTIVE TIME:** 15 MINUTES / **TOTAL TIME:** 1 HOUR AND 15 MINUTES

8 MEDIUM TOMATOES

9 OZ. TUNA IN OLIVE OIL, DRAINED

3 TABLESPOONS MAYONNAISE, PLUS MORE FOR GARNISH

2 TEASPOONS CAPERS IN BRINE, DRAINED

2 ANCHOVIES IN OLIVE OIL, DRAINED

SALT AND PEPPER, TO TASTE

4 PIMENTO-STUFFED OLIVES, HALVED, FOR GARNISH

1. Core the tomatoes and turn them upside down in a colander to drain.
2. Place the tuna, mayonnaise, capers, and anchovies in a food processor and briefly blitz to combine. Season the mixture with salt and pepper, place it in an airtight container, and chill it in the refrigerator for 30 minutes.
3. Stuff the tomatoes with the tuna mixture and arrange them on a serving plate. Garnish the stuffed tomatoes with the olives and additional mayonnaise and enjoy.

Crostini al Pâté di Fegatini

YIELD: 6 SERVINGS / **ACTIVE TIME:** 30 MINUTES / **TOTAL TIME:** 1 HOUR AND 15 MINUTES

1 LB. CHICKEN LIVERS

¼ CUP EXTRA-VIRGIN OLIVE OIL, PLUS MORE AS NEEDED

2 ONIONS, SLICED THIN

1 SPRIG OF FRESH ROSEMARY

5 FRESH SAGE LEAVES

1¾ OZ. CAPERS IN BRINE, DRAINED AND RINSED

1 CUP DRY WHITE WINE

SALT AND PEPPER, TO TASTE

2 CUPS CHICKEN STOCK (SEE PAGE 446), PLUS MORE AS NEEDED

2 LEMON SLICES

½ TEASPOON ANCHOVY PASTE

CRUSTY BREAD, SLICED AND TOASTED, FOR SERVING

1. Rinse the livers under cold water and pat them dry with paper towels. Chop the livers, trimming away any green-hued parts.
2. Place the olive oil in a large skillet and warm it over medium heat. Add the onions and cook, stirring occasionally, until they are translucent, about 3 minutes.
3. Add the livers, rosemary, sage, and capers to the pan and cook, stirring occasionally, until the livers are browned all over, about 10 minutes.
4. Deglaze the pan with the wine, scraping up any browned bits from the bottom. Raise the heat to medium-high and cook until the wine has evaporated.
5. Season with salt and pepper and stir in the stock and lemon slices. Reduce the heat to low and cook for 50 minutes, stirring frequently and adding more stock as needed.
6. Remove the herbs and lemon slices and discard them. Add the anchovy paste, stir until incorporated, and remove the pan from heat. Let the mixture cool.
7. Place the mixture in a food processor. With the food processor running, stream in olive oil until the pâté has the desired texture.
8. Serve the pâté with toasted bread and enjoy.

Crostini Prosciutto e Mozzarella

YIELD: 4 SERVINGS / **ACTIVE TIME:** 10 MINUTES / **TOTAL TIME:** 1 HOUR AND 20 MINUTES

8 SLICES OF DAY-OLD CRUSTY BREAD

8 SLICES OF PROSCIUTTO

3 BALLS OF FRESH MOZZARELLA CHEESE, SLICED AND DRAINED IN THE REFRIGERATOR FOR 1 HOUR

EXTRA-VIRGIN OLIVE OIL, TO TASTE

1. Preheat the oven to 390°F and line a baking sheet with parchment paper. Arrange the bread on the baking sheet and cover each piece with a slice of prosciutto.
2. Top the prosciutto with the mozzarella, distributing it evenly among the slices.
3. Drizzle olive oil over the open-faced sandwiches and place them in the oven. Bake until the mozzarella has melted and the bread is golden brown, about 10 minutes.
4. Remove the open-faced sandwiches from the oven and enjoy.

Tuscan Kale in Padella

YIELD: 4 SERVINGS / **ACTIVE TIME:** 20 MINUTES / **TOTAL TIME:** 50 MINUTES

SALT, TO TASTE

1 LB. TUSCAN KALE, WOODY STEMS REMOVED

3 TABLESPOONS EXTRA-VIRGIN OLIVE OIL

1 GARLIC CLOVE, MINCED

½ HOT CHILE PEPPER, MINCED

2 BALLS OF FRESH MOZZARELLA CHEESE, SLICED AND DRAINED IN THE REFRIGERATOR FOR 1 HOUR

1. Bring water to a boil in a large saucepan and prepare an ice bath. Add salt and the kale to the boiling water and cook until the toughest parts of the kale have softened, about 15 minutes.
2. Drain the kale and plunge it into the ice bath. Drain it again, squeeze the kale to remove any excess water, chop it, and set it aside.
3. Place the olive oil in a large skillet and warm it over low heat. Add the garlic and chile and cook until the garlic is lightly browned, about 1 minute.
4. Add the kale, season with salt, and reduce the heat to low. Cook for 10 to 15 minutes, stirring occasionally.
5. Top the dish with the mozzarella and cook until the cheese has melted. Serve immediately.

Bruschetta al Pomodoro

YIELD: 4 SERVINGS / **ACTIVE TIME:** 10 MINUTES / **TOTAL TIME:** 15 MINUTES

4 LARGE, EXTRA-RIPE TOMATOES, SEEDED AND DICED

2 HANDFULS OF FRESH BASIL LEAVES, TORN

EXTRA-VIRGIN OLIVE OIL, TO TASTE

SALT AND PEPPER, TO TASTE

8 SLICES OF DAY-OLD CRUSTY BREAD

2 GARLIC CLOVES, HALVED

1. Place the tomatoes and basil in a bowl, season with olive oil, salt, and pepper, and toss to combine.
2. Toast both sides of the bread on the grill, or in a grill pan on the stove.
3. Remove the toasted bread from the cooking surface and rub both sides with the garlic.
4. Place the bread on a serving plate, top it with the tomato mixture, and drizzle olive oil over the dish. Serve immediately.

Carciofi alla Giudia

YIELD: 4 SERVINGS / **ACTIVE TIME:** 40 MINUTES / **TOTAL TIME:** 2 HOURS

4 LARGE ARTICHOKES

JUICE OF 1 LEMON

1 CUP EXTRA-VIRGIN OLIVE OIL

3 TABLESPOONS CHOPPED FRESH MINT

3 TABLESPOONS CHOPPED FRESH PARSLEY

2 GARLIC CLOVES, MINCED

⅓ CUP BREAD CRUMBS

SALT AND PEPPER, TO TASTE

1. To trim the artichokes, remove the outer layer of leaves, usually at least the first three layers. Cut the rest of the leaves short, in a way that only the pale green or yellow leaves remain.
2. Open the top of the artichokes and remove as much of the white pieces as possible.
3. Cut the stems, leaving only the edible hearts. Place the artichokes in a bowl of water and add the lemon juice.
4. Place one-third of the olive oil, the mint, parsley, garlic, and bread crumbs in a bowl, season with salt, and stir to combine.
5. Drain the artichokes and fill them with the herb mixture.
6. Place the remaining olive oil in a skillet and warm it over medium-high heat. Add the artichokes, upside down, season them with salt, and fry for about 10 minutes.
7. Carefully add water to the pan until the liquid covers half of the artichokes' heads. Cover the pan, reduce the heat, and cook until the artichokes are fork-tender, 1 to 1½ hours.
8. Season the artichokes with salt and pepper and serve immediately.

Piselli al Prosciutto

YIELD: 4 SERVINGS / **ACTIVE TIME:** 20 MINUTES / **TOTAL TIME:** 50 MINUTES

2 TABLESPOONS UNSALTED BUTTER

3½ OZ. PROSCIUTTO, CUT INTO STRIPS, FATTY PARTS REMOVED AND RESERVED

1 SMALL WHITE ONION, FINELY DICED

2 LBS. PEAS

1 CUP CHICKEN STOCK (SEE PAGE 446), PLUS MORE AS NEEDED

SALT AND PEPPER, TO TASTE

1. Place half of the butter and the fatty pieces of prosciutto in a skillet and warm the mixture over medium heat. Add the onion and cook, stirring occasionally, until it is translucent, about 3 minutes.
2. Add the peas and cook, stirring occasionally, until they start to brown.
3. Add the stock, season with salt and pepper, and cover the pan. Cook until the peas are tender, adding more stock if the mixture starts to look dry.
4. Add the remaining prosciutto and butter and stir to combine. Cook for 5 minutes and serve immediately.

Fricandò di Verdure

YIELD: 4 SERVINGS / **ACTIVE TIME:** 20 MINUTES / **TOTAL TIME:** 1 HOUR

¼ CUP EXTRA-VIRGIN OLIVE OIL

2 GARLIC CLOVES

3 ZUCCHINI, DICED

2 MEDIUM POTATOES, PEELED AND DICED

1 ROUND EGGPLANT, DICED

2 BELL PEPPERS, STEMMED, SEEDED, AND DICED

2 ONIONS, CHOPPED

SALT, TO TASTE

2 TOMATOES, PEELED AND CHOPPED

1. Place the olive oil in a large skillet and warm it over medium-low heat. Add the garlic and cook, stirring frequently, for 2 minutes.
2. Add the zucchini, potatoes, eggplant, peppers, and onions, season with salt, and stir to combine. Raise the heat to high and cook for 10 minutes.
3. Reduce the heat and cover the pan. Cook for about 20 minutes, tossing the vegetables occasionally and taking care not to break them.
4. Add the tomatoes and gently toss to incorporate them. Cover the pan and cook for another 15 minutes. Serve immediately.

Gattafin

YIELD: 15 GATTAFIN / **ACTIVE TIME:** 1 HOUR / **TOTAL TIME:** 1 HOUR AND 30 MINUTES

FOR THE DOUGH

4½ CUPS ALL-PURPOSE FLOUR, PLUS MORE AS NEEDED

1 CUP PLUS 1 TABLESPOON WATER

1¾ OZ. EXTRA-VIRGIN OLIVE OIL

FOR THE FILLING

2 TABLESPOONS EXTRA-VIRGIN OLIVE OIL, PLUS MORE AS NEEDED

1 ONION, FINELY DICED

½ LEEK, WHITE PART ONLY, RINSED WELL AND FINELY DICED

1 LARGE BUNCH OF PREBUGGIÙN (SEE PAGE 88)

2 TABLESPOONS WATER

2 EGGS, LIGHTLY BEATEN

2 HANDFULS OF FRESH MARJORAM, FINELY CHOPPED

1 (HEAPING) CUP GRATED GRANA PADANO CHEESE

1 (HEAPING) CUP GRATED PECORINO CHEESE

SALT, TO TASTE

1. To prepare the dough, place the flour in a large bowl and make a well in the center. Add the water and olive oil to the well and work the mixture until it comes together as a smooth and elastic dough. Form the dough into a ball, cover it with plastic wrap, and chill it in the refrigerator for 30 minutes.
2. To begin preparations for the filling, place the olive oil in a large skillet and warm it over medium heat. Add the onion and leek and cook, stirring occasionally, until they have softened, about 5 minutes.
3. Add the prebuggiùn and water, cover the pan, and cook until the mixture is tender, stirring occasionally.
4. Uncover the pan and cook until the liquids have evaporated. Remove the pan from heat and let the mixture cool.
5. Squeeze the mixture to remove any excess liquid. Place it in a bowl, add the remaining ingredients, and stir to combine. Set the filling aside.
6. Place the dough on a flour-dusted work surface and roll it out into a very thin sheet that is about ⅛ inch thick. Cut 5-inch rounds out of the dough, place a spoonful of the filling in the center, and fold the dough over the filling to create a half-moon. Crimp the edges of the gattafin with a fork.
7. Add olive oil to a skillet until it is about 1 inch deep and warm it to 325°F. Working in batches to avoid crowding the pot, add the gattafin and fry until they are crispy and golden brown, 4 to 6 minutes, turning them as necessary.
8. Transfer the fried gattafin to a paper towel–lined plate to drain before serving.

Gnocco Fritto

YIELD: 40 SERVINGS / **ACTIVE TIME:** 40 MINUTES / **TOTAL TIME:** 4 HOURS

1 CUP WATER

⅔ PACKET OF ACTIVE DRY YEAST

4½ CUPS BREAD FLOUR, PLUS MORE AS NEEDED

6 TABLESPOONS LARD

2 TEASPOONS TABLE SALT

EXTRA-VIRGIN OLIVE OIL, AS NEEDED

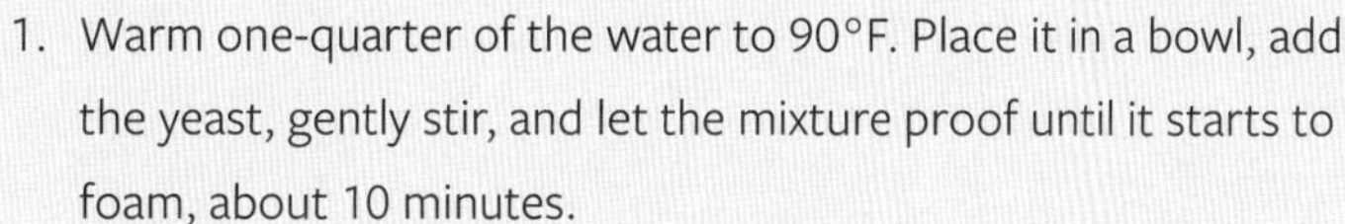

1. Warm one-quarter of the water to 90°F. Place it in a bowl, add the yeast, gently stir, and let the mixture proof until it starts to foam, about 10 minutes.
2. Add ½ cup of flour to the yeast mixture, stir to combine, cover it with plastic wrap, and let the mixture sit in a naturally warm spot for about 1 hour.
3. Place the mixture in the work bowl of a stand mixer fitted with the dough hook. Add the remaining water and flour and work the mixture until it just comes together as a dough.
4. With the mixer running, gradually add the lard and work the dough until it is smooth and elastic. Add the salt and work the dough until it is incorporated.
5. Form the dough into a ball, place it in a clean bowl, and cover it with plastic wrap. Let the dough rise in a naturally warm spot until it has doubled in size, about 2 hours.
6. Place the dough on a flour-dusted work surface. Roll it out into a ⅓-inch-thick rectangle and cut the dough into 2-inch-wide strips.
7. Cut the strips into 2-inch-long diamonds.
8. Add olive oil to a narrow, deep, heavy-bottomed saucepan with high sides until it is about 2 inches deep and warm it to 350°F. Working in batches to avoid crowding the pot, add the gnocco and fry until they are golden brown on both sides, turning them as necessary.
9. Transfer the fried gnocco to a paper towel–lined plate to drain before serving.

Chizze Reggiane

YIELD: 15 CHIZZE / **ACTIVE TIME:** 40 MINUTES / **TOTAL TIME:** 4 HOURS

1 CUP PLUS 1 TABLESPOON WATER, PLUS MORE AS NEEDED

⅔ PACKET OF ACTIVE DRY YEAST

4½ CUPS BREAD FLOUR, PLUS MORE AS NEEDED

6 TABLESPOONS LARD

2 TEASPOONS TABLE SALT

7 OZ. PARMESAN CHEESE, SHAVED

EXTRA-VIRGIN OLIVE OIL, AS NEEDED

1. Warm one-quarter of the water to 90°F. Place it in a bowl, add the yeast, gently stir, and let the mixture proof until it starts to foam, about 10 minutes.
2. Add ½ cup of flour to the yeast mixture, stir to combine, cover it with plastic wrap, and let the mixture sit in a naturally warm spot for about 1 hour.
3. Place the mixture in the work bowl of a stand mixer fitted with the dough hook. Add the remaining water and flour and work the mixture until it just comes together as a dough.
4. With the mixer running, gradually add the lard and work the dough until it is smooth and elastic. Add the salt and work the dough until it is incorporated.
5. Form the dough into a ball, place it in a clean bowl, and cover it with plastic wrap. Let the dough rise in a naturally warm spot until it has doubled in size, about 2 hours.
6. Place the dough on a flour-dusted work surface. Roll it out into a ⅕-inch-thick rectangle and cut the dough into 2-inch-wide strips.
7. Cut the strips into 4-inch-long rectangles. Place a few pieces of Parmesan on each rectangle, moisten the edges of the dough with water, and, working from a long side, fold the dough over itself, pressing down on the edges to seal.
8. Add olive oil to a narrow, deep, heavy-bottomed saucepan with high sides until it is about 2 inches deep and warm it to 350°F. Working in batches to avoid crowding the pot, add the chizze and fry until they are golden brown on both sides, turning them as necessary.
9. Transfer the fried chizze to a paper towel–lined plate to drain before serving.

Fonduta alla Valdostana

YIELD: 4 SERVINGS / **ACTIVE TIME:** 1 HOUR / **TOTAL TIME:** 4 HOURS AND 30 MINUTES

11 OZ. FONTINA CHEESE

⅔ CUP WHOLE MILK

¼ CUP UNSALTED BUTTER

4 EGGS

SALT AND WHITE PEPPER, TO TASTE

5 SLICES OF CRUSTY BREAD, CUBED AND TOASTED, FOR SERVING

1. Remove the rind from the fontina cheese and slice the cheese thin. Place the fontina and milk in a bowl, cover it with plastic wrap, and chill the mixture in the refrigerator for 4 hours.
2. Bring a few inches of water to a gentle simmer in a large saucepan. Place half of the butter in a heatproof bowl and place it over the simmering water. Stir occasionally until the butter has melted.
3. Drain the fontina and add it to the bowl.
4. When the cheese starts to melt, whisk the mixture, making sure all of the lumps dissolve and the temperature does not rise above 140°F.
5. Add the rest of the butter and whisk until it is incorporated. While whisking continually, incorporate the eggs one at a time. Season the fonduta with salt and white pepper.
6. Place the fonduta over a heat source to serve it, accompanied by the toasted bread.

Radicchio e Bruciatini

YIELD: 4 SERVINGS / **ACTIVE TIME:** 15 MINUTES / **TOTAL TIME:** 30 MINUTES

14 OZ. RADICCHIO DI CHIOGGIA

3½ OZ. PANCETTA OR BACON, DICED

2½ TABLESPOONS BALSAMIC VINEGAR

EXTRA-VIRGIN OLIVE OIL, TO TASTE

SALT, TO TASTE

1. Rinse the radicchio and pat it dry.
2. Place the pancetta in a large skillet and cook it over medium heat until the fat has rendered, stirring occasionally.
3. Add the vinegar and cook, stirring occasionally, until the pancetta has browned.
4. Arrange the radicchio leaves on a serving plate, top with the pancetta, and drizzle olive oil over the dish. Season it with salt and serve immediately.

Cavolfiore in Besciamella

YIELD: 4 SERVINGS / **ACTIVE TIME:** 15 MINUTES / **TOTAL TIME:** 40 MINUTES

SALT, TO TASTE

1 HEAD OF CAULIFLOWER, TRIMMED AND CUT INTO 4 PIECES

¼ CUP UNSALTED BUTTER, PLUS MORE AS NEEDED

2 (HEAPING) CUPS BESCIAMELLA (SEE PAGE 452)

2 OZ. PARMESAN CHEESE, GRATED

⅔ CUP BREAD CRUMBS

1. Preheat the oven to 350°F. Bring water to a boil in a large saucepan. Add salt and the cauliflower to the boiling water and cook until the cauliflower is just tender, about 10 minutes. Drain the cauliflower and set it aside.
2. Coat a baking dish with butter and cover the bottom with a layer of béchamel and a generous sprinkle of Parmesan.
3. Chop the cauliflower and place it in the baking dish in an even layer. Cover with the butter and remaining béchamel and Parmesan. Sprinkle the bread crumbs over the top.
4. Place the cavolfiore in the oven and bake until the top is golden brown, about 20 minutes.
5. Remove the cavolfiore from the oven and let it cool slightly before serving.

Cipolle Ripiene

YIELD: 4 SERVINGS / **ACTIVE TIME:** 30 MINUTES / **TOTAL TIME:** 1 HOUR

8 WHITE ONIONS

SALT, TO TASTE

2 OZ. DAY-OLD BREAD

¼ CUP WHOLE MILK

3½ OZ. GROUND PORK

3½ OZ. GROUND VEAL

3½ OZ. HAM, DICED

2 HANDFULS OF FRESH PARSLEY, FINELY CHOPPED

2 EGGS

¼ CUP UNSALTED BUTTER, DICED, PLUS MORE AS NEEDED

¼ CUP GRATED PARMESAN CHEESE

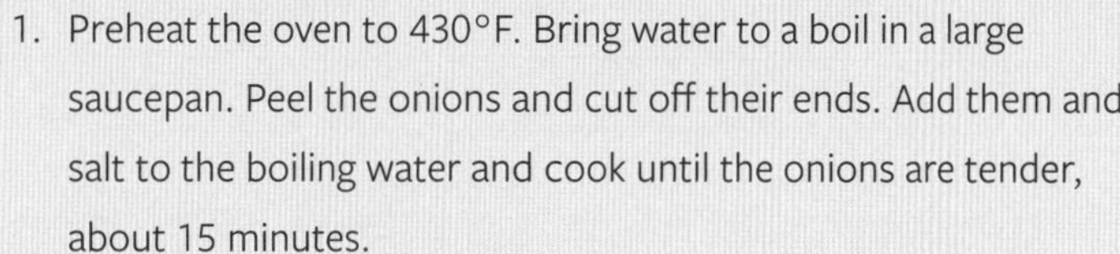

1. Preheat the oven to 430°F. Bring water to a boil in a large saucepan. Peel the onions and cut off their ends. Add them and salt to the boiling water and cook until the onions are tender, about 15 minutes.
2. Drain the onions and remove the inner petals, leaving the 3 outer layers. Finely chop the inner petals and set them aside.
3. Place the stale bread and milk in a bowl and soak for 10 minutes. Drain the bread, reserving the milk. Squeeze the bread to remove any excess moisture and set it aside.
4. Place the pork, veal, ham, parsley, bread, and chopped onions in a bowl and stir to combine.
5. Season the mixture with salt and add one of the eggs, stirring to incorporate.
6. Stuff the onions with the mixture. Coat a baking dish with butter and arrange the stuffed onions in it.
7. Place the remaining egg, the reserved milk, the Parmesan, and a couple of pinches of salt in a bowl and stir to combine. Pour the mixture over the stuffed onions and sprinkle the butter over them.
8. Place the stuffed onions in the oven and bake until the tops are golden brown and crispy, about 20 minutes.
9. Remove the stuffed onions from the oven and let them cool slightly before serving.

Bagna Càuda

YIELD: 4 SERVINGS / **ACTIVE TIME:** 1 HOUR / **TOTAL TIME:** 1 HOUR

2 CUPS EXTRA-VIRGIN OLIVE OIL

CLOVES FROM 4 HEADS OF GARLIC, SLICED THIN

7 OZ. ANCHOVIES PACKED IN SALT, SOAKED IN WARM WATER, DRAINED, AND CHOPPED

2 TABLESPOONS UNSALTED BUTTER

FRESH VEGETABLES, FOR SERVING

1. Place half of the olive oil in a saucepan and warm it over medium-low heat. Add the garlic and cook, stirring continually to ensure it does not brown.
2. Add the anchovies and cook, stirring to dissolve them.
3. Add the remaining olive oil, reduce the heat to low, and cook the bagna càuda for 30 minutes, making sure that it does not start to fry at any point.
4. Add the butter and stir to incorporate. Place the bagna càuda over a heat source to serve it, accompanied by vegetables.

Giardiniera Piemontese

YIELD: 6 PINTS / **ACTIVE TIME:** 1 HOUR / **TOTAL TIME:** 1 MONTH

2½ CUPS WATER

3 CUPS PLUS 3 TABLESPOONS DRY WHITE WINE

3½ CUPS WHITE WINE VINEGAR

8 BAY LEAVES

1½ TABLESPOONS BLACK PEPPERCORNS

4 TEASPOONS COARSE SEA SALT

½ CUP SUGAR

7 OZ. CARROTS, PEELED AND SLICED

9 OZ. CELERY STALKS, LIGHTLY PEELED AND CHOPPED

7 OZ. GREEN BEANS, TRIMMED AND HALVED

3½ OZ. YELLOW BELL PEPPERS, STEMMED, SEEDED, AND SLICED

3½ OZ. RED BELL PEPPERS, STEMMED, SEEDED, AND SLICED

3½ OZ. GREEN BELL PEPPERS, STEMMED, SEEDED, AND SLICED

7 OZ. FENNEL, TRIMMED AND CUT INTO WEDGES

11 OZ. CAULIFLOWER FLORETS

7 OZ. PEARL ONIONS

9 OZ. RADISHES, TRIMMED AND HALVED

7 OZ. CUCUMBERS, CHOPPED

1. Place six mason jars in a canning pot, cover them with cold water, and bring to a boil. Boil the jars for 30 minutes to sterilize them. Remove the jars from the boiling water and place them on a wire rack, upside down, to drain and cool.
2. Place the water, wine, and vinegar in a large pot and bring to a boil.
3. Add the bay leaves, peppercorns, salt, sugar, carrots, celery, and green beans and boil for 2 minutes.
4. Add the peppers, fennel, and cauliflower and boil for another 2 minutes.
5. Add the pearl onions, radishes, and cucumbers, gently stir, and boil for 2 minutes. Drain the vegetables, reserving the brine.
6. Distribute the vegetables among the sterilized jars, leaving about 1 inch free on top. Pour the reserved brine into the jars until it nearly reaches their rims.
7. Seal the jars tight and place them in the canning pot. Cover them with cold water and bring to a boil. Reduce the heat and let the jars simmer for 5 to 10 minutes.
8. Remove the jars from the hot water and place them on the wire rack to cool. As they are cooling, you should hear the classic "ping and pop" sound of the lids creating a seal.
9. After 6 hours, check the lids. There should be no give in them, and they should be suctioned onto the jars. Discard any lids and food that did not seal properly.
10. Keep the giardiniera in a dark place for 1 month before serving.

Cundigiun

YIELD: 4 SERVINGS / **ACTIVE TIME:** 15 MINUTES / **TOTAL TIME:** 2 HOURS

SALT, TO TASTE

6 OZ. GREEN BEANS, TRIMMED AND HALVED

1 TABLESPOON WHITE WINE VINEGAR

1 TABLESPOON WATER

4 GALLETTE DEL MARINAIO (SEE PAGE 363), BROKEN

1 GARLIC CLOVE, HALVED

4 TOMATOES, SLICED

1 RED BELL PEPPER, STEMMED, SEEDED, AND SLICED

1 YELLOW BELL PEPPER, STEMMED, SEEDED, AND SLICED

6 SPRING ONIONS, SLICED

2 HANDFULS OF FRESH BASIL, CHOPPED

2 HANDFULS OF GREEN OLIVES, PITTED

2 HANDFULS OF TAGGIASCA BLACK OLIVES, PITTED

6 OZ. TUNA IN OLIVE OIL, DRAINED

3½ OZ. PIECE OF BOTTARGA, SLICED

¼ CUP EXTRA-VIRGIN OLIVE OIL

1. Bring water to a boil in a large saucepan. Add salt and the green beans and cook until the green beans are just tender, about 3 minutes. Drain the green beans, run them under cold water, and set them aside.
2. Place the vinegar and water in a bowl. Add the sea biscuits and toss until they have absorbed the liquid.
3. Rub the garlic over the inside of a salad bowl. Add the remaining ingredients, green beans, and sea biscuits, season with salt, and toss to combine.
4. Refrigerate the cundigiun for 1 hour before serving.

Radicchio Rosso Fritto

YIELD: 4 SERVINGS / **ACTIVE TIME:** 15 MINUTES / **TOTAL TIME:** 30 MINUTES

5 HEADS OF LATE RED RADICCHIO

1 CUP ALL-PURPOSE FLOUR, PLUS MORE AS NEEDED

⅔ CUP CORNMEAL

1 EGG

1⅓ CUPS PROSECCO

EXTRA-VIRGIN OLIVE OIL, AS NEEDED

SALT, TO TASTE

1. Prepare an ice bath. To trim the radicchio, remove the outer leaves if they are damaged. Remove the base of each radicchio without breaking the bunch. Cut them into wedges and soak them in the ice bath until their tips curl, about 10 minutes.
2. Place the flour, cornmeal, egg, and Prosecco in a bowl and whisk until the mixture comes together as a smooth batter.
3. Drain the radicchio and pat them dry with a paper towel.
4. Add olive oil to a narrow, deep, heavy-bottomed saucepan with high sides until it is 2 inches deep and warm it to 350°F. Dredge the radicchio in the batter until completely coated and, working in batches to avoid crowding the pot, gently slip them into the hot oil. Fry until they are golden brown.
5. Transfer the fritters to a paper towel–lined plate to drain. Season them with salt before serving.

Prosciutto e Melone

YIELD: 4 SERVINGS / **ACTIVE TIME:** 10 MINUTES / **TOTAL TIME:** 10 MINUTES

1 CANTALOUPE

16 SLICES OF PROSCIUTTO

EXTRA-VIRGIN OLIVE OIL, FOR TOPPING

1. Split the cantaloupe in half, remove all of the seeds and the rind, and discard them. Cut the cantaloupe into eight slices.
2. Wrap each slice of cantaloupe with two slices of prosciutto. You can also arrange the slices of prosciutto over the cantaloupe, but if you do, make sure not to cover them entirely.
3. Arrange the wrapped cantaloupe on a serving platter, drizzle olive oil over the top, and either serve immediately or chill in the refrigerator.

Patate in Tecia

YIELD: 4 SERVINGS / **ACTIVE TIME:** 20 MINUTES / **TOTAL TIME:** 1 HOUR

SALT AND PEPPER, TO TASTE

1½ LBS. POTATOES

5 TABLESPOONS UNSALTED BUTTER

1 ONION, FINELY DICED

4½ OZ. PANCETTA OR BACON, CUBED

1 CUP BEEF STOCK (SEE PAGE 446)

1. Bring water to a boil in a large saucepan. Add salt and the potatoes and cook until they are fork-tender.
2. Drain the potatoes and let them cool. When they are cool enough to handle, peel the potatoes and roughly chop them.
3. Place the butter in a large cast-iron skillet and melt it over medium heat. Add the onion and cook, stirring occasionally, until it has softened, about 5 minutes.
4. Add the pancetta and cook, stirring occasionally, until it is browned and crispy.
5. Add the potatoes, season with salt and pepper, and raise the heat to medium-high. Cook, stirring continually and adding the stock a little at a time to keep the potatoes from sticking to the pan, until the potatoes are crispy and golden brown and have absorbed all of the liquid, 10 to 15 minutes. Serve immediately.

Funghi al Funghetto

YIELD: 4 SERVINGS / **ACTIVE TIME:** 15 MINUTES / **TOTAL TIME:** 30 MINUTES

1 LB. PORCINI MUSHROOMS

3 TABLESPOONS EXTRA-VIRGIN OLIVE OIL

1 GARLIC CLOVE, MINCED

1 TABLESPOON FINELY CHOPPED FRESH PARSLEY

2 TABLESPOONS WATER

SALT, TO TASTE

DRIED OREGANO, TO TASTE

1. Gently brush the mushrooms to remove any residual soil and then pat them with a moist kitchen towel. Cut the mushrooms into 1-inch-thick slices and set them aside.
2. Place the olive oil in a large skillet and warm it over medium heat. Add the garlic and parsley and cook until the garlic is golden brown.
3. Add the mushrooms and water and cook until the mushrooms start to brown, 10 to 12 minutes, stirring occasionally.
4. Season with salt and oregano and serve warm or at room temperature.

Funghi Trifolati

YIELD: 4 SERVINGS / **ACTIVE TIME:** 15 MINUTES / **TOTAL TIME:** 30 MINUTES

14 OZ. FRESH MUSHROOMS

¼ CUP EXTRA-VIRGIN OLIVE OIL

1 GARLIC CLOVE, HALVED

SALT, TO TASTE

2 HANDFULS OF FRESH PARSLEY, FINELY CHOPPED

½ CHILE PEPPER, MINCED (OPTIONAL)

1. Gently brush the mushrooms to remove any residual soil and then pat them with a moist kitchen towel. Cut the mushrooms into 1-inch-thick slices and set the mushrooms aside.
2. Place the olive oil in a large skillet and warm it over medium heat. Add the garlic and cook, stirring continually, for 1 minute.
3. Remove the garlic and discard it. Add the mushrooms, reduce the heat to low, and cover the pan. Cook the mushrooms for 7 minutes, stirring occasionally.
4. Season the mushrooms with salt, add two-thirds of the parsley and the chile (if desired), cover the pan, and cook for 7 minutes.
5. Stir in the remaining parsley and serve warm or at room temperature.

Asparagi al Prosciutto

YIELD: 6 SERVINGS / **ACTIVE TIME:** 15 MINUTES / **TOTAL TIME:** 40 MINUTES

SALT, TO TASTE

24 TO 36 ASPARAGUS STALKS, TRIMMED

12 SLICES OF PROSCIUTTO

¼ CUP UNSALTED BUTTER, CHOPPED, PLUS MORE AS NEEDED

2 OZ. PARMESAN CHEESE, GRATED

1. Preheat the oven to 350°F. Bring water to a boil in a tall, narrow pot. Add salt to the boiling water, tie the asparagus tightly with kitchen twine, and stand them in the pot with their tips facing up. Cook until the asparagus is al dente, about 5 minutes. Drain the asparagus and let it cool.
2. Wrap two to three asparagus stalks in each piece of prosciutto—how many asparagus stalks you put in each one depends on how thick they are.
3. Coat a baking dish with high sides with butter and arrange the prosciutto-wrapped asparagus in it.
4. Top with the butter and Parmesan and place the dish in the oven. Bake until the cheese has melted and the prosciutto is golden brown, about 10 minutes.
5. Remove the dish from the oven and serve immediately, drizzling any pan juices over the top.

Polpette alla Vedova

YIELD: 20 MEATBALLS / **ACTIVE TIME:** 30 MINUTES / **TOTAL TIME:** 1 HOUR

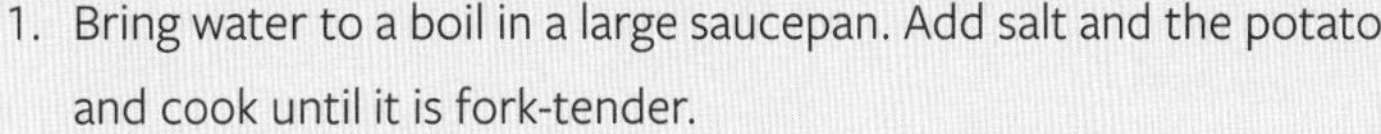

SALT AND PEPPER, TO TASTE

1 MEDIUM POTATO

¾ LB. GROUND BEEF

2 EGGS

3 OZ. MORTADELLA, FINELY DICED

HANDFUL OF FRESH PARSLEY, FINELY CHOPPED

1 GARLIC CLOVE, MINCED

BREAD CRUMBS, AS NEEDED

EXTRA-VIRGIN OLIVE OIL, AS NEEDED

1. Bring water to a boil in a large saucepan. Add salt and the potato and cook until it is fork-tender.
2. Drain the potato and let it cool. When it is cool enough to handle, peel the potato and mash it.
3. Place the ground beef, eggs, mortadella, parsley, garlic, and mashed potato in a mixing bowl, season with salt and pepper, and stir to combine. Check the consistency of the mixture: if it seems to be too soft, incorporate bread crumbs until it is the right consistency.
4. Add olive oil to a narrow, deep, heavy-bottomed saucepan with high sides until it is about 2 inches deep and warm it to 350°F.
5. Place some bread crumbs in a shallow bowl. Form the mixture into small meatballs that are about the size of a walnut. Roll the meatballs in the bread crumbs until they are coated all over.
6. Working in batches to avoid crowding the pot, gently slip the meatballs into the hot oil and fry until they are cooked through and golden brown, turning as necessary.
7. Transfer the fried meatballs to a paper towel–lined plate to drain before serving.

Crostini alla Salsa Peverada

YIELD: 4 SERVINGS / **ACTIVE TIME:** 20 MINUTES / **TOTAL TIME:** 40 MINUTES

3 TABLESPOONS EXTRA-VIRGIN OLIVE OIL

1 GARLIC CLOVE, MINCED

2 HANDFULS OF FRESH PARSLEY, FINELY CHOPPED

2 ANCHOVIES PACKED IN SALT, SOAKED IN WARM WATER, DRAINED, AND MINCED

3 CHICKEN LIVERS, FINELY DICED

3½ OZ. SOPRESSA VENETA, FINELY DICED

ZEST OF ½ LEMON

SALT AND PEPPER, TO TASTE

¼ CUP WHITE WINE VINEGAR

4 SLICES OF CRUSTY BREAD, TOASTED

1. Place the olive oil in a large skillet and warm it over medium heat. Add the garlic and parsley and cook until the garlic is golden brown.
2. Add the anchovies, chicken livers, salami, and lemon zest, season generously with salt and pepper, and toss to combine.
3. Add the vinegar and bring to a simmer. Reduce the heat to low and cook, stirring occasionally, for 10 minutes.
4. Spread the peverada over the toasted slices of bread and serve immediately.

Baccalà Mantecato

YIELD: 4 SERVINGS / **ACTIVE TIME:** 25 MINUTES / **TOTAL TIME:** 50 MINUTES

11 OZ. STOCKFISH, SOAKED, DRAINED, SKIN REMOVED, AND DEBONED

4 CUPS WATER, PLUS MORE AS NEEDED

SALT AND PEPPER, TO TASTE

½ LEMON

2 BAY LEAVES

1½ CUPS EXTRA-VIRGIN OLIVE OIL

FRESH PARSLEY, CHOPPED, FOR GARNISH

CRUSTY BREAD, TOASTED, FOR SERVING

1. Place the stockfish and water in a saucepan, season with salt, and then add the lemon and bay leaves. Bring to a boil and cook the stockfish for 20 minutes.
2. Remove the stockfish with a slotted spoon, place it in a bowl, and add the olive oil. Stir to combine, breaking the stockfish into small pieces.
3. Using a handheld mixer, whip the mixture until it is dense and creamy and there are only a few pieces of stockfish left whole, adding water as necessary to get the proper consistency.
4. Season the cream with salt and pepper, garnish with parsley, and serve alongside crusty bread.

Octopus alla Veneziana

YIELD: 4 SERVINGS / **ACTIVE TIME:** 20 MINUTES / **TOTAL TIME:** 40 MINUTES

4 CUPS WATER

2 TABLESPOONS WHITE WINE VINEGAR

SALT AND PEPPER, TO TASTE

12 BABY OCTOPUS, CLEANED AND RINSED

JUICE OF 1 LEMON

¼ CUP EXTRA-VIRGIN OLIVE OIL

HANDFUL OF FRESH PARSLEY, FINELY CHOPPED, FOR GARNISH

1. Place the water and vinegar in a saucepan, season with salt, and bring to a boil. Submerge the ends of the octopus in the boiling water, holding them by the head, until the tentacles curl up. Drop the octopus in the water and cook for 30 minutes.
2. Remove the octopus, cut them in half, and season with salt and pepper.
3. Place the lemon juice and olive oil in a bowl and whisk until it has emulsified. Drizzle the emulsion over the octopus, sprinkle the parsley on top, and serve.

Scallops alla Veneziana

YIELD: 4 SERVINGS / **ACTIVE TIME:** 15 MINUTES / **TOTAL TIME:** 20 MINUTES

12 LARGE SCALLOPS IN THEIR SHELLS

½ CUP EXTRA-VIRGIN OLIVE OIL

1 GARLIC CLOVE, MINCED

HANDFUL OF FRESH PARSLEY, FINELY CHOPPED

SALT AND PEPPER, TO TASTE

JUICE OF ½ LEMON

1. Preheat the oven to 200°F. Using a sharp knife, remove the scallops from their shells, including the orange part, and rinse them under cold water.
2. Rinse and dry the four largest scallop shells. Place them in the oven to keep them warm.
3. Place half of the olive oil in a large skillet and warm it over medium heat. Add the garlic and parsley and cook, stirring continually, for 2 minutes.
4. Add the scallops and sear on both sides until they are browned and just cooked through. Season them with salt and pepper.
5. Place three scallops in each shell, drizzle the lemon juice and remaining olive oil over them, and serve.

Sarde in Saor

YIELD: 4 SERVINGS / **ACTIVE TIME:** 25 MINUTES / **TOTAL TIME:** 50 MINUTES

6 TABLESPOONS EXTRA-VIRGIN OLIVE OIL

1 CUP ALL-PURPOSE FLOUR

1⅓ LBS. FRESH SARDINES, CLEANED AND DEBONED

SALT AND PEPPER, TO TASTE

1 TABLESPOON CORIANDER SEEDS

1 TABLESPOON GREEN PEPPERCORNS

2 WHOLE CLOVES

2 WHITE ONIONS, SLICED THIN

2 OZ. SULTANAS, SOAKED IN WARM WATER, DRAINED, AND SQUEEZED DRY

2 OZ. PINE NUTS

1⅓ CUPS WHITE WINE VINEGAR

1 CUP DRY WHITE WINE

1. Place two-thirds of the olive oil in a large skillet and warm it over medium heat. Place the flour in a shallow bowl and dredge the sardines in it until they are coated all over.
2. Add the sardines to the pan and fry until they are golden brown and crispy on both sides, taking care not to break them. Transfer the fried sardines to a paper towel–lined plate, season with salt and pepper, and let them drain.
3. Using a mortar and pestle, grind the coriander seeds, green peppercorns, and cloves into a fine powder.
4. Place the remaining olive oil in a small saucepan and warm it over medium heat. Add the onions and cook, stirring occasionally, until they have browned, about 10 minutes.
5. Stir in the raisins, pine nuts, and ground spices, cover the mixture with the vinegar and white wine, and bring to a simmer. Cook until the liquid has reduced and thickened, 10 to 15 minutes.
6. Top the onion stew with the fried sardines and serve.

Cappon Magro

YIELD: 6 SERVINGS / **ACTIVE TIME:** 1 HOUR / **TOTAL TIME:** 3 HOURS

2 WHITEFISH FILLETS

EXTRA-VIRGIN OLIVE OIL, TO TASTE

FRESH LEMON JUICE, TO TASTE

SALT, TO TASTE

1 SMALL HEAD OF CAULIFLOWER, TRIMMED AND CHOPPED

1 BEET, PEELED AND CHOPPED

3 CARROTS, PEELED AND CHOPPED

7 OZ. GREEN BEANS, TRIMMED

3 SCORZONERA ROOTS OR 11 OZ. CELERIAC, TRIMMED

6 ARTICHOKE HEARTS

WHITE WINE VINEGAR, TO TASTE

4 GALLETTE DEL MARINAIO (SEE PAGE 363)

3½ OZ. BOTTARGA, SLICED

2 BATCHES OF BAGNET VERT (SEE PAGE 452)

1 LB. ASSORTED SEAFOOD, COOKED, FOR SERVING

1. Fill a large saucepan with water and bring to a simmer. Place the fish in a steaming basket, place the steaming basket over the simmering water, and steam the fish until it is cooked through, 12 to 15 minutes.
2. Remove the fish from the steaming basket, drizzle olive oil and lemon juice over it, season with salt, and set it aside.
3. Bring the water to a boil. Add the cauliflower, beet, carrots, green beans, scorzonera, and artichoke hearts one at a time and cook until they are al dente.
4. Cut the cooked vegetables into small pieces, place them in separate bowls, season with olive oil, salt, and vinegar, and toss to combine. Set the vegetables aside.
5. Place the gallettes in a bowl, sprinkle water and vinegar over them, and let them soak for a few minutes. Press down on the gallettes to remove excess moisture and set them aside.
6. Line a 9 x 5–inch loaf pan with plastic wrap. Layer the fish and each of the vegetables in the pan, inserting 2 layers of bottarga between the vegetable layers and topping each layer with some of the salsa verde.
7. Top the cappon magro with the gallettes and press down on it to compact it slightly.
8. Chill the cappon magro in the refrigerator for 2 hours.
9. Invert the cappon magro onto a serving dish and remove the plastic wrap. Spread any remaining salsa verde over it and serve alongside the seafood.

PIZZA & FOCACCIA

Neapolitan Pizza Dough

YIELD: 4 BALLS OF DOUGH / **ACTIVE TIME:** 30 MINUTES / **TOTAL TIME:** 8 TO 12 HOURS

1¾ CUPS (419.5 ML) WATER

⅛ TEASPOON PLUS 1 PINCH (0.2 G) ACTIVE DRY YEAST

5⅔ CUPS (677.5 G) BREAD FLOUR OR "00" FLOUR, PLUS MORE AS NEEDED

1 TABLESPOON (17 G) TABLE SALT

EXTRA-VIRGIN OLIVE OIL, AS NEEDED

1. Warm 3½ tablespoons of the water until it is 105°F. Add the water and yeast to a bowl and gently stir. Let it sit until it starts to foam, about 10 minutes.
2. In a large bowl, combine the flour, yeast mixture, and remaining water and work the mixture until it just holds together. If kneading by hand, transfer the dough to a flour-dusted work surface. Work the dough until it is smooth and elastic.
3. Add the salt and knead until the dough is very developed, elastic, and extensible. A Neapolitan-style pizza dough needs to be very well-developed, which means the gluten in the dough should be at maximum strength. The resulting dough needs to be both extensible and elastic, meaning it needs to be easy to spread out thin but it also needs to spring back quite energetically, in order not to lose its shape.
4. Coat an airtight container that allows the dough to get at least three times bigger with olive oil. Form the dough into a ball, place it in the container, and cover the container. Let it rest in a naturally warm spot (in the oven with the light on is a good option) until it has doubled in size, about 1 hour. For a classic Neapolitan dough, the room temperature should be 73°F. If your kitchen is colder, let the dough rest for longer before shaping it into balls.
5. Transfer the dough to a flour-dusted work surface, divide it into four pieces, and shape them into very tight balls. Coat a baking dish with high sides with olive oil and place the balls in it, leaving enough space between them so that they won't touch when fully risen. Coat plastic wrap with olive oil, cover the baking dish with it, and let the dough rest for 6 to 8 hours before using it to make pizza.

Pizza Dough with Biga

YIELD: 4 BALLS OF DOUGH / **ACTIVE TIME:** 40 MINUTES / **TOTAL TIME:** 24 HOURS

FOR THE BIGA

⅚ CUP (100 G) BREAD FLOUR

2 TABLESPOONS PLUS 4 TEASPOONS (50 ML) WATER

⅛ TEASPOON PLUS 1 PINCH (0.2 G) ACTIVE DRY YEAST

EXTRA-VIRGIN OLIVE OIL, AS NEEDED

FOR THE DOUGH

1½ CUPS PLUS 4 TEASPOONS (380 ML) WATER

¼ TEASPOON PLUS 1 PINCH (0.4 G) ACTIVE DRY YEAST

4¾ CUPS (569.7 G) BREAD FLOUR OR "00" FLOUR, PLUS MORE AS NEEDED

⅔ CUP (150 G) BIGA

1 TABLESPOON (18 G) TABLE SALT

EXTRA-VIRGIN OLIVE OIL, AS NEEDED

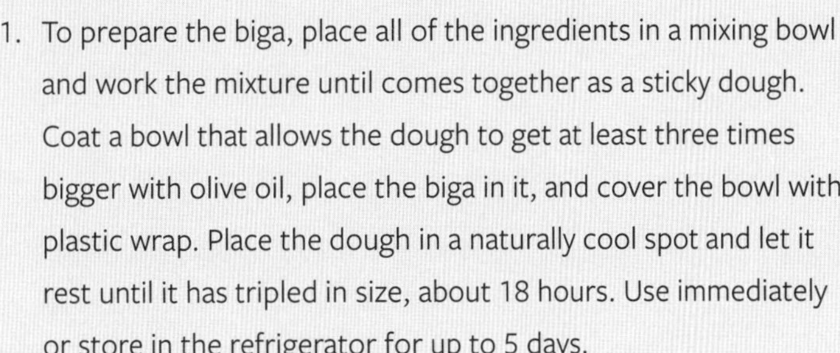

1. To prepare the biga, place all of the ingredients in a mixing bowl and work the mixture until comes together as a sticky dough. Coat a bowl that allows the dough to get at least three times bigger with olive oil, place the biga in it, and cover the bowl with plastic wrap. Place the dough in a naturally cool spot and let it rest until it has tripled in size, about 18 hours. Use immediately or store in the refrigerator for up to 5 days.
2. To begin preparations for the dough, warm 3½ tablespoons of the water until it is 105°F. Add the water and yeast to a bowl and gently stir. Let it sit until it starts to foam, about 10 minutes.
3. In a large bowl, combine the flour, yeast mixture, remaining water, and biga and work the mixture until it just holds together. If kneading by hand, transfer the dough to a flour-dusted work surface. Work the dough until it is smooth and elastic.
4. Add the salt and knead until the dough is developed, elastic, and extensible, about 5 minutes. Coat an airtight container that allows the dough to get at least three times bigger with olive oil. Form the dough into a ball, place it in the container, and cover the container. Let it rest in a naturally warm spot until it has doubled in size, 2 to 3 hours.
5. Transfer the dough to a flour-dusted work surface, divide it into four pieces, and shape them into tight balls. Coat a baking dish with high sides with olive oil and place the balls in it, leaving enough space between them so that they won't touch when fully risen. Coat plastic wrap with olive oil, cover the baking dish with it, and chill the dough in the refrigerator for a minimum of 20 hours.
6. After this period of cold fermentation, remove the dough from the refrigerator and let it sit at room temperature for 1 to 2 hours before using it to make pizza.

Pizza al Taglio Dough

YIELD: DOUGH FOR 1 LARGE PAN PIZZA / **ACTIVE TIME:** 30 MINUTES / **TOTAL TIME:** 5 HOURS

2 CUPS PLUS 2 TEASPOONS (490 ML) WATER

1¼ TEASPOONS (3.7 G) ACTIVE DRY YEAST

3¾ CUPS (450 G) BREAD FLOUR OR STRONG "00" FLOUR

2 CUPS PLUS 1 TABLESPOON (250 G) ALL-PURPOSE FLOUR, PLUS MORE AS NEEDED

1 TABLESPOON (13 G) EXTRA-VIRGIN OLIVE OIL, PLUS MORE AS NEEDED

1 TABLESPOON (17 G) TABLE SALT

1. Warm 3½ tablespoons of the water until it is 105°F. Add the water and yeast to a bowl and gently stir. Let it sit until it starts to foam, about 10 minutes.
2. In a large bowl, combine the flours, yeast mixture, and remaining water and work the mixture until it just holds together. If kneading by hand, transfer the dough to a flour-dusted work surface. Work the dough until it is smooth and elastic.
3. Add the olive oil and salt and knead until the dough is developed, elastic, and extensible, about 5 minutes. Coat an airtight container that allows the dough to get at least three times bigger with olive oil. Form the dough into a ball, place it in the container, and cover the container. Let it rest in a naturally warm spot until it has doubled in size, 3 to 4 hours.

Pizza Marinara

YIELD: 1 PIZZA / **ACTIVE TIME:** 15 MINUTES / **TOTAL TIME:** 45 MINUTES

SEMOLINA FLOUR, AS NEEDED

1 BALL OF PIZZA DOUGH

⅓ CUP PIZZA SAUCE (SEE PAGE 451)

1 GARLIC CLOVE, SLICED THIN

SALT, TO TASTE

DRIED OREGANO, TO TASTE

EXTRA-VIRGIN OLIVE OIL, TO TASTE

1. Place a baking stone or steel on the middle rack of the oven and preheat the oven to the maximum temperature.
2. Dust a work surface with semolina flour, place the dough on the work surface, and gently stretch it into a round. Cover the dough with the sauce and top it with the garlic. Season the pizza with salt and dried oregano and drizzle olive oil over the pizza.
3. Using a peel or a flat baking sheet, transfer the pizza to the heated baking implement in the oven. Bake for about 15 minutes, until the crust is golden brown and starting to char. Remove the pizza from the oven and let it cool slightly before slicing and serving.

Pizza alla Pala Dough

YIELD: 2 BALLS OF DOUGH / **ACTIVE TIME:** 30 MINUTES / **TOTAL TIME:** 7 HOURS

2⅙ CUPS (524 ML) WATER

1¼ TEASPOONS (3.7 G) ACTIVE DRY YEAST

5⅚ CUPS (700 G) BREAD FLOUR OR STRONG "00" FLOUR, PLUS MORE AS NEEDED

2 TEASPOONS (6 G) DIASTATIC MALT

1¾ TEASPOONS (7 G) SUGAR

3 TABLESPOONS (40 G) EXTRA-VIRGIN OLIVE OIL, PLUS MORE AS NEEDED

1 TABLESPOON (17 G) TABLE SALT, PLUS MORE TO TASTE

1. Warm 3½ tablespoons of the water until it is 105°F. Add the water and yeast to a bowl and gently stir. Let it sit until it starts to foam, about 10 minutes.
2. In a large bowl, combine the flour and three-quarters of the remaining water and work the mixture until combined. Add the yeast mixture, malt, sugar, and olive oil and work the mixture until it just holds together. If kneading by hand, transfer the dough to a flour-dusted work surface. Work the dough until it is smooth and elastic, about 10 minutes.
3. Add the salt and remaining water and knead until the dough is developed, elastic, and extensible, about 5 minutes. Coat an airtight container that allows the dough to get at least three times bigger with olive oil. Form the dough into a ball, place it in the container, and cover the container. Let it rest in a naturally warm spot until it has doubled in size and is full of bubbles, about 5 hours.
4. Line two baking sheets with parchment paper and dust the parchment paper with flour. Place the dough on a flour-dusted work surface and divide it into two pieces. Place a piece of dough on each baking sheet, shape the pieces into ovals, and let them rest in a naturally warm spot for 2 to 3 hours, stretching the dough lengthwise every 30 minutes and taking care not to deflate them.
5. After the last stretch, generously drizzle olive oil and sprinkle salt over the pieces of dough. Let them rest for another 15 minutes before using them to make pizza.

Pizza Margherita

YIELD: 1 PIZZA / **ACTIVE TIME:** 15 MINUTES / **TOTAL TIME:** 45 MINUTES

SEMOLINA FLOUR, AS NEEDED

1 BALL OF PIZZA DOUGH

⅓ CUP PIZZA SAUCE (SEE PAGE 451)

4 OZ. FRESH MOZZARELLA CHEESE, DRAINED AND CUT INTO SHORT STRIPS

FRESH BASIL LEAVES, TO TASTE

SALT, TO TASTE

EXTRA-VIRGIN OLIVE OIL, TO TASTE

1. Place a baking stone or steel on the middle rack of the oven and preheat the oven to the maximum temperature.
2. Dust a work surface with semolina flour, place the dough on the work surface, and gently stretch it into a round. Cover the dough with the sauce and top it with the mozzarella and basil. Season with salt and drizzle olive oil over the pizza.
3. Using a peel or a flat baking sheet, transfer the pizza to the heated baking implement in the oven. Bake for about 15 minutes, until the crust is golden brown and starting to char. Remove the pizza from the oven and let it cool slightly before slicing and serving.

Pizza Quattro Formaggi

YIELD: 1 PIZZA / **ACTIVE TIME:** 15 MINUTES / **TOTAL TIME:** 45 MINUTES

SEMOLINA FLOUR, AS NEEDED

1 BALL OF PIZZA DOUGH

⅓ CUP PIZZA SAUCE (OPTIONAL; SEE PAGE 451)

2 OZ. FRESH MOZZARELLA CHEESE, DRAINED AND CUT INTO SHORT STRIPS

2 OZ. FONTINA OR PROVOLONE CHEESE, SHREDDED

2 OZ. GORGONZOLA CHEESE, CRUMBLED

2 OZ. PECORINO OR PARMESAN CHEESE, GRATED

SALT AND PEPPER, TO TASTE

EXTRA-VIRGIN OLIVE OIL, TO TASTE

1. Place a baking stone or steel on the middle rack of the oven and preheat the oven to the maximum temperature.
2. Dust a work surface with semolina flour, place the dough on the work surface, and gently stretch it into a round. If using, top the dough with the sauce. Top the pizza with the cheeses, season with salt and pepper, and drizzle olive oil over the pizza.
3. Using a peel or a flat baking sheet, transfer the pizza to the heated baking implement in the oven. Bake for about 15 minutes, until the crust is golden brown and starting to char. Remove the pizza from the oven and let it cool slightly before slicing and serving.

Pizza Boscaiola

YIELD: 1 PIZZA / **ACTIVE TIME:** 25 MINUTES / **TOTAL TIME:** 55 MINUTES

EXTRA-VIRGIN OLIVE OIL, AS NEEDED

1 LINK OF ITALIAN SAUSAGE, CASING REMOVED AND CRUMBLED

SEMOLINA FLOUR, AS NEEDED

1 BALL OF PIZZA DOUGH

⅓ CUP PIZZA SAUCE (SEE PAGE 451)

½ CUP MUSHROOMS

SALT, TO TASTE

3 OZ. FRESH MOZZARELLA CHEESE, DRAINED AND CUT INTO SHORT STRIPS

1. Place a baking stone or steel on the middle rack of the oven and preheat the oven to the maximum temperature.
2. Coat the bottom of a skillet with olive oil and warm it over medium-high heat. Add the sausage and cook until it starts to brown, about 6 minutes, stirring occasionally. Remove the pan from heat and set the sausage aside.
3. Dust a work surface with semolina flour, place the dough on the work surface, and gently stretch it into a round. Cover the dough with the sauce and top it with the mushrooms and sausage. Season with salt and drizzle olive oil over the pizza.
4. Using a peel or a flat baking sheet, transfer the pizza to the heated baking implement in the oven. Bake for about 5 minutes, until the crust starts to brown. Remove the pizza, distribute the mozzarella over the top, and return the pizza to the oven. Bake for about 10 minutes, until the crust is golden brown and starting to char. Remove the pizza from the oven and let it cool slightly before slicing and serving.

Pizza Romana

YIELD: 1 PIZZA / **ACTIVE TIME:** 15 MINUTES / **TOTAL TIME:** 45 MINUTES

SEMOLINA FLOUR, AS NEEDED

1 BALL OF PIZZA DOUGH

⅓ CUP PIZZA SAUCE (SEE PAGE 451)

2½ OZ. FRESH MOZZARELLA CHEESE, DRAINED AND CUT INTO SHORT STRIPS

4 ANCHOVY FILLETS IN OLIVE OIL, DRAINED AND CHOPPED

1 TABLESPOON CAPERS, DRAINED

SALT, TO TASTE

DRIED OREGANO, TO TASTE

EXTRA-VIRGIN OLIVE OIL, TO TASTE

1. Place a baking stone or steel on the middle rack of the oven and preheat the oven to the maximum temperature.
2. Dust a work surface with semolina flour, place the dough on the work surface, and gently stretch it into a round. Cover the dough with the sauce and top it with the mozzarella, anchovies, and capers. Season with salt and oregano and drizzle olive oil over the pizza.
3. Using a peel or a flat baking sheet, transfer the pizza to the heated baking implement in the oven. Bake for about 15 minutes, until the crust is golden brown and starting to char. Remove the pizza from the oven and let it cool slightly before slicing and serving.

Pizza Capricciosa

YIELD: 1 PIZZA / **ACTIVE TIME:** 15 MINUTES / **TOTAL TIME:** 45 MINUTES

SEMOLINA FLOUR, AS NEEDED

1 BALL OF PIZZA DOUGH

⅓ CUP PIZZA SAUCE (SEE PAGE 451)

2 ARTICHOKE HEARTS, CHOPPED

¼ CUP MUSHROOMS

SALT, TO TASTE

EXTRA-VIRGIN OLIVE OIL, TO TASTE

3 OZ. FRESH MOZZARELLA CHEESE, DRAINED AND CUT INTO SHORT STRIPS

2 SLICES OF PROSCIUTTO, TORN

1 SMALL HANDFUL OF PITTED BLACK OLIVES, SLICED OR LEFT WHOLE

1. Place a baking stone or steel on the middle rack of the oven and preheat the oven to the maximum temperature.
2. Dust a work surface with semolina flour, place the dough on the work surface, and gently stretch it into a round. Cover the dough with the sauce and top it with the artichokes and mushrooms. Season with salt and drizzle olive oil over the pizza.
3. Using a peel or a flat baking sheet, transfer the pizza to the heated baking implement in the oven. Bake for about 5 minutes, until the crust starts to brown. Remove the pizza, distribute the mozzarella, prosciutto, and olives over the top, and return the pizza to the oven. Bake for about 10 minutes, until the crust is golden brown and starting to char. Remove the pizza from the oven and let it cool slightly before slicing and serving.

Pizza Stagioni

YIELD: 1 PIZZA / **ACTIVE TIME:** 35 MINUTES / **TOTAL TIME:** 1 HOUR AND 15 MINUTES

EXTRA-VIRGIN OLIVE OIL, AS NEEDED

4 OZ. SEAFOOD MIXTURE (SHRIMP, CALAMARI, MUSSELS, CRAB, AND/OR TUNA RECOMMENDED)

SALT, TO TASTE

SEMOLINA FLOUR, AS NEEDED

1 BALL OF PIZZA DOUGH

⅓ CUP PIZZA SAUCE (SEE PAGE 451)

3 OZ. FRESH MOZZARELLA CHEESE, DRAINED AND CUT INTO SHORT STRIPS

2 ARTICHOKE HEARTS IN OLIVE OIL, DRAINED AND CUT INTO WEDGES

8 SLICES OF PEPPERONI

1 TOMATO, SLICED

1. Place a baking stone or steel on the middle rack of the oven and preheat the oven to the maximum temperature.
2. Coat the bottom of a skillet with olive oil and warm it over medium-high heat. Add the seafood, season with salt, and cook until the seafood is just cooked through, about 4 minutes. Remove the pan from heat and set the seafood aside. If using mussels, discard any mussels that did not open and remove the meat from those that did open.
3. Dust a work surface with semolina flour, place the dough on the work surface, and gently stretch it into a round. Cover the dough with the sauce and top it with the mozzarella. Place each of the artichokes, pepperoni, seafood, and tomato on their own section of the pizza. Season with salt and drizzle olive oil over the pizza.
4. Using a peel or a flat baking sheet, transfer the pizza to the heated baking implement in the oven. Bake for about 10 minutes, until the crust is golden brown and starting to char. Remove the pizza from the oven and let it cool slightly before slicing and serving.

Pizza Diavola

YIELD: 1 PIZZA / **ACTIVE TIME:** 15 MINUTES / **TOTAL TIME:** 50 MINUTES

2 TABLESPOONS EXTRA-VIRGIN OLIVE OIL

RED PEPPER FLAKES, TO TASTE

SEMOLINA FLOUR, AS NEEDED

1 BALL OF PIZZA DOUGH

⅓ CUP PIZZA SAUCE (SEE PAGE 451)

2½ OZ. CACIOCAVALLO OR PROVOLA CHEESE, CUBED

5 SLICES OF SPICY SALAMI

SALT, TO TASTE

DRIED OREGANO, TO TASTE

1. Place a baking stone or steel on the middle rack of the oven and preheat the oven to the maximum temperature. Combine the olive oil and red pepper flakes in a small bowl and set the mixture aside.
2. Dust a work surface with semolina flour, place the dough on the work surface, and gently stretch it into a round. Cover the dough with the sauce and top it with the cheese and salami. Season with salt and oregano and drizzle the spicy olive oil over the pizza.
3. Using a peel or a flat baking sheet, transfer the pizza to the heated baking implement in the oven. Bake for about 15 minutes, until the crust is golden brown and starting to char. Remove the pizza from the oven and let it cool slightly before slicing and serving.

Pizza Pescatora

YIELD: 1 PIZZA / **ACTIVE TIME:** 25 MINUTES / **TOTAL TIME:** 1 HOUR

- EXTRA-VIRGIN OLIVE OIL, AS NEEDED
- 5 LARGE SHRIMP, SHELLED AND DEVEINED
- HANDFUL OF CALAMARI RINGS
- 6 MUSSELS, RINSED WELL AND DEBEARDED
- HANDFUL OF BABY OCTOPUS
- ½ GARLIC CLOVE, MINCED
- SALT AND PEPPER, TO TASTE
- RED PEPPER FLAKES, TO TASTE
- SEMOLINA FLOUR, AS NEEDED
- 1 BALL OF PIZZA DOUGH
- ½ CUP PIZZA SAUCE (SEE PAGE 451)
- DRIED OREGANO, TO TASTE
- FRESH BASIL LEAVES, TO TASTE

1. Place a baking stone or steel on the middle rack of the oven and preheat the oven to the maximum temperature.
2. Coat the bottom of a skillet with olive oil and warm it over medium-high heat. Add all of the seafood and garlic, season with salt and red pepper flakes, and cook until most of the mussels have opened and the rest of the seafood is just cooked through, about 4 minutes. Remove from heat, discard any mussels that did not open, and remove the meat from those that did open.
3. Dust a work surface with semolina flour, place the dough on the work surface, and gently stretch it into a round. Cover the dough with the sauce and season with oregano and pepper.
4. Using a peel or a flat baking sheet, transfer the pizza to the heated baking implement in the oven. Bake for about 5 minutes, until the crust starts to brown. Remove the pizza, distribute the seafood over it, drizzle olive oil and sprinkle basil on top, and return the pizza to the oven. Bake for about 10 minutes, until the crust is golden brown and starting to char. Remove the pizza from the oven and let it cool slightly before slicing and serving.

Pizza Ortolana

YIELD: 1 PIZZA / **ACTIVE TIME:** 30 MINUTES / **TOTAL TIME:** 1 HOUR AND 15 MINUTES

¼ CUP MUSHROOMS, CHOPPED

SALT AND PEPPER, TO TASTE

EXTRA-VIRGIN OLIVE OIL, TO TASTE

½ BELL PEPPER, SLICED

½ SMALL EGGPLANT, SLICED

SEMOLINA FLOUR, AS NEEDED

1 BALL OF PIZZA DOUGH

⅓ CUP PIZZA SAUCE (SEE PAGE 451)

¼ ONION, SLICED

FRESH BASIL LEAVES, TO TASTE

DRIED OREGANO, TO TASTE

1. Place a baking stone or steel on the middle rack of the oven and preheat the oven to the maximum temperature. Place the mushrooms in a bowl, season with salt and pepper, and generously drizzle olive oil over them. Stir to combine and let the mixture sit for 10 minutes. Drain the mushrooms and set them aside.
2. Place the bell pepper and eggplant on an aluminum foil–lined baking sheet, season with salt and pepper, drizzle olive oil over the vegetables, and place them in the oven. Roast until they are tender and browned, about 25 minutes. Remove the vegetables from the oven and let them cool.
3. Dust a work surface with semolina flour, place the dough on the work surface, and gently stretch it into a round. Cover the dough with the sauce and top it with the mushrooms, bell pepper, eggplant, onion, and basil. Season with salt and oregano and drizzle olive oil over the pizza.
4. Using a peel or a flat baking sheet, transfer the pizza to the heated baking implement in the oven. Bake for about 15 minutes, until the crust is golden brown and starting to char. Remove the pizza from the oven and let it cool slightly before slicing and serving.

Pizza Carrettiera

YIELD: 1 PIZZA / **ACTIVE TIME:** 25 MINUTES / **TOTAL TIME:** 1 HOUR

EXTRA-VIRGIN OLIVE OIL, AS NEEDED

½ GARLIC CLOVE, MINCED

5 OZ. BROCCOLI RABE, TRIMMED

SALT AND PEPPER, TO TASTE

1 LINK OF ITALIAN SAUSAGE, CHOPPED

SEMOLINA FLOUR, AS NEEDED

1 BALL OF PIZZA DOUGH

3 OZ. FRESH MOZZARELLA CHEESE, DRAINED AND CUT INTO SHORT STRIPS

1. Place a baking stone or steel on the middle rack of the oven and preheat the oven to the maximum temperature.
2. Coat the bottom of a skillet with olive oil and warm it over medium-high heat. Add the garlic and broccoli rabe and cook, stirring frequently, until the broccoli rabe has softened, about 8 minutes. Season with salt and pepper, add the sausage, and cook until the sausage is browned, about 6 minutes, stirring as necessary. Remove the pan from heat and let the mixture cool.
3. Dust a work surface with semolina flour, place the dough on the work surface, and gently stretch it into a round. Distribute the broccoli rabe and sausage over the dough, top it with the mozzarella, and drizzle olive oil over the pizza.
4. Using a peel or a flat baking sheet, transfer the pizza to the heated baking implement in the oven. Bake for about 15 minutes, until the crust is golden brown and starting to char. Remove the pizza from the oven and let it cool slightly before slicing and serving.

Pizza Caprese

YIELD: 1 PIZZA / **ACTIVE TIME:** 15 MINUTES / **TOTAL TIME:** 45 MINUTES

SEMOLINA FLOUR, AS NEEDED

1 BALL OF PIZZA DOUGH

⅓ CUP PIZZA SAUCE (SEE PAGE 451)

4½ OZ. FRESH MOZZARELLA CHEESE, DRAINED AND SLICED

1 TOMATO, SLICED

SALT AND PEPPER, TO TASTE

DRIED OREGANO, TO TASTE

EXTRA-VIRGIN OLIVE OIL, TO TASTE

FRESH BASIL LEAVES, FOR GARNISH

1. Place a baking stone or steel on the middle rack of the oven and preheat the oven to the maximum temperature.
2. Dust a work surface with semolina flour, place the dough on the work surface, and gently stretch it into a round. Cover the dough with the sauce and top it with the mozzarella and tomato. Season with salt, pepper, and oregano and drizzle olive oil over the pizza.
3. Using a peel or a flat baking sheet, transfer the pizza to the heated baking implement in the oven. Bake for about 15 minutes, until the crust is golden brown and starting to char. Remove the pizza from the oven and let it cool slightly before garnishing with basil, slicing, and serving.

Pizza al Taglio with Wild Mushrooms & Two Cheeses

YIELD: 1 LARGE PAN PIZZA / **ACTIVE TIME:** 1 HOUR / **TOTAL TIME:** 3 HOURS AND 30 MINUTES

PIZZA AL TAGLIO DOUGH (SEE PAGE 274)

ALL-PURPOSE FLOUR, AS NEEDED

EXTRA-VIRGIN OLIVE OIL, AS NEEDED

SALT, TO TASTE

14 OZ. MUSHROOMS, SLICED

7 OZ. CACIOCAVALLO CHEESE, SLICED

13 OZ. BUFFALO MOZZARELLA CHEESE, DRAINED AND TORN

¼ CUP FRESH PARSLEY, CHOPPED

RED PEPPER FLAKES, TO TASTE

1. Once the dough has finished its initial rise, place it on a flour-dusted work surface and form it into a loose ball, making sure not to compress the core of the dough. Coat an 18 × 13–inch baking pan with olive oil, place the dough in the center, and gently stretch it into an oval. Brush the dough with olive oil, cover it with plastic wrap, and let it rest at room temperature for 1 hour. Preheat the oven to 445°F.
2. Use your hands to flatten the dough and stretch it toward the edges of the pan.
3. Drizzle olive oil over the dough and let it rest at room temperature for another 30 minutes.
4. Season the pizza with salt, place it in the oven, and bake it for 20 to 25 minutes, until the edges are slightly crispy.
5. While the pizza is in the oven, coat the bottom of a skillet with olive oil and warm it over medium-high heat. Add the mushrooms, season with salt, and cook, stirring occasionally, until they start to brown, about 10 minutes. Remove the pan from heat and let the mushrooms cool.
6. Remove the pizza from the oven and let it cool slightly. Top it with the caciocavallo, mozzarella, parsley, red pepper flakes, and sautéed mushrooms, slice, and serve.

Pizza Caprese

SEE PAGE 284

Pizza al Taglio with Bufala, Eggplant & Garlic

YIELD: 1 LARGE PAN PIZZA / **ACTIVE TIME:** 1 HOUR / **TOTAL TIME:** 3 HOURS AND 30 MINUTES

PIZZA AL TAGLIO DOUGH (SEE PAGE 274)

ALL-PURPOSE FLOUR, AS NEEDED

EXTRA-VIRGIN OLIVE OIL, AS NEEDED

14 OZ. EGGPLANT, SLICED

SALT, TO TASTE

6 GARLIC CLOVES, MINCED

RED PEPPER FLAKES, TO TASTE

13 OZ. BUFFALO MOZZARELLA CHEESE, DRAINED AND TORN

¼ CUP FRESH PARSLEY, CHOPPED

1. Once the dough has finished its initial rise, place it on a flour-dusted work surface and form it into a loose ball, making sure not to compress the core of the dough. Coat an 18 × 13–inch baking pan with olive oil, place the dough in the center, and gently stretch it into an oval. Brush the dough with olive oil, cover it with plastic wrap, and let it rest at room temperature for 1 hour. Preheat the oven to 445°F.
2. Prepare a gas or charcoal grill for medium heat (about 400°F). Place the eggplant in a mixing bowl, drizzle olive oil over it, and season with salt. Toss to combine and then place the eggplant on the grill. Cook until it is tender and charred all over, about 8 minutes, turning it occasionally. Remove the eggplant from the grill and let it cool. When the eggplant is cool enough to handle, chop it and set it aside.
3. Use your hands to flatten the dough and stretch it toward the edges of the pan.
4. Drizzle olive oil over the dough and let it rest at room temperature for another 30 minutes.
5. Season the pizza with salt, place it in the oven, and bake it for 20 to 25 minutes, until the edges are slightly crispy.
6. While the pizza is in the oven, coat the bottom of a skillet with olive oil and warm it over medium-high heat. Add the garlic, season with salt and red pepper flakes, and cook, stirring occasionally, until the garlic starts to brown, about 2 minutes. Remove the pan from heat and set the garlic aside.
7. Remove the pizza from the oven and let it cool slightly. Top it with the mozzarella, parsley, eggplant, and garlic, drizzle olive oil over the pizza, slice, and serve.

Pizza al Taglio with Prosciutto & Bocconcini

YIELD: 1 LARGE PAN PIZZA / **ACTIVE TIME:** 1 HOUR / **TOTAL TIME:** 3 HOURS AND 30 MINUTES

PIZZA AL TAGLIO DOUGH (SEE PAGE 274)

ALL-PURPOSE FLOUR, AS NEEDED

EXTRA-VIRGIN OLIVE OIL, AS NEEDED

SALT AND PEPPER, TO TASTE

11 OZ. PROSCIUTTO, SLICED THIN

½ LB. FRESH BOCCONCINI, HALVED

FRESH BASIL, FOR GARNISH

1. Once the dough has finished its initial rise, place it on a flour-dusted work surface and form it into a loose ball, making sure not to compress the core of the dough. Coat an 18 × 13–inch baking pan with olive oil, place the dough in the center, and gently stretch it into an oval. Brush the dough with olive oil, cover it with plastic wrap, and let it rest at room temperature for 1 hour. Preheat the oven to 445°F.
2. Use your hands to flatten the dough and stretch it toward the edges of the pan.
3. Drizzle olive oil over the dough and let it rest at room temperature for another 30 minutes.
4. Season the pizza with salt, place it in the oven, and bake it for 20 to 25 minutes, until the edges are slightly crispy.
5. Remove the pizza from the oven and let it cool slightly. Top it with the prosciutto and bocconcini, drizzle olive oil over the top, and season with pepper. Garnish the pizza with basil, slice, and serve.

Pizza alla Pala with Prosciutto & Endive

YIELD: 1 PIZZA ALLA PALA / **ACTIVE TIME:** 25 MINUTES / **TOTAL TIME:** 3 HOURS

½ LB. ENDIVE

EXTRA-VIRGIN OLIVE OIL, TO TASTE

SALT AND PEPPER, TO TASTE

1 BALL OF PIZZA ALLA PALA DOUGH (SEE PAGE 275)

9 OZ. BUFFALO MOZZARELLA CHEESE, DRAINED AND TORN

7 OZ. PROSCIUTTO, SLICED

1. Preheat the oven to 480°F and place a baking stone or steel in the oven as it warms.
2. Prepare a gas or charcoal grill for medium-high heat (about 450°F). Place the endive in a mixing bowl, drizzle olive oil over it, and season with salt and pepper. Toss to combine and place the endive on the grill. Cook until it is charred all over, about 5 minutes, turning it as necessary. Remove the endive from the grill, let it cool slightly, and chop it. Set the endive aside.
3. Generously drizzle olive oil over the dough and season it with salt.
4. Using a peel or a flat baking sheet, transfer the pizza to the heated baking implement in the oven. Bake for 10 to 15 minutes, until the crust is golden brown and starting to char. Remove the pizza from the oven and distribute the endive over it. Drizzle olive oil over the endive, top it with the mozzarella and prosciutto, slice, and serve.

Pizza alla Pala with Zucchini Blossoms, Anchovies & Burrata

YIELD: 1 PIZZA ALLA PALA / **ACTIVE TIME:** 25 MINUTES / **TOTAL TIME:** 3 HOURS

EXTRA-VIRGIN OLIVE OIL, AS NEEDED

7 OZ. ZUCCHINI BLOSSOMS, STAMENS REMOVED

SALT, TO TASTE

1 BALL OF PIZZA ALLA PALA DOUGH (SEE PAGE 275)

3 OZ. ANCHOVIES, HALVED

9 OZ. BURRATA CHEESE, TORN

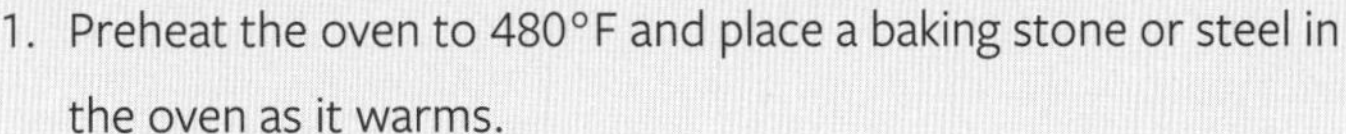

1. Preheat the oven to 480°F and place a baking stone or steel in the oven as it warms.
2. Coat a large skillet with olive oil and warm it over medium heat. Add the zucchini blossoms, season them with salt, and cook, stirring occasionally, until they start to wilt, 2 to 3 minutes. Remove the pan from heat and set the zucchini blossoms aside.
3. Generously drizzle olive oil over the dough and season it with salt.
4. Using a peel or a flat baking sheet, transfer the pizza to the heated baking implement in the oven. Bake for 10 to 15 minutes, until the crust is golden brown and starting to char. Remove the pizza from the oven, distribute the zucchini blossoms and anchovies over the pizza, and top it with the burrata. Drizzle olive oil over the pizza, slice, and serve.

Quick Focaccia Dough

YIELD: DOUGH FOR 1 FOCACCIA / **ACTIVE TIME:** 15 MINUTES / **TOTAL TIME:** 1 HOUR AND 30 MINUTES

I2 CUPS PLUS 1 TABLESPOON (454 G) WARM WATER (105°F)

3½ TEASPOONS (10.5 G) ACTIVE DRY YEAST

4⅙ CUPS (500 G) BREAD FLOUR

1⅔ CUPS (198 G) ALL-PURPOSE FLOUR, PLUS MORE AS NEEDED

2 TEASPOONS (8 G) SUGAR

5 TABLESPOONS (65 G) EXTRA-VIRGIN OLIVE OIL, PLUS MORE AS NEEDED

2½ TEASPOONS (13 G) TABLE SALT

1. Place the water and yeast in a bowl, gently stir to combine, and let the mixture sit until it starts to foam, about 10 minutes.
2. In a large bowl, combine the flours, sugar, and yeast mixture and work the mixture until it just holds together. Place the dough on a flour-dusted work surface and knead the dough until it is compact, smooth, and elastic.
3. Add the olive oil and salt and knead until the dough is developed, elastic, and extensible, about 5 minutes. Coat a large, clean bowl with olive oil, shape the dough into a ball, and place it in the bowl. Cover the bowl with plastic wrap, place the dough in a naturally warm spot, and let it rest until it has doubled in size, about 1 hour.
4. After 1 hour, the dough can be stretched and flavored as desired. It will need another 30 minutes to 1 hour for the second rise before baking.

Low-Hydration Focaccia Dough

YIELD: DOUGH FOR 1 LARGE FOCACCIA / **ACTIVE TIME:** 30 MINUTES / **TOTAL TIME:** 27 HOURS

1½ CUPS PLUS 1½ TEASPOONS (368.5 G) WARM WATER (105°F)

1 (HEAPING) TEASPOON (3.2 G) ACTIVE DRY YEAST

2½ CUPS (300 G) BREAD FLOUR

2½ CUPS (300 G) ALL-PURPOSE FLOUR, PLUS MORE AS NEEDED

2⅔ TEASPOONS (14⅔ G) TABLE SALT

2 TABLESPOONS (26 G) EXTRA-VIRGIN OLIVE OIL, PLUS MORE AS NEEDED

1. Place the water and yeast in a bowl, gently stir to combine, and let the mixture sit until it starts to foam, about 10 minutes.
2. In a large bowl, combine the flours and yeast mixture. Work the mixture until it just comes together as a dough. Place the dough on a flour-dusted work surface and knead until it is compact, smooth, and elastic.
3. Add the salt and knead until the dough is developed, elastic, and extensible, about 5 minutes. Add the olive oil and knead until it has been incorporated. Coat a large, clean bowl with olive oil, shape the dough into a ball, and place it in the bowl. Cover the bowl with plastic wrap and let it rest in the refrigerator for 24 hours.
4. Remove the dough from the refrigerator and let it warm to room temperature before making focaccia.

High-Hydration Focaccia Dough

YIELD: DOUGH FOR 1 LARGE FOCACCIA / **ACTIVE TIME:** 30 MINUTES / **TOTAL TIME:** 27 HOURS

2 CUPS PLUS 2 TEASPOONS (490 G) WARM WATER (105°F)

1⅔ TEASPOONS (5 G) ACTIVE DRY YEAST

4⅙ CUPS (500 G) BREAD FLOUR OR "00" FLOUR

1⅔ CUPS (198 G) ALL-PURPOSE FLOUR, PLUS MORE AS NEEDED

1 TABLESPOON (17 G) TABLE SALT

2 TABLESPOONS (26 G) EXTRA-VIRGIN OLIVE OIL, PLUS MORE AS NEEDED

1. Place the water and yeast in a bowl, gently stir to combine, and let the mixture sit until it starts to foam, about 10 minutes.
2. In a large bowl, combine the flours and yeast mixture. Work the mixture until it just comes together as a dough. Place the dough on a flour-dusted work surface and knead until it is compact, smooth, and elastic.
3. Add the salt and knead until the dough is developed, elastic, and extensible, about 5 minutes. Add the olive oil and knead until it has been incorporated. Coat a large, clean bowl with olive oil, shape the dough into a ball, and place it in the bowl. Cover the bowl with plastic wrap and let it rest in the refrigerator for 24 hours.
4. Remove the dough from the refrigerator and let it warm to room temperature before making focaccia.

Classic Focaccia Dough

YIELD: DOUGH FOR 1 LARGE FOCACCIA / **ACTIVE TIME:** 30 MINUTES / **TOTAL TIME:** 5 HOURS

2 CUPS (482 G) WARM WATER (105°F)

¾ TEASPOON (2.2 G) ACTIVE DRY YEAST

5 CUPS (595 G) BREAD FLOUR

⅔ CUP (85 G) ALL-PURPOSE FLOUR, PLUS MORE AS NEEDED

2 TABLESPOONS (26 G) EXTRA-VIRGIN OLIVE OIL, PLUS MORE AS NEEDED

2 TEASPOONS (11 G) TABLE SALT

1. Place the water and yeast in a bowl, gently stir to combine, and let the mixture sit until it starts to foam, about 10 minutes.
2. In a large bowl, combine the flours and yeast mixture. Work the mixture until it just comes together. Place the dough on a flour-dusted work surface and knead the dough until it is compact, smooth, and elastic.
3. Add the olive oil and salt and knead the dough until it is developed, elastic, and extensible, about 5 minutes. Coat a large, clean bowl with olive oil, shape the dough into a ball, and place it in the bowl. Cover the bowl with plastic wrap, place the dough in a naturally warm spot, and let it rest until it has doubled in size, 3 to 4 hours.
4. Stretch and flavor the dough as desired. It will need another 1½ to 2 hours for the second rise before baking. The extra rising time can only benefit the dough, as the relatively low amount of yeast in this recipe means the risk of overproofing is small.

Pizza di Granturco

YIELD: 8 SMALL FOCACCIA / **ACTIVE TIME:** 10 MINUTES / **TOTAL TIME:** 45 MINUTES

3⅓ CUPS (500 G) CORNMEAL, PLUS MORE AS NEEDED

1 TEASPOON (5.5 G) TABLE SALT

3¾ CUPS (900 ML) BOILING WATER

1. Preheat the oven to 430°F and place a baking stone or steel on the middle rack of the oven as it warms.
2. In a large bowl, combine the cornmeal and salt. Using a wooden spoon, gradually incorporate the boiling water and work the mixture until it just comes together as a dough. Place the dough on a cornmeal-dusted work surface and knead until it is smooth. Divide the dough into eight pieces, shape them into rounds, and flatten them into rather thick disks.
3. Place the disks directly on the heated baking implement and bake for about 25 minutes, until the tops are crispy. Remove the focaccia from the oven and let them cool slightly before serving.

Pizz'onta

YIELD: 12 SMALL FOCACCIA / **ACTIVE TIME:** 30 MINUTES / **TOTAL TIME:** 4 HOURS

1 CUP (241 ML) WATER

1¼ TEASPOONS (3.7 G) ACTIVE DRY YEAST

3¼ CUPS (397 G) BREAD FLOUR, PLUS MORE AS NEEDED

2 TEASPOONS (8 G) SUGAR

1 TEASPOON (6 G) TABLE SALT, PLUS MORE TO TASTE

2 TABLESPOONS (26 G) EXTRA-VIRGIN OLIVE OIL, PLUS MORE AS NEEDED

1. Warm 3½ tablespoons of the water until it is 105°F. Add the yeast and water to a bowl and gently stir to combine. Let the mixture sit until it starts to foam, about 10 minutes.
2. In a large bowl, combine the flour, yeast mixture, remaining water, and the sugar. Work the mixture until it just comes together as a dough. If kneading by hand, place the dough on a flour-dusted work surface. Work the dough until it is compact, smooth, and elastic.
3. Add the salt and olive oil and work the dough until it is developed, elastic, and extensible, about 5 minutes. Coat a large, clean bowl with olive oil, shape the dough into a ball, and place it in the bowl. Cover the bowl with plastic wrap, place it in a naturally warm spot, and let it rest until it has doubled in size, about 2 hours.
4. Place the dough on a flour-dusted work surface, divide it into 12 pieces, and shape them into rounds, taking care not to overwork the dough. Cover the dough with a kitchen towel and let it rest for 30 minutes.
5. Add olive oil to a Dutch oven until it is approximately 2 inches deep and warm it to 350°F. Flatten the rounds and, working in batches, fry them until they are golden brown on both sides, about 4 minutes.
6. Transfer the fried focaccia to a paper towel–lined plate to drain and season them with salt before serving.

Pizza Assettata

YIELD: 1 LARGE FOCACCIA / **ACTIVE TIME:** 25 MINUTES / **TOTAL TIME:** 1 HOUR AND 15 MINUTES

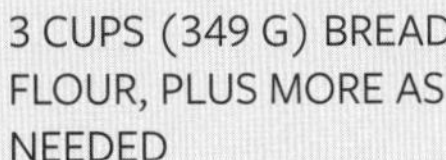

3 CUPS (349 G) BREAD FLOUR, PLUS MORE AS NEEDED

3 CUPS (349 G) FINELY GROUND DURUM WHEAT FLOUR

2 TEASPOONS (11 G) TABLE SALT

2 CUPS (471 G) WARM WATER (105°F)

1¾ OZ. (50 G) EXTRA-VIRGIN OLIVE OIL, PLUS MORE AS NEEDED

1 TABLESPOON FENNEL SEEDS

1 TEASPOON RED PEPPER FLAKES

COARSE SEA SALT, FOR TOPPING

1. In a large bowl, combine the flours and table salt. Gradually incorporate the water and work the mixture with your hands until it just comes together as a dough. Add the olive oil, fennel seeds, and red pepper flakes and work the dough until they have been incorporated.
2. If kneading by hand, place the dough on a flour-dusted work surface. Work it until it is smooth, compact, and elastic, about 10 minutes. Shape the dough into a ball, cover it with plastic wrap, and let it rest at room temperature for 30 minutes.
3. Preheat the oven to 430°F. Coat an 18 × 13–inch baking pan with olive oil. Place the dough on a flour-dusted work surface and roll it out into a rectangle that will fit in the pan. Place the dough in the pan, drizzle olive oil over the dough, and sprinkle coarse salt on top.
4. Place the focaccia in the oven and bake for 20 to 25 minutes, until it is a light golden brown. Remove the focaccia from the oven and let it cool slightly before serving.

Montanare

YIELD: 20 MINIATURE FOCACCIA / **ACTIVE TIME:** 45 MINUTES / **TOTAL TIME:** 2 HOURS AND 45 MINUTES

½ BATCH OF NEAPOLITAN PIZZA DOUGH (SEE PAGE 272)

ALL-PURPOSE FLOUR, AS NEEDED

EXTRA-VIRGIN OLIVE OIL, AS NEEDED

1¾ CUPS (748 G) SUGO AL BASILICO (SEE PAGE 447), WARMED, FOR TOPPING

PECORINO CHEESE, GRATED, FOR TOPPING

FRESH BASIL, FOR TOPPING

MOZZARELLA CHEESE, SLICED, FOR TOPPING (OPTIONAL)

1. Place the dough on a flour-dusted work surface, divide it into 20 pieces, and shape each piece into a ball. Coat a piece of plastic wrap with olive oil, place it over the balls of dough, and let them rest at room temperature until they have doubled in size, about 2 hours.
2. Add olive oil to a deep skillet until it is about 1 inch deep and warm it to 350°F. Flatten the balls of dough. Working in batches of three, gently slip them into the hot oil and cook until they are golden brown, turning them frequently, about 5 minutes. Place the cooked focaccia on paper towel–lined plates to drain.
3. When all of the focaccia have been cooked, top them with the sauce, pecorino, basil, and, if desired, mozzarella. Drizzle olive oil over the focaccia and serve.

Parigina

YIELD: 1 LARGE FOCACCIA / **ACTIVE TIME:** 20 MINUTES / **TOTAL TIME:** 3 HOURS AND 30 MINUTES

EXTRA-VIRGIN OLIVE OIL, AS NEEDED

LOW-HYDRATION FOCACCIA DOUGH (SEE PAGE 292)

23 OZ. CANNED WHOLE PEELED TOMATOES, DRAINED AND CRUSHED BY HAND

SALT, TO TASTE

7 OZ. HAM, SLICED

14 OZ. CACIOCAVALLO CHEESE OR LOW-MOISTURE MOZZARELLA CHEESE, SLICED THIN

1 SHEET OF FROZEN PUFF PASTRY, THAWED

2 EGG YOLKS

¼ CUP HEAVY CREAM

1. Coat an 18 x 13–inch baking sheet with olive oil, place the dough on it, and stretch the dough toward the edges of the pan, taking care not to tear it. Cover the dough with olive oil–coated plastic wrap and let it rest at room temperature for 2 hours. As the dough rests, stretch it toward the edges of the pan every 20 minutes until it covers the entire pan.
2. Preheat the oven to 390°F. Spread the tomatoes over the dough, making sure to leave a 1-inch border of dough at the edges. Season the tomatoes with salt. Cover the tomatoes with a layer of ham and top this with a layer of cheese. Cover the focaccia with the puff pastry, beat the egg yolks and cream together until combined, and brush the puff pastry with the egg wash.
3. Place the focaccia in the oven and bake until it is golden brown, 30 to 35 minutes.
4. Remove the focaccia from the oven and let it cool slightly before cutting it into squares and serving.

Panuozzo

YIELD: 6 SMALL FOCACCIA / **ACTIVE TIME:** 20 MINUTES / **TOTAL TIME:** 3 HOURS AND 30 MINUTES

HIGH-HYDRATION FOCACCIA DOUGH (SEE PAGE 292)

ALL-PURPOSE FLOUR, AS NEEDED

EXTRA-VIRGIN OLIVE OIL, TO TASTE

¾ LB. PANCETTA OR BACON, SLICED THIN

26 OZ. FRESH MOZZARELLA CHEESE, DRAINED AND SLICED

2 TOMATOES, SLICED

12 LETTUCE LEAVES

RED PEPPER FLAKES, TO TASTE

SALT, TO TASTE

1. Place the dough on a flour-dusted work surface and cut it into six pieces. Stretch the pieces of dough into 8- to 10-inch-long ovals, place them on pieces of flour-dusted parchment paper, and cover them with kitchen towels or plastic wrap coated with olive oil. Let the dough rest in a naturally warm spot for 2 to 3 hours.
2. Preheat the oven to 410°F and place a baking stone or steel on the middle rack of the oven as it warms.
3. Using a peel or a flat baking sheet, slide the focaccia onto the heated baking implement and bake for 15 to 20 minutes, until the crust is set. Remove the focaccia from the oven and let them cool before cutting a slit along the equator of each focaccia.
4. Fill each focaccia with an equal amount of the pancetta, mozzarella, tomatoes, and lettuce. Sprinkle red pepper flakes and salt over the filling and drizzle olive oil over it.
5. Return the focaccia to the oven and bake for about 10 minutes, until the pancetta or bacon looks cooked through and the mozzarella has melted. Remove the focaccia from the oven and let them cool briefly before serving.

Grupariata

YIELD: 1 FOCACCIA / **ACTIVE TIME:** 30 MINUTES / **TOTAL TIME:** 3 HOURS AND 30 MINUTES

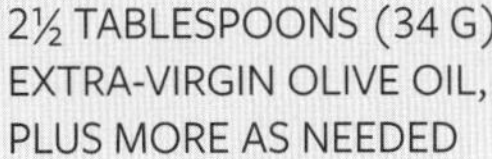

2½ TABLESPOONS (34 G) EXTRA-VIRGIN OLIVE OIL, PLUS MORE AS NEEDED

1¾ CUPS (397 G) WARM WATER (105°F)

2½ TEASPOONS (7.5 G) ACTIVE DRY YEAST

4⅙ CUPS (500 G) BREAD FLOUR

2½ CUPS (300 G) "00" FLOUR

1 LB. (454 G) CANNED WHOLE PEELED TOMATOES, DRAINED AND CHOPPED

2 TABLESPOONS (16 G) CHILI POWDER

2½ TEASPOONS (13 G) TABLE SALT, PLUS MORE TO TASTE

2 GARLIC CLOVES, MINCED

FRESH OREGANO, FINELY CHOPPED, TO TASTE

ANCHOVIES IN OLIVE OIL, DRAINED AND TORN, TO TASTE

1 FRESH TOMATO, SLICED

FRESH ROSEMARY, TO TASTE

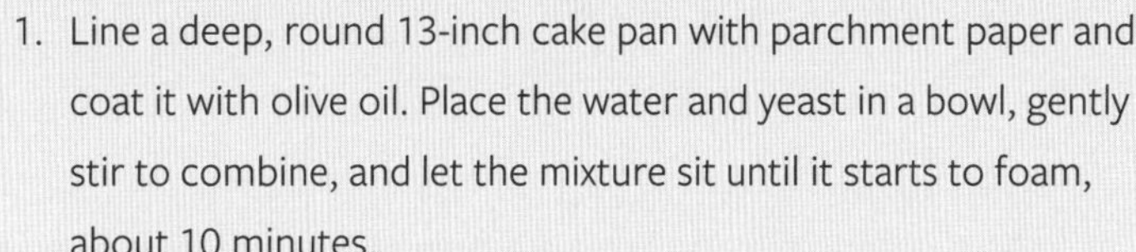

1. Line a deep, round 13-inch cake pan with parchment paper and coat it with olive oil. Place the water and yeast in a bowl, gently stir to combine, and let the mixture sit until it starts to foam, about 10 minutes.
2. In a large bowl, combine the flours, peeled tomatoes, chili powder, olive oil, salt, and yeast mixture and work the mixture until it comes together as a smooth, developed dough.
3. Incorporate the garlic and a few pinches of oregano into the dough and transfer it into the cake pan. Cover the pan with a kitchen towel and let the dough rest at room temperature until it has doubled in size, about 2½ hours.
4. Preheat the oven to 390°F. Cover the focaccia with anchovies and the fresh tomato slices, pressing down on them so that they are embedded deep within the dough. Sprinkle rosemary, additional oregano, and salt over the dough and drizzle some olive oil over the top.
5. Place the focaccia in the oven and bake for 30 to 35 minutes, until it is golden brown. Remove the focaccia from the oven and let it cool slightly before serving.

Pizza Scima

YIELD: 1 LARGE FOCACCIA / **ACTIVE TIME:** 25 MINUTES / **TOTAL TIME:** 1 HOUR AND 15 MINUTES

4⅙ CUPS (500 G) BREAD FLOUR

1⅔ CUPS (198 G) ALL-PURPOSE FLOUR, PLUS MORE AS NEEDED

¼ TEASPOON (1.5 G) BAKING SODA

2 TEASPOONS (11 G) TABLE SALT

6 TABLESPOONS (79 G) EXTRA-VIRGIN OLIVE OIL

6 TABLESPOONS (79 ML) WHITE WINE

¾ CUP (179 ML) WATER

1. In a large bowl, combine the flours, baking soda, and salt. Incorporate the olive oil, wine, and water gradually and work the mixture until it just holds together. Place the dough on a flour-dusted work surface and knead until it is compact, smooth, and elastic. Shape the dough into a ball, cover it with plastic wrap, and let it rest at room temperature for 30 minutes.
2. Preheat the oven to 430°F and place a baking stone or steel on the middle rack of the oven as it warms.
3. Place the dough on a flour-dusted work surface. Using a rolling pin, roll the dough out until it is approximately ¾ inch thick. Place the dough on a piece of parchment paper and make deep cuts in it, working in a crosshatch pattern and taking care not to cut all the way through.
4. Using a peel or flat baking sheet, transfer the dough onto the heated baking implement and bake for 20 to 30 minutes, until it is golden brown. Remove the focaccia from the oven and let it cool slightly before serving.

Focaccia di Altamura

YIELD: 2 SMALL FOCACCIA / **ACTIVE TIME:** 30 MINUTES / **TOTAL TIME:** 4 HOURS

1¾ CUPS (397 ML) WARM WATER (105°F)

2 TEASPOONS (6 G) ACTIVE DRY YEAST

5 CUPS (598 G) FINELY GROUND DURUM WHEAT FLOUR, PLUS MORE AS NEEDED

2½ TEASPOONS (13.7 G) TABLE SALT, PLUS MORE TO TASTE

EXTRA-VIRGIN OLIVE OIL, AS NEEDED

1 LARGE ONION, SLICED

2 VERY RIPE TOMATOES, SLICED

FRESH OREGANO, FINELY CHOPPED, TO TASTE

1. Place the water and yeast in a bowl, gently stir to combine, and let the mixture sit until it starts to foam, about 10 minutes.
2. In a large bowl, combine the flour and yeast mixture and work the mixture until it just holds together. If kneading by hand, place the dough on a flour-dusted work surface. Work it until it is compact, smooth, and elastic.
3. Add the salt and work the dough until it is developed, elastic, and extensible, about 5 minutes. Coat a large, clean bowl with olive oil, shape the dough into a ball, and place it in the bowl. Cover the bowl with plastic wrap, place it in a naturally warm spot, and let it rest until it has doubled in size, about 2 hours.
4. Generously coat two 10-inch cast-iron skillets or round cake pans with olive oil. Place the dough on a flour-dusted work surface and divide it in half. Place a piece of dough in each pan and spread it to the edge, making sure not to press down too hard on the dough and deflate the focaccia. Let the dough rest at room temperature for 1 hour.
5. Preheat the oven to the maximum temperature. Top the focaccia with the onion, press the tomatoes into the dough, season with salt and oregano, and drizzle olive oil over the focaccia. Place the pans directly on the bottom of the oven and bake for 10 minutes.
6. Transfer the pans to the middle rack and bake until the edges look brown and crunchy, 5 to 7 more minutes.
7. Remove the focaccia from the oven and let them cool slightly before serving.

Puddica Salentina

YIELD: 2 SMALL FOCACCIA / **ACTIVE TIME:** 30 MINUTES / **TOTAL TIME:** 4 HOURS

1¾ CUPS (397 ML) WATER

2 TEASPOONS (6 G) ACTIVE DRY YEAST

3⅓ CUPS (397 G) BREAD FLOUR

1⅔ CUPS (198 G) ALL-PURPOSE FLOUR, PLUS MORE AS NEEDED

2½ TEASPOONS (15 G) TABLE SALT, PLUS MORE TO TASTE

EXTRA-VIRGIN OLIVE OIL, AS NEEDED

CAPERS, DRAINED AND RINSED, TO TASTE

2 VERY RIPE TOMATOES, CHOPPED

FRESH OREGANO, CHOPPED, TO TASTE

1. Warm 3½ tablespoons of the water until it is 105°F. Add the yeast and water to a bowl and gently stir to combine. Let the mixture sit until it starts to foam, about 10 minutes.
2. In a large bowl, combine the flours, yeast mixture, and remaining water and work the mixture until it comes together as a dough. If kneading by hand, place the dough on a flour-dusted work surface. Work it until it is compact, smooth, and elastic.
3. Add the salt and work the dough until it is developed, elastic, and extensible, about 5 minutes. Coat a large, clean bowl with olive oil, shape the dough into a ball, and place it in the bowl. Cover the bowl with plastic wrap, place it in a naturally warm spot, and let it rest until it has doubled in size, about 2 hours.
4. Generously coat two 10-inch cast-iron skillets or round cake pans with olive oil. Place the dough on a flour-dusted work surface and divide it in half. Place a piece of dough in each pan and spread it to the edge, making sure not to press down too hard on the dough and deflate it. Let the dough rest at room temperature for 1 hour.
5. Preheat the oven to the maximum temperature. Top the focaccia with capers, press the tomatoes into the dough, season with salt and oregano, and drizzle olive oil over the focaccia. Place the pans directly on the bottom of the oven and bake for 10 minutes.
6. Transfer the pans to the middle rack and bake until the edges look brown and crunchy, 5 to 7 more minutes.
7. Remove the focaccia from the oven and let them cool slightly before serving.

Cavicione

YIELD: 1 MEDIUM FOCACCIA / **ACTIVE TIME:** 45 MINUTES / **TOTAL TIME:** 5 HOURS

1 CUP PLUS 2 TEASPOONS (249 G) WARM WATER (105°F), PLUS MORE AS NEEDED

2 TEASPOONS (6 G) ACTIVE DRY YEAST

4⅙ CUPS (500 G) ALL-PURPOSE FLOUR, PLUS MORE AS NEEDED

1½ TEASPOONS (8.2 G) TABLE SALT, PLUS MORE TO TASTE

EXTRA-VIRGIN OLIVE OIL, AS NEEDED

1 LB. SPRING ONIONS, CHOPPED

5 OZ. PITTED BLACK OLIVES

4 OZ. ANCHOVIES IN OLIVE OIL, DRAINED

1. Place the water and yeast in a bowl, gently stir to combine, and let the mixture sit until it starts to foam, about 10 minutes.
2. In a large bowl, combine the flour and yeast mixture and work the mixture until it just holds together. Place the dough on a flour-dusted work surface and knead until it is compact, smooth, and elastic.
3. Add the salt and knead until the dough is smooth, elastic, and extensible. Coat a large, clean bowl with olive oil, shape the dough into a ball, and place it in the bowl. Cover the bowl with plastic wrap, place it in a naturally warm spot, and let it rest until it has doubled in size, about 2 hours.
4. Coat the bottom of a skillet with olive oil and warm it over medium-high heat. Add the onions and cook, stirring occasionally, until they are tender and starting to brown, about 10 minutes. Remove the pan from heat and let the onions cool completely.
5. Coat a 10-inch cast-iron skillet or round cake pan with olive oil. Place the dough on a flour-dusted work surface and divide it into two pieces, making sure one piece is slightly bigger than the other. Roll out that piece into a disk that is slightly larger than the pan. Place the disk in the pan and top it with the onions, olives, and anchovies.
6. Roll out the second piece of dough so that it will fit within the pan, place it over the filling, and crimp the edge to seal the focaccia. Brush the top of the focaccia with olive oil and use a fork to poke holes in it. Coat a piece of plastic wrap with olive oil, place it over the pan, and let the focaccia rest for 1 hour.
7. Preheat the oven to 430°F. Place the focaccia in the oven and bake for 20 minutes. Reduce the temperature to 350°F and bake for another 20 to 25 minutes, until the focaccia is golden brown on the top and bottom.
8. Remove the focaccia from the oven and let it cool slightly before serving.

Focaccia Barese

YIELD: 2 SMALL FOCACCIA / **ACTIVE TIME:** 30 MINUTES / **TOTAL TIME:** 4 HOURS

1¾ CUPS (397 ML) WATER

2 TEASPOONS (6 G) ACTIVE DRY YEAST

3⅓ CUPS (397 G) BREAD FLOUR, PLUS MORE AS NEEDED

1⅔ CUPS (198 G) FINELY GROUND DURUM WHEAT FLOUR

1 POTATO, BOILED, PEELED, AND MASHED

2½ TEASPOONS (15 G) TABLE SALT, PLUS MORE TO TASTE

EXTRA-VIRGIN OLIVE OIL, AS NEEDED

2 VERY RIPE TOMATOES, CHOPPED

GREEN OLIVES, PITTED AND CHOPPED, TO TASTE

FRESH OREGANO, CHOPPED, TO TASTE

1. Warm 3½ tablespoons of the water until it is 105°F. Add the yeast and water to a bowl and gently stir to combine. Let the mixture sit until it starts to foam, about 10 minutes.
2. In a large bowl, combine the flours, potato, yeast mixture, and remaining water. Work the mixture until it comes together as a dough. If kneading by hand, place the dough on a flour-dusted work surface. Work it until it is compact, smooth, and elastic.
3. Add the salt and work the dough until it is developed, elastic, and extensible, about 5 minutes. Coat a large, clean bowl with olive oil, shape the dough into a ball, and place it in the bowl. Cover the bowl with plastic wrap, place it in a naturally warm spot, and let it rest until it has doubled in size, about 2 hours.
4. Generously coat two 10-inch cast-iron skillets or round cake pans with olive oil. Place the dough on a flour-dusted work surface and divide it in half. Place a piece of dough in each pan and spread it to the edge, making sure not to press down too hard on the dough and deflate it. Let the dough rest in a naturally warm spot for 1 hour.
5. Preheat the oven to the maximum temperature. Top the focaccia with the tomatoes, olives, and oregano, season it with salt, and drizzle olive oil over the top. Place the pans directly on the bottom of the oven and bake for 10 minutes.
6. Transfer the pans to the middle rack and bake until the edges of the focaccia look brown and crunchy, 5 to 7 more minutes.
7. Remove the focaccia from the oven and let them cool slightly before serving.

Sceblasti & Pizzo Leccese

YIELD: 1 LARGE FOCACCIA / **ACTIVE TIME:** 45 MINUTES / **TOTAL TIME:** 3 HOURS

1¾ CUPS (420 ML) WARM WATER (105°F)

2 TEASPOONS (6 G) ACTIVE DRY YEAST

5 CUPS (600 G) ALL-PURPOSE FLOUR, PLUS MORE AS NEEDED

2½ TEASPOONS (13.7 G) TABLE SALT, PLUS MORE TO TASTE

6 TABLESPOONS (79 G) EXTRA-VIRGIN OLIVE OIL, PLUS MORE AS NEEDED

2 MEDIUM ONIONS, SLICED

7 OZ. CHERRY TOMATOES

1 ZUCCHINI (OMIT IF MAKING PIZZO LECCESE)

7 OZ. COOKED FRESH PUMPKIN (OMIT IF MAKING PIZZO LECCESE)

7 OZ. PITTED BLACK OLIVES

½ CUP PIZZA SAUCE (SEE PAGE 451)

FRESH OREGANO, FINELY CHOPPED, TO TASTE

RED PEPPER FLAKES, TO TASTE

1. Place the water and yeast in a bowl, gently stir to combine, and let the mixture sit until it starts to foam, about 10 minutes.
2. In a large bowl, combine the flour and yeast mixture and work the mixture until it just comes together as a dough. Place the dough on a flour-dusted work surface and knead until it is compact, smooth, and elastic.
3. Add the salt and knead until the dough is smooth, elastic, and extensible. Coat a large, clean bowl with olive oil, shape the dough into a ball, and place it in the bowl. Cover the bowl with plastic wrap, place it in a naturally warm spot, and let it rest until it has doubled in size, about 2 hours.
4. Preheat the oven to the maximum temperature and place a baking stone or steel on the middle rack of the oven as it warms. While the dough is rising, mince all of the vegetables and combine them with the sauce, olive oil, salt, oregano, and, if desired, red pepper flakes.
5. Flatten the dough and spread the vegetables over it, folding the dough over the vegetables and working with your hands to incorporate them into the dough. Using a peel or flat baking sheet, transfer the focaccia onto the heated baking implement. Bake the focaccia until it is golden brown, about 20 minutes.
6. Remove the focaccia from the oven and let it cool briefly before serving.

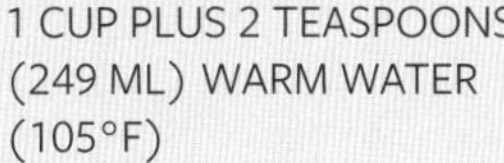

Calzone Pugliese

YIELD: 1 MEDIUM FOCACCIA / **ACTIVE TIME:** 45 MINUTES / **TOTAL TIME:** 4 HOURS

1 CUP PLUS 2 TEASPOONS (249 ML) WARM WATER (105°F)

2 TEASPOONS (6 G) ACTIVE DRY YEAST

4⅙ CUPS (500 G) ALL-PURPOSE FLOUR, PLUS MORE AS NEEDED

1½ TEASPOONS (8.2 G) TABLE SALT, PLUS MORE TO TASTE

EXTRA-VIRGIN OLIVE OIL, AS NEEDED

3 ONIONS, SLICED

5 OZ. CHERRY TOMATOES

5 OZ. PITTED BLACK OLIVES

2 TO 3 ANCHOVIES, DRAINED

2 TABLESPOONS CAPERS IN BRINE, DRAINED AND RINSED

1. Place the water and yeast in a bowl, gently stir to combine, and let the mixture sit until it starts to foam, about 10 minutes.
2. In a large bowl, combine the flour and yeast mixture and work the mixture until it just holds together. Place the dough on a flour-dusted work surface and knead until it is compact, smooth, and elastic.
3. Add the salt and knead until the dough is smooth, elastic, and extensible. Coat a large, clean bowl with olive oil, shape the dough into a ball, and place it in the bowl. Cover the bowl with plastic wrap, place it in a naturally warm spot, and let it rest until it has doubled in size, about 2 hours.
4. Coat the bottom of a skillet with olive oil and warm it over medium-high heat. Add the onions and cook, stirring occasionally, until they are translucent, about 3 minutes. Add the cherry tomatoes and cook until they start to collapse, about 10 minutes. Remove the pan from heat and let the mixture cool completely.
5. Coat a 10-inch cast-iron skillet or round cake pan with olive oil. Place the dough on a flour-dusted work surface and divide it into two pieces, making sure one piece is slightly larger than the other. Roll out that piece into a disk that is slightly larger than the pan. Place the disk in the pan, top it with the onion-and-tomato mixture, and distribute the olives, anchovies, and capers over the top.
6. Roll out the second piece of dough so that it will fit within the pan, place it over the filling, and crimp the edge to seal the focaccia. Brush the top of the focaccia with olive oil and use a fork to poke holes in it. Coat a piece of plastic wrap with olive oil, place it over the pan, and let the focaccia rest for 1 hour.
7. Preheat the oven to 430°F. Place the focaccia in the oven and bake for 20 minutes. Reduce the temperature to 350°F and bake for another 20 to 25 minutes, until the focaccia is golden brown on the top and bottom.
8. Remove the focaccia from the oven and let it cool slightly before serving.

Vastedda con Sambuco

YIELD: 1 MEDIUM FOCACCIA / **ACTIVE TIME:** 30 MINUTES / **TOTAL TIME:** 4 HOURS

1½ CUPS (350 G) WARM WATER (105°F)

2½ TEASPOONS (7.5 G) ACTIVE DRY YEAST

5 CUPS (600 G) ALL-PURPOSE FLOUR, PLUS MORE AS NEEDED

7 TABLESPOONS (100 G) LARD OR BUTTER

ELDERFLOWERS, FRESH OR DRIED, TO TASTE

1½ TEASPOONS (8.2 G) TABLE SALT

5 EGGS

EXTRA-VIRGIN OLIVE OIL, AS NEEDED

1 LB. SALAMI, SLICED

1 LB. CACIOCAVALLO OR TUMA CHEESE, CUBED

1. Place the water and yeast in a bowl, gently stir to combine, and let the mixture sit until it starts to foam, about 10 minutes.
2. In a large bowl, combine the flour, lard or butter, a handful of elderflowers, and the yeast mixture and work the mixture until it just comes together as a dough. Place the dough on a flour-dusted work surface and knead until it is compact, smooth, and elastic.
3. Add the salt and eggs and knead until the dough is smooth, elastic, and extensible. Coat a large, clean bowl with olive oil, shape the dough into a ball, and place it in the bowl. Cover the bowl with plastic wrap, place it in a naturally warm spot, and let it rest until it has doubled in size, about 2 hours.
4. Coat a 10-inch cast-iron skillet or round cake pan with olive oil. Place the dough on a flour-dusted work surface and divide it into two pieces, making sure one piece is slightly larger than the other. Roll out that piece into a round that is slightly larger than the pan. Place the round in the pan and layer the salami and caciocavallo or tuma on top.
5. Roll out the second piece of dough so that it will fit within the pan, place it over the filling, and crimp the edge to seal the focaccia. Brush the top of the focaccia with olive oil and use a fork to poke holes in it. Coat a piece of plastic wrap with olive oil, place it over the pan, and let the focaccia rest for 1 hour.
6. Preheat the oven to 390°F. Sprinkle elderflowers over the focaccia and drizzle olive oil over the top. Place the focaccia in the oven and bake for 30 to 35 minutes, until it is golden brown and crispy.
7. Remove the focaccia from the oven and let it cool slightly before serving.

Focaccia di Carnevale Salentina

YIELD: 1 SMALL FOCACCIA / **ACTIVE TIME:** 45 MINUTES / **TOTAL TIME:** 4 HOURS

1 CUP PLUS 2 TEASPOONS (250 ML) WATER

2 TEASPOONS (6 G) ACTIVE DRY YEAST

4 CUPS PLUS 2 TABLESPOONS (496 G) ALL-PURPOSE FLOUR, PLUS MORE AS NEEDED

1½ TEASPOONS (9 G) TABLE SALT, PLUS MORE TO TASTE

EXTRA-VIRGIN OLIVE OIL, AS NEEDED

1 ONION, SLICED

14 OZ. ITALIAN SAUSAGE, CHOPPED

BLACK PEPPER, TO TASTE

3 SMALL TOMATOES, PEELED, SEEDED, AND SLICED

2½ OZ. PECORINO CHEESE, GRATED

10 OZ. FRESH MOZZARELLA CHEESE, DRAINED AND TORN

1. Warm 3½ tablespoons of the water until it is 105°F. Add the yeast and water to a bowl and gently stir to combine. Let the mixture sit until it starts to foam, about 10 minutes.
2. In a large bowl, combine the flour, yeast mixture, and remaining water and work the mixture until it comes together as a dough. If kneading by hand, place the dough on a flour-dusted work surface. Work it until it is compact, smooth, and elastic.
3. Add the salt and work the dough until it is developed, elastic, and extensible, about 5 minutes. Coat a large, clean bowl with olive oil, shape the dough into a ball, and place it in the bowl. Cover the bowl with plastic wrap, place it in a naturally warm spot, and let it rest until it has doubled in size, about 2 hours.
4. Coat the bottom of a skillet with olive oil and warm it over medium-high heat. Add the onion and sausage, season with salt and pepper, and cook, stirring frequently, until the sausage is browned and the onion is tender, about 10 minutes. Remove the pan from heat and let the mixture cool.
5. Coat a 10-inch cast-iron skillet or a round cake pan with olive oil. Place the dough on a flour-dusted work surface and divide it into two pieces, making sure one piece is slightly bigger than the other. Roll out that piece into a disk that is slightly larger than the pan. Place it in the pan, top it with the onion-and-sausage mixture, and distribute the tomatoes, pecorino, and mozzarella over the mixture.
6. Roll out the second piece of dough so it will fit within the pan, place it over the filling, and crimp the edge to seal the focaccia. Brush the top of the focaccia with olive oil and use a fork to poke holes in it. Coat a piece of plastic wrap with olive oil, place it over the pan, and let it rest for 1 hour.
7. Preheat the oven to 430°F. Place the focaccia in the oven and bake for 20 minutes. Reduce the temperature to 350°F and bake for another 20 to 25 minutes, until the focaccia is golden brown on the top and bottom.
8. Remove the focaccia from the oven and let it cool slightly before serving.

Sfincione Palermitano

YIELD: 1 LARGE FOCACCIA / **ACTIVE TIME:** 1 HOUR / **TOTAL TIME:** 4 HOURS AND 30 MINUTES

2⅔ CUPS (638 ML) WATER

2½ TEASPOONS (7.5 G) ACTIVE DRY YEAST

4⅔ CUPS (560 G) BREAD FLOUR, PLUS MORE AS NEEDED

2 CUPS (238 G) FINE SEMOLINA FLOUR

1 TABLESPOON (18 G) TABLE SALT, PLUS MORE TO TASTE

EXTRA-VIRGIN OLIVE OIL, AS NEEDED

2 ONIONS, SLICED

23 OZ. CRUSHED TOMATOES

12 ANCHOVIES IN OLIVE OIL, DRAINED AND TORN

BLACK PEPPER, TO TASTE

1 LB. CACIOCAVALLO CHEESE, TWO-THIRDS CUBED, ONE-THIRD GRATED

FRESH OREGANO, CHOPPED, TO TASTE

BREAD CRUMBS, TO TASTE

1. Warm 3½ tablespoons of the water until it is 105°F. Add the yeast and water to a bowl and gently stir to combine. Let the mixture sit until it starts to foam, about 10 minutes.
2. In a large bowl, combine the flours, yeast mixture, and remaining water until the mixture comes together as a dough. If kneading by hand, place the dough on a flour-dusted work surface. Work the dough until it is compact, smooth, and elastic.
3. Add the salt and work the dough until it is developed, elastic, and extensible, about 5 minutes. Coat a large, clean bowl with olive oil, shape the dough into a ball, and place it in the bowl. Cover the bowl with plastic wrap, place it in a naturally warm spot, and let it rest until it has doubled in size, about 2 hours.
4. Coat the bottom of a skillet with olive oil and warm it over medium-low heat. Add the onions and cook, stirring frequently, until they are starting to brown, about 12 minutes. Add the tomatoes and three anchovies, cover the skillet, reduce the heat, and simmer until the flavor is to your liking, 20 to 30 minutes.
5. Season with salt and pepper, remove the pan from heat, and let the mixture cool completely.
6. Coat an 18 x 13–inch baking pan with olive oil, place the dough in the pan, and gently stretch it until it covers the entire pan. Cover the dough with plastic wrap and let it rest for 1 hour.
7. Preheat the oven to 430°F. Top the focaccia with the cubed caciocavallo and remaining anchovies and press down on them until they are embedded in the dough. Cover them with the tomato sauce, generously sprinkle oregano over the sauce, and drizzle olive oil over everything. Sprinkle the grated caciocavallo and a generous handful of bread crumbs over the focaccia.
8. Place the focaccia in the oven and bake for 20 minutes. Reduce the temperature to 350°F and bake for another 15 to 20 minutes, until the focaccia is golden brown on the edges and on the bottom.
9. Remove the focaccia from the oven and let it cool slightly before serving.

Mustazzeddu

YIELD: 1 LARGE FOCACCIA / **ACTIVE TIME:** 40 MINUTES / **TOTAL TIME:** 4 HOURS AND 30 MINUTES

28 OZ. CHERRY TOMATOES, CHOPPED

2 GARLIC CLOVES, CHOPPED

4 FRESH BASIL LEAVES

1 TABLESPOON (12.5 G) EXTRA-VIRGIN OLIVE OIL, PLUS MORE AS NEEDED

1½ TEASPOONS (9 G) TABLE SALT, PLUS MORE TO TASTE

1⅓ CUPS PLUS 2 TEASPOONS (330 ML) WATER

2 TEASPOONS (6 G) ACTIVE DRY YEAST

3 CUPS (349 G) FINELY GROUND DURUM WHEAT FLOUR

1¼ CUPS (150 G) BREAD FLOUR, PLUS MORE AS NEEDED

BLACK PEPPER, TO TASTE

1. Place the tomatoes, garlic, basil leaves, and a generous amount of olive oil in a bowl, season the mixture with salt, and stir to combine. Let the mixture sit for 2 hours, drain it in a colander, and let it drain further for 1 hour.
2. Warm 3½ tablespoons of the water until it is about 105°F. Add the yeast and water to a bowl and gently stir to combine. Let the mixture sit until it starts to foam, about 10 minutes.
3. In a large bowl, combine the flours, olive oil, yeast mixture, and remaining water until the dough holds together. Add the salt and work the dough until it is compact, smooth, and elastic. Cover the bowl with a damp kitchen towel and let it rest at room temperature until it has doubled in size, about 2 hours.
4. Place the dough on a flour-dusted work surface and roll it out until it is an approximately ¾-inch-thick disk. Line a baking sheet with parchment paper, place the dough on it, cover it with the kitchen towel, and let it rest for another hour.
5. Position a rack in the middle of the oven and preheat the oven to 430°F. Place the tomato mixture on the focaccia, making sure to leave some dough uncovered at the edges. Season the focaccia with salt and pepper and fold the dough over the filling. You can leave the filling exposed or cover it completely; both are traditional in Sardinia.
6. Brush the dough with olive oil, place the pan directly on the bottom of the oven, and bake for 10 minutes. Reduce the temperature to 390°F, transfer the focaccia to the center rack, and bake for 30 to 40 minutes, until it is golden brown on the edges and on the bottom. Remove the focaccia from the oven and let it cool slightly before serving.

Focaccia Portoscusese

YIELD: 4 MEDIUM FOCACCIA / **ACTIVE TIME:** 40 MINUTES / **TOTAL TIME:** 3 HOURS AND 45 MINUTES

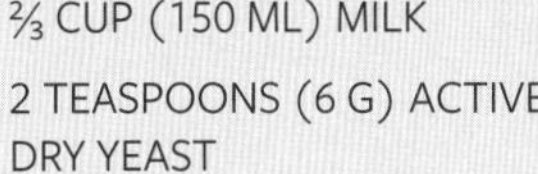

⅔ CUP (150 ML) MILK

2 TEASPOONS (6 G) ACTIVE DRY YEAST

2½ CUPS (300 G) BREAD FLOUR, PLUS MORE AS NEEDED

1¾ LBS. (800 G) POTATOES, BOILED, PEELED, AND MASHED

1½ TEASPOONS (8.2 G) TABLE SALT, PLUS MORE TO TASTE

EXTRA-VIRGIN OLIVE OIL, AS NEEDED

14 OZ. ONIONS, SLICED THIN

14 OZ. CANNED WHOLE PEELED TOMATOES, DRAINED AND GENTLY CRUSHED BY HAND

7 OZ. PECORINO CHEESE, GRATED

1. Warm 3½ tablespoons of the milk until it is 105°F. Add the milk and yeast to a bowl and gently stir to combine. Let the mixture sit until it starts to foam, about 10 minutes.
2. In a large bowl, combine the flour, potatoes, and yeast mixture until a soft and not-too-sticky dough forms. If needed, gradually add the remaining milk; how much you need depends on how watery the potatoes are.
3. Work the salt into the dough, place the dough on a flour-dusted work surface, and work the dough until it is smooth. Coat a large, clean bowl with olive oil, shape the dough into a ball, and place it in the bowl. Cover the bowl with plastic wrap, place it in a naturally warm spot, and let it rest until it has doubled in size, about 2 hours.
4. Coat the bottom of a skillet with olive oil and warm it over medium-low heat. Add the onions and cook, stirring occasionally, until they are tender, about 10 minutes. Add the tomatoes, cover the skillet, reduce the heat to low, and cook until the flavor of the mixture is to your liking, 20 to 30 minutes. Remove the pan from heat, season the mixture with salt, and let it cool completely.
5. Place the dough on a flour-dusted work surface and divide it into four pieces. Shape the pieces into balls, coat a piece of plastic wrap with olive oil, and place it over the dough. Let the dough rest for 1 hour.
6. Preheat the oven to 390°F and place a baking stone or steel on the middle rack of the oven as it warms. Gently flatten the balls of dough and cover them with the tomato sauce. Sprinkle the pecorino over the focaccia and drizzle olive oil on top. Use a peel to transfer the focaccia onto the heated baking implement and bake for 20 to 25 minutes, until the edges and bottom are golden brown.
7. Remove the focaccia from the oven and let them cool slightly before serving.

Focaccia Messinese

YIELD: 1 LARGE FOCACCIA / **ACTIVE TIME:** 40 MINUTES / **TOTAL TIME:** 4 HOURS AND 30 MINUTES

1¾ CUPS (420 G) WARM WATER (105°F)

2½ TEASPOONS (7.5 G) ACTIVE DRY YEAST

3¾ CUPS (454 G) BREAD FLOUR, PLUS MORE AS NEEDED

2 CUPS PLUS 1½ TABLESPOONS (249 G) FINELY GROUND DURUM WHEAT FLOUR

1½ TABLESPOONS (20 G) EXTRA-VIRGIN OLIVE OIL, PLUS MORE AS NEEDED

1 TABLESPOON (17 G) TABLE SALT, PLUS MORE TO TASTE

12 ANCHOVIES IN OLIVE OIL, DRAINED AND TORN

21 OZ. (598 G) CACIOCAVALLO CHEESE, CUBED

14 OZ. (397 G) ESCAROLE, CHOPPED

3 TOMATOES, CHOPPED

FRESH OREGANO, FINELY CHOPPED, TO TASTE

BLACK PEPPER, TO TASTE

1. Place the water and yeast in a bowl, gently stir to combine, and let the mixture sit until it starts to foam, about 10 minutes.
2. In a large bowl, combine the flours, olive oil, and yeast mixture and work the mixture until it just comes together as a dough. Place the dough on a flour-dusted work surface and knead until it is compact, smooth, and elastic.
3. Add the salt and knead until the dough is smooth, elastic, and extensible. Coat a large, clean bowl with olive oil, shape the dough into a ball, and place it in the bowl. Cover the bowl with plastic wrap, place it in a naturally warm spot, and let it rest until it has doubled in size, about 2 hours.
4. Coat an 18 × 13–inch baking pan with olive oil, place the dough on it, and brush the dough with more olive oil. Cover the pan with a kitchen towel and let the dough rest for 30 minutes.
5. Gently stretch the dough until it covers the entire pan. Let it rest for another hour.
6. Preheat the oven to 390°F. Press the anchovies and caciocavallo into the dough and top it with the escarole and tomatoes. Season the focaccia with oregano, salt, and pepper and drizzle olive oil over the top.
7. Place the focaccia in the oven and bake for 20 to 30 minutes, until it is golden brown and crispy on the edges and on the bottom.
8. Remove the focaccia from the oven and let it cool slightly before slicing and serving.

Rianata

YIELD: 1 LARGE FOCACCIA / **ACTIVE TIME:** 40 MINUTES / **TOTAL TIME:** 4 HOURS AND 45 MINUTES

1¾ CUPS (420 ML) WATER

2½ TEASPOONS (7.5 G) ACTIVE DRY YEAST

3¾ CUPS (454 G) BREAD FLOUR, PLUS MORE AS NEEDED

2 CUPS PLUS 1½ TABLESPOONS (249 G) FINELY GROUND DURUM WHEAT FLOUR

1 TABLESPOON PLUS 1 TEASPOON (17 G) EXTRA-VIRGIN OLIVE OIL, PLUS MORE AS NEEDED

1 TABLESPOON (18 G) TABLE SALT, PLUS MORE TO TASTE

8 ANCHOVIES IN OLIVE OIL, DRAINED

30 CHERRY TOMATOES, HALVED

½ LB. PECORINO CHEESE, GRATED

FRESH OREGANO, CHOPPED, TO TASTE

1. Warm 3½ tablespoons of the water until it is 105°F. Add the yeast and water to a bowl and gently stir to combine. Let the mixture sit until it starts to foam, about 10 minutes.
2. In a large bowl, combine the flours, olive oil, yeast mixture, and remaining water until the mixture comes together as a dough. Place the dough on a flour-dusted work surface and knead the dough until it is compact, smooth, and elastic.
3. Add the salt and knead until the dough is developed, elastic, and extensible, about 5 minutes. Coat a large, clean bowl with olive oil, shape the dough into a ball, and place it in the bowl. Cover the bowl with plastic wrap, place it in a naturally warm spot, and let it rest until it has doubled in size, about 2 hours.
4. Coat an 18 x 13-inch baking sheet with olive oil, place the dough on it, and brush the dough with more olive oil. Cover the dough with a kitchen towel and let the dough rest for 30 minutes.
5. Gently stretch the dough until it covers the entire pan. Let it rest for another hour.
6. Preheat the oven to 430°F. Press the anchovies and tomatoes into the dough, sprinkle the pecorino over the top, season with salt and oregano, and drizzle olive oil over the focaccia.
7. Place the focaccia in the oven and bake for 20 to 30 minutes, until the focaccia is golden brown and crispy on the edges and on the bottom.
8. Remove the focaccia from the oven and let it cool slightly before serving.

Schiaccia Toscana

YIELD: 1 LARGE FOCACCIA / **ACTIVE TIME:** 30 MINUTES / **TOTAL TIME:** 4 HOURS AND 30 MINUTES

$\frac{5}{6}$ CUP (198 ML) WARM WATER (105°F)

$1\frac{3}{4}$ TEASPOONS (5.2 G) ACTIVE DRY YEAST

$4\frac{1}{6}$ CUPS (500 G) ALL-PURPOSE FLOUR, PLUS MORE AS NEEDED

2 TABLESPOONS PLUS 4 TEASPOONS (50 ML) WHITE WINE

2 TABLESPOONS PLUS 4 TEASPOONS (50 ML) MILK

1 TABLESPOON (13 G) SUGAR

1 TEASPOON (5.5 G) TABLE SALT, PLUS MORE TO TASTE

EXTRA-VIRGIN OLIVE OIL, AS NEEDED

1. Place the water and yeast in a bowl, gently stir to combine, and let the mixture sit until it starts to foam, about 10 minutes.
2. In a large bowl, combine the flour, wine, milk, sugar, and yeast mixture. Work the mixture until it just comes together as a dough. If kneading by hand, place the dough on a flour-dusted work surface. Knead the dough until it is compact, smooth, and elastic.
3. Add the salt and work the dough until it is developed, elastic, and extensible, about 5 minutes. Coat a large, clean bowl with olive oil, shape the dough into a ball, and place it in the bowl. Cover the bowl with plastic wrap, place it in a naturally warm spot, and let it rest until it has doubled in size, about 2 hours.
4. Generously coat an 18 × 13–inch baking pan with olive oil, place the dough in the center of the pan, and gently flatten it into an oval. Brush the dough with olive oil, cover it with plastic wrap, and let it rest for 30 minutes.
5. Use your hands to flatten the dough and spread it toward the edges of the baking pan. If the dough does not want to extend to the edges of the pan right away, let it rest for 15 to 20 minutes before trying again.
6. Brush the focaccia with more olive oil and use your fingers to make indentations in the dough. Cover the focaccia with plastic wrap and let it rest for another 30 minutes.
7. Preheat the oven to 480°F.
8. Brush the dough with more olive oil and season it with salt. Place the focaccia in the oven and bake for 15 minutes, until the valleys between the bubbles are a deep golden brown. As this focaccia is supposed to be slightly crunchy, you want the bottom to be golden brown as well.
9. Remove the focaccia from the oven and let it cool slightly before serving.

Schiacciata con Cipolla e Salvia

YIELD: 1 LARGE FOCACCIA / **ACTIVE TIME:** 40 MINUTES / **TOTAL TIME:** 4 HOURS AND 30 MINUTES

1¼ CUPS (300 ML) WARM WATER (105°F)

1¾ TEASPOONS (5.2 G) ACTIVE DRY YEAST

4⅙ CUPS (500 G) ALL-PURPOSE FLOUR, PLUS MORE AS NEEDED

2½ TEASPOONS (10 G) SUGAR

1 TEASPOON (5.5 G) TABLE SALT, PLUS MORE TO TASTE

30 FRESH SAGE LEAVES, FINELY CHOPPED

EXTRA-VIRGIN OLIVE OIL, AS NEEDED

4 LARGE YELLOW ONIONS, SLICED THIN

1. Place the water and yeast in a bowl, gently stir to combine, and let the mixture sit until it starts to foam, about 10 minutes.
2. In a large bowl, combine the flour, sugar, and yeast mixture. Work the mixture until it just comes together as a dough. If kneading by hand, place the dough on a flour-dusted work surface. Work it until it is compact, smooth, and elastic.
3. Add the salt and half of the sage and knead until they have been incorporated and the dough appears smooth and elastic again. Coat a large, clean bowl with olive oil, shape the dough into a ball, and place it in the bowl. Cover the bowl with plastic wrap, place it in a naturally warm spot, and let it rest until it has doubled in size, about 2 hours.
4. Place the onions on a piece of parchment paper, sprinkle salt over them, and let them dry out.
5. Generously coat an 18 × 13–inch baking pan with olive oil, place the dough in the center of the pan, and gently flatten it into an oval. Brush the dough generously with olive oil, cover it with a kitchen towel, and let it rest for 30 minutes.
6. Use your hands to flatten the dough and stretch it toward the edges of the baking pan. If the dough does not want to extend to the edges of the pan right away, let it rest for 15 to 20 minutes before trying again.
7. Brush the focaccia with more olive oil and use your fingers to make indentations in the dough. Cover it with plastic wrap and let it rest for another 30 minutes. Preheat the oven to 390°F.
8. Distribute the onions and remaining sage over the focaccia. Drizzle olive oil over the top and season with just a bit of salt, keeping in mind that the onions have been salted.
9. Place the focaccia in the oven and bake for 30 to 35 minutes, until the edges are golden brown.
10. Remove the focaccia from the oven and let it cool slightly before serving.

Schiaccia All'uva

YIELD: 1 LARGE FOCACCIA / **ACTIVE TIME:** 40 MINUTES / **TOTAL TIME:** 3 HOURS

2⅙ CUPS (519 ML) WATER

1 TABLESPOON (9 G) ACTIVE DRY YEAST

7½ CUPS (900 G) ALL-PURPOSE FLOUR, PLUS MORE AS NEEDED

2 TEASPOONS (14 G) HONEY

6 TABLESPOONS (79 G) EXTRA-VIRGIN OLIVE OIL, PLUS MORE AS NEEDED

½ CUP PLUS 1 TABLESPOON (113 G) SUGAR

2½ LBS. SEEDLESS PURPLE GRAPES

CASTER SUGAR, FOR TOPPING

1. Place the water and yeast in a bowl, gently stir to combine, and let the mixture sit until it starts to foam, about 10 minutes.
2. In a large bowl, combine the flour, honey, and yeast mixture. Work the mixture until it just holds together. If kneading by hand, place the dough on a flour-dusted work surface. Work it until it is compact, smooth, and elastic. Coat a large, clean bowl with olive oil, shape the dough into a ball, and place it in the bowl. Cover the bowl with plastic wrap, place it in a naturally warm spot, and let it rest until it has doubled in size, about 2 hours.
3. Preheat the oven to 360°F. Working the dough with your hands, incorporate the sugar and olive oil. Divide the dough in half and roll each piece into a rectangle that is approximately the size of an 18 × 13–inch baking sheet.
4. Coat the baking sheet with olive oil and place one piece of dough on it. Place half of the grapes on top of the dough and gently press down on them. Sprinkle caster sugar and drizzle olive oil over the grapes.
5. Cover the grapes with the remaining piece of dough and crimp the edges to seal the focaccia. Place the remaining grapes on top of the focaccia and gently press down on them. Sprinkle caster sugar and drizzle olive oil over the grapes.
6. Place the focaccia in the oven and bake for 40 minutes, until it is golden brown. Remove the focaccia from the oven and let it cool briefly before serving.

Pizza Bianca Romana

YIELD: 2 SMALL FOCACCIA / **ACTIVE TIME:** 30 MINUTES / **TOTAL TIME:** 8 HOURS

2⅙ CUPS (524 ML) WARM WATER (105°F)

1¼ TEASPOONS (3.7 G) ACTIVE DRY YEAST

5⅚ CUPS (700 G) BREAD FLOUR OR "00" PIZZA FLOUR, PLUS MORE AS NEEDED

2 TEASPOONS (6 G) DIASTATIC MALT

1¾ TEASPOONS (44 G) SUGAR

3 TABLESPOONS (40 G) EXTRA-VIRGIN OLIVE OIL, PLUS MORE AS NEEDED

1 TABLESPOON (17 G) TABLE SALT, PLUS MORE TO TASTE

1. Place the water and yeast in a bowl, gently stir to combine, and let the mixture sit until it starts to foam, about 10 minutes.
2. In a large bowl, combine the flour, yeast mixture, malt, sugar, and olive oil and work the mixture until it just holds together. Using your hands or a stand mixer, work the dough until it is smooth and elastic, 10 to 15 minutes.
3. Add the salt and knead the dough until it is extremely elastic. Coat a large, clean bowl with olive oil, shape the dough into a ball, and place it in the bowl. Cover the bowl with plastic wrap, place it in a naturally warm spot, and let it rest until it has doubled in size and is full of bubbles, about 5 hours.
4. Line two baking sheets with parchment paper. Invert the dough onto a flour-dusted work surface and divide it in half. Place each piece of dough on a baking sheet and flatten it into an oval. Let it rest for 2 to 3 hours in a naturally warm spot, stretching the dough lengthwise every 30 minutes and being careful not to press down on it too much. After the last stretch, generously drizzle olive oil and sprinkle salt over the pieces of dough.
5. Preheat the oven to 480°F and place a baking stone or steel in the oven as it warms.
6. Using a peel or flat baking sheet, transfer one of the focaccia and its parchment paper onto the heated baking implement. Bake for 10 to 15 minutes, until it is golden brown. Remove the focaccia from the oven and brush it with olive oil. Repeat with the remaining focaccia.

Torta al Testo

YIELD: 2 SMALL FOCACCIA / **ACTIVE TIME:** 25 MINUTES / **TOTAL TIME:** 1 HOUR

4⅙ CUPS (500 G) ALL-PURPOSE FLOUR, PLUS MORE AS NEEDED

1 TEASPOON (5.5 G) TABLE SALT

1 TEASPOON (6 G) BAKING SODA

1 CUP PLUS 2 TEASPOONS (250 ML) WATER

1. In a large bowl, combine the flour, salt, and baking soda. Incorporate the water gradually and work the mixture until it comes together. Place the dough on a flour-dusted work surface and work it until it is compact, smooth, and elastic. Divide the dough in half and shape each piece into a ball. Cover the balls with plastic wrap and let them rest at room temperature for 30 minutes.
2. Warm a 10-inch cast-iron skillet over medium heat. Using a rolling pin, flatten each ball until it is a disk that is approximately ¼ inch thick. Use a fork to poke holes in the disks.
3. Working with one disk at a time, place it in the pan and cook until it is golden brown all over, about 6 minutes per side.
4. Cut the cooked focaccia into wedges. These can be enjoyed as is, or filled with cold cuts, cheese, or sautéed vegetables.

Smacafam

YIELD: 1 MEDIUM FOCACCIA / **ACTIVE TIME:** 10 MINUTES / **TOTAL TIME:** 1 HOUR

BUTTER, AS NEEDED

3⅓ CUPS (397 G) ALL-PURPOSE FLOUR, PLUS MORE AS NEEDED

2½ CUPS (569 ML) WHOLE MILK

2 EGGS

½ LB. SWEET ITALIAN SAUSAGE, CHOPPED

2 TEASPOONS (12 G) TABLE SALT

2 PINCHES OF BLACK PEPPER

1. Preheat the oven to 360°F and coat a 13 x 9–inch baking pan with butter. Place all of the ingredients, except for about 3 oz. of the sausage, in a mixing bowl and stir until the batter looks smooth. Pour the batter into the pan and sprinkle the remaining sausage over the top.
2. Place the focaccia in the oven and bake for 30 to 40 minutes, until the edges are golden brown. Remove the focaccia from the oven and let it cool briefly before serving.

Crescia Sfogliata

YIELD: 6 SMALL FOCACCIA / **ACTIVE TIME:** 45 MINUTES / **TOTAL TIME:** 4 HOURS

4⅙ CUPS (500 G) ALL-PURPOSE FLOUR, PLUS MORE AS NEEDED

⅚ CUP (198 ML) WATER

7 TABLESPOONS (100 G) LARD, PLUS MORE AS NEEDED

2 EGGS

1¾ TEASPOONS (10.5 G) TABLE SALT

2 PINCHES OF BLACK PEPPER

1. In a large bowl, combine the flour, water, lard, eggs, salt, and pepper and work the mixture until it just comes together as a dough. If kneading by hand, place the dough on a flour-dusted work surface. Work it until it is compact, smooth, and elastic.
2. Shape the dough into a ball, cover it with plastic wrap, and let it rest at room temperature for 30 minutes.
3. Divide the dough into six pieces and shape them into balls. Flatten each ball into a disk, brush them with lard, and roll them up as tightly as possible. Twist the rolls into spirals. Line a baking sheet with parchment paper, place the spirals on it, and cover them with plastic wrap. Refrigerate for 30 minutes to 1 hour.
4. Remove the spirals from the refrigerator and flatten them into disks that are approximately ⅛ inch thick.
5. Warm a 10-inch skillet over medium heat. Working with one disk at a time, cook the focaccia until dark spots appear all over them, about 5 minutes per side.
6. Let the cooked focaccia cool briefly before enjoying.

Focaccia Genovese

YIELD: 1 LARGE FOCACCIA / **ACTIVE TIME:** 30 MINUTES / **TOTAL TIME:** 2 HOURS

CLASSIC FOCACCIA DOUGH (SEE PAGE 293)

ALL-PURPOSE FLOUR, AS NEEDED

3 TABLESPOONS EXTRA-VIRGIN OLIVE OIL, PLUS MORE AS NEEDED

⅔ CUP WATER

1 TEASPOON TABLE SALT

COARSE SEA SALT, TO TASTE

1. Place the dough on a flour-dusted work surface and shape it into a loose ball, making sure not to compress the core of the dough and deflate it. Coat an 18 × 13–inch baking pan with olive oil, place the dough on the pan, and gently flatten the dough into an oval. Cover the dough with a kitchen towel and let it rest at room temperature for 30 minutes to 1 hour.
2. Stretch the dough toward the edges of the baking pan. If the dough does not want to extend to the edges of the pan right away, let it rest for 15 to 20 minutes before trying again. Cover the dough with the kitchen towel and let it rest for another 30 minutes to 1 hour.
3. Place the olive oil, water, and table salt in a mixing bowl and stir to combine. Set the mixture aside. Lightly dust the focaccia with flour and press down on the dough with two fingers to make deep indentations in it. Cover the focaccia with half of the olive oil mixture and let it rest for another 30 minutes.
4. Preheat the oven to 445°F. Cover the focaccia with the remaining olive oil mixture and sprinkle coarse sea salt over the top. Place the focaccia in the oven and bake for 15 to 20 minutes, until the focaccia is a light golden brown. As this focaccia is supposed to be soft, it's far better to remove it too early as opposed to too late. Remove the focaccia from the oven and let it cool briefly before serving.

Caccіannanze

YIELD: 1 LARGE FOCACCIA / **ACTIVE TIME:** 30 MINUTES / **TOTAL TIME:** 3 HOURS

CLASSIC FOCACCIA DOUGH (SEE PAGE 293)

ALL-PURPOSE FLOUR, AS NEEDED

EXTRA-VIRGIN OLIVE OIL, AS NEEDED

2 TABLESPOONS FRESH ROSEMARY

3 GARLIC CLOVES, SLICED THIN

SALT, TO TASTE

LARD, AS NEEDED (OPTIONAL)

1. Place the dough on a flour-dusted work surface and shape it into a loose ball, making sure not to press down on the dough and deflate it. Coat an 18 × 13–inch baking sheet with olive oil, place the dough in the center, and gently flatten it into an oval. Brush the dough with olive oil, cover it with plastic wrap, and let it rest at room temperature for 1 hour.
2. Place the rosemary, garlic, and a few pinches of salt in a mixing bowl and stir to combine. Use your hands to flatten the dough and stretch it toward the edges of the baking sheet. If the dough does not want to extend to the edges of the pan right away, let it rest for 15 to 20 minutes before trying again.
3. Brush the dough with olive oil, sprinkle the rosemary-and-garlic mixture over the top, and let the focaccia rest at room temperature for another 30 minutes. If desired, you can also sprinkle chunks of lard over the focaccia. Preheat the oven to 390°F.
4. Place the focaccia in the oven and bake for 15 to 20 minutes, until it is golden brown and slightly crispy on the edges. Remove the focaccia from the oven and let it cool slightly before serving.

Pinza Onta Polesana

YIELD: 1 LARGE FOCACCIA / **ACTIVE TIME:** 40 MINUTES / **TOTAL TIME:** 4 HOURS

7 OZ. PANCETTA, DICED

½ CUP PLUS 2 TEASPOONS (130 G) LUKEWARM WATER (90°F)

2 TEASPOONS (6 G) ACTIVE DRY YEAST

5 CUPS (600 G) ALL-PURPOSE FLOUR, PLUS MORE AS NEEDED

⅚ CUP (198 G) WHOLE MILK

½ CUP (119 G) LARD, CHOPPED AND AT ROOM TEMPERATURE, PLUS MORE AS NEEDED

2 TEASPOONS (11 G) TABLE SALT

2 PINCHES OF BLACK PEPPER

EXTRA-VIRGIN OLIVE OIL, AS NEEDED

BREAD CRUMBS, AS NEEDED

COARSE SEA SALT, TO TASTE

1. Place the pancetta in a skillet and cook over medium heat until the fat has rendered, about 4 minutes. Transfer the pancetta to a paper towel–lined plate to cool.
2. Place the water and yeast in a bowl, gently stir to combine, and let the mixture sit until it starts to foam, about 10 minutes.
3. In a large bowl, combine the flour, milk, half of the lard, and the yeast mixture and work the mixture until it just holds together. If kneading by hand, place the dough on a flour-dusted work surface. Work the dough until it is compact, smooth, and elastic.
4. Add the table salt, pepper, and cooled pancetta and work the dough until it is developed, elastic, and extensible, about 5 minutes. Coat a large, clean bowl with olive oil, shape the dough into a ball, and place it in the bowl. Cover the bowl with plastic wrap, place it in a naturally warm spot, and let it rest until it has doubled in size, about 2 hours.
5. Coat an 18 × 13–inch baking pan with lard and sprinkle a light coating of bread crumbs over the pan. Place the dough in the pan and stretch it into a thick rectangle, making sure not to stretch it all the way to the edges of the pan. Cover the pan with plastic wrap and let the dough rest at room temperature for 1 hour.
6. Gently stretch the dough until it covers the entire pan. Let it rest for another 30 minutes. Preheat the oven to 410°F.
7. Sprinkle coarse sea salt over the focaccia and top it with the remaining lard. Place the focaccia in the oven and bake until it is golden brown and crispy, 30 to 35 minutes.
8. Remove the focaccia from the oven and let it cool briefly before slicing and serving.

Tirot

YIELD: 1 LARGE FOCACCIA / **ACTIVE TIME:** 40 MINUTES / **TOTAL TIME:** 4 HOURS AND 45 MINUTES

1½ CUPS (368.5 ML) LUKEWARM WATER (90°F)

2 TEASPOONS (6 G) ACTIVE DRY YEAST

5 CUPS (600 G) ALL-PURPOSE FLOUR, PLUS MORE AS NEEDED

⅔ CUP (150 G) LARD, AT ROOM TEMPERATURE AND CHOPPED, PLUS MORE AS NEEDED

1 LB. YELLOW ONIONS, SLICED THIN

2 TEASPOONS (11 G) TABLE SALT, PLUS MORE TO TASTE

EXTRA-VIRGIN OLIVE OIL, AS NEEDED

BREAD CRUMBS, AS NEEDED

1. Place the water and yeast in a bowl, gently stir to combine, and let the mixture sit until it starts to foam, about 10 minutes.
2. In a large bowl, combine the flour, two-thirds of the lard, and the yeast mixture and work the mixture until it just holds together. If kneading by hand, place the dough on a flour-dusted work surface. Work the dough until it is compact, smooth, and elastic.
3. Add the onions and salt and work the dough until the onions are well incorporated. Coat a large, clean bowl with olive oil, shape the dough into a ball, and place it in the bowl. Cover the bowl with plastic wrap, place it in a naturally warm spot, and let it rest until it has doubled in size, about 2 hours.
4. Coat an 18 × 13-inch baking pan with lard and sprinkle a light coating of bread crumbs on top to prevent the focaccia from sticking to the pan. Place the dough on a flour-dusted work surface and press it out into a thick rectangle that is smaller than the pan. Place the dough in the pan, brush the surface with olive oil, and cover the dough with a kitchen towel. Let it rest for 30 minutes.
5. Gently stretch the dough until it covers the whole pan. Let it rest for another hour.
6. Preheat the oven to 390°F.
7. Season the focaccia with salt and top it with the remaining lard. Place it in the oven and bake until the focaccia is golden brown and crispy, 30 to 35 minutes.
8. Remove the focaccia from the oven and let it cool briefly before serving.

Pizza al Padellino

YIELD: 1 SMALL FOCACCIA / **ACTIVE TIME:** 15 MINUTES / **TOTAL TIME:** 4 HOURS AND 30 MINUTES

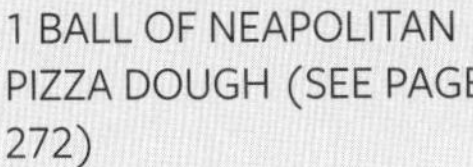

1 BALL OF NEAPOLITAN PIZZA DOUGH (SEE PAGE 272)

1 TABLESPOON EXTRA-VIRGIN OLIVE OIL, PLUS MORE TO TASTE

1 CUP CRUSHED TOMATOES

½ (SCANT) TEASPOON TABLE SALT, PLUS MORE TO TASTE

2 PINCHES OF DRIED OREGANO

7 OZ. FRESH MOZZARELLA CHEESE, DRAINED AND SLICED

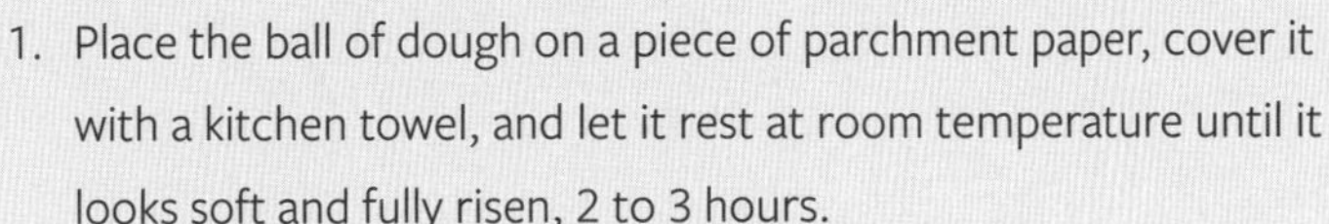

1. Place the ball of dough on a piece of parchment paper, cover it with a kitchen towel, and let it rest at room temperature until it looks soft and fully risen, 2 to 3 hours.
2. Place the dough in a 10-inch cast-iron skillet and gently spread it to the edge of the pan, making sure not to press down too hard on the dough and deflate it. Brush the dough with olive oil, cover the skillet with plastic wrap, and let the dough rest at room temperature for 30 minutes.
3. Preheat the oven to 480°F.
4. Place the tomatoes, salt, oregano, and olive oil in a mixing bowl and stir to combine. Spread the sauce over the focaccia, season it with salt, and generously drizzle olive oil over the top.
5. Place the focaccia in the oven and bake for about 10 minutes, until it is a light golden brown. Remove the focaccia, top it with the mozzarella, and return it to the oven. Bake until the mozzarella has melted and the edges of the focaccia are golden brown, about 10 minutes.
6. Remove the focaccia from the oven and let it cool briefly before serving.

Focaccia con le Olive

YIELD: 1 LARGE FOCACCIA / **ACTIVE TIME:** 20 MINUTES / **TOTAL TIME:** 3 HOURS AND 30 MINUTES

CLASSIC FOCACCIA DOUGH (SEE PAGE 293)

ALL-PURPOSE FLOUR, AS NEEDED

3½ TABLESPOONS EXTRA-VIRGIN OLIVE OIL, PLUS MORE AS NEEDED

5⅓ OZ. WATER

1 TEASPOON TABLE SALT

10 OZ. GREEN OLIVES, PITTED

1. Place the dough on a flour-dusted work surface and shape it into a loose ball, making sure not to compress the core of the dough and deflate it. Coat an 18 x 13–inch baking sheet with olive oil, place the dough on the pan, and gently flatten the dough into an oval. Cover the dough with a kitchen towel and let it rest at room temperature for 1 hour.
2. Stretch the dough toward the edges of the baking sheet. If the dough does not want to extend to the edges of the pan right away, let it rest for 15 to 20 minutes before trying again. Cover the dough with the kitchen towel and let it rest for another 30 minutes.
3. Place the olive oil, water, and salt in a mixing bowl and stir to combine. Cover the focaccia with half of the mixture and let it rest for another hour.
4. Preheat the oven to 445°F. Distribute the olives over the focaccia, pressing them into the dough until it doesn't bounce back. Brush the focaccia with the remaining olive oil mixture.
5. Place the focaccia in the oven and bake until it is golden brown, about 15 minutes. Remove the focaccia from the oven and let it cool briefly before serving.

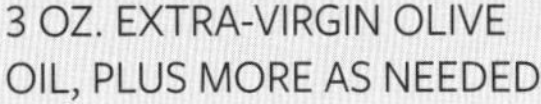

Pissalandrea

YIELD: 1 SMALL FOCACCIA / **ACTIVE TIME:** 45 MINUTES / **TOTAL TIME:** 3 HOURS AND 30 MINUTES

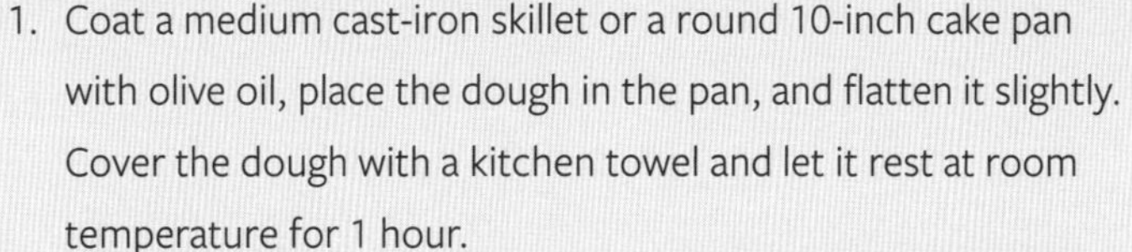

3 OZ. EXTRA-VIRGIN OLIVE OIL, PLUS MORE AS NEEDED

½ BATCH OF CLASSIC FOCACCIA DOUGH (SEE PAGE 293)

1 ONION, SLICED THIN

21.1 OZ. CANNED WHOLE PEELED TOMATOES, CRUSHED BY HAND

¾ TEASPOON TABLE SALT, PLUS MORE TO TASTE

2 PINCHES OF DRIED OREGANO

4 ANCHOVIES IN OLIVE OIL, DRAINED AND CHOPPED

½ LB. BLACK OLIVES, PITTED

9 GARLIC CLOVES, UNPEELED (OPTIONAL)

1 TABLESPOON CAPERS IN BRINE, DRAINED AND RINSED (OPTIONAL)

1. Coat a medium cast-iron skillet or a round 10-inch cake pan with olive oil, place the dough in the pan, and flatten it slightly. Cover the dough with a kitchen towel and let it rest at room temperature for 1 hour.
2. Place the onion and olive oil in a saucepan and cook, stirring occasionally, over medium-high heat until the onion starts to soften, about 5 minutes. Add the tomatoes, salt, and oregano and simmer until the flavor is to your liking, about 30 minutes. Remove the pan from heat and let the sauce cool completely.
3. Gently stretch the dough toward the edge of the pan. If the dough does not want to extend to the edge of the pan right away, let it rest for 15 to 20 minutes before trying again. When the dough is covering the pan, brush it with olive oil, cover it with the kitchen towel, and let it rest until it looks completely risen, about 45 minutes.
4. Preheat the oven to 430°F.
5. Spread the sauce over the focaccia, making sure not to press down too hard on the dough and deflate it. Top the focaccia with the anchovies, olives, and, if desired, the garlic and capers. Season with salt and drizzle olive oil over the focaccia.
6. Place the focaccia in the oven and bake until it is golden brown, 20 to 30 minutes.
7. Remove the focaccia from the oven and let it cool briefly before serving.

Farinata

YIELD: 1 LARGE FOCACCIA / **ACTIVE TIME:** 20 MINUTES / **TOTAL TIME:** 3 HOURS

4½ CUPS (397 G) CHICKPEA FLOUR

2 TEASPOONS (11 G) TABLE SALT

5 CUPS (1.135 L) WATER

½ CUP (100 G) EXTRA-VIRGIN OLIVE OIL, PLUS MORE AS NEEDED

1 TABLESPOON (2 G) FRESH ROSEMARY (OPTIONAL)

BLACK PEPPER, TO TASTE

1. In a large bowl, combine the chickpea flour and salt. While whisking constantly, gradually add the water. If possible, use a handheld mixer, as you do not want lumps to form in the dough. When all of the water has been incorporated, cover the batter with a kitchen towel and let it rest at room temperature for 2 to 3 hours.
2. Preheat the oven to 480°F.
3. Remove the foam that has gathered on the surface of the batter. Discard the foam. Stir the olive oil and, if desired, the rosemary into the batter.
4. Coat an 18 x 13-inch baking sheet with olive oil, pour the batter into the pan, and use a rubber spatula to even the surface. Generously drizzle olive oil over the focaccia.
5. Place the focaccia on the upper rack of the oven and bake until it is set and lightly brown, 10 to 15 minutes.
6. Remove the focaccia from the oven and let it cool briefly before seasoning it with pepper and cutting it into squares.

Chisola Piacentina

YIELD: 1 SMALL FOCACCIA / **ACTIVE TIME:** 40 MINUTES / **TOTAL TIME:** 4 HOURS

7 OZ. PANCETTA, DICED

3 TABLESPOONS LARD, PLUS MORE AS NEEDED

½ CUP PLUS 2 TABLESPOONS (150 G) LUKEWARM WATER (90°F)

1¾ TEASPOONS (5.2 G) ACTIVE DRY YEAST

2½ CUPS (300 G) BREAD FLOUR

2½ CUPS (300 G) ALL-PURPOSE FLOUR, PLUS MORE AS NEEDED

7 TABLESPOONS (100 ML) WHITE WINE

1½ TEASPOONS (8.2 G) TABLE SALT

EXTRA-VIRGIN OLIVE OIL, AS NEEDED

1. Place the pancetta and lard in a skillet and cook over medium heat, stirring occasionally, until the pancetta is browned, 6 to 8 minutes. Transfer the pancetta to a bowl, making sure to reserve the rendered fat as well.
2. Place the water and yeast in a bowl, gently stir to combine, and let the mixture sit until it starts to foam, about 10 minutes.
3. In a large bowl, combine the flours, wine, and yeast mixture and work the mixture until it just comes together. If kneading by hand, place the dough on a flour-dusted work surface. Work it until it is compact, smooth, and elastic.
4. Add the salt, pancetta, and its rendered fat and work the dough until they have been incorporated and the dough is developed, elastic, and extensible, about 5 minutes. Coat a large, clean bowl with olive oil, shape the dough into a ball, and place it in the bowl. Cover the bowl with plastic wrap, place it in a naturally warm spot, and let it rest until it has doubled in size, about 2 hours.
5. Place the dough on a flour-dusted work surface and roll it out until it is an approximately ⅓-inch-thick disk. Coat a medium cast-iron skillet or a round 10-inch cake pan with lard and place the focaccia in the pan. Brush the focaccia with lard, cover it with a kitchen towel, and let it rest for 1 hour.
6. Preheat the oven to 390°F.
7. Top the focaccia with more lard, place it in the oven, and bake until it is golden brown, about 30 minutes.
8. Remove the focaccia from the oven and let it cool briefly before serving.

Piadina

YIELD: 4 PIADINA / **ACTIVE TIME:** 30 MINUTES / **TOTAL TIME:** 1 HOUR AND 30 MINUTES

2 TEASPOONS (11 G) TABLE SALT

4.8 OZ. (136 ML) LUKEWARM WATER (90°F)

18 OZ. (510 G) ALL-PURPOSE FLOUR, PLUS MORE AS NEEDED

1½ TEASPOONS (9 G) BAKING SODA

7 TABLESPOONS (100 G) LARD, PLUS MORE AS NEEDED

1. Combine the salt and water in a bowl and stir until the salt has dissolved. In a large bowl, combine the flour and baking soda. Add the lard and salted water and work the mixture until it just comes together. Place the dough on a flour-dusted work surface and knead the dough until it is compact, smooth, and elastic. Coat an airtight container with lard, shape the dough into a ball, place it in the container, and let the dough rest at room temperature for 30 minutes.
2. Place the dough on a flour-dusted work surface and divide it into four pieces. Shape the pieces into balls and roll each one until it is an approximately ⅛-inch-thick disk.
3. Warm a dry skillet over medium-high heat. When the skillet is hot, cook one piadina at a time. Cook until dark brown spots appear on both sides, about 5 minutes per side. Pop any big bubbles with a fork as the piadina cooks.
4. Serve once all of the piadina have been cooked.

Crescenta Bolognese

YIELD: 1 LARGE FOCACCIA / **ACTIVE TIME:** 45 MINUTES / **TOTAL TIME:** 5 HOURS

1 CUP PLUS 6 TABLESPOONS (312 G) LUKEWARM WATER (90°F)

⅔ TEASPOON (2 G) ACTIVE DRY YEAST

½ LB. PROSCIUTTO

½ LB. PANCETTA

5⅚ CUPS (700 G) BREAD FLOUR, PLUS MORE AS NEEDED

⅓ CUP (71 G) LARD, PLUS MORE AS NEEDED

½ LB. (227 G) BIGA (SEE PAGE 273)

1 TABLESPOON (13 G) SUGAR

2⅔ TEASPOONS (14.6 G) TABLE SALT

EXTRA-VIRGIN OLIVE OIL, AS NEEDED

1. Place the water and yeast in a bowl, gently stir to combine, and let the mixture sit until it starts to foam, about 10 minutes.
2. Place the prosciutto and pancetta in a food processor and blitz until very finely chopped. Set the mixture aside.
3. In a large bowl, combine the flour, lard, biga, sugar, and yeast mixture and work the mixture until it just comes together. Place the dough on a flour-dusted work surface and knead the dough until it is compact, smooth, and elastic.
4. Add the salt and cured meat mixture and knead the dough until it is developed, elastic, and extensible, about 5 minutes. Coat a large, clean bowl with olive oil, shape the dough into a ball, and place it in the bowl. Cover the bowl with plastic wrap, place it in a naturally warm spot, and let it rest until it has doubled in size, about 2 hours.
5. Place the dough on a flour-dusted work surface and shape it into a ball. Coat an 18 x 13–inch baking sheet with lard and place the dough in the center. Brush the surface of the dough with lard and gently press it into an oval. Cover the dough with a kitchen towel and let it rest for 1 hour.
6. Stretch the dough toward the edges of the baking sheet. If the dough does not want to extend to the edges of the pan right away, let it rest for 15 to 20 minutes before trying again. Once it has been stretched to the edges of the pan, cover it with a kitchen towel and let it rest until fully risen, about 1 hour. You may need to stretch the dough again halfway through this final rise to get the desired result.
7. Position a rack in the middle of the oven and preheat the oven to 430°F. Brush the focaccia with lard, place it in the oven, and bake until it is golden brown, 25 to 30 minutes.
8. Remove the focaccia from the oven and let it cool slightly before serving.

BREADS

Casatiello

YIELD: 1 LOAF / **ACTIVE TIME:** 1 HOUR / **TOTAL TIME:** 6 HOURS

FOR THE DOUGH

1 PACKET (7 G) OF ACTIVE DRY YEAST

1¾ CUPS (420 ML) WARM WATER (105°F)

5⅚ CUPS (700 G) BREAD FLOUR, PLUS MORE AS NEEDED

2 TEASPOONS (11 G) TABLE SALT

1 TABLESPOON (6 G) BLACK PEPPER

10 TABLESPOONS (140 G) LARD, SOFTENED, PLUS MORE AS NEEDED

FOR THE FILLING

5 OZ. PROVOLONE CHEESE, CUBED

3½ OZ. CACIOCAVALLO CHEESE, CUBED

6 OZ. SALAMI, CHOPPED

2 OZ. PANCETTA, CUBED

¼ CUP GRATED PECORINO CHEESE

1 TEASPOON BLACK PEPPER

5 EGGS, LEFT WHOLE, FOR TOPPING

1. To begin preparations for the dough, place the yeast and water in a mixing bowl, gently stir, and let the mixture proof until it is foamy, about 10 minutes.
2. Add the flour and work the mixture until it comes together as a smooth dough.
3. Place the dough on a flour-dusted work surface, add the salt and pepper, and then gradually incorporate the lard. Knead the dough until it is smooth and elastic. Shape the dough into a ball, place it in a clean mixing bowl, and cover it with plastic wrap. Place the dough in a naturally warm place and let it rise for 2 hours.
4. To prepare the filling, place all of the ingredients, except for the eggs, in a mixing bowl and stir to combine.
5. Remove a handful of dough, cover it with plastic wrap, and set it aside. Place the remaining dough on a flour-dusted work surface and roll it out into a ½-inch-thick rectangle.
6. Distribute the filling evenly over the dough and gently fold the dough over itself, lengthwise. Gently pinch the seam to seal it.
7. Coat a 10-inch Bundt pan with lard, place the dough in the pan, seam side down, and pinch the ends of the dough together to join them.
8. Cover the dough with a kitchen towel, place it in a naturally warm spot, and let it rise for 2 hours.
9. Preheat the oven to 390°F. Arrange the eggs on the top of the casatiello, spaced regularly, and secure them using cross strips made from the reserved dough. Brush the dough with melted lard and place it in the oven.
10. Bake for 10 minutes, reduce the oven's temperature to 340°F, and bake until a toothpick inserted into the center of the bread comes out clean, about 35 minutes.
11. Remove the bread from the oven and let it cool completely before serving.

Tortano

YIELD: 1 LOAF / **ACTIVE TIME:** 1 HOUR / **TOTAL TIME:** 6 HOURS

FOR THE DOUGH

1 PACKET (7 G) OF ACTIVE DRY YEAST

1¾ CUPS (420 ML) WARM WATER (105°F)

5⅚ CUPS (700 G) BREAD FLOUR, PLUS MORE AS NEEDED

2 TEASPOONS (11 G) TABLE SALT

1 TABLESPOON (6 G) BLACK PEPPER

10 TABLESPOONS (140 G) LARD, SOFTENED, PLUS MORE AS NEEDED

FOR THE FILLING

5 OZ. PROVOLONE CHEESE, CUBED

3½ OZ. CACIOCAVALLO CHEESE, CUBED

6 OZ. SALAMI, CHOPPED

2 OZ. PANCETTA, CUBED

4 HARD-BOILED EGGS, CHOPPED

¼ CUP GRATED PECORINO CHEESE

1 TEASPOON BLACK PEPPER

1. To begin preparations for the dough, place the yeast and water in a mixing bowl, gently stir, and let the mixture proof until it is foamy, about 10 minutes.
2. Add the flour and work the mixture until it comes together as a smooth dough.
3. Place the dough on a flour-dusted work surface, add the salt and pepper, and then gradually incorporate the lard. Knead the dough until it is smooth and elastic. Shape the dough into a ball, place it in a clean mixing bowl, and cover it with plastic wrap. Place the dough in a naturally warm place and let it rise for 2 hours.
4. To prepare the filling, place all of the ingredients in a mixing bowl and stir to combine. Place the dough on a flour-dusted work surface and roll it out into a ½-inch-thick rectangle. Distribute the filling evenly over the dough and gently fold the dough over itself, lengthwise. Gently pinch the seam to seal it.
5. Coat a 10-inch Bundt pan with lard, place the dough in the pan, seam side down, and pinch the ends of the dough together to join them.
6. Cover the dough with a kitchen towel, place it in a naturally warm spot, and let it rise for 2 hours.
7. Preheat the oven to 390°F.
8. Brush the dough with melted lard and place it in the oven.
9. Bake for 10 minutes, reduce the oven's temperature to 340°F, and bake until a toothpick inserted into the center of the bread comes out clean, about 35 minutes. Remove the bread from the oven and let it cool completely before serving.

Tortano

SEE PAGE 337

Pane Aquilano

YIELD: 1 LOAF / **ACTIVE TIME:** 1 HOUR / **TOTAL TIME:** 15 HOURS

2¾ CUPS (329 G) BREAD FLOUR, PLUS MORE AS NEEDED

⅞ CUP (99 G) FINELY GROUND WHOLE WHEAT FLOUR

1¼ CUPS PLUS 2 TEASPOONS (309 ML) WATER

7 TABLESPOONS (99 G) PASTA MADRE (SEE PAGE 372)

1 SMALL POTATO, BOILED, PEELED, AND PRESSED THROUGH A POTATO RICER

2 TEASPOONS (11 G) TABLE SALT

SEMOLINA FLOUR, AS NEEDED

1. Place the bread flour, whole wheat flour, and two-thirds of the water in the work bowl of a stand mixer fitted with the dough hook and work the mixture on low. Gradually add the starter and work the mixture until it comes together as a shaggy dough.
2. Add the potato and continue to work the dough until it is smooth. Gradually add the salt and remaining water and work the dough until they have been incorporated. Shape the dough into a ball, place it in a clean bowl, and cover it with plastic wrap. Let the dough rise at room temperature for 1 hour, fold it, and let it rest for another hour. Fold the dough again and let it rest for 6 hours.
3. Place the dough on a flour-dusted work surface and fold it over itself. Cover the dough with a kitchen towel and let it rest for 30 minutes.
4. Using your hands, spread the dough into a rectangle. Fold a long side toward the center of the dough and then fold the other long side over it.
5. Place the dough, seam side down, on a semolina-dusted kitchen towel that is large enough to also cover the top of the dough. Let it rest for 1 hour.
6. Preheat the oven to 390°F and place a baking stone or steel on the middle rack of the oven as it warms.
7. Place the dough on a semolina-dusted peel and slide it onto the heated baking implement. Bake until the bread is dark brown, feels lighter when lifted, and makes a hollow sound when tapped, about 50 minutes.
8. Remove the bread from the oven, place it on a wire rack, and let it cool for at least 4 hours before serving.

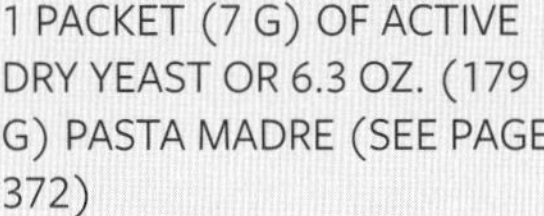

Pitta Calabrese

YIELD: 3 LOAVES / **ACTIVE TIME:** 1 HOUR / **TOTAL TIME:** 14 HOURS

1 PACKET (7 G) OF ACTIVE DRY YEAST OR 6.3 OZ. (179 G) PASTA MADRE (SEE PAGE 372)

2 CUPS (479 ML) WATER

2 TEASPOONS (14 G) HONEY (OPTIONAL)

3 CUPS (350 G) BREAD FLOUR

3 CUPS (350 G) STONE-GROUND ALL-PURPOSE FLOUR, PLUS MORE AS NEEDED

1 TEASPOON (5.5 G) TABLE SALT

EXTRA-VIRGIN OLIVE OIL, AS NEEDED

1. If using active dry yeast, warm the water until it is about 105°F, place it in the work bowl of a stand mixer fitted with the dough hook, and add the yeast and, if desired, honey. Gently stir to combine and let the mixture sit until it starts to foam, about 10 minutes.
2. Add the flours and work the mixture on low until combined. If using a starter, add it gradually and work the mixture until it comes together as a dough.
3. Raise the speed and work the dough until it is smooth and elastic. Add the salt and work the dough for another 10 minutes.
4. Coat a clean bowl with olive oil, place the dough in it, and cover the bowl with plastic wrap. Place the dough in a naturally warm spot and let it rest for 3 hours.
5. Place the dough on a flour-dusted work surface, divide it into three pieces, and shape them into rounds. Cover the dough with a kitchen towel and let it rest for another 3 hours.
6. Preheat the oven to 410°F and place a baking stone or steel on the middle rack of the oven as it warms.
7. Roll out each round into a disk and make a hole in the center with a glass or ring cutter. Use a parchment-lined peel to slide the dough onto the heated baking implement and bake for 15 minutes.
8. Reduce the temperature to 355°F and bake until the bread is golden brown, feels lighter when lifted, and makes a hollow sound when tapped, about 15 minutes.
9. Remove the bread from the oven, place it on a wire rack, and let it cool for 2 hours before serving.

Friselle

YIELD: 6 LOAVES / **ACTIVE TIME:** 1 HOUR / **TOTAL TIME:** 5 HOURS

1 CUP PLUS 1 TABLESPOON (255 G) WARM WATER (105°F)

3½ TEASPOONS (10.5 G) ACTIVE DRY YEAST

4⅙ CUPS (499 G) BREAD FLOUR

4⅙ CUPS (499 G) FINELY GROUND DURUM WHEAT FLOUR, PLUS MORE AS NEEDED

2 TEASPOONS (11 G) TABLE SALT

1. Place the water and yeast in the work bowl of a stand mixer fitted with the dough hook, gently stir to combine, and let the mixture sit until it starts to foam, about 10 minutes.
2. Add the remaining ingredients and work the mixture until it comes together as a smooth, elastic dough. Shape the dough into a ball, cover the work bowl with plastic wrap, and let the dough rest for 2 hours.
3. Line two baking sheets with parchment paper. Place the dough on a flour-dusted work surface, divide it into six pieces, and shape them into 14-inch-long logs.
4. Shape the logs into circles and pinch the ends of the circles to join them together. Place them on the baking sheets, cover them with kitchen towels, and let them rest for 1 hour.
5. Preheat the oven to 430°F. Place the friselle in the oven and bake them for 20 minutes. Remove the friselle from the oven and let them cool.
6. Cut them in half at their equators and place them back on the baking sheets, cut side up.
7. Reduce the temperature to 340°F. Place the friselle back in the oven and bake them until they are golden brown, about 1 hour.
8. Remove the friselle from the oven, place them on wire racks, and let them cool before serving.

Cuddura c'a Ciuciulena

YIELD: 1 LOAF / **ACTIVE TIME:** 1 HOUR / **TOTAL TIME:** 6 HOURS

1¼ CUPS (300 ML) WARM WATER (105°F), PLUS MORE AS NEEDED

1 PACKET (7 G) OF ACTIVE DRY YEAST

1 TEASPOON (4 G) SUGAR

5 CUPS (598 G) FINELY GROUND DURUM WHEAT FLOUR, PLUS MORE AS NEEDED

½ CUP (99 G) EXTRA-VIRGIN OLIVE OIL

2 TEASPOONS (12 G) TABLE SALT

⅓ CUP SESAME SEEDS, FOR TOPPING

1. Line a baking sheet with parchment paper. Place the water, yeast, and sugar in the work bowl of a stand mixer fitted with the dough hook, gently stir to combine, and let the mixture sit until it starts to foam, about 10 minutes.
2. Add the flour and olive oil and work the mixture until it comes together as a smooth and elastic dough, incorporating the salt toward the end.
3. Place the dough on a flour-dusted work surface and divide it into two pieces, keeping one piece half the size of the other. Roll the pieces into logs that are the same length.
4. Place the larger piece of dough on the baking sheet and shape it into a circle. Shape the smaller piece of dough into a circle and place it on top of the larger piece of dough. Cover the dough with a kitchen towel, place it in a naturally warm spot, and let it rest for 3 hours.
5. Preheat the oven to 350°F and set it on convection mode, if available. Moisten the dough with a bit of water and sprinkle the sesame seeds over it. Using scissors, make incisions that resemble ears of wheat all over the top circle.
6. Place the bread in the oven. Toss three ice cubes onto the bottom of the oven to bake with steam. Bake until the bread is golden brown, feels lighter when lifted, and makes a hollow sound when tapped, about 30 minutes.
7. Remove the bread from the oven, place it on a wire rack, and let it cool for 2 hours before serving.

Pane di Altamura

YIELD: 2 LOAVES / **ACTIVE TIME:** 2 HOURS / **TOTAL TIME:** 24 HOURS

6⅔ CUPS (799 G) FINELY GROUND DURUM WHEAT FLOUR, PLUS MORE AS NEEDED

1⅚ CUPS (218 G) BREAD FLOUR

3 (SCANT) CUPS (689 ML) WATER

¾ CUP (179 G) PASTA MADRE (SEE PAGE 372), FED TWICE WITH FINELY GROUND DURUM WHEAT FLOUR

1 TABLESPOON (17.5 G) TABLESPOON SALT

1. Place the flours and 2½ cups of the water in the work bowl of a stand mixer fitted with the dough hook and work the mixture until it just comes together and there are no lumps. Cover the bowl and let the dough rest for 1 hour.
2. Add the starter and remaining water and work the dough until it is smooth and elastic. Add the salt and work the dough until it has been incorporated. Transfer the dough to a large bowl, cover it with plastic wrap, and let it rest for 30 minutes.
3. Stretch and fold the dough over itself a few times. Cover the dough, let it rest for 30 minutes, and stretch and fold the dough over itself a few times. Rest for another 30 minutes, repeat the stretches and folds, and place the dough back in the bowl. Cover the bowl and store the dough in the refrigerator overnight.
4. Remove the dough from the refrigerator and let it rest at room temperature for 30 minutes.
5. Place the dough on a flour-dusted work surface, divide it in half, and shape the pieces into rounds. Cover the rounds with a kitchen towel and let them rest for 2½ hours.
6. Preheat the oven to 480°F and place a baking stone or steel on the middle rack of the oven as it warms.
7. Using a lame or sharp knife, make two cuts in the shape of a cross on the top of each round. Use a parchment-lined peel to slide the loaves onto the heated baking implement and toss three ice cubes onto the bottom of the oven to bake with steam. Bake for 10 minutes, reduce the temperature to 390°F, and bake for 30 minutes.
8. Reduce the temperature to 350°F and open the oven door a crack. Leave it open and bake until the bread is golden brown, feels lighter when lifted, and makes a hollow sound when tapped, 15 to 20 minutes.
9. Remove the bread from the oven, place it on a wire rack, and let it cool for 2 hours before serving.

Pane di Altamura

SEE PAGE 345

Pane Coccoi

YIELD: 2 LOAVES / **ACTIVE TIME:** 1 HOUR / **TOTAL TIME:** 7 HOURS

1 CUP (227 ML) WATER

2 TEASPOONS (12 G) TABLE SALT

4⅙ CUPS (499 G) FINELY GROUND DURUM WHEAT FLOUR, PLUS MORE AS NEEDED

7 TABLESPOONS (99 G) PASTA MADRE (SEE PAGE 372), FED 8 TO 12 HOURS EARLIER WITH FINELY GROUND DURUM WHEAT FLOUR

1. Place the water and salt in the work bowl of a stand mixer fitted with the dough hook and stir to combine.
2. Add the flour and work the mixture until it just comes together as a dough. Add the starter and work the dough until it is smooth and elastic. Shape the dough into a ball, place it in a clean bowl, and cover the bowl with plastic wrap. Let the dough rest for 1 hour.
3. Place the dough on a flour-dusted work surface, divide it in half, and shape the pieces into logs.
4. Flatten the logs, dust them with flour, and use your hands to create a depression in the center of each log. The depressions should run the entire length of the logs.
5. Fold each log over itself, like a long pocket, and make incisions along the edges.
6. You can shape the log into a crown or just curve it a bit, making the cuts open up slightly.
7. Line two baking sheets with parchment paper, place the loaves on them, cover them with kitchen towels, and let them rest until they have doubled in size, about 1½ hours.
8. Preheat the oven to 450°F. If the cuts became less visible during the rise, redo them.
9. Place the loaves in the oven and bake until they are golden brown, feel lighter when lifted, and make a hollow sound when tapped, about 35 minutes.
10. Remove the loaves from the oven, place them on a wire rack, and let them cool for 2 hours before serving.

Torta di Pasqua

YIELD: 1 TORTA / **ACTIVE TIME:** 30 MINUTES / **TOTAL TIME:** 4 HOURS AND 30 MINUTES

⅓ CUP (76 ML) LUKEWARM WHOLE MILK (90°F)

1 PACKET (7 G) OF ACTIVE DRY YEAST

5 EGGS

½ CUP (100 G) EXTRA-VIRGIN OLIVE OIL, PLUS MORE AS NEEDED

2 CUPS (200 G) GRATED PARMESAN CHEESE

½ CUP (50 G) GRATED PECORINO CHEESE

4⅙ CUPS (499 G) BREAD FLOUR

1½ TEASPOONS (8.2 G) TABLE SALT

BLACK PEPPER, TO TASTE

3½ OZ. (99 G) EMMENTAL CHEESE, CUBED

1. Place the milk and yeast in a bowl, gently stir to combine, and let the mixture sit until it starts to foam, about 10 minutes.
2. Place the eggs, olive oil, Parmesan, pecorino, and yeast mixture in the work bowl of a stand mixer fitted with the dough hook. Work the mixture until it comes together as a dough.
3. Add the flour, salt, and a generous pinch of pepper and knead the dough until it is smooth and elastic.
4. Coat a deep, round 9-inch cake pan with olive oil, place the dough in it, and distribute the Emmental over it, pushing the cubes deep into the dough. Cover the pan with plastic wrap and let the dough rise until it has reached the edge of the pan, 2 to 3 hours.
5. Preheat the oven to 350°F.
6. Place the bread in the oven and bake until it is just dark brown, about 1 hour. If the bread is darkening too much, cover it with aluminum foil toward the end of baking. Remove the bread from the oven and let it cool completely before removing it from the pan, slicing, and serving.

Pane Toscano

YIELD: 1 LOAF / **ACTIVE TIME:** 1 HOUR / **TOTAL TIME:** 30 HOURS

FOR THE BIGA

⅓ CUP (76 G) LUKEWARM WATER (90°F)

⅓ TEASPOON (1 G) ACTIVE DRY YEAST

1 CUP (120 G) BREAD FLOUR

FOR THE DOUGH

1 CUP (241 ML) WATER

½ TEASPOON (1.5 G) ACTIVE DRY YEAST

3⅓ CUPS (397 G) BREAD FLOUR, PLUS MORE AS NEEDED

1. To prepare the biga, place the water and yeast in a bowl, gently stir to combine, and let the mixture sit until it starts to foam, about 10 minutes. Add the flour and stir until it has been incorporated. Cover the bowl and let the biga chill in the refrigerator for 1 day.
2. To begin preparations for the dough, warm one-third of the water to 90°F. Add the yeast, gently stir to combine, and let the mixture sit until it starts to foam, about 10 minutes.
3. Place the flour, yeast mixture, and remaining water in the work bowl of a stand mixer fitted with the dough hook and work the mixture until combined. Add the biga and work the mixture until it comes together as a smooth, elastic dough.
4. Shape the dough into a round and place it in a large, clean bowl. Cover the bowl with plastic wrap and let the dough rest until it has almost doubled in size, about 3 hours.
5. Place the dough on a flour-dusted work surface and flatten it into a rectangle. Working from the short sides, fold the dough over itself like a letter and shape it into a log.
6. Place the dough on a flour-dusted kitchen towel, fold the towel over the loaf, and let it rest, seam side up, for 2 hours. Preheat the oven to 480°F and place a baking stone or steel on the middle rack of the oven as it warms.
7. Invert the dough onto a parchment-lined peel and make two diagonal cuts in it with a razor. Slide the bread onto the heated baking implement and toss three ice cubes onto the bottom of the oven to bake with steam.
8. Bake for 15 minutes, reduce the temperature to 420°F, and bake until a pale crust has formed and the bread feels lighter, 20 to 25 minutes. Keep in mind that this bread won't take on much color because there is no salt. Remove the bread from the oven, place it on a wire rack, and let it cool completely before slicing and serving.

Pane di Matera

YIELD: 2 LOAVES / **ACTIVE TIME:** 2 HOURS / **TOTAL TIME:** 24 HOURS

8⅓ CUPS (997 G) FINELY GROUND DURUM WHEAT FLOUR, PLUS MORE AS NEEDED

3 (SCANT) CUPS (689 ML) WATER

¾ CUP (179 G) PASTA MADRE (SEE PAGE 372), FED TWICE WITH FINELY GROUND DURUM WHEAT FLOUR

1 TABLESPOON (17.5 G) TABLE SALT

1. Place the flour and 21.1 oz. of the water in the work bowl of a stand mixer fitted with the dough hook and work the mixture until it just comes together and there are no lumps. Cover the bowl and let the dough rest for 1 hour.
2. Add the starter and remaining water and work the dough until it is smooth and elastic. Add the salt and work the dough until it has been incorporated.
3. Transfer the dough to a large bowl, cover it with plastic wrap, and let it rest for 30 minutes.
4. Stretch and fold the dough over itself a few times. Cover the dough, let it rest for 30 minutes, and stretch and fold the dough over itself a few times. Rest for another 30 minutes, repeat the stretches and folds, and place the dough back in the bowl. Cover the bowl and store the dough in the refrigerator overnight.
5. Remove the dough from the refrigerator and let it rest at room temperature for 3 hours.
6. Place the dough on a flour-dusted work surface and divide it in half.
7. Preheat the oven to 480°F and place a baking stone or steel on the middle rack of the oven as it warms.
8. Slightly flatten each piece of the dough and shape the pieces into ovals. Fold the edges of both sides of the ovals underneath the dough, roll the edges up tightly, and shape the pieces of dough into logs. Bend the logs into half-moons and score three perpendicular cuts on the curved sides of the half-moons, where the two halves meet. Squeeze a bit of the loaves from the side opposite to the cuts so that they open.
9. Use a parchment-lined peel to slide the loaves onto the heated baking implement and toss three ice cubes onto the bottom of the oven to bake with steam.
10. Reduce the temperature to 390°F and bake for 30 minutes. Reduce the temperature to 350°F and leave the oven door open a crack. Bake until the bread is golden brown, feels lighter when lifted, and makes a hollow sound when tapped, about 15 minutes.
11. Remove the bread from the oven, place it on a wire rack, and let it cool for 2 hours before serving.

Pane di Genzano

YIELD: 2 LOAVES / **ACTIVE TIME:** 1 HOUR / **TOTAL TIME:** 32 HOURS

FOR THE BIGA

⅓ CUP (74 G) PASTA MADRE (SEE PAGE 372)

5 TABLESPOONS (74 ML) WATER

1¼ CUPS (150 G) BREAD FLOUR

FOR THE DOUGH

7⅓ CUPS (879 G) BREAD FLOUR, PLUS MORE AS NEEDED

2⅔ CUPS PLUS 2 TEASPOONS (649 ML) WATER

1 TABLESPOON (17 G) TABLE SALT

WHEAT BRAN, AS NEEDED

1. To prepare the biga, place all of the ingredients in a bowl and stir until combined. Cover the bowl and let the biga chill in the refrigerator for 1 day.
2. To begin preparations for the dough, place the flour and four-fifths of the water in the work bowl of a stand mixer fitted with the dough hook and work the mixture until combined. Let the mixture rest for 1 hour.
3. Add the biga and work the mixture until it has been incorporated. Add the salt and remaining water and work the mixture until it comes together as a smooth, elastic dough.
4. Shape the dough into a round and place it in a large, clean bowl. Cover the bowl with plastic wrap and let the dough rise until it has almost doubled in size, about 4 hours.
5. Place the dough on a flour-dusted work surface and divide it in half. Flatten the pieces into rectangles. Working from the short sides, fold the rectangles over themselves like a letter and shape them into loaves.
6. Dust two kitchen towels with wheat bran. Place the loaves on the towels, fold the towels over them, and let them rest, seam side down, for 2 to 3 hours.
7. Preheat the oven to the maximum temperature and place a baking stone or steel on the middle rack of the oven as it warms.
8. Invert the loaves onto a parchment-lined peel. Slide them onto the heated baking implement and toss three ice cubes onto the bottom of the oven to bake with steam.
9. Bake for 15 minutes, reduce the temperature to 420°F, and bake until the bread has a dark crust, feels lighter when lifted, and makes a hollow sound when tapped, 30 to 35 minutes. Remove the loaves from the oven, place them on a wire rack, and let them cool completely before slicing and serving.

Pane di Lariano

YIELD: 2 LOAVES / **ACTIVE TIME:** 1 HOUR / **TOTAL TIME:** 32 HOURS

FOR THE BIGA

⅓ CUP (74 G) PASTA MADRE (SEE PAGE 372)

5 TABLESPOONS (74 ML) WATER

1¼ CUPS (150 G) BREAD FLOUR

FOR THE DOUGH

5½ CUPS (658 G) BREAD FLOUR, PLUS MORE AS NEEDED

2 CUPS (230 G) FINELY GROUND WHOLE WHEAT FLOUR

2¾ CUPS PLUS 2 TEASPOONS (649 ML) WATER

1 TABLESPOON (17 G) TABLE SALT

WHEAT BRAN, AS NEEDED

1. To prepare the biga, place all of the ingredients in a bowl and stir until combined. Cover the bowl and let the biga chill in the refrigerator for 1 day.
2. To begin preparations for the dough, place the flours and four-fifths of the water in the work bowl of a stand mixer fitted with the dough hook and work the mixture until combined. Let the mixture rest for 1 hour.
3. Add the biga and work the mixture until it has been incorporated. Add the salt and remaining water and work the mixture until it comes together as a smooth, elastic dough.
4. Shape the dough into a round and place it in a large, clean bowl. Cover the bowl with plastic wrap and let the dough rest until it has almost doubled in size, about 4 hours.
5. Place the dough on a flour-dusted work surface and divide it in half. Flatten the pieces into rectangles. Working from the short sides, fold the rectangles over themselves like a letter and shape them into logs.
6. Dust two kitchen towels with wheat bran. Place the loaves on the towels, fold the towels over the loaves, and let them rest, seam side down, for 2 to 3 hours.
7. Preheat the oven to 480°F and place a baking stone or steel on the middle rack of the oven as it warms.
8. Invert the loaves onto a parchment-lined peel. Slide them onto the heated baking implement and toss three ice cubes onto the bottom of the oven to bake with steam.
9. Bake for 15 minutes, reduce the temperature to 420°F, and bake until the bread has a dark crust, feels lighter when lifted, and makes a hollow sound when tapped, 30 to 35 minutes. Remove the loaves from the oven, place them on a wire rack, and let them cool completely before slicing and serving.

Pane Biove

YIELD: 2 LOAVES / **ACTIVE TIME:** 40 MINUTES / **TOTAL TIME:** 2 HOURS AND 30 MINUTES

1⅙ CUPS (281 ML) LUKEWARM WATER (90°F)

1 PACKET (7 G) OF ACTIVE DRY YEAST

4⅙ CUPS (499 G) BREAD FLOUR

1 TABLESPOON (7 G) BARLEY MALT

1½ TEASPOONS (8.2 G) TABLE SALT

2 TABLESPOONS (28 G) LARD, PLUS MORE AS NEEDED

SEMOLINA FLOUR, AS NEEDED

1. Line a baking sheet with parchment paper. Place the water and yeast in the work bowl of a stand mixer fitted with the dough hook, gently stir to combine, and let the mixture sit until it starts to foam, about 10 minutes.

2. Add the flour and work the mixture on low until incorporated. Add the malt, salt, and lard and work the mixture until it comes together as a firm dough.

3. Raise the speed to high and work the dough until it is smooth and elastic, about 10 minutes. Shape the dough into a ball and place it on the baking sheet. Cover it with a kitchen towel and let it rest for 30 minutes.

4. Place the dough on a semolina-dusted work surface, divide it in half, and shape each piece into a round. Stretch each round into a log.

5. Use a rolling pin to flatten each log into a 2⅓-inch-thick rectangle. Starting from a long side, roll each rectangle up tightly.

6. Roll each piece of dough into a long, 2-inch-wide strip. Roll each strip up and place the dough, seam side down, on the work surface. Cover the dough with kitchen towels and use some object to prevent the dough from expanding horizontally. Let the dough rest for 30 minutes.

7. Preheat the oven to 390°F and line a baking sheet with parchment paper. Place the loaves on the baking sheet and make a deep cut in each one.

8. Place the loaves in the oven and bake until they are golden brown, feel lighter when lifted, and make a hollow sound when tapped, about 30 minutes.

9. Remove the bread from the oven, place it on a wire rack, and let it cool completely before slicing and serving.

Pane Pugliese

YIELD: 1 LOAF / **ACTIVE TIME:** 30 MINUTES / **TOTAL TIME:** 6 HOURS

7 TABLESPOONS (100 G) PASTA MADRE (SEE PAGE 372)

1⅓ CUPS (317 ML) WATER

2½ CUPS (400 G) FINELY GROUND DURUM WHEAT FLOUR, PLUS MORE AS NEEDED

⅚ CUP (100 G) BREAD FLOUR

2 TEASPOONS (12 G) TABLE SALT

1. In the work bowl of a stand mixer fitted with the dough hook, combine the starter and water. Add the flours and work the mixture on low for 8 minutes.
2. Add the salt and work the dough until it is incorporated. Knead at low speed for 5 minutes, raise the speed to medium, and work the dough until it is smooth, 2 to 3 minutes.
3. Place the dough in a clean bowl, cover it with plastic wrap, and let it rest until it has increased to 1½ times its original size, 2 to 2½ hours. Make a series of folds during the first 1½ hours.
4. Place the dough on a flour-dusted work surface and shape it into a tight round. Place the shaped round, seam side up, in a banneton or a bowl lined with a floured kitchen towel. Cover it with a kitchen towel and let the dough rest at room temperature for 1½ to 2 hours.
5. Preheat the oven to 480°F and place a baking stone or steel on the middle rack of the oven as it warms.
6. Invert the dough onto a parchment-lined peel or flat baking sheet and score a cross on the top. Slide it onto the heated baking implement and bake for 10 minutes, then gradually reduce the temperature to 360°F and bake until the bread is golden brown, feels lighter when lifted, and makes a hollow sound when tapped, 30 to 40 minutes.
7. Remove the bread from the oven, place it on a wire rack, and let it cool completely before slicing and serving.

Marocca di Casola

YIELD: 2 LOAVES / **ACTIVE TIME:** 30 MINUTES / **TOTAL TIME:** 8 HOURS

1 MEDIUM POTATO, PEELED AND CHOPPED

7 TABLESPOONS (100 G) PASTA MADRE (SEE PAGE 372)

3¾ CUPS (337 G) CHESTNUT FLOUR, PLUS MORE AS NEEDED

1 CUP (120 G) ALL-PURPOSE FLOUR, PLUS MORE AS NEEDED

1 CUP (227 ML) WATER

1 TEASPOON (6 G) TABLE SALT

1½ TABLESPOONS (20 G) EXTRA-VIRGIN OLIVE OIL

1. Place the potato in a saucepan, cover it with water, and bring it to a boil. Cook until the potato is fork-tender, about 15 minutes. Drain and let the potato cool completely.
2. In the work bowl of a stand mixer fitted with the dough hook, combine the starter, flours, and water and work the mixture on low until it comes together as a dough. Shape the dough into a round, place it in a clean mixing bowl, and cover it with plastic wrap. Let the dough rest at room temperature for 2 to 3 hours.
3. Knead the salt, olive oil, and potato into the dough. Divide the dough into two rounds and place them in small bannetons that have been dusted with a combination of chestnut flour and all-purpose flour. Let the rounds rest at room temperature for 3 to 4 hours, until they look proofed: they will not rise much, but cracks on the surface indicate that the loaves are proofed.
4. Preheat the oven to 390°F.
5. Invert the rounds onto a parchment-lined baking sheet and score each one with a slash in the center. Place the loaves in the oven and bake until they are golden brown, feel lighter when lifted, and make a hollow sound when tapped, 35 to 40 minutes.
6. Remove the loaves from the oven, place them on a wire rack, and let them cool completely before slicing and serving.

Pane Siciliano

YIELD: 2 LOAVES / **ACTIVE TIME:** 30 MINUTES / **TOTAL TIME:** 3 HOURS AND 50 MINUTES

1¼ CUPS (302 ML) WATER

1 PACKET (7 G) OF ACTIVE DRY YEAST

1 TEASPOON (5 G) HONEY

2½ CUPS (400 G) FINELY GROUND DURUM WHEAT FLOUR, PLUS MORE AS NEEDED

1¼ CUPS (150 G) BREAD FLOUR

2 TEASPOONS (9 G) EXTRA-VIRGIN OLIVE OIL

2 TEASPOONS (12 G) TABLE SALT

SESAME SEEDS, FOR TOPPING

1. Warm 3½ tablespoons of the water until it is about 105°F. Add the yeast and water to the work bowl of a stand mixer fitted with the dough hook and gently stir to combine. Let the mixture sit until it starts to foam, about 10 minutes.
2. Add the honey, flours, olive oil, and remaining water and work the mixture on low until it comes together as a dough. Add the salt and work the dough until it is incorporated. Knead at low speed for 5 minutes, raise the speed to medium, and work the dough until it is smooth, 2 to 3 minutes.
3. Shape the dough into a ball and place it in a clean mixing bowl. Cover the bowl with plastic wrap and let the dough rest until it has doubled in size, about 1½ hours.
4. Sprinkle the sesame seeds over a baking sheet and set them aside.
5. Place the dough on a flour-dusted work surface and divide it in half. Flatten each piece and then shape them into rectangles. Flatten each piece once again, fold the top side down, and fold the bottom side up. Pull both sides together and press down on the seam to seal. Place the loaves on the baking sheet with the sesame seeds, seam side up. Cover the loaves with a floured kitchen towel and let them rest at room temperature for 1 hour.
6. Preheat the oven to 430°F and place a baking stone or steel on the middle rack of the oven as it warms.
7. Invert the loaves onto a parchment-lined peel and score each one, making one shallow lengthwise cut and two shallow crosswise cuts. Slide the loaves onto the heated baking implement and bake for 15 minutes.
8. Reduce the temperature to 375°F and bake until the loaves are golden brown, feel lighter when lifted, and make a hollow sound when tapped, 25 to 30 minutes.
9. Remove the loaves from the oven, place them on a wire rack, and let them cool completely before slicing and serving.

Pane Cafone

YIELD: 2 LOAVES / **ACTIVE TIME:** 30 MINUTES / **TOTAL TIME:** 8 HOURS

7 TABLESPOONS (100 G) PASTA MADRE (SEE PAGE 372)

1 TEASPOON (5 G) HONEY

1⅘ CUPS (440 ML) WATER

5 CUPS (600 G) BREAD FLOUR, PLUS MORE AS NEEDED

2½ TEASPOONS (15 G) TABLE SALT

SEMOLINA FLOUR, AS NEEDED

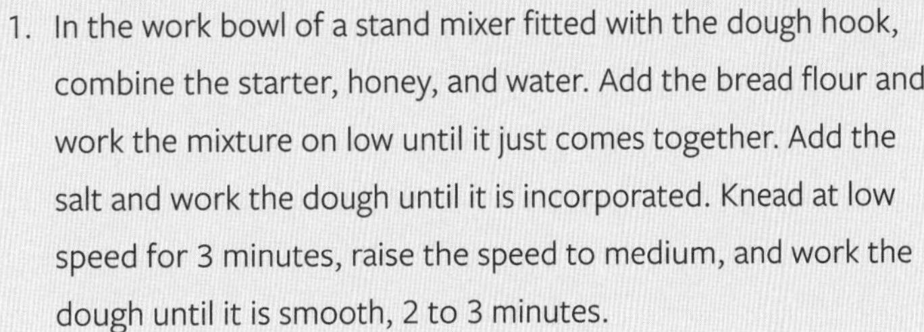

1. In the work bowl of a stand mixer fitted with the dough hook, combine the starter, honey, and water. Add the bread flour and work the mixture on low until it just comes together. Add the salt and work the dough until it is incorporated. Knead at low speed for 3 minutes, raise the speed to medium, and work the dough until it is smooth, 2 to 3 minutes.

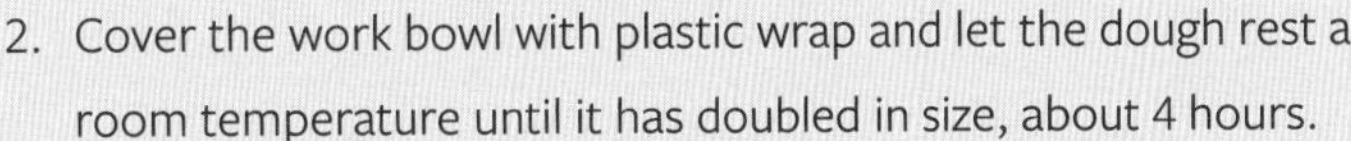

2. Cover the work bowl with plastic wrap and let the dough rest at room temperature until it has doubled in size, about 4 hours.
3. Place the dough on a flour-dusted work surface and divide it in half. Flatten each piece and then shape them into rectangles. Flatten the dough once again, fold the top side down, and fold the bottom side up. Pull both sides together and press down on the seam to seal the pieces of dough. Place the loaves on a generously flour-dusted baking sheet, seam side up. Cover the loaves with a floured kitchen towel and let them rest at room temperature for 3 hours, until they can be poked with a finger without bouncing back, as it is OK to slightly overproof this type of bread.
4. Preheat the oven to the maximum temperature and place a baking stone or steel on the middle rack of the oven as it warms.
5. Invert the loaves onto a semolina-dusted peel and score them on the sides. Slide them onto the heated baking implement.
6. Reduce the temperature to 480°F and bake for 20 minutes, then reduce the temperature to 430°F and bake until the bread is golden brown, feels lighter when lifted, and makes a hollow sound when tapped, 20 to 30 minutes.
7. Remove the loaves from the oven, place them on a wire rack, and let them cool completely before slicing and serving.

Coppia Ferrarese

YIELD: 3 LOAVES / **ACTIVE TIME:** 50 MINUTES / **TOTAL TIME:** 5 HOURS

¾ CUP (176 ML) WATER

⅔ PACKET (4.5 G) OF ACTIVE DRY YEAST

4 CUPS PLUS 2 TABLESPOONS (496 G) ALL-PURPOSE FLOUR, PLUS MORE AS NEEDED

¼ CUP (50 G) EXTRA-VIRGIN OLIVE OIL

2 TEASPOONS (12 G) TABLE SALT

1. Place the water and yeast in the work bowl of a stand mixer fitted with the dough hook, gently stir to combine, and let the mixture sit until it starts to foam, about 10 minutes.
2. Add the flour and work the mixture on low until incorporated. Add the olive oil and work the mixture, gradually increasing the speed with the intent to reach medium speed after 10 to 15 minutes.
3. Add the salt and work the dough until it is smooth and elastic, about 5 minutes. Shape the dough into a ball and place it in a mixing bowl. Cover it with plastic wrap and let the dough rest until it has doubled in size, 2 to 2½ hours.
4. Preheat the oven to 430°F and line a baking sheet with parchment paper.
5. Remove a small piece from the dough (smaller than a golf ball), cover it, and set aside. Shape the remaining dough into a ball, place it on a flour-dusted work surface, and roll it out into a large, ⅛-inch-thick disk. Using a pizza cutter or another sharp implement, cut the disk into six triangles.
6. Roll each triangle up into a log, starting from the base. Take two rolled-up logs and place them next to each other, lengthwise, on the baking sheet. Use a small piece of the dough you put aside to join the rolled-up logs at their centers, leaving most of each log uncovered. Turn the free ends of each log so that they form an arch facing away from the center. Repeat with the remaining rolled-up logs.
7. Cover the coppia with a kitchen towel and let them rest for 20 minutes.
8. Place the coppia in the oven and bake until they are golden brown, about 20 minutes.
9. Remove the coppia from the oven, transfer them to wire racks, and let them cool completely before enjoying.

Parrozzo Molisano

YIELD: 1 LOAF / **ACTIVE TIME:** 1 HOUR / **TOTAL TIME:** 10 HOURS

1¼ CUPS (150 G) BREAD FLOUR, PLUS MORE AS NEEDED

¾ CUP PLUS 2 TABLESPOONS (99 G) WHOLE WHEAT FLOUR

1⅔ CUPS PLUS 2 TEASPOONS (329 ML) WATER

⅔ CUP (150 G) PASTA MADRE (SEE PAGE 372)

⅔ CUP (150 G) POLENTA, COOKED AND COOLED

⅔ CUP (150 G) MASHED POTATOES, COOLED

1½ TEASPOONS (9 G) TABLE SALT

SEMOLINA FLOUR, AS NEEDED

1. Place the bread flour, whole wheat flour, and two-thirds of the water in the work bowl of a stand mixer fitted with the dough hook and work the mixture on low. Gradually add the starter and work the mixture until it comes together as a shaggy dough.
2. Add the polenta and potatoes and continue to work the dough until it is smooth.
3. Gradually add the salt and remaining water and work the dough until they have been incorporated. Shape the dough into a ball, place it in a clean bowl, and cover it with plastic wrap. Let the dough rest at room temperature for 30 minutes, fold it, and let it rest for another 30 minutes. Fold the dough again and let it rest for another hour.
4. Place the dough on a flour-dusted work surface and fold it over itself. Cover the dough with a kitchen towel and let it rest for 30 minutes.
5. Spread the dough into a rectangle with your hands. Fold a long side toward the center of the dough and then fold the other long side over it.
6. Place the dough, seam side down, on a semolina-dusted kitchen towel that is large enough to also cover the top of the dough. Let it rest for 4 hours.
7. Preheat the oven to the maximum temperature and place a baking stone or steel on the middle rack of the oven as it warms.
8. Place the dough on a semolina-dusted peel and slide it onto the heated baking implement. Bake for 15 minutes and reduce the temperature to 390°F. Bake until the bread is dark brown, feels lighter when lifted, and makes a hollow sound when tapped, about 30 minutes.
9. Remove the bread from the oven, place it on a wire rack, and let it cool for 2 hours before serving.

Gallette del Marinaio

YIELD: 8 TO 9 GALLETTE / **ACTIVE TIME:** 30 MINUTES / **TOTAL TIME:** 2 HOURS AND 30 MINUTES

½ TEASPOON (1.5 G) ACTIVE DRY YEAST

1 CUP PLUS 2 TEASPOONS (250 G) LUKEWARM WATER (90°F)

4⅙ CUPS (500 G) BREAD FLOUR, PLUS MORE AS NEEDED

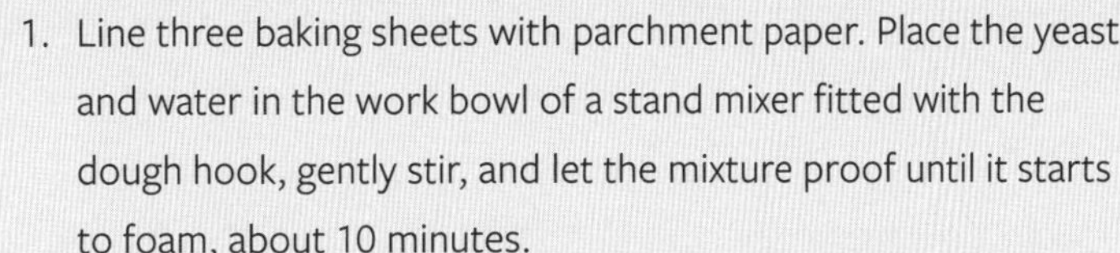

1. Line three baking sheets with parchment paper. Place the yeast and water in the work bowl of a stand mixer fitted with the dough hook, gently stir, and let the mixture proof until it starts to foam, about 10 minutes.
2. Add the flour and work the mixture on low until it comes together as a firm dough.
3. Raise the speed to high and work the dough until it is smooth and elastic, about 10 minutes.
4. Divide the dough into 3 oz. pieces and shape them into tight rounds.
5. Place the dough balls on one of the baking sheets, cover them with a kitchen towel, and let them rise for 1 hour.
6. Roll each ball into a ¼-inch-thick disk, place them on the baking sheets, and cover with a kitchen towel. Let them rest for 45 minutes.
7. Preheat the oven to 430°F. Poke holes in the tops of the gallette with a fork and place them in the oven. Bake for about 10 minutes.
8. Remove the gallette from the baking sheets and place them directly on the oven's racks. Bake until golden brown, about 5 minutes.
9. Turn the oven off, crack open the oven door, and let the gallette cool in the oven.

Gubana

YIELD: 1 GUBANA / **ACTIVE TIME:** 30 MINUTES / **TOTAL TIME:** 24 HOURS

FOR THE FILLING

EXTRA-VIRGIN OLIVE OIL, AS NEEDED

⅔ CUP RAISINS

1 CUP RUM OR MARSALA, PLUS MORE AS NEEDED

½ CUP SUGAR, PLUS MORE FOR TOPPING

3 TABLESPOONS WATER

½ TEASPOON WHITE VINEGAR

2 CUPS WALNUTS

2 TABLESPOONS UNSALTED BUTTER, CHOPPED, PLUS MORE AS NEEDED

⅔ CUP PINE NUTS

7 AMARETTI (SEE PAGE 378)

1½ OZ. DRY, BISCUIT-STYLE COOKIES (PETIT BEURRE OR SIMILAR)

ZEST OF ½ LEMON

1 TEASPOON PURE VANILLA EXTRACT

2 TEASPOONS CINNAMON

FOR THE DOUGH

¼ CUP (60 ML) WHOLE MILK

⅔ PACKET (4.6 G) OF ACTIVE DRY YEAST

2½ CUPS (300 G) STRONG BREAD FLOUR, PLUS MORE AS NEEDED

1 EGG

2 EGG YOLKS

⅓ TEASPOON (2 G) TABLE SALT

1 TABLESPOON (20 G) HONEY

¼ CUP (60 G) UNSALTED BUTTER, SOFTENED

¼ CUP (50 G) SUGAR

1 EGG WHITE, LIGHTLY BEATEN

1. The day before you are going to prepare the dough, begin preparations for the filling. Coat a clean, heat-resistant work surface with olive oil. Place the raisins and the rum in a bowl and let the raisins soak.
2. Place half of the sugar, the water, and vinegar in a medium saucepan and cook over medium heat, swirling the pan occasionally, until the mixture starts to caramelize. Add half of the walnuts and cook, stirring continually, until they are coated. Pour the mixture onto the work surface and let it cool.
3. Place the butter in a large skillet and melt it over low heat. Add the pine nuts and toast, stirring occasionally, until they are browned, about 5 minutes. Remove the pan from heat and let the pine nuts cool.
4. Crush the Amaretti and the biscuits and place them in a bowl. Chop the caramelized walnuts and remaining walnuts and add them to the bowl.
5. Drain the raisins and squeeze them dry. Add them, the toasted pine nuts, butter, lemon zest, salt, vanilla, cinnamon, remaining sugar, and enough rum for the mixture to be spreadable to the bowl. Stir to combine, cover the mixture with plastic wrap, and chill the filling in the refrigerator overnight.
6. To begin preparations for the dough, warm the milk to 90°F. Add the yeast, gently stir, and let the mixture proof until it starts to foam, about 10 minutes.

7. Place two-thirds of the flour, the egg, egg yolks, and yeast mixture in the work bowl of a stand mixer fitted with the dough hook and work the mixture until it comes together as a soft, smooth dough. Cover the work bowl with a kitchen towel, place it in a naturally warm spot, and let the dough rise for 1 hour.
8. Add the remaining flour, the salt, honey, butter, and sugar to the work bowl and work the dough vigorously until it is elastic. Cover the bowl with a kitchen towel, place it in a naturally warm spot, and let it rise for 30 minutes. Remove the filling from the refrigerator and let it sit at room temperature.
9. Place the dough on a flour-dusted work surface and roll it into an 8 x 12–inch rectangle. Spread the filling over the dough and dot it with pieces of butter. Working from a long side, roll the dough up, finishing with the seam side down. Pinch the dough at both of the short sides to seal the gubana.
10. Stretch the gubana until it is about 30 inches long. Coat a round, 10-inch cake pan with high edges with butter. Place the gubana in the pan in a tight spiral, making sure one end is underneath to seal it. Cover the pan with a kitchen towel and let the gubana rise until it has doubled in size, about 1½ hours.
11. Preheat the oven to 320°F. Brush the gubana with the egg white, sprinkle some sugar over the top, and place it in the oven.
12. Bake until the gubana is golden brown and a toothpick inserted into the center comes out clean, about 1 hour. Remove it from the oven and let it cool before slicing and serving.

Grissini

YIELD: 50 GRISSINI / **ACTIVE TIME:** 30 MINUTES / **TOTAL TIME:** 2 HOURS

1 PACKET (7 G) OF ACTIVE DRY YEAST

1¼ CUPS (300 ML) LUKEWARM WATER (90°F)

4⅙ CUPS (500 G) BREAD FLOUR

1 TEASPOON (2 G) BARLEY MALT

2 TEASPOONS (12 G) TABLE SALT

¼ CUP PLUS 1 TABLESPOON (60 G) EXTRA-VIRGIN OLIVE OIL, PLUS MORE AS NEEDED

SEMOLINA FLOUR, AS NEEDED

1. Line a baking sheet with parchment paper. Place the yeast and water in the work bowl of a stand mixer fitted with the dough hook, gently stir, and let the mixture proof until it starts to foam, about 10 minutes.
2. Add the flour and work the mixture on low until incorporated. Add the malt, salt, and olive oil and work the mixture until it comes together as a firm dough.
3. Raise the speed to high and work the dough until it is smooth and elastic, about 10 minutes.
4. Place the dough on the baking sheet, flatten it into a ⅛-inch-thick rectangle, and brush the top with olive oil. Cover with plastic wrap and let the dough rise for 1 hour.
5. Preheat the oven to 375°F and line two more baking sheets with parchment paper. Cut the dough into ⅓-inch-wide strips and place them on the baking sheets.
6. Sprinkle semolina flour over the grissini and place them in the oven.
7. Bake until the grissini are golden brown, 15 to 20 minutes. Remove the grissini from the oven and let them cool slightly before serving.

Schüttelbrot

YIELD: 8 SCHÜTTELBROT / **ACTIVE TIME:** 40 MINUTES / **TOTAL TIME:** 2 HOURS AND 30 MINUTES

1½ CUPS (340 ML) WARM WATER (105°F)

2½ TEASPOONS (7 G) ACTIVE DRY YEAST

3½ CUPS (365 G) MEDIUM RYE FLOUR

1¼ CUPS (150 G) ALL-PURPOSE FLOUR, PLUS MORE AS NEEDED

2 TEASPOONS (6 G) MIXED SEEDS (FENNEL, CARAWAY, CORIANDER, ETC.)

1½ TEASPOONS (9 G) TABLE SALT

1 TEASPOON (4 G) SUGAR

3⅓ TABLESPOONS (50 ML) BUTTERMILK

1. Place the water and yeast in the work bowl of a stand mixer fitted with the dough hook and gently stir to combine. Let the mixture sit until it starts to foam, about 10 minutes.
2. Add the remaining ingredients and work the mixture on low until it comes together as a smooth dough, about 15 minutes.
3. Knead the dough by hand or with the stand mixer for about 15 minutes.
4. Coat a large, clean bowl with nonstick cooking spray, shape the dough into a ball, and place it in the bowl. Cover the bowl with plastic wrap, place it in a naturally warm spot, and let it rest for 40 minutes.
5. Place the dough on a flour-dusted work surface, roll it into a long log, and cut it into eight pieces. Shape each piece into a round, place them on a parchment-lined baking sheet, and cover them with a kitchen towel. Let the schüttelbrot rest for 1 hour.
6. Place the schüttelbrot on a flour-dusted work surface and roll them out until they are ⅕ inch thick. Cover the flatbreads with a kitchen towel and let them rest for 20 minutes.
7. Preheat the oven to 410°F and place a baking stone on the middle rack of the oven as it warms.
8. Using a peel or a flat baking sheet, transfer the flatbreads to the heated baking implement and bake for about 20 minutes, until they are a light golden brown.
9. Remove the schüttelbrot from the oven and let them cool on wire racks before serving.

Pane Carasau

YIELD: 20 CARASAU / **ACTIVE TIME:** 1 HOUR / **TOTAL TIME:** 3 HOURS

1 CUP PLUS 2 TABLESPOONS (264 ML) WARM WATER (105°F)

1¾ TEASPOONS (5.2 G) ACTIVE DRY YEAST

1 TEASPOON (4 G) SUGAR

4⅙ CUPS (500 G) FINELY GROUND DURUM WHEAT FLOUR, PLUS MORE AS NEEDED

1 TEASPOON (5.5 G) TABLE SALT

EXTRA-VIRGIN OLIVE OIL, AS NEEDED

1. Place the water, yeast, and sugar in the work bowl of a stand mixer fitted with the dough hook, gently stir to combine, and let the mixture sit until it starts to foam, about 10 minutes.
2. Add the flour and work the mixture until it just comes together as a dough.
3. Add the salt and work the dough until it is smooth and elastic. Coat a large, clean bowl with olive oil, shape the dough into a ball, and place it in the bowl. Cover the bowl with plastic wrap, place it in a naturally warm spot, and let it rest for 1 hour.
4. Place the dough on a flour-dusted work surface, divide it into 10 pieces, and shape them into rounds. Cover the rounds with kitchen towels and let them rest for 30 minutes.
5. Preheat the oven to the maximum temperature and place a baking stone or steel in the oven as it warms. Flatten the rounds into ⅒-inch-thick disks, cover them with kitchen towels, and let them rest for another 30 minutes.
6. Using a peel or a flat baking sheet, slide one round at a time onto the heated baking implement and bake until it puffs up, 3 to 5 minutes.
7. Remove the bread from the oven and let it cool slightly.
8. When all of the carasau have been baked, cut them in half at their equators and gently press down to flatten them.
9. Slide a few carasau at a time onto the baking stone and bake until they are crispy, about 30 seconds. Remove them from the oven and let the carasau cool before serving.

Ciabatta

YIELD: 2 LOAVES / **ACTIVE TIME:** 2 HOURS AND 30 MINUTES / **TOTAL TIME:** 24 HOURS

FOR THE LEVAIN

¼ CUP (30 G) ALL-PURPOSE FLOUR

1 TABLESPOON PLUS 2 TEASPOONS (24 ML) WATER

1 TABLESPOON (12 G) PASTA MADRE (SEE PAGE 372)

FOR THE DOUGH

8¼ CUPS (1 KG) WHOLE WHEAT FLOUR

¼ CUP (35 G) LEVAIN

3¾ CUPS (908 ML) WATER

2⅓ TABLESPOONS (37 G) TABLE SALT

1 TEASPOON (2 G) INSTANT YEAST

3 TABLESPOONS (40 G) EXTRA-VIRGIN OLIVE OIL, PLUS MORE AS NEEDED

¼ CUP (28 G) TOASTED WHEAT GERM

1. To prepare the levain, place all of the ingredients in a mixing bowl and stir to combine. Let the levain rest in a naturally warm spot for 4 hours before using.
2. To begin preparations for the dough, place the flour, levain, and 90 percent of the water in the work bowl of a stand mixer fitted with the dough hook and work the mixture on low until it comes together as a shaggy mass. Sprinkle the salt, yeast, olive oil, wheat germ, and remaining water on top and mix by hand. Once combined, the ingredients should have a temperature of 78°F. If the dough's temperature is different, cover the bowl and place the dough in a drafty or warmer area of the kitchen to adjust its overall temperature. Let the dough rest for 1½ hours.
3. Fold the dough five to seven times, waiting 12 minutes between each fold, until the dough is smooth and elastic.
4. Coat a large container with olive oil, place the dough in it, and store it in the refrigerator overnight.
5. Remove the dough from the refrigerator and divide it in half. Let the dough rest at room temperature for 30 minutes.
6. Preheat the oven to 500°F and place a baking stone or steel on the middle rack of the oven as it warms. Invert the loaves onto a parchment-lined peel and slide them onto the heated baking implement. Reduce the temperature to 450ºF and cook until they are golden brown and feel lighter when lifted, about 25 minutes.
7. Remove the ciabattas from the oven, place them on a wire rack, and let them cool completely before slicing and serving.

SEE PAGE 369

Panettone

YIELD: 3 PANETTONE / **ACTIVE TIME:** 3 HOURS / **TOTAL TIME:** 2 TO 3 DAYS

FOR THE PASTA MADRE

1 TABLESPOON (14 G) SOURDOUGH STARTER

WATER, AS NEEDED

ALL-PURPOSE FLOUR, AS NEEDED

FOR THE FIRST DOUGH

3½ OZ. (100 G) EGG YOLKS

1 CUP (227 ML) WATER

4 CUPS (480 G) STRONG BREAD FLOUR OR PANETTONE FLOUR

½ CUP (100 G) SUGAR

6.3 OZ. (180 G) PASTA MADRE

4.3 OZ. (121 G) UNSALTED BUTTER, CHOPPED

FOR THE SECOND DOUGH

2 CUPS (240 G) STRONG BREAD FLOUR OR PANETTONE FLOUR

6.7 OZ. (190 G) EGG YOLKS

1 TABLESPOON (10 G) POWDERED MILK

1 (SCANT) TEASPOON (6 G) BARLEY MALT

1 (HEAPING) TABLESPOON (25 G) HONEY

1 TEASPOON (4.5 G) ORANGE EXTRACT

SEEDS OF 2 VANILLA BEANS

2 TEASPOONS (11 G) TABLE SALT

¾ (SCANT) CUP (139 G) SUGAR

½ CUP (113 G) UNSALTED BUTTER, CHOPPED, PLUS MORE AS NEEDED

5 OZ. DICED CANDIED ORANGE PEELS

5 OZ. CHOPPED CANDIED CITRUS PEELS

10 OZ. RAISINS

1. Begin preparations for the pasta madre 2 to 3 days before you are going to start baking the panettone. Combine the starter with 50 ml water and 100 g flour in a large bowl. Cover the bowl with plastic wrap and let it rest for 12 hours.
2. Combine 50 g of the pasta madre with 50 ml water and 100 g flour.
3. Perform three feedings of the pasta madre, one every 3 to 4 hours. The fed starter should be kept in a naturally warm spot, ideally about 79°F. The schedule should look like this: first feeding (morning): 50 g of the stiff starter with 50 ml water and 100 g flour; second feeding (lunchtime): 100 g stiff starter, 50 ml water, and 100 g flour; final feeding (late afternoon): 100 g stiff starter, 50 ml water, and 100 g flour.
4. To begin preparations for the first dough, place the egg yolks and water in the work bowl of a stand mixer fitted with the paddle attachment and beat to combine. Fit the mixer with the dough hook, add the flour and sugar, and work the mixture on low until combined. Gradually add the pasta madre and knead to incorporate.
5. Add the butter in three increments and knead the dough for about 6 minutes on low. The first dough should be mixed for no more than 10 minutes after the flour has been added.
6. Place the dough in a large, deep bowl and let the dough rest at room temperature until it is 3 to 4 times its original size, 10 to 12 hours.

7. To begin preparations for the second dough, place the first dough and two-thirds of the flour in the work bowl of a stand mixer fitted with the dough hook and mix on low speed for 2 minutes. Add the egg yolks and the remaining flour and knead on medium speed for about 2 minutes.
8. Add the powdered milk and barley malt and mix for 1 minute. Add the honey, orange extract, vanilla seeds, and salt and mix for 1 minute. Add the sugar and mix at medium-high speed until the sugar is fully dissolved and the dough sticks to the hook, 2 to 5 minutes.
9. Gradually add the butter and work the dough at medium speed until it wraps tightly around the hook and is elastic, about 10 minutes. Add the candied peels and raisins and work the dough until they are evenly distributed.
10. Let the dough rest in the mixing bowl for 30 minutes.
11. Coat a work surface with butter and place the dough on it. Shape the dough into three tight balls that are each 30 oz. and place them in three 26 oz. panettone molds.
12. Place the panettone molds on baking sheets. Let the rounds rise in a naturally warm spot until the dough reaches the edges of the molds, 5 to 10 hours.
13. Preheat the oven to 350°F. Gently score a cross on top of each panettone and slightly pull up on the edges of each cross. Ideally you want to perform a scarpatura, detaching the edges from the dough with a razor, but if you are making your first attempt at making panettone, just place a small piece of butter in the center of each cross, on top of the panettone.
14. Place the panettone in the oven and bake until their internal temperature is around 200°F, 35 to 45 minutes. Do not open the oven until at least 35 minutes have passed.
15. Remove the panettone from the oven, put 2 skewers in the bottom part of the panettone, and flip them upside down. Hang the panettone by the skewers and let them remain upside down until cool, 2 to 3 hours.
16. Spray fitted plastic sheets with grain alcohol and wrap the panettone with them. Stored this way, the panettone will keep for several weeks.

DESSERTS

Mostaccioli

YIELD: 15 COOKIES / **ACTIVE TIME:** 40 MINUTES / **TOTAL TIME:** 1 HOUR

4⅙ CUPS (500 G) ALL-PURPOSE FLOUR, PLUS MORE AS NEEDED

1½ CUPS (150 G) ALMOND FLOUR

7½ TABLESPOONS (150 G) HONEY

¾ CUP (150 G) SUGAR

1½ TEASPOONS (6 G) BAKER'S AMMONIA

2 TEASPOONS (5 G) PISTO

½ (SCANT) CUP (35 G) UNSWEETENED COCOA POWDER

ZEST AND JUICE OF 1 ORANGE

7 TABLESPOONS (100 ML) HOT WATER (140°F), PLUS MORE AS NEEDED

7 OZ. BITTERSWEET CHOCOLATE, CHOPPED

1. Preheat the oven to 350°F and line two baking sheets with parchment paper. Place the flours, honey, sugar, baker's ammonia, pisto, cocoa powder, orange zest, and orange juice in the work bowl of a stand mixer fitted with the paddle attachment. With the mixer running, gradually add the hot water and work the mixture until it comes together as a soft, smooth dough. Depending on the all-purpose flour you end up using, you may not need to use all of the water; you also may need to add more water if the dough is too stiff.
2. Place the dough on a flour-dusted work surface and roll it out until it is about ½ inch thick. Cut the dough into diamonds and place them on the baking sheets.
3. Place the cookies in the oven and bake until they are golden brown, 10 to 15 minutes. Remove the cookies from the oven and let them cool.
4. While the cookies are cooling, bring a few inches of water to a simmer in a medium saucepan. Place the chocolate in a heatproof bowl, place it over the simmering water, and stir until the chocolate has melted.
5. Using kitchen tongs, dip the cookies into the melted chocolate and place them on wire racks. Let the chocolate set before serving.

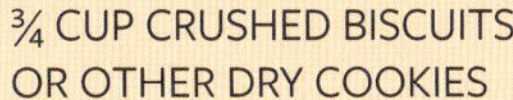

Celli Pieni

YIELD: 40 COOKIES / **ACTIVE TIME:** 40 MINUTES / **TOTAL TIME:** 1 HOUR AND 30 MINUTES

¾ CUP CRUSHED BISCUITS OR OTHER DRY COOKIES

⅔ CUP BLANCHED AND TOASTED ALMONDS, FINELY CHOPPED

1⅓ CUPS GRAPE JAM

ZEST OF 1 LEMON

2 TEASPOONS (3 G) UNSWEETENED COCOA POWDER

½ TEASPOON (1 G) CINNAMON

⅓ CUP (155 ML) DRY WHITE WINE

2 TABLESPOONS (25 G) SUGAR, PLUS MORE FOR TOPPING

⅔ CUP (135 G) EXTRA-VIRGIN OLIVE OIL

4⅙ CUPS (500 G) ALL-PURPOSE FLOUR, PLUS MORE AS NEEDED

1. Place the cookies and almonds in a bowl and stir to combine. Add the jam, lemon zest, cocoa powder, and cinnamon and stir to incorporate. Let the mixture rest for 30 minutes.
2. Place the wine and sugar in a saucepan and warm the mixture over medium heat, stirring to dissolve the sugar.
3. Place the wine syrup in a heatproof bowl, add the olive oil and flour, and work the mixture with your hands until it comes together as a smooth dough. Cover the dough and let it rest for 30 minutes.
4. Preheat the oven to 350°F and line two baking sheets with parchment paper. Place the dough on a flour-dusted work surface and roll it out into a very thin sheet. It is also possible to use a pasta maker to get the dough thin enough.
5. Distribute teaspoons of the jam mixture on the dough, leaving 1 inch between each dollop. Use a glass or ring cutter to cut out rounds of dough with the jam mixture in the center. Fold the rounds over the filling, shape them into crescents, and pinch the seams to seal the cookies. Bring the two points of the crescents together to form the shape of a fortune cookie. Dust the cookies with sugar and place them on the baking sheets.
6. Place the cookies in the oven and bake until they are a light golden brown, about 15 minutes.
7. Remove the cookies from the oven and let them cool on the baking sheets for a few minutes before transferring them to wire racks to cool completely.

Amaretti

YIELD: 50 COOKIES / **ACTIVE TIME:** 40 MINUTES / **TOTAL TIME:** 24 HOURS

1¼ CUPS (175 G) BLANCHED ALMONDS

1⅓ CUPS (150 G) CONFECTIONERS' SUGAR

2 TABLESPOONS (16 G) CHOPPED BITTER ALMONDS

2 (60 G) EGG WHITES

1 TEASPOON (5 G) BAKER'S AMMONIA

1. Preheat the oven to 390°F. Place the blanched almonds on a sheet pan, place them in the oven, and toast until they are golden brown, about 8 minutes. Remove the toasted almonds from the oven and let them cool.
2. Place the toasted almonds in a food processor, add the confectioners' sugar and bitter almonds, and pulse until the mixture is finely ground, taking care not to overwork the mixture and release the fat in the almonds.
3. Transfer the mixture to the work bowl of a stand mixer fitted with the paddle attachment. Add the egg whites and baker's ammonia and beat until the resulting mixture comes together as a smooth dough, scraping down the work bowl as necessary. Cover the bowl with plastic wrap and chill it in the refrigerator overnight.
4. Preheat the oven to 300°F and line two sheet pans with parchment paper. Working with damp hands, form the mixture into balls the size of a small walnut and place them on the pans, making sure to leave 1 inch between them.
5. Place one pan of cookies in the oven at a time. Bake until they are golden brown and starting to crack, about 20 minutes, rotating the pans halfway through.
6. Remove the amaretti from the oven, transfer them to wire racks, and let them cool completely before enjoying.

Susamielli

YIELD: 12 COOKIES / **ACTIVE TIME:** 40 MINUTES / **TOTAL TIME:** 1 HOUR

¾ CUP BLANCHED ALMONDS, PLUS MORE FOR TOPPING

½ CUP (100 G) SUGAR

2 CUPS PLUS 1½ TABLESPOONS (250 G) ALL-PURPOSE FLOUR

½ TEASPOON (2 G) BAKER'S AMMONIA

2 TEASPOONS (5 G) PISTO

¾ CUP (255 G) HONEY

1 EGG WHITE, BEATEN

1. Preheat the oven to 350°F and line a baking sheet with parchment paper. Place the almonds and sugar in a food processor and blitz until the almonds are finely ground.
2. Place the almond mixture, flour, baker's ammonia, pisto, and honey in the work bowl of a stand mixer fitted with the paddle attachment and beat until the mixture comes together as a smooth dough.
3. Divide the dough into two pieces and form them into logs. Tear each log into 2-oz. pieces, roll these pieces into thin logs, and shape them into an S.
4. Place the cookies on the baking sheet, brush them with the egg white, and press almonds into the tops.
5. Place the cookies in the oven and bake until they are golden brown, about 15 minutes.
6. Remove the cookies from the oven and let them cool on the baking sheet for a few minutes before transferring them to wire racks to cool completely.

Taralli di Avigliano

YIELD: 4 LARGE TARALLI / **ACTIVE TIME:** 1 HOUR / **TOTAL TIME:** 2 HOURS

FOR THE DOUGH

5 EGGS, PLUS MORE AS NEEDED

PINCH OF TABLE SALT

4⅙ CUPS (500 G) ALL-PURPOSE FLOUR, PLUS MORE AS NEEDED

½ CUP (100 G) SUGAR

1 TEASPOON (4 G) BAKING POWDER

7 TABLESPOONS (100 G) LARD

½ CUP (120 ML) ANISE LIQUEUR

FOR THE GLAZE

½ CUP WATER

2½ CUPS SUGAR

4 DROPS OF ANISE EXTRACT

1. To begin preparations for the dough, place the eggs and salt in a bowl and whisk to combine. Place this mixture and the remaining ingredients in a large bowl and stir to combine. Work the mixture until it comes together as a shaggy dough.
2. Transfer the dough to a flour-dusted work surface and knead it until it is soft and smooth. If the dough feels too dry, incorporate another egg.
3. Tear the dough into four pieces and form them into logs that are about 8 inches long and 1 inch thick (each one should weigh just under 1 lb.). Join the ends together to form large rings and pinch the seams.
4. Bring water to a boil in a large pot. Add the taralli a few at a time and cook until they rise to the surface. Remove, score the taralli at their equators, and place them on a paper towel–lined plate to dry.
5. Preheat the oven to 350°F and line a baking sheet with parchment paper.
6. Place the taralli on the baking sheet, place them in the oven, and bake until they are golden brown, about 20 minutes.
7. Remove the taralli from the oven and let them cool completely.
8. To prepare the glaze, place the water and sugar in a saucepan and bring to a boil, stirring to dissolve the sugar. Remove the pan from heat and place it on a heat-resistant surface. Work the syrup quickly and energetically with a spatula until it becomes a white paste. Transfer the paste to a heatproof bowl.
9. Bring a few inches of water to a boil in a saucepan. Place the paste over the simmering water and let it melt slowly. Add the anise, stir to incorporate, and then add the taralli, turning them to ensure they are coated evenly.
10. Remove the taralli from the glaze and place them on wire racks. Enjoy once the glaze has hardened.

Paste di Mandorla Siciliane

YIELD: 20 COOKIES / **ACTIVE TIME:** 20 MINUTES / **TOTAL TIME:** 40 MINUTES

2 EGG WHITES

2 CUPS (200 G) ALMOND FLOUR

1¼ CUPS (140 G) CONFECTIONERS' SUGAR

3 TABLESPOONS (45 ML) WATER OR LIQUEUR, PLUS MORE AS NEEDED

3 DROPS OF BITTER ALMOND EXTRACT

ALMONDS, FOR TOPPING (OPTIONAL)

CANDIED CHERRIES, HALVED, FOR TOPPING (OPTIONAL)

1. Place the egg whites in the work bowl of a stand mixer fitted with the whisk attachment and whip them until they are very firm.
2. Place the flour and sugar in a bowl and stir to combine. Add the water and almond extract and stir until the mixture comes together.
3. Add the egg whites and fold until the mixture is soft enough to be squeezed out of a piping bag. If the mixture feels too hard, incorporate a splash of water.
4. Place the dough in a piping bag and chill it in the refrigerator for 1 hour.
5. Preheat the oven to 330°F and line a baking sheet with parchment paper. Pipe small dollops of the dough onto the baking sheet.
6. Press either almonds or candied cherries into the centers of the cookies. Place them in the oven and bake until they are golden brown, about 15 minutes.
7. Remove the cookies from the oven and let them cool on the baking sheet for a few minutes before transferring them to wire racks to cool completely.

Buccellati

YIELD: 20 COOKIES / **ACTIVE TIME:** 40 MINUTES / **TOTAL TIME:** 3 HOURS

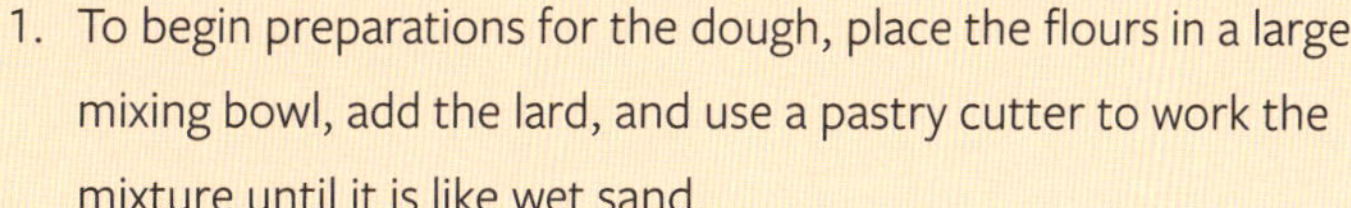

FOR THE DOUGH

2¼ CUPS (270 G) ALL-PURPOSE FLOUR, PLUS MORE AS NEEDED

2 (SCANT) CUPS (225 G) FINELY GROUND DURUM WHEAT FLOUR

½ CUP PLUS 2 TABLESPOONS (140 G) LARD

¾ CUP (150 G) SUGAR

2 TEASPOONS (8 G) BAKER'S AMMONIA

1 TEASPOON (5 ML) PURE VANILLA EXTRACT

1 CUP (240 ML) LUKEWARM WHOLE MILK (90°F)

FOR THE FILLING

3 CUPS DRIED FIGS, CHOPPED

⅓ CUP ALMONDS, FINELY CHOPPED

⅓ CUP HONEY OR FIG JAM

1¾ OZ. DARK CHOCOLATE, GRATED

1 CUP CANDIED ORANGE PEELS

COLORED SUGAR SPRINKLES, FOR TOPPING

1. To begin preparations for the dough, place the flours in a large mixing bowl, add the lard, and use a pastry cutter to work the mixture until it is like wet sand.
2. Add the sugar, baker's ammonia, vanilla, and milk and work the mixture until it just comes together as a dough. Transfer the dough to a flour-dusted work surface and quickly knead the dough until it is smooth and dense. Cover the dough with plastic wrap and chill it in the refrigerator for 1 hour.
3. To prepare the filling, place all of the ingredients, except for the sugar sprinkles, in a mixing bowl and stir to combine.
4. Preheat the oven to 350°F and line a baking sheet with parchment paper. Place the dough on a flour-dusted work surface and roll it out into a ½-inch-thick rectangle. Spread the filling over the dough and then roll the dough up tightly, starting from a long side.
5. Cut the dough into 1-inch-wide slices, place them on the baking sheet, and gently press down on them to flatten them slightly.
6. Sprinkle sugar sprinkles over the cookies, place them in the oven, and bake until they are golden brown, about 25 minutes.
7. Remove the cookies from the oven and let them cool on the baking sheet for a few minutes before transferring them to wire racks to cool completely.

Taralli Dolci Pugliesi

YIELD: 60 COOKIES / **ACTIVE TIME:** 40 MINUTES / **TOTAL TIME:** 1 HOUR AND 15 MINUTES

4⅙ CUPS (500 G) ALL-PURPOSE FLOUR, PLUS MORE AS NEEDED

2 TEASPOONS (12 G) BAKING SODA

⅔ CUP (130 G) SUGAR, PLUS MORE FOR COATING

¾ CUP (150 G) EXTRA-VIRGIN OLIVE OIL

¾ CUP (180 ML) SWEET WHITE WINE

1. Preheat the oven to 340°F and line two baking sheets with parchment paper. Sift the flour into a mixing bowl, add the baking soda and sugar, and stir to combine. Add the olive oil and wine and work the mixture until it comes together as a shaggy dough.
2. Transfer the dough to a flour-dusted work surface and knead it until it is soft and smooth.
3. Tear the dough into walnut-sized pieces and roll them into 4-inch-long logs. Join the ends together to form rings and gently press down on the seams.
4. Fill a small bowl with sugar and dip the taralli in it until evenly coated.
5. Place the taralli on the baking sheets, place them in the oven, and bake until they are golden brown, about 25 minutes.
6. Remove the taralli from the oven and let them cool on the baking sheets for a few minutes before transferring them to wire racks to cool completely.

Biscotti all'Amarena

YIELD: 10 COOKIES / **ACTIVE TIME:** 1 HOUR / **TOTAL TIME:** 1 HOUR AND 30 MINUTES

FOR THE FROLLA

2½ CUPS (300 G) ALL-PURPOSE FLOUR, PLUS MORE AS NEEDED

⅔ CUP (120 G) SUGAR

1 CUP PLUS 2 TEASPOONS (120 G) UNSALTED BUTTER, SOFTENED AND CHOPPED INTO PIECES

1 EGG

1 EGG YOLK

1 TEASPOON (4 G) BAKING POWDER

1 TEASPOON (5 ML) PURE VANILLA EXTRACT

FOR THE FILLING

¾ LB. LEFTOVER SPONGE CAKE, CHOPPED

5½ TABLESPOONS UNSWEETENED COCOA POWDER

1 CUP PLUS 2 TABLESPOONS SOUR CHERRIES OR BLACK CHERRY JAM

2 TABLESPOONS ALCHERMES OR ANOTHER SWEET LIQUEUR

FOR THE GLAZE

1 CUP PLUS 2 TABLESPOONS CONFECTIONERS' SUGAR

2 TABLESPOONS EGG WHITES

BLACK CHERRY JAM, AS NEEDED

1. To begin preparations for the frolla, place all of the ingredients in a mixing bowl and quickly work the mixture with your hands until it just comes together as a dough. Place the dough on a flour-dusted surface and shape it into a compact ball. Cover the dough with plastic wrap and chill it in the refrigerator for 30 minutes.
2. To prepare the filling, place all of the ingredients in a bowl and stir until well combined. Place the dough on a flour-dusted work surface and roll it into a rectangle.
3. Line a baking sheet with parchment paper. Shape the filling into a log that is the same length as the dough. Place the filling in the center of the dough and roll the long sides of the dough over the filling, making sure the sides meet at the center. Pinch the seam closed, turn the dough over, and place it on the baking sheet. Chill the dough in the refrigerator for 15 minutes.
4. To prepare the glaze, place the confectioners' sugar and egg whites in a small bowl and beat until the mixture is a thick glaze. Set the glaze aside.
5. Preheat the oven to 350°F. Take the dough out of the refrigerator and trim away the 2 ends that have little filling inside. Spread the glaze evenly over the dough.
6. Using a toothpick, cut two long strips in the glaze. Place cherry jam in a piping bag fitted with a fine tip and pipe the jam into the strips. Cut the dough into 1½-inch-wide slices, place them in the oven, and bake until they are golden brown, about 20 minutes.
7. Remove the cookies from the oven and let them cool on the baking sheet for a few minutes before transferring them to a wire rack to cool completely.

Pistoccheddus de Cappa

YIELD: 40 COOKIES / **ACTIVE TIME:** 1 HOUR / **TOTAL TIME:** 2 HOURS

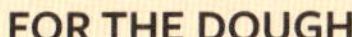

FOR THE DOUGH

2 CUPS PLUS 1½ TABLESPOONS (250 G) ALL-PURPOSE FLOUR, PLUS MORE AS NEEDED

2 CUPS PLUS 1½ TABLESPOONS (250 G) FINELY GROUND DURUM WHEAT FLOUR

1 TEASPOON (4 G) BAKING POWDER

1 TEASPOON (4 G) BAKER'S AMMONIA

½ CUP (120 ML) WHOLE MILK

4 EGG YOLKS

½ CUP (100 G) SUGAR

1 TEASPOON (5 ML) PURE VANILLA EXTRACT

ZEST OF 1 LEMON

¼ CUP (56 G) LARD, SOFTENED

FOR THE GLAZE

4 EGG WHITES

2 CUPS CONFECTIONERS' SUGAR

COLORED SUGAR SPRINKLES, FOR TOPPING (SILVER ARE THE MOST TYPICAL)

1. Preheat the oven to 350°F and line two baking sheets with parchment paper. To begin preparations for the dough, sift the flours into a mixing bowl, add the baking powder, and stir to combine.
2. Place the baker's ammonia and milk in a separate bowl, stir to dissolve the baker's ammonia, and set the mixture aside.
3. Place the egg yolks and sugar in a separate mixing bowl and whisk until the mixture is pale yellow. Stir in the vanilla, lemon zest, and lard, add the flour mixture, and work the mixture until it comes together.
4. Place the mixture on a flour-dusted work surface, add the milk mixture, and work the mixture until it is a smooth dough. Tear the dough into pieces that are the size of a large walnut and roll each piece into a cylinder. Shape the cylinders into ovals, circles, hearts, or S-shaped cookies.
5. Place the cookies on the baking sheets, place them in the oven, and bake until they are a light golden brown, about 20 minutes.
6. To prepare the glaze, place the egg whites and confectioners' sugar in a heatproof bowl and whisk to combine. Bring a few inches of water to a boil in a medium saucepan and place the bowl over it. Whisk until the sugar has dissolved.
7. Remove the cookies from the oven, turn them over, and brush their bottoms with the glaze. Reduce the oven's temperature to 250°F. Place the cookies back in the oven and bake for 10 minutes, making sure the glaze does not brown.
8. Remove the cookies from the oven, turn them over, and brush their tops with the glaze. Sprinkle the sugar sprinkles over the cookies, place them back in the oven, and bake for 10 minutes.
9. Remove the cookies from the oven and let them cool on the baking sheets for a few minutes before transferring them to wire racks to cool completely.

Reginelle

YIELD: 40 COOKIES / **ACTIVE TIME:** 30 MINUTES / **TOTAL TIME:** 2 HOURS

4⅙ CUPS (500 G) ALL-PURPOSE FLOUR, PLUS MORE AS NEEDED

¾ CUP (150 G) SUGAR

¼ TEASPOON (0.1 G) SAFFRON THREADS

1 TEASPOON (4 G) BAKER'S AMMONIA

1½ TABLESPOONS (22.5 ML) WHOLE MILK

½ CUP PLUS 2 TABLESPOONS (140 G) LARD OR UNSALTED BUTTER

2 EGGS

ZEST OF 1 LEMON

PINCH OF TABLE SALT

1 CUP SESAME SEEDS

1. Place the flour, sugar, and saffron in a mixing bowl and stir to combine. Place the baker's ammonia and milk in a bowl and stir until the baker's ammonia has dissolved. Add the milk mixture, lard, eggs, lemon zest, and salt to the mixing bowl and work the mixture until it just comes together.
2. Place the dough on a flour-dusted work surface and knead it until it is smooth. Form the dough into a ball, cover it with plastic wrap, and chill it in the refrigerator for 30 minutes.
3. Preheat the oven to 390°F and line two baking sheets with parchment paper. Place the dough on a flour-dusted work surface, divide it into 8 pieces, and roll each piece into a 1-inch-thick cylinder. Cut the cylinders into 2-inch-long pieces.
4. Place the sesame seeds in a bowl, spray the pieces of dough with water, and roll them in the sesame seeds until they are completely coated.
5. Place the cookies on the baking sheets, place them in the oven, and bake them until they are golden brown, 10 to 15 minutes.
6. Reduce the oven's temperature to 300°F and bake the cookies for another 15 minutes.
7. Remove the cookies from the oven and let them cool on the baking sheets for a few minutes before transferring them to wire racks to cool completely.

Pasticciotti Leccesi

YIELD: 15 PASTICCIOTTI / **ACTIVE TIME:** 1 HOUR / **TOTAL TIME:** 2 HOURS

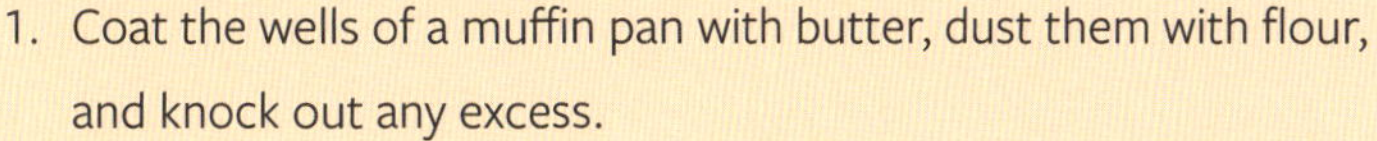

UNSALTED BUTTER, AS NEEDED

ALL-PURPOSE FLOUR, AS NEEDED

PASTA FROLLA AL LARDO (SEE PAGE 457)

1½ CUPS CREMA PASTICCERA NAPOLETANA (SEE PAGE 460)

1 EGG YOLK

½ TEASPOON WATER

CONFECTIONERS' SUGAR, FOR TOPPING

1. Coat the wells of a muffin pan with butter, dust them with flour, and knock out any excess.
2. Preheat the oven to 350°F. Place the frolla on a flour-dusted work surface and beat it with a rolling pin to soften it. Roll out the frolla into a ¼-inch-thick rectangle and use a glass or ring cutter to cut out rounds that are large enough to cover the bottom and sides of the wells in the muffin pan. Place the rounds in the wells and trim away any excess dough. Roll the excess dough out into a thin sheet that will cover the muffin pan. Fill each pastry with a generous spoonful of the pastry cream.
3. Cut rounds slightly larger than the wells from the sheet of dough. Place them over the pasticciotti and press down on the edges to seal so that the tops hold tight in the oven.
4. Prick the tops of the pasticciotti with a toothpick. Place the egg yolk and water in a small bowl, beat to combine, and brush the pasticciotti with the egg wash.
5. Place the pasticciotti in the oven. Baking times will depend on the depth of the wells in the muffin pan. For deeper wells, bake for about 30 minutes. For shallower wells, bake for about 20 minutes. Also, do not worry if the tops detach, they will be reattached later.
6. Remove the pasticciotti from the oven and let them cool for 5 minutes. Cover the pan with a similarly sized tray, invert the pan, and let it rest on the counter for 1 hour.
7. Turn the pan back over, remove the pasticciotti from the pan, dust them generously with confectioners' sugar, and enjoy.

Crostata di Ricotta

YIELD: 1 PIE / **ACTIVE TIME:** 1 HOUR / **TOTAL TIME:** 2 HOURS

2 LBS. RICOTTA CHEESE, DRAINED

1 TEASPOON PURE VANILLA EXTRACT

4 EGGS

ZEST OF 1 LEMON

ZEST OF 1 ORANGE

1½ CUPS SUGAR

½ TEASPOON CINNAMON

½ CUP RAISINS, SOAKED IN WARM WATER FOR 10 MINUTES, DRAINED, AND SQUEEZED DRY

PASTA FROLLA (SEE PAGE 456)

ALL-PURPOSE FLOUR, AS NEEDED

UNSALTED BUTTER, AS NEEDED

CONFECTIONERS' SUGAR, FOR TOPPING

1. Place the ricotta, vanilla, eggs, lemon zest, orange zest, sugar, and cinnamon in a mixing bowl and stir until the mixture is thick and creamy.
2. Place the ricotta mixture in a saucepan and bring it to a simmer over low heat. Let the mixture simmer for 3 minutes and remove the pan from heat. Let the mixture cool until it is lukewarm. Add the raisins to the mixture and stir to combine.
3. Preheat the oven to 340°F. Place the frolla on a flour-dusted work surface, remove a 3½ oz. piece of dough, and set it aside. Beat the remaining dough with a rolling pin to soften it and roll it out into a ⅛-inch-thick disk.
4. Coat a 9-inch pie plate with butter, dust it with flour, and knock out any excess. Place the dough in the pie plate, prick it with a fork, and trim away any excess dough.
5. Roll out the 3½ oz. piece of dough into a ⅛-inch-thick disk and cut it into seven strips.
6. Pour the filling into the dough and arrange the strips of dough in a lattice pattern over the filling.
7. Place the crostata in the oven and bake until the crust is golden brown, about 1 hour.
8. Remove the crostata from the oven, let it cool completely, and dust with confectioners' sugar before serving.

Pepatelli Molisani

YIELD: 40 COOKIES / **ACTIVE TIME:** 30 MINUTES / **TOTAL TIME:** 1 HOUR

4½ CUPS (500 G) WHOLE WHEAT FLOUR

1 TEASPOON (6 G) BAKING SODA

1½ CUPS (500 G) HONEY

3 CUPS BLANCHED AND TOASTED ALMONDS

ZEST OF 1 ORANGE

1 TABLESPOON BLACK PEPPER

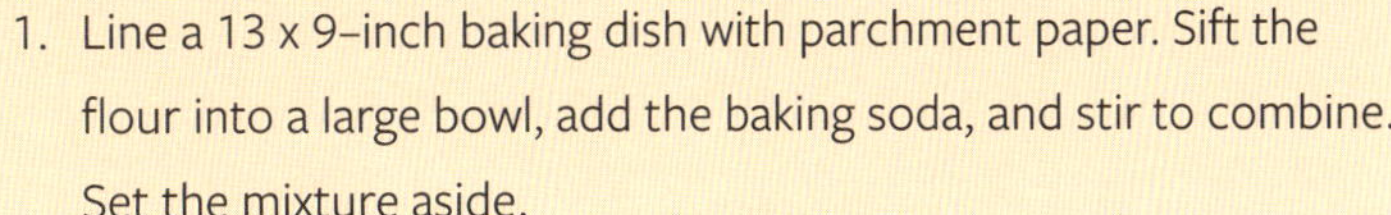

1. Line a 13 x 9–inch baking dish with parchment paper. Sift the flour into a large bowl, add the baking soda, and stir to combine. Set the mixture aside.

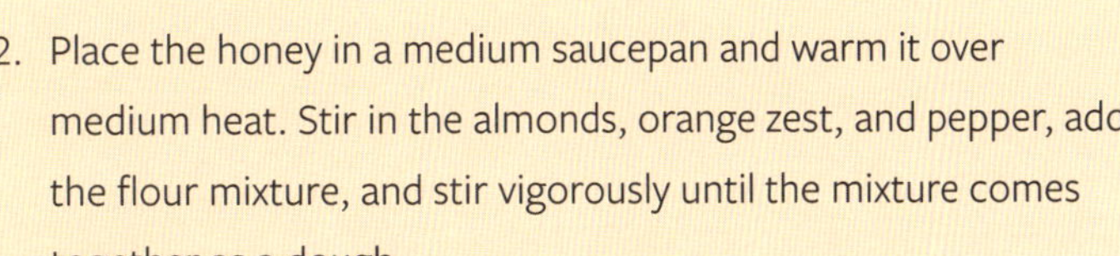

2. Place the honey in a medium saucepan and warm it over medium heat. Stir in the almonds, orange zest, and pepper, add the flour mixture, and stir vigorously until the mixture comes together as a dough.
3. Pour the dough into the baking dish and level it until it is about 1 inch thick. Let the dough cool completely.
4. Preheat the oven to 340°F. Line two baking sheets with parchment paper. Cut the dough into 2 x ½–inch strips and place them on the baking sheets.
5. Place the cookies in the oven and bake until they are a light golden brown, about 15 minutes. Turn off the oven and leave the cookies in the cooling oven for 5 minutes.
6. Remove the cookies from the oven and let them cool on the baking sheets for a few minutes before transferring them to wire racks to cool completely.

Sfogliatelle di Frolla

YIELD: 12 SFOGLIATELLE / **ACTIVE TIME:** 1 HOUR / **TOTAL TIME:** 3 HOURS

1⅔ CUPS WHOLE MILK

PINCH OF TABLE SALT

½ CUP UNSALTED BUTTER

1 LEMON PEEL, PITH REMOVED

¾ CUP COARSE SEMOLINA FLOUR

1 EGG

2 (SCANT) CUPS CONFECTIONERS' SUGAR

1 TEASPOON PURE VANILLA EXTRACT

1 TEASPOON ORANGE BLOSSOM WATER

PINCH OF CINNAMON

½ CUP CANDIED CITRUS PEELS, FINELY CHOPPED

1 CUP RICOTTA CHEESE

PASTA FROLLA NAPOLETANA (SEE PAGE 457)

ALL-PURPOSE FLOUR, AS NEEDED

1 EGG YOLK, BEATEN

1. Place the milk, salt, half of the butter, and the lemon peel in a medium saucepan and bring the mixture to a boil. Remove the lemon peel and discard it. Add the semolina and stir continually until the mixture thickens.
2. Remove the pan from heat, cover it with plastic wrap, and let the mixture cool.
3. Place the egg, confectioners' sugar, vanilla, orange blossom water, cinnamon, and candied citrus peels in another bowl and whisk to combine. Incorporate the ricotta a little bit at a time. When all of the ricotta has been incorporated, add the semolina mixture gradually and whisk until incorporated.
4. Cover the mixture with plastic wrap and chill it in the refrigerator for 1 hour.
5. Line two baking sheets with parchment paper. Place the frolla on a flour-dusted work surface and beat it with a rolling pin to soften it. Divide the frolla into 12 pieces and roll out each piece into a ¼-inch-thick oval.
6. Place 1 tablespoon of the ricotta cream on the bottom half of each oval, making sure to maintain a small border around the edge, and fold the other half of the dough over the filling.
7. Press down on the edges of the sfogliatelle to seal them and trim away any excess dough.
8. Place the sfogliatelle on the baking sheets and chill them in the refrigerator for 1 hour.
9. Preheat the oven to 390°F (if your oven has convection mode, set it to that).
10. Brush the sfogliatelle with the egg yolk, place them in the oven, and bake until they are golden brown, about 15 minutes. Remove the sfogliatelle from the oven and let them cool slightly before serving.

Cassatelle Siciliane

YIELD: 20 CASSATELLE / **ACTIVE TIME:** 1 HOUR / **TOTAL TIME:** 1 HOUR AND 30 MINUTES

1 LB. RICOTTA CHEESE, DRAINED IN THE REFRIGERATOR FOR A FEW HOURS

1 (SCANT) CUP CONFECTIONERS' SUGAR, PLUS MORE FOR TOPPING

3½ OZ. BITTERSWEET CHOCOLATE CHIPS

1 EGG YOLK

½ TEASPOON CINNAMON

ZEST OF 1 ORANGE

PASTA FROLLA AL MARSALA (SEE PAGE 458)

ALL-PURPOSE FLOUR, AS NEEDED

EXTRA-VIRGIN OLIVE OIL, AS NEEDED

1. Place all of the ingredients, except for the frolla, flour, and olive oil, in a large bowl and stir until well combined.
2. Place the frolla on a flour-dusted work surface and roll it out into a ¼-inch-thick rectangle. Use a glass or ring cutter to cut 4-inch rounds out of the dough.
3. Place a teaspoon of the ricotta mixture in the center of each round and fold the rounds into half-moons. Press down on the edge to seal the dumplings and trim away any excess dough using a pasta wheel.
4. Add olive oil to a large, deep skillet until it is about 1 inch deep and warm it to 350°F. Add the cassatelle and fry until they are crispy and golden brown, 4 to 6 minutes, turning them as necessary.
5. Transfer the fried cassatelle to a paper towel–lined plate to drain. Dust them with confectioners' sugar and enjoy.

Genovesi di Erice

YIELD: 20 GENOVESI / **ACTIVE TIME:** 45 MINUTES / **TOTAL TIME:** 1 HOUR

PASTA FROLLA DI SEMOLA (SEE PAGE 459)

ALL-PURPOSE FLOUR, AS NEEDED

CREMA PASTICCERA SICILIANA (SEE PAGE 461)

CONFECTIONERS' SUGAR, FOR TOPPING

1. Preheat the oven to 375°F and line two baking sheets with parchment paper. Place the frolla on a flour-dusted work surface and beat it with a rolling pin to soften it. Roll out the frolla into a ¼-inch-thick rectangle. Use a glass or ring cutter to cut 4-inch rounds out of the dough.
2. Place a teaspoon of the pastry cream in the center of each round. Roll the remaining dough into a ¼-inch-thick rectangle. Use a glass or ring cutter to cut 4-inch rounds out of the dough. Place the rounds over the filling and press down on the edges to seal the genovesi. Trim away any excess dough using a pasta wheel.
3. Place the genovesi on the baking sheets, place them in the oven, and bake until they are just about to brown, 10 to 15 minutes.
4. Remove the genovesi from the oven and let them cool.
5. Dust the genovesi generously with confectioners' sugar and enjoy.

Sfogliatelle di Frolla

SEE PAGE 392

Pizza di Crema e Amarene

YIELD: 1 PIE / **ACTIVE TIME:** 30 MINUTES / **TOTAL TIME:** 3 HOURS AND 15 MINUTES

PASTA FROLLA (SEE PAGE 456)

ALL-PURPOSE FLOUR, AS NEEDED

UNSALTED BUTTER, AS NEEDED

1 CUP CHERRIES IN SYRUP, DRAINED

CREMA PASTICCERA NAPOLETANA (SEE PAGE 460)

CONFECTIONERS' SUGAR, FOR TOPPING

1. Preheat the oven to 350°F. Place the frolla on a flour-dusted work surface, remove a 3½-oz. piece of dough, and set it aside. Beat the remaining dough with a rolling pin to soften it and roll it out into a ⅛-inch-thick disk.
2. Coat a 9-inch pie plate with butter, dust it with flour, and knock out any excess. Place the dough in the pie plate, prick it with a fork, and trim away any excess dough.
3. Roll out the 3½-oz. piece of dough into a ⅛-inch-thick disk and cut it into seven strips.
4. Distribute half of the cherries in the crust, cover them with the pastry cream, and then top the pastry cream with the remaining cherries.
5. Arrange the strips of dough in a lattice pattern over the cherries. Place the pie in the oven and bake until the crust is golden brown, about 45 minutes.
6. Remove the pie from the oven and let it cool for a few hours.
7. Dust the pie with confectioners' sugar and serve.

Migliaccio

YIELD: 1 CAKE / **ACTIVE TIME:** 1 HOUR / **TOTAL TIME:** 2 HOURS AND 30 MINUTES

4 CUPS (1.060 ML) WHOLE MILK

¼ TEASPOON (1.5 G) TABLE SALT

¼ CUP (55 G) UNSALTED BUTTER, PLUS MORE AS NEEDED

½ ORANGE PEEL, PITH REMOVED

½ LEMON PEEL, PITH REMOVED

1½ CUPS (180 G) COARSE SEMOLINA FLOUR

6 EGGS

1¾ CUPS (350 G) SUGAR

2 TEASPOONS (10 ML) PURE VANILLA EXTRACT

2 TABLESPOONS (30 ML) LIMONCELLO

2 TEASPOONS (10 ML) ORANGE BLOSSOM WATER

¼ TEASPOON (0.7 G) CINNAMON

ZEST OF ½ ORANGE

ZEST OF ½ LEMON

2 CUPS (450 G) RICOTTA CHEESE, DRAINED

CONFECTIONERS' SUGAR, FOR TOPPING

1. Preheat the oven to 350°F. Place the milk, salt, butter, orange peel, and lemon peel in a saucepan and bring the mixture to a boil.
2. Remove the orange peel and lemon peel and discard them. Add the semolina and stir continually until the mixture thickens. Remove the pan from heat, cover it with plastic wrap, and let the mixture cool.
3. Place the eggs, sugar, vanilla, limoncello, orange blossom water, cinnamon, orange zest, and lemon zest in a bowl and whisk to combine. Incorporate the ricotta a little bit at a time. When all of the ricotta has been incorporated, add the semolina mixture gradually and whisk until incorporated.
4. Coat a round 12-inch cake pan with low edges with butter. Pour the mixture into the pan, place it in the oven, and bake for 1½ hours.
5. Remove the migliaccio from the oven and let it cool completely. Dust it with confectioners' sugar before serving.

Bocconotti Abruzzesi

YIELD: 15 BOCCONOTTI / **ACTIVE TIME:** 1 HOUR / **TOTAL TIME:** 4 HOURS

1½ CUPS WATER

5 OZ. BITTERSWEET CHOCOLATE

½ CUP PLUS 2 TABLESPOONS SUGAR

4 EGG YOLKS

⅔ CUP BLANCHED AND TOASTED ALMONDS, FINELY CHOPPED

LARGE PINCH OF CINNAMON

UNSALTED BUTTER, AS NEEDED

ALL-PURPOSE FLOUR, AS NEEDED

PASTA FROLLA (SEE PAGE 456)

CONFECTIONERS' SUGAR, FOR TOPPING

1. Place the water in a saucepan and warm it until it is lukewarm. Add the chocolate and sugar and bring to a boil. Remove the pan from heat and let the mixture cool until it is lukewarm.
2. Stir in three of the egg yolks, place the mixture over medium heat, and let it come to a gentle simmer.
3. Stir in the almonds and gently simmer the mixture until it thickens. Stir in the cinnamon, remove the pan from heat, and cover the custard with plastic wrap, placing it directly on the surface to prevent a skin from forming. Chill the custard in the refrigerator for 1 hour.
4. Coat the wells of a muffin pan with butter, dust them with flour, and knock out any excess.
5. Preheat the oven to 350°F. Place the frolla on a flour-dusted work surface and beat it with a rolling pin to soften it. Roll out the frolla into a ¼-inch-thick rectangle and use a glass or ring cutter to cut out rounds that are large enough to cover the bottom and sides of the wells in the muffin pan. Place the rounds in the wells and trim away any excess dough. Roll the excess dough out into a thin sheet that will cover the muffin pan.
6. Fill each pastry with a spoonful of the custard, keeping in mind that it will expand in the oven. Lay the thin sheet of dough over the muffin pan and trim away the dough that is not directly over the bocconotti, leaving just a little bit over the edge of each well. You can also cut out properly sized rounds from the sheet of dough instead of placing the sheet over the pan all at once. Press down on the edges to seal so that the tops hold tight in the oven. Prick the tops of the bocconotti with a toothpick. Beat the remaining egg yolk and brush the bocconotti with it.
7. Place the bocconotti in the oven. Baking times will depend on the depth of the wells in the muffin pan. For deeper wells, bake for about 30 minutes. For shallower wells, bake for about 20 minutes. Also, do not worry if the tops detach; they will be reattached later.
8. Remove the bocconotti from the oven and let them cool for 5 minutes. Cover the pan with a similarly sized tray, invert the pan, and let it rest on the counter for 1 hour.
9. Turn the pan back over, remove the bocconotti from the pan, dust them generously with confectioners' sugar, and enjoy.

Bocconotti Calabresi

YIELD: 15 BOCCONOTTI / **ACTIVE TIME:** 1 HOUR / **TOTAL TIME:** 2 HOURS

UNSALTED BUTTER, AS NEEDED

ALL-PURPOSE FLOUR, AS NEEDED

PASTA FROLLA (SEE PAGE 456)

1½ CUPS BLACK GRAPE MARMALADE (MOSTARDA D'UVA)

1 EGG YOLK

CONFECTIONERS' SUGAR, FOR TOPPING

1. Coat the wells of a muffin pan with butter, dust them with flour, and knock out any excess.
2. Preheat the oven to 350°F. Place the frolla on a flour-dusted work surface and beat it with a rolling pin to soften it. Roll out the frolla into a ¼-inch-thick rectangle and use a glass or ring cutter to cut out rounds that are large enough to cover the bottom and sides of the wells in the muffin pan. Place the rounds in the wells and trim away any excess dough. Roll the excess dough out into a thin sheet that will cover the muffin pan.
3. Fill each pastry with a heaping spoonful of the marmalade.
4. Cut rounds slightly larger than the wells from the sheet of dough. Place them over the bocconotti and press down on the edges to seal so that the tops hold tight in the oven.
5. Prick the tops of the bocconotti with a toothpick. Beat the egg yolk and brush the bocconotti with it.
6. Place the bocconotti in the oven. Baking times will depend on the depth of the wells in the muffin pan. For deeper wells, bake for about 30 minutes. For shallower wells, bake for about 20 minutes. Also, do not worry if the tops detach, they will be reattached later.
7. Remove the bocconotti from the oven and let them cool for 5 minutes. Cover the pan with a similarly sized tray, invert the pan, and let it rest on the counter for 1 hour.
8. Turn the pan back over, remove the bocconotti from the pan, dust them generously with confectioners' sugar, and enjoy.

Bocconotti Molisani

YIELD: 15 BOCCONOTTI / **ACTIVE TIME:** 1 HOUR / **TOTAL TIME:** 2 HOURS

UNSALTED BUTTER, AS NEEDED

ALL-PURPOSE FLOUR, AS NEEDED

2 BATCHES OF PASTA FROLLA (SEE PAGE 456)

½ LB. CHERRIES IN SYRUP, DRAINED AND PATTED DRY

1½ CUPS CREMA PASTICCERA NAPOLETANA (SEE PAGE 460)

1 EGG YOLK

½ TEASPOON WATER

CONFECTIONERS' SUGAR, FOR TOPPING

1. Coat the wells of a muffin pan with butter, dust them with flour, and knock out any excess.
2. Preheat the oven to 350°F. Place the frolla on a flour-dusted work surface and beat it with a rolling pin to soften it. Roll out the frolla into a ¼-inch-thick rectangle and use a glass or ring cutter to cut out rounds that are large enough to cover the bottom and sides of the wells in the muffin pan. Place the rounds in the wells and trim away any excess dough. Roll the excess dough out into a thin sheet that will cover the muffin pan.
3. Fill each pastry with a few cherries and a generous spoonful of the pastry cream.
4. Cut rounds slightly larger than the wells from the sheet of dough. Place them over the bocconotti and press down on the edges to seal so that the tops hold tight in the oven.
5. Prick the tops of the bocconotti with a toothpick. Place the egg yolk and water in a small bowl, beat to combine, and brush the bocconotti with the egg wash.
6. Place the bocconotti in the oven. Baking times will depend on the depth of the wells in the muffin pan. For deeper wells, bake for about 30 minutes. For shallower wells, bake for about 20 minutes. Also, do not worry if the tops detach, they will be reattached later.
7. Remove the bocconotti from the oven and let them cool for 5 minutes. Cover the pan with a similarly sized tray, invert the pan, and let it rest on the counter for 1 hour.
8. Turn the pan back over, remove the bocconotti from the pan, dust them generously with confectioners' sugar, and enjoy.

Cassatelle di Partinico

YIELD: 20 CASSATELLE / **ACTIVE TIME:** 1 HOUR / **TOTAL TIME:** 24 HOURS

3 CUPS DRIED CHICKPEAS

1 TEASPOON BAKING SODA

SALT, TO TASTE

3½ OZ. ROASTED BUTTERNUT SQUASH, DICED

¼ CUP HONEY

½ CUP BITTERSWEET CHOCOLATE CHIPS

PASTA FROLLA DI SEMOLA (SEE PAGE 459; SUBSTITUTE LARD FOR THE BUTTER)

ALL-PURPOSE FLOUR, AS NEEDED

EXTRA-VIRGIN OLIVE OIL, AS NEEDED

SUGAR, FOR TOPPING

CINNAMON, FOR TOPPING

1. Place the chickpeas in a bowl, cover them with water, and stir in the baking soda. Let the chickpeas soak overnight.
2. Drain the chickpeas and place them in a large saucepan. Cover them with water, add a few pinches of salt, and bring to a boil. Cook the chickpeas until they are tender, drain them, and let them cool.
3. Add the butternut squash, honey, and chocolate chips to the chickpeas and stir to combine.
4. Preheat the oven to 350°F and line two baking sheets with parchment paper. Place the frolla on a flour-dusted work surface and roll it out until it is a ⅛-inch-thick rectangle. Use a glass or ring cutter to cut 4-inch rounds out of the dough.
5. Place a teaspoon of the filling in the center of each round and fold the rounds into half-moons. Press down on the edge to seal the dumplings and trim away any excess dough using a pasta wheel.
6. Add olive oil to a large, deep skillet until it is about 1 inch deep and warm it to 350°F. Add the cassatelle and fry until they are crispy and golden brown, 4 to 6 minutes, turning them as necessary.
7. Transfer the fried cassatelle to a paper towel–lined plate to drain. Place sugar and cinnamon in a shallow bowl and stir to combine. Sprinkle the mixture over the cassatelle and enjoy.

Cannoli Siciliani

YIELD: 30 CANNOLI / **ACTIVE TIME:** 1 HOUR / **TOTAL TIME:** 4 HOURS

FOR THE SHELLS

4⅙ CUPS (500 G) ALL-PURPOSE FLOUR, PLUS MORE AS NEEDED

3 TABLESPOONS (40 G) SUGAR

PINCH OF TABLE SALT

1 TEASPOON (1.5 G) UNSWEETENED COCOA POWDER

1 TEASPOON (2.6 G) CINNAMON

3 TABLESPOONS (40 G) LARD

2⅔ TABLESPOONS (40 ML) MARSALA OR WHITE WINE

2⅔ TABLESPOONS (40 ML) VINEGAR

1 EGG

1 EGG WHITE, BEATEN

EXTRA-VIRGIN OLIVE OIL, AS NEEDED

FOR THE RICOTTA CREAM

3 CUPS RICOTTA CHEESE (MADE FROM SHEEP'S MILK PREFERRED), DRAINED FOR A FEW HOURS IN THE REFRIGERATOR

1½ CUPS CONFECTIONERS' SUGAR

½ CUP SMALL BITTERSWEET CHOCOLATE CHIPS (OPTIONAL)

BITTERSWEET CHOCOLATE CHIPS, CANDIED CHERRIES, CHOPPED PISTACHIOS, CANDIED ORANGE PEELS, AND CONFECTIONERS' SUGAR, FOR GARNISH

1. To begin preparations for the shells, place the flour, sugar, salt, cocoa powder, and cinnamon in a mixing bowl and stir to combine.
2. Add the lard, wine, vinegar, and egg and work the mixture until it just comes together as a shaggy dough. Place the dough on a flour-dusted work surface and knead it until it is smooth and elastic, about 10 minutes. Cover the dough in plastic wrap and chill it in the refrigerator for 3 hours.
3. To prepare the ricotta cream, place all of the ingredients, except for the garnishes, in a mixing bowl and stir until well combined. Store it in the refrigerator.
4. Place the dough on a flour-dusted work surface and roll it out into a ⅛-inch-thick sheet.
5. Cut the dough into 4-inch rounds and form them into shells around cannoli molds, brushing the edges with the beaten egg white and pressing down to seal them.
6. Add olive oil to a narrow, deep, heavy-bottomed saucepan with high edges until it is about 2 inches deep and warm it to 340°F. Working in batches to avoid crowding the pot, add the cannoli shells and fry until they are golden brown, 3 to 4 minutes. Transfer the fried cannoli shells to a paper towel–lined plate to drain and cool.
7. When the cannoli shells are cold, place the ricotta cream in a piping bag and fill the shells with them. Garnish the two ends with chocolate chips, candied cherries, pistachios, or candied orange peels, dust the cannoli with confectioners' sugar, and enjoy.

Parrozzo

YIELD: 1 CAKE / **ACTIVE TIME:** 30 MINUTES / **TOTAL TIME:** 2 HOURS

FOR THE CAKE

4 LARGE EGGS, SEPARATED

½ CUP (100 G) SUGAR

ZEST OF 1 LEMON

⅓ CUP (80 G) UNSALTED BUTTER, MELTED, PLUS MORE AS NEEDED

2 TABLESPOONS (30 ML) AMARETTO

1 CUP (120 G) SEMOLINA FLOUR

⅚ CUP (100 G) BLANCHED ALMONDS, VERY FINELY GROUND

FOR THE CHOCOLATE GANACHE

7 OZ. BITTERSWEET CHOCOLATE, CHOPPED

1½ TABLESPOONS UNSALTED BUTTER

1. Preheat the oven to 320°F. To begin preparations for the cake, place the egg yolks and sugar in a bowl and whisk until the mixture is pale yellow. Add the remaining ingredients, except for the egg whites, and stir until the mixture comes together as a smooth batter.
2. Place the egg whites in the work bowl of a stand mixer fitted with the whisk attachment and whip until they hold soft peaks. Add the egg whites to the batter and fold to incorporate them.
3. Coat a 6 x 3-inch hemisphere pan with butter and pour the batter into it.
4. Place the cake in the oven and bake until a toothpick inserted into the center of it comes out clean, about 20 minutes.
5. Remove the cake from the oven, let it cool for 10 minutes, and then remove it from the pan. Place the cake on a wire rack and let it cool completely.
6. To prepare the ganache, bring a few inches of water to a simmer in a medium saucepan. Place the chocolate and butter in a heatproof bowl, place it over the simmering water, and stir until the mixture is melted and smooth.
7. Place a piece of waxed paper beneath the cake on the wire rack and pour the ganache over the cake. Collect the ganache from the waxed paper and spread it over the cake.
8. Let the ganache set before slicing and serving the cake.

Cannoli Siciliani

SEE PAGE 402

Seadas Sarde

YIELD: 20 SEADAS / **ACTIVE TIME:** 1 HOUR AND 30 MINUTES / **TOTAL TIME:** 2 HOURS

3½ CUPS PLUS 3 TABLESPOONS (440 G) FINELY GROUND DURUM WHEAT FLOUR, PLUS MORE AS NEEDED

1 CUP (240 ML) WARM WATER (105°F), PLUS MORE AS NEEDED

PINCH OF TABLE SALT

¼ CUP (55 G) LARD

2 CUPS (450 G) RICOTTA CHEESE (MADE FROM SHEEP'S MILK PREFERRED)

ZEST OF 1 LEMON

EXTRA-VIRGIN OLIVE OIL, AS NEEDED

HONEY, FOR TOPPING

1. Place 3 cups of flour and the water in the work bowl of a stand mixer fitted with the dough hook and stir to combine. Add the salt and lard and work the mixture until it comes together as a smooth dough. Cover the dough with plastic wrap and chill it in the refrigerator for 30 minutes.
2. Place the ricotta, lemon zest, and remaining flour in a saucepan and warm the mixture over low heat, stirring occasionally, until it is creamy and not watery. Remove the pan from heat and let the mixture cool.
3. Place the dough on a flour-dusted work surface and roll it out until it is about ⅒ inch thick. You can also use a pasta maker to get the dough to the proper thinness. Cut the dough into 5-inch rounds.
4. Place a tablespoon of the ricotta mixture in the center of each round.
5. Roll out the leftover dough until it is ⅒ inch thick and cut it into 5-inch rounds. Place them over the filling and press down on the edges to seal the seadas. Trim away any excess dough, using a pasta wheel.
6. Add olive oil to a large, deep skillet until it is about 1 inch deep and warm it to 350°F. Add the seadas and fry until they are crispy and golden brown, 4 to 6 minutes, turning them as necessary.
7. Transfer the fried seadas to a paper towel–lined plate to drain. Drizzle honey over them and enjoy.

Cassata Siciliana

YIELD: 1 CAKE / **ACTIVE TIME:** 1 HOUR / **TOTAL TIME:** 5 HOURS

FOR THE RICOTTA CREAM

2 LBS. RICOTTA CHEESE (MADE FROM SHEEP'S MILK PREFERRED), DRAINED FOR A FEW HOURS IN THE REFRIGERATOR

2 CUPS SUGAR

1 TABLESPOON VANILLA SUGAR OR 1 TEASPOON PURE VANILLA EXTRACT

1¾ CUPS BITTERSWEET CHOCOLATE CHIPS

FOR THE MARZIPAN

1 CUP SUGAR

3½ TABLESPOONS WATER

2 TO 3 DROPS BRIGHT GREEN FOOD COLORING

2 CUPS ALMOND FLOUR

FOR THE BAGNA

⅓ CUP MARSALA, LUXARDO MARASCHINO LIQUEUR, OR SWEET LIQUEUR

⅔ CUP WATER

¼ CUP SUGAR

2.3 LBS. PAN DI SPAGNA (SEE PAGE 459)

FOR THE ICING

2 (SCANT) CUPS CONFECTIONERS' SUGAR

¼ CUP WATER

CANDIED FRUIT, FOR TOPPING

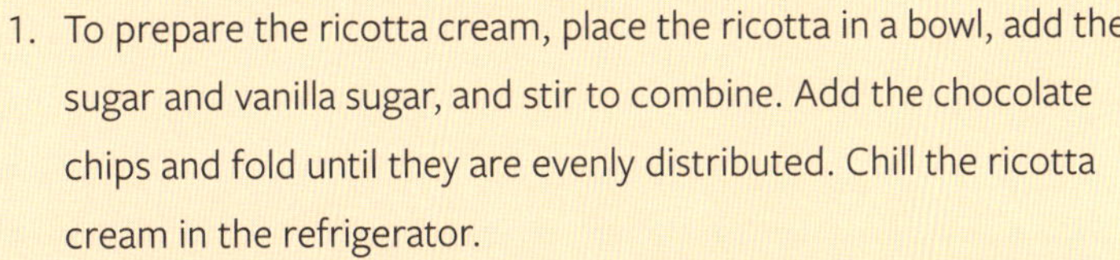

1. To prepare the ricotta cream, place the ricotta in a bowl, add the sugar and vanilla sugar, and stir to combine. Add the chocolate chips and fold until they are evenly distributed. Chill the ricotta cream in the refrigerator.
2. To begin preparations for the marzipan, place the sugar, water, and food coloring in a saucepan and bring to a boil, stirring to dissolve the sugar. Turn off the heat, add the almond flour, and stir until the mixture is dense, smooth, and soft, and starts to pull away from the side of the pan.
3. Spray a pastry board or cutting board with water, pour the marzipan onto it, and let it cool.
4. Knead the marzipan for a few minutes until it feels smoother. Roll it out into a ¼-inch-thick rectangle and cut the marzipan into 7 or 8 trapezoids that are approximately one-third as high as the edge of the pan on which the cassata will be arranged.
5. To prepare the bagna, place all of the ingredients, except for the Pan di Spagna, in a bowl and whisk until combined.
6. Cut the Pan di Spagna, horizontally, into three equally thick pieces. Place the top piece in a round cake pan, cut side up. Cut out trapezoids from the middle piece of cake and line the side of the pan with them and the pieces of marzipan, alternating between them.
7. Pour the bagna over the pieces of the cake and then spread the ricotta cream inside the cake. Place the remaining piece of cake on top, cut side down, and place the cassata in the refrigerator for 2 to 3 hours.
8. To prepare the icing, place the confectioners' sugar in a bowl and incorporate the water 1 tablespoon at a time until the icing has the desired consistency. Set the mixture aside.
9. Remove the cake from the refrigerator, place a large plate over the pan, and invert the cake. Spread the icing over the top and sides of the cake, top it with candied fruit, and enjoy.

Sise delle Monache

YIELD: 10 PASTRIES / **ACTIVE TIME:** 40 MINUTES / **TOTAL TIME:** 1 HOUR

4 EGGS, SEPARATED

½ CUP (100 G) SUGAR

⅚ CUP (100 G) ALL-PURPOSE OR CAKE FLOUR

7 TABLESPOONS (50 G) CORNSTARCH

½ BATCH OF CREMA PASTICCERA NAPOLETANA (SEE PAGE 460)

CONFECTIONERS' SUGAR, FOR TOPPING

1. Preheat the oven to 360°F and line a baking sheet with parchment paper. Place the egg whites in the work bowl of a stand mixer fitted with the whisk attachment and whip until they hold medium peaks. Add half of the sugar and whip until the meringue holds stiff peaks.
2. Place the egg yolks and remaining sugar in a separate bowl and beat until the mixture is pale and well combined. Add the flour and cornstarch and whisk to combine.
3. Add the meringue and fold to incorporate it. Place the batter in a piping bag.
4. In groups of three, pipe small cones of the batter onto the baking sheet. Place the pan in the oven and bake until the sise delle monache are lightly golden brown, 15 to 20 minutes.
5. Turn off the oven and let the sise delle monache rest in the cooling oven for 5 minutes.
6. Remove the sise delle monache from the oven and let them cool completely.
7. Cut off the tips of the sise delle monache with a sharp knife, fill them with the pastry cream, and put the tips back on. Dust the sise delle monache with confectioners' sugar and enjoy.

Cassata Abruzzese

YIELD: 1 CAKE / **ACTIVE TIME:** 1 HOUR / **TOTAL TIME:** 1 HOUR AND 30 MINUTES

½ CUP WHOLE MILK

2 TABLESPOONS CENTERBE

⅞ CUP UNSALTED BUTTER

1 CUP SUGAR

6 EGG YOLKS (FROM VERY FRESH EGGS)

½ CUP HAZELNUTS, BLANCHED, TOASTED, AND FINELY CHOPPED

2 OZ. TORRONE, FINELY DICED

⅓ CUP MILK CHOCOLATE, FINELY CHOPPED

¼ CUP UNSWEETENED COCOA POWDER

1 LB. PAN DI SPAGNA (SEE PAGE 459)

CANDIED ALMONDS, FOR TOPPING (OPTIONAL)

CHERRIES IN SYRUP, DRAINED, FOR TOPPING (OPTIONAL)

1. Place the milk and liqueur in a bowl, stir to combine, and set it aside.
2. Place the butter and sugar in the work bowl of a stand mixer fitted with the paddle attachment and cream it on medium speed until pale and fluffy. With the mixer running, incorporate the egg yolks one at a time. Divide the mixture into three equal portions.
3. Add the hazelnuts to the first portion, the torrone and chocolate to the second portion, and the cocoa powder to the third portion. Stir until the additions have been incorporated.
4. Place a spoonful of each frosting in a separate bowl and stir to combine.
5. Cut the Pan di Spagna, horizontally, into four equally thick pieces.
6. Place a piece of cake on a plate, moisten it with the liqueur mixture, and spread the cocoa powder frosting over the cake.
7. Place another piece of cake on top, moisten it with the liqueur mixture, and spread the hazelnut frosting over the cake.
8. Place another piece of cake on top, moisten it with the liqueur mixture, and spread the torrone frosting over the cake.
9. Top with the final piece of cake, moisten it with the liqueur mixture, and spread the mixture of all three frostings over the top.
10. Top the cake with candied almonds and/or cherries (if desired) and enjoy.

Torta Fedora

YIELD: 1 CAKE / **ACTIVE TIME:** 30 MINUTES / **TOTAL TIME:** 3 HOURS

FOR THE RICOTTA CREAM

4 CUPS RICOTTA CHEESE (MADE FROM SHEEP'S MILK PREFERRED), DRAINED FOR A FEW HOURS IN THE REFRIGERATOR

1¼ CUPS CONFECTIONERS' SUGAR

½ CUP BITTERSWEET CHOCOLATE CHIPS

FOR THE BAGNA

¾ CUP WATER

½ CUP SUGAR

ZEST OF 1 ORANGE

2 TABLESPOONS ORANGE LIQUEUR

PAN DI SPAGNA (SEE PAGE 459)

1 CUP SLIVERED ALMONDS, TOASTED, FOR TOPPING

1 CUP UNSALTED PISTACHIOS, FINELY CHOPPED, FOR TOPPING

1. To prepare the ricotta cream, place all of the ingredients in a bowl and stir until well combined. Chill the ricotta cream in the refrigerator.
2. To prepare the bagna, place the water, sugar, and orange zest in a small saucepan and bring to a boil, stirring to dissolve the sugar. Remove the pan from heat and let the syrup cool. When the syrup has cooled, stir in the liqueur.
3. Cut the Pan di Spagna, horizontally, into two equally thick pieces and moisten them both with the bagna.
4. Spread two-thirds of the ricotta cream over the bottom piece of cake. Place the other piece of cake on top and coat the entire cake with the remaining ricotta cream.
5. Top the sides of the cake with the almonds and the top with the pistachios. Place the cake in the refrigerator and chill it for at least 1 hour before serving.

Casadinas

YIELD: 15 CASADINAS / **ACTIVE TIME:** 1 HOUR / **TOTAL TIME:** 2 HOURS

2½ CUPS (300 G) FINELY GROUND DURUM WHEAT FLOUR, PLUS MORE AS NEEDED

⅓ CUP (75 G) LARD

⅔ CUP (160 ML) LUKEWARM WATER (90°F)

PINCH OF TABLE SALT

2 CUPS (450 G) RICOTTA CHEESE (MADE FROM SHEEP'S MILK PREFERRED)

1 (SCANT) CUP (100 G) CONFECTIONERS' SUGAR

2 TABLESPOONS (15 G) ALL-PURPOSE FLOUR

1 EGG

PINCH OF SAFFRON THREADS

ZEST OF 1 ORANGE

ZEST OF 1 LEMON

1. Place the flour, lard, water, and salt in a mixing bowl and work the mixture until it comes together as a smooth dough. Cover the dough with plastic wrap and let it rest for 30 minutes.
2. Place the remaining ingredients in a mixing bowl and stir until well combined.
3. Preheat the oven to 350°F and line two baking sheets with parchment paper.
4. Place the dough on a flour-dusted work surface and roll it out until it is about ⅛ inch thick. Cut the dough into 4-inch rounds and place them on the baking sheets.
5. Place a tablespoon of the ricotta mixture in the center of each round.
6. To shape the casadinas, pinch the edge of the rounds around the filling, forming a sort of small basket that encases it. Generally, the perimeter of the pastry has 7 or 8 corners.
7. Place the casadinas in the oven and bake until the filling is golden brown and puffy, about 30 minutes.
8. Remove the casadinas from the oven and let them cool slightly before enjoying.

Cassatine Siciliane

YIELD: 15 CASSATINE / **ACTIVE TIME:** 1 HOUR / **TOTAL TIME:** 5 HOURS

FOR THE RICOTTA CREAM

1 LB. RICOTTA CHEESE (MADE FROM SHEEP'S MILK PREFERRED), DRAINED FOR A FEW HOURS IN THE REFRIGERATOR

1 CUP SUGAR

2 TEASPOONS VANILLA SUGAR OR ½ TEASPOON PURE VANILLA EXTRACT

1 CUP BITTERSWEET CHOCOLATE CHIPS

FOR THE MARZIPAN

½ CUP SUGAR

1½ TABLESPOONS WATER

2 DROPS BRIGHT GREEN FOOD COLORING

1 CUP ALMOND FLOUR

PAN DI SPAGNA (SEE PAGE 459)

FOR THE ICING

1 (SCANT) CUP CONFECTIONERS' SUGAR

2 TABLESPOONS WATER

CANDIED FRUIT, FOR TOPPING

1. To prepare the ricotta cream, place the ricotta in a bowl, add the sugar and vanilla sugar, and stir to combine. Add the chocolate chips and fold until they are evenly distributed. Chill the ricotta cream in the refrigerator.
2. To begin preparations for the marzipan, place the sugar, water, and food coloring in a saucepan and bring to a boil, stirring to dissolve the sugar. Turn off the heat, add the almond flour, and stir until the mixture is dense, smooth, and soft, and starts to pull away from the side of the pan.
3. Spray a pastry board or cutting board with water, pour the marzipan onto it, and let it cool.
4. Knead the marzipan for a few minutes until it feels smoother. Roll it out into a ¼-inch-thick rectangle and cut the marzipan into rounds that are the size of the bottom of the wells in a cupcake pan. Place the rounds in the wells of the cupcake pan.
5. Cut the Pan di Spagna, horizontally, into three equally thick pieces. Cut rounds large enough to cover the marzipan out of the pieces of cake.
6. Place pieces of cake on top of the marzipan and spread some of the ricotta cream over the top, almost filling the wells of the cupcake pan. Place the remaining pieces of cake on top of each portion of ricotta cream. Place the cassatine in the refrigerator for 2 to 3 hours.
7. To prepare the icing, place the confectioners' sugar in a bowl and incorporate the water a little at a time until the icing has the desired consistency. Set the mixture aside.
8. Remove the cassatine Siciliane from the refrigerator, place a large tray over the pan, and invert the cakes. Spread the icing over the top and sides of the cakes, top them with candied fruit, and enjoy.

Zippula Sarde

YIELD: 12 TO 14 ZIPPULA / **ACTIVE TIME:** 40 MINUTES / **TOTAL TIME:** 2 HOURS

1 PACKET (7 G) OF ACTIVE DRY YEAST

½ CUP (120 ML) LUKEWARM WATER (90°F)

4⅙ CUPS (500 G) SEMOLINA FLOUR

½ CUP (120 ML) LUKEWARM WHOLE MILK

1 EGG

ZEST AND JUICE OF 1 ORANGE

¼ CUP (60 ML) BRANDY OR ANISE LIQUEUR

1½ TEASPOONS (9 G) TABLE SALT

EXTRA-VIRGIN OLIVE OIL, AS NEEDED

3 CUPS SUGAR

1. Place the yeast and water in a mixing bowl, gently stir, and let the mixture proof until it is foamy, about 10 minutes.
2. Add the remaining ingredients, except for the olive oil and sugar, and work the mixture until it comes together as a smooth batter that is soft enough to be extruded from a piping bag. Cover the bowl with plastic wrap and let the batter rest at room temperature until bubbles start forming on the surface, about 1 hour.
3. Add extra-virgin olive oil to a narrow, deep, heavy-bottomed saucepan with high edges until it is 2 inches deep and warm it to 340°F. Pipe a few spirals of batter at a time into the hot oil and fry until they are just golden brown, turning as necessary.
4. Place the fried zippula on a paper towel–lined plate to drain.
5. Place the sugar in a bowl, add the zippula, toss until they are completely coated, and enjoy.

Sorbetto al Limone

YIELD: 4 CUPS / **ACTIVE TIME:** 30 MINUTES / **TOTAL TIME:** 9 HOURS

2¼ CUPS WATER

1¼ CUPS SUGAR

2 LEMON PEELS, PITH REMOVED

¾ CUP FRESH LEMON JUICE

1. Place the water, sugar, and lemon peels in a saucepan and bring to a boil, stirring to dissolve the sugar. Remove the pan from heat and let the syrup cool.
2. Remove the lemon peels, discard them, and stir in the lemon juice.
3. Pour the lemon syrup into a container and freeze it for 5 to 6 hours.
4. Remove the syrup from the freezer and let it thaw at room temperature for at least 25 minutes. Scoop the sorbet into a blender and briefly mix until it is creamy.

Iris

YIELD: 12 IRIS / **ACTIVE TIME:** 50 MINUTES / **TOTAL TIME:** 6 HOURS

FOR THE DOUGH

1¼ CUPS (280 ML) WHOLE MILK

⅓ PACKET (2.3 G) OF ACTIVE DRY YEAST

5⅚ CUPS (700 G) BREAD FLOUR

1¼ CUPS (150 G) ALL-PURPOSE FLOUR, PLUS MORE AS NEEDED

1 MEDIUM EGG

2 TABLESPOONS (25 G) SUGAR

¼ CUP (56 G) UNSALTED BUTTER

FOR THE FILLING

1½ CUPS RICOTTA CHEESE (MADE FROM SHEEP'S MILK PREFERRED), DRAINED IN THE REFRIGERATOR FOR A FEW HOURS

1¼ CUPS CONFECTIONERS' SUGAR

2 OZ. BITTERSWEET CHOCOLATE CHIPS, FROZEN FOR 30 MINUTES BEFORE USING (OPTIONAL)

2 EGGS

1½ CUPS BREAD CRUMBS

EXTRA-VIRGIN OLIVE OIL, AS NEEDED

1. To begin preparations for the dough, warm the milk to 90°F, place it in a bowl, and add the yeast. Gently stir and let the mixture proof until it starts to foam, about 10 minutes.
2. Place the mixture in the work bowl of a stand mixer fitted with the dough hook, add the flours and egg, and work the mixture on low speed until it is combined. Add the sugar and work the mixture until it comes together as a smooth and elastic dough.
3. Add the butter, raise the mixer's speed to medium, and knead until the dough is very elastic. Cover the bowl with plastic wrap, place it in a warm spot, and let the dough rise until it doubles in size, about 4 hours.
4. To prepare the filling, place all of the ingredients in a mixing bowl and stir to combine.
5. Line a baking sheet with parchment paper. Place the dough on a flour-dusted work surface, divide it into 12 pieces, and shape them into rounds. Place the rounds on the baking sheet, cover them with a kitchen towel, and let them rise for 1 hour.
6. Working with one round at a time, place it on a flour-dusted work surface, flatten it, and place 1 tablespoon of filling in the center. Form the dough around the filling, seal it, and flip it over. Work the dough in a circular motion until it is a seamless round.
7. Place the eggs in a bowl and beat until scrambled. Place the bread crumbs in a shallow bowl. Dredge the iris in the eggs and then in the bread crumbs until it is completely coated.
8. Repeat Steps 6 and 7 with the remaining rounds and filling.
9. Add olive oil to a narrow, deep, heavy-bottomed saucepan with high edges until it is about 2 inches deep and warm it to 350°F. Add two iris to the hot oil at a time and fry until they are golden brown, turning them over halfway through. Transfer the fried iris to a paper towel–lined plate to drain and serve once all of the iris have been cooked.

Torta Savoia

YIELD: 1 CAKE / **ACTIVE TIME:** 1 HOUR / **TOTAL TIME:** 5 HOURS

1½ BATCHES OF PAN DI SPAGNA (SEE PAGE 459), FULL BATCH PREPARED IN 1 PAN, ½ BATCH PREPARED IN ANOTHER PAN, AT ROOM TEMPERATURE

FOR THE CHOCOLATE & HAZELNUT CREAM

2 (HEAPING) CUPS BLANCHED HAZELNUTS

¼ CUP SUGAR

10 OZ. MILK CHOCOLATE, CHOPPED

1 CUP NUTELLA

FOR THE GLAZE

15 OZ. BITTERSWEET CHOCOLATE, CHOPPED

¼ CUP COCONUT OIL

1. Cut the larger Pan di Spagna, horizontally, into three equally thick rounds. Cut the smaller one, horizontally, into three equally thick rounds. Set them aside.
2. To begin preparations for the chocolate and hazelnut cream, place the hazelnuts and sugar in a food processor and blitz until the mixture is a smooth paste.
3. Bring a few inches of water to a simmer in a medium saucepan. Place the chocolate in a heatproof bowl, place it over the simmering water, and stir until it is melted and smooth. Add the Nutella, stir to incorporate, and then incorporate the hazelnut paste. Remove the bowl from heat.
4. Spread the chocolate and hazelnut cream over the pieces of cake, stacking the frosted pieces on top of one another and pressing down gently on them to make sure they stay together. Chill the cake in the refrigerator or freezer for 2 to 3 hours.
5. Bring a few inches of water to a simmer in a medium saucepan. To prepare the glaze, place the chocolate in a heatproof bowl, place it over the simmering water, and stir until it is melted and smooth. Add the coconut oil and stir until the mixture is very smooth and shiny. Remove the bowl from heat.
6. Reserve a few tablespoons of the glaze and pour the rest over the cake. Use a rubber spatula to smooth out any smudges on the bottom of the cake.
7. Using two spatulas, transfer the cake onto a clean serving plate. Place it back in the freezer or refrigerator and chill until the icing has set.
8. Place the reserved glaze in a piping bag fitted with a fine tip and pipe the word "Savoia" on the top of the cake. Decorate the cake with any remaining glaze and enjoy.

Torta Caprese

YIELD: 1 CAKE / **ACTIVE TIME:** 30 MINUTES / **TOTAL TIME:** 3 HOURS

⅞ CUP (200 G) UNSALTED BUTTER, PLUS MORE AS NEEDED

1 CUP (200 G) SUGAR

6 EGGS, SEPARATED

ZEST OF 1 ORANGE

2 TABLESPOONS (30 ML) ORANGE LIQUEUR

9 OZ. (255 G) BITTERSWEET CHOCOLATE

2½ CUPS (250 G) ALMOND FLOUR

UNSWEETENED COCOA POWDER, AS NEEDED

CONFECTIONERS' SUGAR, FOR TOPPING

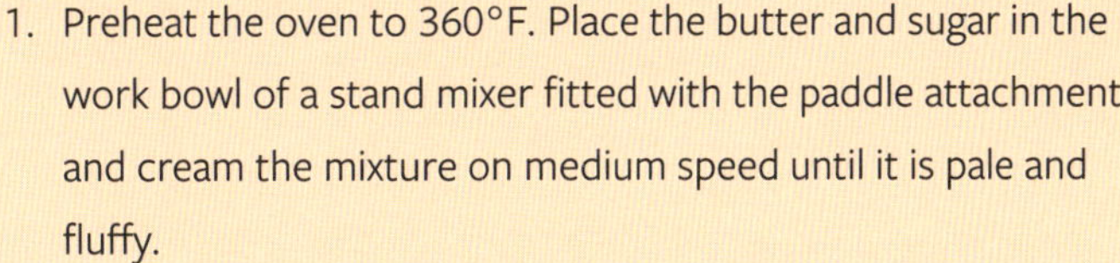

1. Preheat the oven to 360°F. Place the butter and sugar in the work bowl of a stand mixer fitted with the paddle attachment and cream the mixture on medium speed until it is pale and fluffy.
2. Add the egg yolks, orange zest, and liqueur and beat until incorporated.
3. Bring a few inches of water to a simmer in a medium saucepan. Place the chocolate in a heatproof bowl, place it over the simmering water, and stir until it is melted and smooth. Remove the bowl from heat, add the almond flour to the melted chocolate, and stir to combine. Add the butter mixture to the melted chocolate mixture and stir until well combined.
4. Clean out the work bowl of the stand mixer and fit the mixer with the whisk attachment. Place the egg whites in the work bowl and whip until they hold stiff peaks. Add the whipped egg whites to the batter and fold to incorporate.
5. Coat a round 9-inch cake pan with butter, dust it with cocoa powder, and knock out any excess. Pour the batter into the pan, place it in the oven, and bake until a toothpick inserted into the center comes out clean, about 40 minutes.
6. Remove the cake from the oven and let it cool. Dust the cake with cocoa powder and confectioners' sugar and enjoy.

Ricciarelli

YIELD: 25 COOKIES / **ACTIVE TIME:** 40 MINUTES / **TOTAL TIME:** 25 HOURS

2 EGG WHITES

1 TEASPOON (5 ML) FRESH LEMON JUICE

SEEDS OF 1 VANILLA POD

2 DROPS OF BITTER ALMOND EXTRACT

ZEST OF 1 ORANGE

2 CUPS (200 G) ALMOND FLOUR

1¾ CUPS (200 G) CONFECTIONERS' SUGAR, PLUS MORE AS NEEDED

1. Place the egg whites, lemon juice, vanilla seeds, bitter almond extract, and orange zest in a mixing bowl and whisk until the mixture is foamy.
2. Add the almond flour and confectioners' sugar and whisk until the mixture comes together as a soft dough.
3. Form the dough into a ball, cover it with plastic wrap, and chill in the refrigerator for 24 hours.
4. Preheat the oven to 300°F and line a baking sheet with parchment paper. Generously dust a work surface with confectioners' sugar and place more on a plate. Place the dough on the work surface and shape it into a 1-inch-thick cylinder. Slice it into 1 oz. pieces, roll them in the confectioners' sugar until coated all over, and form them into ovals or diamonds, flattening and lengthening them.
5. Place the ricciarelli on the baking sheet. Wet your fingers, moisten the cookies, and generously sprinkle more confectioners' sugar over the cookies.
6. Place the cookies in the oven and bake for 5 minutes. Raise the oven's temperature to 350°F and cook until the cookies start to crack, about 5 minutes.
7. Reduce the oven's temperature to 320°F and cook for another 5 minutes.
8. Remove the ricciarelli from the oven, transfer them to a wire rack, and let them cool before serving.

Babà

YIELD: 1 CAKE / **ACTIVE TIME:** 40 MINUTES / **TOTAL TIME:** 8 HOURS

FOR THE LIEVITINO

1 PACKET (7 G) OF INSTANT YEAST

3 TABLESPOONS (45 ML) LUKEWARM WATER (90°F)

1 TEASPOON (4 G) SUGAR

2 TABLESPOONS (15 G) BREAD FLOUR

FOR THE DOUGH

2½ CUPS (300 G) STRONG BREAD FLOUR (SUCH AS MANITOBA FLOUR), PLUS MORE AS NEEDED

5 EGGS

2 TABLESPOONS (25 G) SUGAR

PINCH OF TABLE SALT

7 TABLESPOONS (100 G) UNSALTED BUTTER, PLUS MORE AS NEEDED

FOR THE BAGNA

2 CUPS SUGAR

3⅓ CUPS WATER

1 LEMON PEEL, PITH REMOVED

2 CUPS RUM

1. To prepare the lievitino, place all of the ingredients in a bowl and stir to combine. Cover the bowl with plastic wrap and let the lievitino rest for 1 hour.
2. To begin preparations for the dough, place the lievitino and flour in the work bowl of a stand mixer fitted with the dough hook and work the mixture at low speed until combined. Incorporate the eggs one at a time. Add the sugar and salt and work the mixture until they have been incorporated.
3. Work the mixture until it is a smooth and elastic dough. Gradually add the butter and knead the dough until it has been incorporated. Raise the speed to medium and knead the dough until it is soft, very elastic, and not sticky. Cover the bowl with plastic wrap and let the dough rest in a naturally warm spot (86°F is ideal). Let the dough rise until it has tripled in size, about 4 hours.
4. Dust a pastry board or cutting board with flour, place the dough on it, and shape it into a round. Make a hole in the center of the round.
5. Coat a 10-inch Bundt pan with butter, place the dough in it, and place it in a naturally warm spot. Let the dough rise until it has almost reached the edge of the pan.
6. Preheat the oven to 350°F.
7. Place the cake in the oven and bake until a toothpick inserted into the center comes out clean, about 30 minutes. Remove the cake from the oven and let it cool completely.
8. To prepare the bagna, place the sugar, water, and lemon peel in a saucepan and bring to a boil, stirring to dissolve the sugar. Remove the pan from heat and stir in the rum. Pour one-quarter of the bagna over the cake and let it soak for 20 minutes. Repeat two more times. Invert the cake onto a serving platter, pour the remaining bagna over the cake, and serve.

Sfince di San Giuseppe

YIELD: 20 SFINCE / **ACTIVE TIME:** 1 HOUR / **TOTAL TIME:** 2 HOURS

FOR THE RICOTTA CREAM

2 LBS. RICOTTA CHEESE, DRAINED IN THE REFRIGERATOR FOR A FEW HOURS

3¼ CUPS CONFECTIONERS' SUGAR, PLUS MORE FOR TOPPING

1 (SCANT) CUP BITTERSWEET CHOCOLATE CHIPS

FOR THE BATTER

7 TABLESPOONS (100 G) LARD OR UNSALTED BUTTER

1 CUP PLUS 2 TEASPOONS (250 ML) WATER

⅔ TEASPOON (4 G) TABLE SALT

1¼ CUPS (150 G) ALL-PURPOSE FLOUR

4 MEDIUM EGGS

EXTRA-VIRGIN OLIVE OIL, AS NEEDED

CANDIED ORANGE PEELS, FOR TOPPING

CANDIED CHERRIES, FOR TOPPING

UNSALTED ROASTED PISTACHIOS, CHOPPED, FOR TOPPING

CONFECTIONERS' SUGAR, FOR TOPPING

1. To prepare the ricotta cream, place all of the ingredients in a mixing bowl, stir to combine, and store the ricotta cream in the refrigerator.
2. To begin preparations for the batter, place the butter, water, and salt in a saucepan and bring to a simmer over medium-low heat. Remove the pan from heat, add the flour, and stir quickly until it has been incorporated.
3. Place the saucepan over low heat and cook for a few minutes, stirring continually. Remove the pan from heat and let the batter cool until it is just warm.
4. Incorporate the eggs into the batter one at a time.
5. Add olive oil to a narrow, deep, heavy-bottomed saucepan with high edges until it is 2 inches deep and warm it to 340°F. Add two or three dollops of the batter to the hot oil and fry until golden brown, turning them as necessary.
6. Place the fried sfince on a paper towel–lined plate. To serve, top them with the ricotta cream, candied orange peels, candied cherries, pistachios, and confectioners' sugar.

Struffoli Napoletani

YIELD: 60 STRUFFOLI / **ACTIVE TIME:** 40 MINUTES / **TOTAL TIME:** 2 HOURS

3⅓ CUPS (400 G) ALL-PURPOSE FLOUR, PLUS MORE AS NEEDED

3 TABLESPOONS (40 G) SUGAR

1 TEASPOON (6 G) TABLE SALT

3 EGGS

⅓ CUP (80 G) UNSALTED BUTTER

ZEST OF 1 ORANGE

ZEST OF 1 LEMON

1½ TABLESPOONS (22.5 ML) RUM OR ANISE LIQUEUR

EXTRA-VIRGIN OLIVE OIL, AS NEEDED

1 (SCANT) CUP HONEY

¼ CUP CONFECTIONERS' SUGAR

COLORED SUGAR SPRINKLES, FOR TOPPING

CANDIED FRUIT, FOR TOPPING

1. Place the flour, sugar, and salt in a mixing bowl and stir to combine. Add the eggs and work the mixture until they have been incorporated.
2. Add the butter, orange zest, lemon zest, and rum and work the mixture until it comes together as a smooth dough. Cover the dough with plastic wrap and chill it in the refrigerator for 1 hour.
3. Place the dough on a flour-dusted work surface, flatten it slightly, and cut it into ½-inch-wide strips. Roll the strips into long, thin logs, cut each log into ½-inch-long pieces, and shape the pieces into rounds.
4. Add olive oil to a narrow, deep, heavy-bottomed saucepan with high edges until it is 2 inches deep and warm it to 340°F. Add a handful of struffoli at a time and fry until they are just golden, about 1 minute. Remove the fried struffoli with a slotted spoon and place them on a paper towel–lined plate to drain.
5. Place the honey and confectioners' sugar in a saucepan and warm the mixture over low heat until the honey has liquefied. Add all of the struffoli to the pan and gently stir until they are all coated.
6. Pile the struffoli on a serving dish or arrange them in a circle. Top with sugar sprinkles and candied fruit and enjoy.

Zeppole di San Giuseppe

YIELD: 9 ZEPPOLE / **ACTIVE TIME:** 1 HOUR / **TOTAL TIME:** 1 HOUR AND 30 MINUTES

¾ CUP (170 G) UNSALTED BUTTER

2 CUPS (480 ML) WATER

1 TEASPOON (6 G) TABLE SALT

2 TEASPOONS (8 G) SUGAR

2½ CUPS (300 G) BREAD FLOUR

10 MEDIUM EGGS

EXTRA-VIRGIN OLIVE OIL, AS NEEDED

CREMA PASTICCERA NAPOLETANA (SEE PAGE 460)

9 CHERRIES IN SYRUP, DRAINED

CONFECTIONERS' SUGAR, FOR TOPPING

1. Place the butter, water, salt, and sugar in a saucepan and bring to a simmer over medium-low heat. Remove the pan from heat, add the flour, and stir quickly until it has been incorporated.
2. Place the saucepan over low heat and cook for a few minutes, stirring continually. Remove the pan from heat and let the batter cool until it is just warm.
3. Incorporate the eggs into the batter two at a time, using either a whisk or the paddle attachment on a stand mixer.
4. Place the batter in a piping bag fitted with a star tip and pipe 4-inch rings of the batter onto a large piece of parchment paper, making sure to leave space between each ring.
5. Add olive oil to a narrow, deep, heavy-bottomed saucepan with high edges until it is 2 inches deep and warm it to 340°F. Cut the parchment paper into squares around each zeppola and gently slip the zeppola and parchment paper into the hot oil, frying one at a time. Fry the zeppole until they are golden brown, turn them over, and remove the parchment paper. Fry for another 1 to 2 minutes.
6. Place the fried zeppole on a paper towel–lined plate. To serve, top each one with some pastry cream, a cherry, and confectioners' sugar.

Ciambelline al Vino Rosso

YIELD: 20 COOKIES / **ACTIVE TIME:** 30 MINUTES / **TOTAL TIME:** 1 HOUR AND 15 MINUTES

3⅓ CUPS (400 G) ALL-PURPOSE FLOUR, PLUS MORE AS NEEDED

½ CUP (100 G) SUGAR, PLUS MORE FOR TOPPING

1½ TEASPOONS (6 G) BAKER'S AMMONIA

PINCH OF TABLE SALT

PINCH OF GROUND STAR ANISE (OPTIONAL)

½ CUP (100 G) EXTRA-VIRGIN OLIVE OIL

1 (SCANT) CUP (225 ML) RED WINE

1. Place the flour, sugar, baker's ammonia, salt, and star anise (if desired) in a mixing bowl and stir to combine.
2. Add the olive oil and wine and work the mixture quickly until it just comes together as a dough. Form the dough into a ball, cover it with plastic wrap, and let it rest for 20 minutes.
3. Preheat the oven to 350°F and line a baking sheet with parchment paper. Place some sugar on a plate.
4. Place the dough on a flour-dusted work surface and divide it into 2 oz. pieces. Roll each piece into a log, shape them into small rings, and pinch the ends together.
5. Dip each cookie in the sugar until coated all over and place them on the baking sheet.
6. Place the cookies in the oven and bake until they are just golden brown, about 20 minutes.
7. Remove the cookies from the oven, transfer them to a wire rack, and let them cool completely before serving.

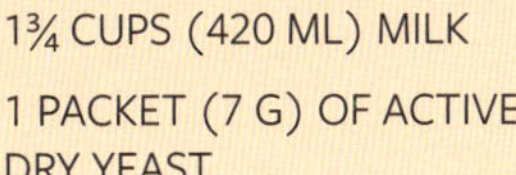

Bomboloni

YIELD: 25 BOMBOLONI / **ACTIVE TIME:** 1 HOUR / **TOTAL TIME:** 7 HOURS

1¾ CUPS (420 ML) MILK

1 PACKET (7 G) OF ACTIVE DRY YEAST

5 CUPS (600 G) ALL-PURPOSE FLOUR, PLUS MORE AS NEEDED

3½ CUPS (300 G) STRONG BREAD FLOUR (SUCH AS MANITOBA FLOUR)

ZEST OF 1 ORANGE

ZEST OF 1 LEMON

¼ CUP (60 ML) SWEET LIQUEUR

½ CUP (100 G) SUGAR, PLUS MORE FOR TOPPING

4 EGGS

7 TABLESPOONS (100 G) LARD

1½ TEASPOONS (9 G) TABLE SALT

EXTRA-VIRGIN OLIVE OIL, AS NEEDED

CREMA PASTICCERA NAPOLETANA (SEE PAGE 460)

1. Warm half of the milk to 90°F. Add the yeast, gently stir, and let the mixture proof until it starts to foam, about 10 minutes.
2. Place the flours, yeast mixture, remaining milk, citrus zests, and liqueur in the work bowl of a stand mixer fitted with the dough hook and work the mixture until combined. Add the sugar and work the mixture to incorporate it.
3. Incorporate the eggs one at a time, with the mixer running on low speed. Add the lard and salt and work the mixture until it is a smooth, elastic dough. Cover the bowl with plastic wrap and let the dough rise until it has nearly doubled in size, 3 to 4 hours.
4. Line two large baking dishes with parchment paper. Dust a work surface with all-purpose flour, place the dough on it, and divide it into 25 pieces. Shape them into rounds, place them in the baking dishes, and gently press down on the rounds to flatten them slightly.
5. Cover the rounds with kitchen towels and let them rise until nearly doubled in size, about 2 hours.
6. Add olive oil to a narrow, deep, and heavy-bottomed saucepan with high edges until it is 2 inches deep and warm it to 350°F. Working in batches to avoid crowding the pot, gently slip the bomboloni into the hot oil and fry until they are golden brown.
7. Transfer the fried bomboloni to a paper towel–lined plate to drain.
8. Place the pastry cream in a piping bag fitted with a plain tip and insert the tip into the centers of the bomboloni's tops. Fill them with the pastry cream and serve.

Ciaramicola

YIELD: 1 CAKE / **ACTIVE TIME:** 40 MINUTES / **TOTAL TIME:** 1 HOUR AND 30 MINUTES

FOR THE CAKE

⅔ CUP (150 G) UNSALTED BUTTER, SOFTENED, PLUS MORE AS NEEDED

1 CUP (200 G) SUGAR

SEEDS OF 1 VANILLA POD

ZEST OF 1 LEMON

3 EGGS

7 TABLESPOONS (100 ML) WHOLE MILK

1 (SCANT) CUP (110 ML) ALCHERMES LIQUEUR

2½ CUPS (300 G) ALL-PURPOSE FLOUR, PLUS MORE AS NEEDED

2 TEASPOONS (8 G) BAKING POWDER

FOR THE GLAZE

2 EGG WHITES

1 CUP SUGAR

SEEDS OF 1 VANILLA POD

COLORED SUGAR SPRINKLES, FOR TOPPING

1. Preheat the oven to 350°F. To begin preparations for the cake, place the butter, sugar, vanilla seeds, and lemon zest in the work bowl of a stand mixer fitted with the whisk attachment and whip the mixture for 10 to 15 minutes, until it is foamy.
2. With the mixer running, incorporate the eggs one at a time. Add the milk and liqueur and whisk to incorporate.
3. Place the flour and baking powder in a mixing bowl and stir to combine. Add the flour mixture to the work bowl and fold to incorporate it into the batter.
4. Coat a 10-inch Bundt pan with butter, dust it with flour, and knock out any excess. Pour the batter into the pan and place it in the oven.
5. Bake until a toothpick inserted into the center of the cake comes out clean, about 40 minutes. Remove the cake from the oven and let it cool in the pan.
6. While the cake is cooling, prepare the glaze. Wipe out the stand mixer's work bowl and clean the whisk. Place the egg whites in the work bowl and whip until they hold stiff peaks. With the mixer running, add the sugar in three increments. Add the vanilla seeds and whip until they are incorporated. Set the glaze aside.
7. Invert the cake onto a serving plate and cover it with the glaze. Top with the sugar sprinkles and serve.

Pinoccata

YIELD: 40 CANDIES / **ACTIVE TIME:** 20 MINUTES / **TOTAL TIME:** 1 HOUR

2.2 LBS. SUGAR

1½ CUPS WATER

5 TABLESPOONS ALL-PURPOSE FLOUR

2 CUPS PINE NUTS

ZEST OF 1 LEMON

2 TEASPOONS PURE VANILLA EXTRACT

1. Preheat the oven to 350°F and line two baking dishes with parchment paper, making sure it overlaps the sides. Place the sugar and water in a saucepan and bring to a boil, stirring to dissolve the sugar.
2. Whisking continually, add the flour. Reduce the heat to low and cook the mixture for 30 minutes, stirring frequently.
3. Place the pine nuts on a baking sheet, place them in the oven, and toast for 5 minutes. Remove the pine nuts from the oven and set them aside. Remove the pan from heat and stir in the pine nuts, lemon zest, and vanilla.
4. Pour the mixture into the parchment-lined baking dishes and let it cool.
5. Cut the candies into large diagonal strips, make diagonal cuts in the opposite direction, creating diamond-shaped candies, and enjoy.

Zaletti

YIELD: 25 ZALETTI / **ACTIVE TIME:** 40 MINUTES / **TOTAL TIME:** 1 HOUR

1 CUP (150 G) RAISINS

GRAPPA, AS NEEDED

1¾ CUPS (210 G) ALL-PURPOSE FLOUR

1 CUP (156 G) FINE CORNMEAL

1 TEASPOON (4 G) BAKING POWDER

¾ CUP (160 G) BROWN SUGAR

PINCH OF TABLE SALT

7 TABLESPOONS (100 G) UNSALTED BUTTER, SOFTENED

2 EGGS

ZEST OF ½ LEMON

1. Preheat the oven to 375°F and line two baking sheets with parchment paper. Place the raisins in a bowl, cover them with grappa, and let them soak for 30 minutes.
2. Drain the raisins and squeeze them dry.
3. Sift the flour, cornmeal, baking powder, brown sugar, and salt into the work bowl of a stand mixer fitted with the paddle attachment. Add the butter, eggs, lemon zest, and raisins and beat until the mixture comes together as a smooth dough.
4. Divide the dough into 25 pieces and form them into rounds. Place the zaletti on the baking sheets and place them in the oven.
5. Bake the zaletti until they are golden brown, about 20 minutes. Remove the zaletti from the oven, transfer them to wire racks, and let them cool completely before enjoying.

Bignè di San Giuseppe

YIELD: 10 BIGNÈ / **ACTIVE TIME:** 50 MINUTES / **TOTAL TIME:** 1 HOUR AND 15 MINUTES

6 TABLESPOONS (85 G) UNSALTED BUTTER

⅞ CUP (200 ML) WATER

PINCH OF TABLE SALT

1¼ CUPS (150 G) ALL-PURPOSE FLOUR

4 EGGS

⅓ CUP (67 G) SUGAR

EXTRA-VIRGIN OLIVE OIL, AS NEEDED

CREMA PASTICCERA NAPOLETANA (SEE PAGE 460)

CONFECTIONERS' SUGAR, FOR TOPPING

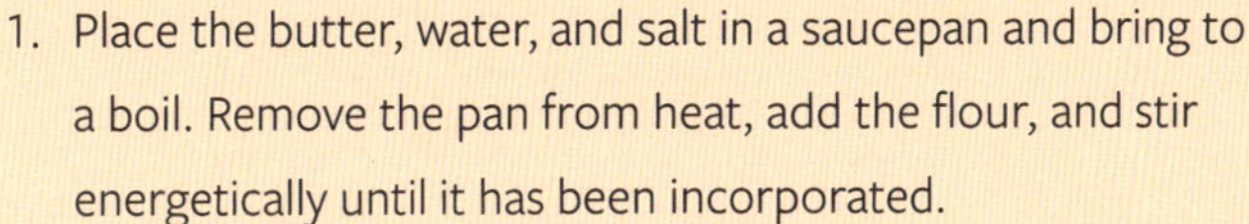

1. Place the butter, water, and salt in a saucepan and bring to a boil. Remove the pan from heat, add the flour, and stir energetically until it has been incorporated.
2. Place the saucepan over medium heat and cook until the dough starts to detach from the side of the pan, stirring continually. Reduce the heat to low and cook for 2 to 3 minutes, stirring continually.
3. Remove the pan from heat and let the dough cool for a few minutes.
4. Incorporate one egg at a time. Add the sugar and stir until it has been incorporated.
5. Pour the dough into a heatproof bowl, cover it with plastic wrap, and let the dough cool for 30 minutes.
6. Add olive oil to a narrow, deep, and heavy-bottomed saucepan with high edges until it is 2 inches deep and warm it to 350°F. Using two spoons, drop balls of dough into the hot oil, working in batches to avoid crowding the pot. Fry the bignè until they are golden brown.
7. Transfer the fried bignè to a paper towel–lined plate to drain.
8. Place the pastry cream in a piping bag fitted with a plain tip and fill the bignè with it. Sprinkle confectioners' sugar over them and serve.

Budino di Riso alla Toscana

YIELD: 18 BUDINO / **ACTIVE TIME:** 40 MINUTES / **TOTAL TIME:** 2 HOURS

2½ CUPS WHOLE MILK

½ CUP SUGAR

PINCH OF TABLE SALT

ZEST OF 1 ORANGE

ZEST OF ½ LEMON

1 (SCANT) CUP RISOTTO RICE (CARNAROLI, VIALONE, ROMA, OR ORIGINARIO PREFERRED)

1 TABLESPOON UNSALTED BUTTER, PLUS MORE AS NEEDED

1¾ CUPS CREMA PASTICCERA NAPOLETANA (SEE PAGE 460)

PASTA FROLLA (SEE PAGE 456)

ALL-PURPOSE FLOUR, AS NEEDED

CONFECTIONERS' SUGAR, FOR TOPPING

1. Place the milk, sugar, salt, and citrus zests in a saucepan and bring to a simmer, stirring to dissolve the sugar.
2. Add the rice, reduce the heat to low, and cook, stirring frequently, until the rice is tender, 20 to 30 minutes.
3. Remove the pan from heat and stir in the butter. Let the rice pudding cool to room temperature. Stir the pastry cream into the rice pudding and set the mixture aside.
4. Place the frolla on a flour-dusted work surface and roll it out into a ¼-inch-thick rectangle.
5. Preheat the oven to 350°F. Coat the wells of two muffin pans with butter. Please note that the recipe is for 1½ pans, so not all of the wells need to be greased.
6. Use a glass or ring cutter to cut the dough into rounds that are large enough to cover the bottom and sides of the wells in the muffin pan. Place the rounds in the wells and trim away any excess dough.
7. Fill the crusts with the rice pudding and place the budino in the oven.
8. Bake for 20 minutes, reduce the oven's temperature to 320°F, and bake until the budino are golden brown, about 15 minutes.
9. Remove the budino from the oven, transfer them to a wire rack, and let them cool completely. Dust the budino with confectioners' sugar before serving.

Torcolo

YIELD: 1 CAKE / **ACTIVE TIME:** 40 MINUTES / **TOTAL TIME:** 1 HOUR AND 30 MINUTES

¾ CUP (170 G) UNSALTED BUTTER, SOFTENED, PLUS MORE AS NEEDED

1¼ CUPS (250 G) SUGAR

PINCH OF TABLE SALT

SEEDS OF 1 VANILLA POD

ZEST OF 1 LEMON

5 EGGS

1 CUP PLUS 2 TEASPOONS (250 ML) WHOLE MILK

4⅙ CUPS (500 G) ALL-PURPOSE FLOUR, PLUS MORE AS NEEDED

1 TABLESPOON (12 G) BAKING POWDER

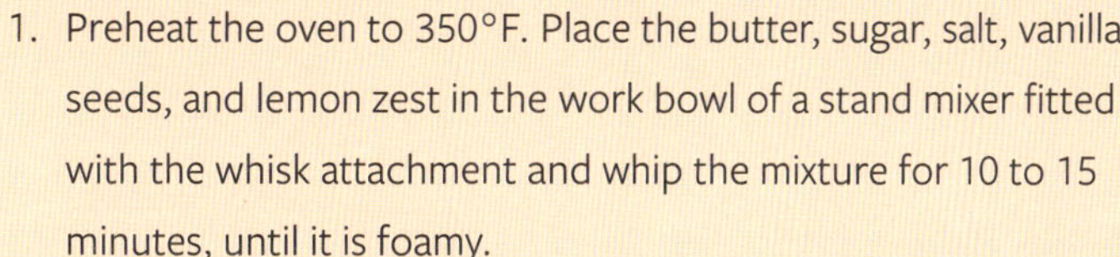

1. Preheat the oven to 350°F. Place the butter, sugar, salt, vanilla seeds, and lemon zest in the work bowl of a stand mixer fitted with the whisk attachment and whip the mixture for 10 to 15 minutes, until it is foamy.
2. With the mixer running, incorporate the eggs one at a time. Add the milk and whisk to incorporate. Place the flour and baking powder in a mixing bowl and stir to combine.
3. Add the flour mixture to the work bowl and fold to incorporate it into the batter.
4. Coat a 10-inch Bundt pan with butter, dust it with flour, and knock out any excess. Pour the batter into the pan and place it in the oven.
5. Bake until a toothpick inserted into the center of the cake comes out clean, about 40 minutes.
6. Remove the cake from the oven and let it cool in the pan.
7. Invert the cake onto a serving plate and enjoy.

Rocciata

YIELD: 1 CAKE / **ACTIVE TIME:** 40 MINUTES / **TOTAL TIME:** 1 HOUR AND 30 MINUTES

FOR THE FILLING

½ CUP RAISINS

½ CUP RUM

⅓ CUP SUGAR

1½ TABLESPOONS CINNAMON

2 TABLESPOONS UNSWEETENED COCOA POWDER

1 TABLESPOON ANISE SEEDS, GROUND (OPTIONAL)

ZEST OF 1 LEMON

4 MEDIUM GOLDEN DELICIOUS APPLES, PEELED, CORED, AND DICED

1 (SCANT) CUP WALNUTS

⅔ CUP PINE NUTS

FOR THE DOUGH

2 CUPS PLUS 1½ TABLESPOONS (250 G) ALL-PURPOSE FLOUR, PLUS MORE AS NEEDED

¼ CUP (50 G) EXTRA-VIRGIN OLIVE OIL

½ CUP (120 ML) WATER

2 PINCHES OF TABLE SALT

ALCHERMES LIQUEUR, FOR TOPPING

CONFECTIONERS' SUGAR, FOR TOPPING

1. To begin preparations for the filling, place the raisins and rum in a bowl and let the mixture steep.
2. To begin preparations for the dough, place all of the ingredients in a mixing bowl and work the mixture until it comes together as a smooth dough. Form the dough into a ball, cover it with plastic wrap, and let it rest for 30 minutes.
3. Preheat the oven to 390°F and line a baking sheet with parchment paper. Place the dough on a flour-dusted work surface and roll it out into a paper-thin sheet. Transfer the sheet of dough to a flour-dusted tablecloth.
4. Resume preparations for the filling. Sprinkle the sugar over the dough and then sprinkle the cinnamon and cocoa powder over it. Sprinkle the anise seeds (if desired) and lemon zest over the dough.
5. Distribute the apples evenly over the dough. Drain the raisins and distribute them, the walnuts, and pine nuts over the dough.
6. With the help of the tablecloth, roll up the dough into a not-too-tight log and pinch the ends to seal, taking care not to break the thin sheet.
7. Transfer the rocciata to the baking sheet and shape it into a spiral. Place the rocciata in the oven and bake until it is golden brown, about 25 minutes, taking care not to burn it.
8. Remove the rocciata from the oven, drizzle alchermes over the top, sprinkle confectioners' sugar over it, and serve.

Panpepato

YIELD: 4 CAKES / **ACTIVE TIME:** 40 MINUTES / **TOTAL TIME:** 27 HOURS

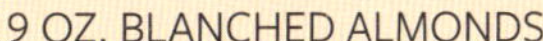

9 OZ. BLANCHED ALMONDS

9 OZ. WALNUTS

9 OZ. BLANCHED HAZELNUTS

¾ CUP PINE NUTS

9 OZ. RAISINS, SOAKED IN WARM WATER FOR 1 HOUR, DRAINED, AND SQUEEZED DRY

3½ OZ. CANDIED FRUIT, DICED

4⅙ CUPS (500 G) ALL-PURPOSE FLOUR, PLUS MORE AS NEEDED

2 TABLESPOONS (12 G) BLACK PEPPER

1 TABLESPOON (8 G) CINNAMON

¼ TEASPOON (0.5 G) FRESHLY GRATED NUTMEG

1½ CUPS (510 G) HONEY

3½ OZ. (100 G) BITTERSWEET CHOCOLATE

1. Line a baking sheet with parchment paper. Place the almonds, walnuts, hazelnuts, pine nuts, raisins, and candied fruit in a mixing bowl and stir to combine. Add the flour, pepper, cinnamon, and nutmeg and toss to combine. Set the mixture aside.
2. Place the honey and chocolate in a saucepan and warm over medium heat until the mixture has liquefied.
3. Pour the mixture into the mixing bowl and stir until everything is combined. Working with flour-dusted hands, form the mixture into four rounds and place them on the baking sheet. Press down on the rounds to flatten them slightly. Cover the rounds with a kitchen towel and let them rest at room temperature for 2 hours.
4. Preheat the oven to 320°F.
5. Place the panpepato in the oven and bake for 20 minutes. Remove them from the oven and shape them into compact rounds.
6. Cover each panpepato with plastic wrap. Let them rest for 1 day before serving.

Pangiallo

YIELD: 4 CAKES / **ACTIVE TIME:** 40 MINUTES / **TOTAL TIME:** 27 HOURS

9 OZ. BLANCHED ALMONDS

9 OZ. WALNUTS

9 OZ. BLANCHED HAZELNUTS

¾ CUP PINE NUTS

9 OZ. RAISINS, SOAKED IN WARM WATER FOR 1 HOUR, DRAINED, AND SQUEEZED DRY

1⅚ CUPS (220 G) ALL-PURPOSE FLOUR, PLUS MORE AS NEEDED

1½ CUPS (510 G) HONEY

2 TABLESPOONS (26 G) EXTRA-VIRGIN OLIVE OIL

1. Line a baking sheet with parchment paper. Place the almonds, walnuts, hazelnuts, pine nuts, and raisins in a mixing bowl and stir to combine. Add the flour and toss to combine. Set the mixture aside.
2. Place the honey in a saucepan and warm it over medium heat until it has completely liquefied.
3. Add the olive oil and stir to combine. Pour the mixture into the mixing bowl and stir until everything is combined.
4. Working with flour-dusted hands, form the mixture into four rounds and place them on the baking sheet. Press down on the rounds to flatten them slightly. Cover the rounds with a kitchen towel and let them rest at room temperature for 2 hours.
5. Preheat the oven to 320°F.
6. Place the pangiallo in the oven and bake for 20 minutes. Remove them from the oven and shape them into compact rounds.
7. Cover each pangiallo with plastic wrap. Let them rest for 1 day before serving.

Canestrelli Liguri

YIELD: 100 CANESTRELLI / **ACTIVE TIME:** 40 MINUTES / **TOTAL TIME:** 2 HOURS

2½ CUPS (300 G) ALL-PURPOSE FLOUR, PLUS MORE AS NEEDED

1⅓ CUPS (200 G) POTATO STARCH

1⅓ CUPS (150 G) CONFECTIONERS' SUGAR, PLUS MORE FOR TOPPING

ZEST OF 1 LEMON

SEEDS FROM 1 VANILLA BEAN

1 CUP PLUS 6 TABLESPOONS (310 G) UNSALTED BUTTER, CHOPPED

6 HARD-BOILED EGG YOLKS, CRUSHED

1. Place the flour, potato starch, confectioners' sugar, lemon zest, and vanilla seeds in the work bowl of a stand mixer fitted with the paddle attachment and beat until combined.
2. Gradually add the butter and beat to incorporate. Add the egg yolks and beat until the dough just comes together.
3. Place the dough on a flour-dusted work surface and flatten it slightly. Cover the dough with plastic wrap and chill it in the refrigerator for 1 hour.
4. Preheat the oven to 350°F and line a baking sheet with parchment paper. Place the dough on a flour-dusted work surface and roll it out into a ⅛-inch-thick round. Cut the dough into cookies with a flower-shaped cookie cutter. Roll out any scraps of dough and cut into cookies.
5. Cut a ⅓-inch hole in the center of each cookie with a ring cutter.
6. Place some canestrelli on the baking sheet, place them in the oven, and bake until they are golden brown, about 15 minutes. Repeat with the remaining canestrelli.
7. Dust the canestrelli with confectioners' sugar before enjoying.

Castagnole

YIELD: 30 CASTAGNOLE / **ACTIVE TIME:** 40 MINUTES / **TOTAL TIME:** 1 HOUR AND 30 MINUTES

2 CUPS PLUS 1½ TABLESPOONS (250 G) ALL-PURPOSE FLOUR, PLUS MORE AS NEEDED

⅓ CUP PLUS 1 TABLESPOON (80 G) SUGAR

ZEST OF ½ ORANGE

PINCH OF TABLE SALT

1½ TEASPOONS (6 G) BAKING POWDER

2 EGGS, LIGHTLY BEATEN

¼ CUP (56 G) UNSALTED BUTTER, SOFTENED

2 TABLESPOONS (30 ML) RUM

EXTRA-VIRGIN OLIVE OIL, AS NEEDED

CONFECTIONERS' SUGAR, FOR TOPPING

1. Place the flour, sugar, orange zest, salt, and baking powder in a mixing bowl and whisk to combine.
2. Add the eggs, butter, and rum and work the mixture until it just comes together. Place the dough on a flour-dusted work surface and knead until it is soft and smooth. Cover the dough with a kitchen towel and let it rest for 30 minutes.
3. Add olive oil to a narrow, deep, heavy-bottomed saucepan with high sides until it is about 2 inches deep and warm it to 350°F. Divide the dough into ¾ oz. pieces and shape them into rounds.
4. Working in batches to avoid crowding the pot, gently slip the castagnole into the hot oil and fry until golden brown.
5. Transfer the fried castagnole to a paper towel–lined plate to drain. Dust them with confectioners' sugar and serve them warm.

Torta Sbrisolona

YIELD: 1 CAKE / **ACTIVE TIME:** 20 MINUTES / **TOTAL TIME:** 1 HOUR

⅞ CUP (200 G) UNSALTED BUTTER, SOFTENED AND CHOPPED, PLUS MORE AS NEEDED

1⅔ CUPS (200 G) ALL-PURPOSE FLOUR

1⅓ CUPS (200 G) FINE CORNMEAL

1 (SCANT) CUP (180 G) SUGAR

PINCH OF TABLE SALT

7 OZ. (200 G) ALMONDS, CHOPPED

2 EGG YOLKS

ZEST OF 1 LEMON

GRAPPA, FOR TOPPING (OPTIONAL)

1. Preheat the oven to 355°F. Coat a round 10-inch cake pan with butter. Place the flour, cornmeal, sugar, and salt in a large mixing bowl and stir to combine.
2. Add the almonds, make a well in the center, place the egg yolks, lemon zest, and butter in the well, and work the mixture with your hands until it comes together as a crumbly dough.
3. Place the dough in the cake pan, leveling it without pressing down. Place the cake in the oven and bake until cooked through, about 30 minutes.
4. Remove the cake from the oven and let it cool completely before removing it from the pan.
5. Torta sbrisolona is generally broken by hand rather than cut. Drizzle grappa over it (if desired) and enjoy.

Zuccotto

YIELD: 1 CAKE / **ACTIVE TIME:** 1 HOUR / **TOTAL TIME:** 4 HOURS

7 OZ. BITTERSWEET CHOCOLATE

14 OZ. PAN DI SPAGNA (SEE PAGE 459)

2 TABLESPOONS CRÈME DE CACAO

3 TABLESPOONS GRAND MARNIER

2 TABLESPOONS BRANDY

4 CUPS WHIPPING CREAM

1 (HEAPING) CUP CONFECTIONERS' SUGAR, PLUS MORE FOR TOPPING

1 TEASPOON PURE VANILLA EXTRACT

½ CUP BLANCHED ALMONDS, TOASTED AND FINELY CHOPPED

½ CUP BLANCHED HAZELNUTS, TOASTED AND FINELY CHOPPED

3 TABLESPOONS UNSWEETENED COCOA POWDER

1. Line a baking sheet with parchment paper. Bring a few inches of water to a simmer in a medium saucepan. Place the chocolate in a heatproof bowl, place it over the simmering water, and stir until it is melted and smooth. Remove the bowl from heat and set one-third of it aside. Place the remaining melted chocolate in a piping bag fitted with a plain tip and pipe short strips of it over the parchment paper.
2. Remove the crust from the Pan di Spagna, cut the cake in half at the equator, and cut triangular slices from one of the halves.
3. Cover a 6 x 3–inch hemisphere pan with plastic wrap and line it with the slices of Pan di Spagna.
4. Place the liqueurs and brandy in a bowl and stir to combine. Brush the slices of cake with the mixture.
5. Place the cream in the work bowl of a stand mixer fitted with the whisk attachment and whip until it holds stiff peaks, adding the confectioners' sugar and vanilla toward the end.
6. Add the chocolate strips and nuts and fold to incorporate.
7. Divide the mixture into two parts. Add the reserved melted chocolate to one portion and stir to combine.
8. Fill the cake-lined pan with the white cream, spreading it evenly with the help of a rubber spatula. Fill the center of the zuccotto, all the way to the top, with the chocolate cream. Cover the zuccotto with an appropriately sized disk of Pan di Spagna. Cover it with plastic wrap and refrigerate for 3 hours.
9. Place a plate over the zuccotto and invert the cake onto the plate.
10. Place the cocoa powder and some confectioners' sugar in a bowl and stir to combine. Sprinkle the mixture over the zuccotto and enjoy.

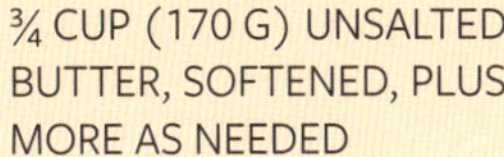

Torta Paradiso

YIELD: 1 CAKE / **ACTIVE TIME:** 40 MINUTES / **TOTAL TIME:** 1 HOUR AND 30 MINUTES

¾ CUP (170 G) UNSALTED BUTTER, SOFTENED, PLUS MORE AS NEEDED

⅚ CUP (100 G) ALL-PURPOSE FLOUR, PLUS MORE AS NEEDED

1½ CUPS (170 G) CONFECTIONERS' SUGAR, PLUS MORE AS NEEDED

½ (SCANT) CUP (70 G) POTATO STARCH

1 (SCANT) TEASPOON (3 G) BAKING POWDER

SEEDS FROM 1 VANILLA POD

ZEST OF ½ LEMON

ZEST OF ½ ORANGE

2.8 OZ. (80 G) EGG YOLKS

PINCH OF TABLE SALT

3½ OZ. (100 G) EGGS

3 TABLESPOONS (40 G) SUGAR

1. Preheat the oven to 340°F. Coat a round 10-inch cake pan with butter and dust it with flour, knocking out any excess. Sift the flour, confectioners' sugar, potato starch, and baking powder into a mixing bowl and set the mixture aside.
2. In a separate bowl, combine the butter, vanilla seeds, lemon zest, and orange zest and beat the mixture with a handheld mixer until it is soft and airy.
3. Add the egg yolks and salt and beat until the mixture is creamy.
4. In a third bowl, whip the eggs and sugar until the mixture is frothy. Add the whole egg mixture to the egg yolk mixture and fold to combine. Gradually add the dry mixture and fold until the mixture is a smooth batter.
5. Pour the batter into the cake pan and knock it on the counter to evenly distribute the batter and remove any air bubbles.
6. Place the cake in the oven and bake until a toothpick inserted into the center comes out clean, about 45 minutes.
7. Remove the cake from the oven and let it cool for 20 minutes.
8. Remove the cake from the pan, dust it with confectioners' sugar, and enjoy.

Zuppa Inglese

YIELD: 1 CAKE / **ACTIVE TIME:** 40 MINUTES / **TOTAL TIME:** 24 HOURS

1¾ CUPS WATER

3½ TABLESPOONS ALCHERMES LIQUEUR

2 TABLESPOONS SUGAR

PAN DI SPAGNA (SEE PAGE 459)

CREMA PASTICCERA (SEE PAGE 458)

½ BATCH OF CREMA PASTICCERA AL CIOCCOLATO (SEE PAGE 462)

COCOA POWDER, FOR TOPPING

1. Place the water, liqueur, and sugar in a bowl and stir to combine. Set the bagna aside.
2. Cut the Pan di Spagna, horizontally, into three equally thick pieces. Cut each layer into large strips and layer one-third of the strips in a 13 x 9–inch baking dish.
3. Drizzle the bagna over the cake. Cover the cake with half of the Pastry Cream, making sure to spread it evenly.
4. Cover the Pastry Cream with the second layer of cake and drizzle half of the remaining bagna over the cake. Spread the Chocolate Pastry Cream over the cake evenly.
5. Top with the last layer of cake, drizzle the remaining bagna over it, and cover with the remaining Pastry Cream.
6. Dust the cake with cocoa powder, cover it with plastic wrap, and refrigerate it for 24 hours before serving.

Pandolce Genovese

YIELD: 1 CAKE / **ACTIVE TIME:** 30 MINUTES / **TOTAL TIME:** 1 HOUR AND 30 MINUTES

4⅙ CUPS (500 G) ALL-PURPOSE FLOUR

2 PINCHES OF TABLE SALT

1 CUP (200 G) SUGAR

1 TABLESPOON (12 G) BAKING POWDER

⅔ CUP (155 G) UNSALTED BUTTER, MELTED

1 EGG

ZEST OF 1 LEMON

7 TABLESPOONS (100 ML) MARSALA

⅔ CUP RAISINS, SOAKED IN WARM WATER, DRAINED, AND SQUEEZED DRY

⅓ CUP PINE NUTS

¼ CUP CANDIED CITRUS PEELS, CHOPPED

1. Preheat the oven to 320°F and line a round 10-inch cake pan with parchment paper. Sift the flour into a large bowl, add the salt, sugar, and baking powder, and stir to combine.
2. Add the melted butter, egg, lemon zest, and Marsala and work the mixture until it comes together as a smooth dough.
3. Add the raisins, pine nuts, and candied citrus peels and work the dough until they have been evenly distributed.
4. Form the dough into a round and flatten it slightly. Place it in the pan, slash a cross on the top of the dough, and place it in the oven.
5. Bake until a toothpick inserted into the center of the cake comes out clean, about 1 hour.
6. Remove the cake from the oven and let it cool completely before slicing and serving.

Torta di Nocciole

YIELD: 1 CAKE / **ACTIVE TIME:** 40 MINUTES / **TOTAL TIME:** 1 HOUR AND 30 MINUTES

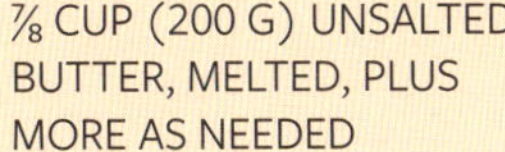

⅞ CUP (200 G) UNSALTED BUTTER, MELTED, PLUS MORE AS NEEDED

⅔ CUP (80 G) ALL-PURPOSE FLOUR, PLUS MORE AS NEEDED

1½ CUPS (220 G) BLANCHED HAZELNUTS, TOASTED

¾ CUP PLUS 1½ TABLESPOONS (170 G) SUGAR

1 TEASPOON (4 G) BAKING POWDER

3 EGGS, SEPARATED

CONFECTIONERS' SUGAR, FOR TOPPING

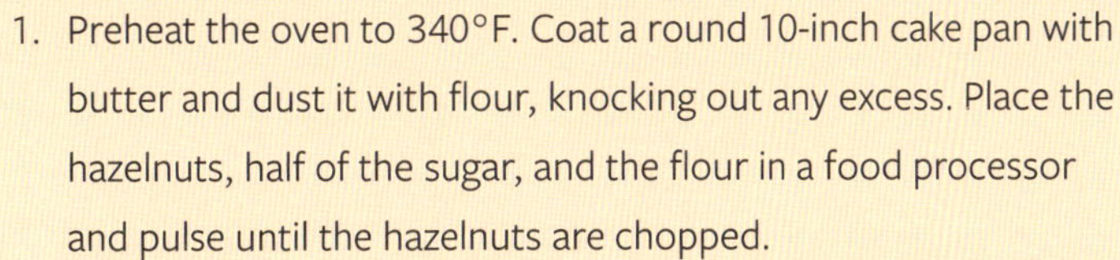

1. Preheat the oven to 340°F. Coat a round 10-inch cake pan with butter and dust it with flour, knocking out any excess. Place the hazelnuts, half of the sugar, and the flour in a food processor and pulse until the hazelnuts are chopped.
2. Place the mixture in a large bowl and add the baking powder. Stir to combine and set the mixture aside.
3. Place the egg yolks and remaining sugar in a separate bowl and beat with a handheld mixer until it is frothy. Add the melted butter and beat to incorporate. Set the mixture aside.
4. Place the egg whites in the work bowl of a stand mixer fitted with the whisk attachment and whip until they hold stiff peaks.
5. Add the whipped egg whites to the egg yolk mixture and fold to combine. Add the dry mixture and fold until the mixture is a smooth batter.
6. Pour the batter into the cake pan and place it in the oven.
7. Bake until the cake is a dark golden brown, 30 to 40 minutes. Remove the cake from the oven and let it cool in the pan.
8. Dust the cake with confectioners' sugar and serve.

Tiramisù

YIELD: 1 CAKE / **ACTIVE TIME:** 20 MINUTES / **TOTAL TIME:** 4 HOURS

3 EGG YOLKS

⅓ CUP SUGAR

11 OZ. MASCARPONE CHEESE

7 OZ. SAVOIARDI (LADYFINGERS)

FRESHLY BREWED ESPRESSO, SLIGHTLY SWEETENED, AS NEEDED

COCOA POWDER, FOR TOPPING

1. Place the egg yolks and sugar in a mixing bowl and beat until frothy. Place the mascarpone in a separate bowl and beat until fluffy. Add the mascarpone to the egg yolk mixture and fold to combine.
2. Soak the sugary sides of the savoiardi in espresso for a few seconds and layer them in a small rectangular baking dish.
3. Cover the savoiardi with some of the mascarpone cream. Repeat with the remaining savoiardi and mascarpone cream.
4. Chill the tiramisù in the refrigerator for 2 to 3 hours.
5. Dust the tiramisù with cocoa powder and serve.

APPENDIX

Beef Stock

YIELD: 6 CUPS / **ACTIVE TIME:** 15 MINUTES / **TOTAL TIME:** 2 TO 3 HOURS

1 LB. STEW BEEF

10 CUPS WATER

1 CARROT, PEELED AND CHOPPED

½ ONION, CHOPPED

1 TOMATO

1 CELERY STALK, CHOPPED

1 TEASPOON FINE SEA SALT

1. Rinse the beef and place it in a stockpot. Add the water and bring to a boil.
2. Add the remaining ingredients, reduce the heat, and simmer the broth until the flavor has developed to your liking, 2 to 3 hours, skimming to remove any impurities that rise to the surface. Halfway through cooking, crush the tomato so that its juices infuse the broth.
3. Strain the broth and use as desired. The meat can be used for other preparations, such as the Bollito Misto alla Piemontese on page 131.

Chicken Stock

YIELD: 6 CUPS / **ACTIVE TIME:** 15 MINUTES / **TOTAL TIME:** 2 HOURS

1 WHOLE CHICKEN

1 CARROT, PEELED AND CHOPPED

1 ONION, CHOPPED

1 CELERY STALK, CHOPPED

10 CUPS WATER

1 SPRIG OF FRESH PARSLEY

1 TABLESPOON WHOLE PEPPERCORNS

1 TEASPOON FINE SEA SALT

1. Rinse the chicken and place it in a stockpot. Add the remaining ingredients and bring to a boil.
2. Reduce the heat and let the broth simmer until the flavor has developed to your liking, about 2 hours, skimming to remove any impurities that rise to the surface.
3. Strain the broth and use as desired. The chicken can be used for another preparation.

Vegetable Stock

YIELD: 6 CUPS / **ACTIVE TIME:** 15 MINUTES / **TOTAL TIME:** 1 HOUR AND 30 MINUTES

2 POTATOES, PEELED AND CHOPPED

1 ZUCCHINI, CHOPPED

1 CARROT, PEELED AND CHOPPED

1 ONION, CHOPPED

1 CELERY STALK WITH LEAVES LEFT ON, CHOPPED

2 TOMATOES

10 CUPS WATER

1 SPRIG OF FRESH PARSLEY

SALT, TO TASTE

1. Place all of the ingredients in a stockpot and bring to a boil.
2. Reduce the heat and let the broth simmer until the flavor has developed to your liking, about 1½ hours, skimming to remove any impurities that rise to the surface. Halfway through cooking, crush the tomatoes and let their juices infuse the broth.
3. Strain the broth and use as desired.

Sugo al Basilico

YIELD: 8 CUPS / **ACTIVE TIME:** 15 MINUTES / **TOTAL TIME:** 1 HOUR

¼ CUP EXTRA-VIRGIN OLIVE OIL

2 GARLIC CLOVES

2 LBS. WHOLE PEELED TOMATOES, CRUSHED BY HAND

SALT, TO TASTE

RED PEPPER FLAKES, TO TASTE

HANDFUL OF FRESH BASIL, TORN

1. Place the olive oil in a medium saucepan and warm it over medium heat. Add the garlic and cook until it starts to brown.
2. Add the tomatoes, partially cover the pan, and cook the sauce for 20 minutes, stirring occasionally.
3. Remove the garlic, season the sauce with salt and red pepper flakes (the latter is optional), and add the basil leaves.
4. Cook until the taste has developed to your liking and the consistency is correct, 5 to 10 minutes. During this last phase, leave the pan uncovered If the sauce is too liquid, or reduce the heat and add a splash of water if it is too thick.

Sugo con Soffritto

YIELD: 8 CUPS / **ACTIVE TIME:** 15 MINUTES / **TOTAL TIME:** 1 HOUR

¼ CUP EXTRA-VIRGIN OLIVE OIL

½ CARROT, PEELED AND CHOPPED

½ ONION, CHOPPED

½ CELERY STALK WITH ITS LEAVES, CHOPPED

½ GARLIC CLOVE, MINCED

2 LBS. WHOLE PEELED TOMATOES, CRUSHED BY HAND

SALT, TO TASTE

RED PEPPER FLAKES, TO TASTE

1. Place the olive oil in a medium saucepan and warm it over low heat. Add the carrot, onion, celery, and garlic and cook, stirring frequently, until the vegetables have softened, about 5 minutes, taking care to make sure that they do not brown.
2. Add the tomatoes, season the sauce with salt and red pepper flakes (the latter is optional, but will benefit the sauce), and partially cover the pan. Raise the heat to medium and cook the sauce for 20 minutes, stirring occasionally.
3. Cook until the taste has developed to your liking and the consistency is correct, 5 to 10 minutes. During this last phase, leave the pan uncovered if the sauce is too liquid, or reduce the heat and add a splash of water if it is too thick.

Sugo ai Peperoni

YIELD: 8 CUPS / **ACTIVE TIME:** 15 MINUTES / **TOTAL TIME:** 1 HOUR

¼ CUP EXTRA-VIRGIN OLIVE OIL

1 GARLIC CLOVE

½ ONION, MINCED

2 RED BELL PEPPERS, STEMMED, SEEDED, AND SLICED THIN

SALT, TO TASTE

2 LBS. WHOLE PEELED TOMATOES, CRUSHED BY HAND

DRIED OREGANO, TO TASTE

RED PEPPER FLAKES, TO TASTE

1. Place the olive oil in a medium saucepan and warm it over medium heat. Add the garlic and onion and cook until the onion is translucent, about 3 minutes.
2. Add the bell peppers, season with salt, and cook, stirring frequently, until they have softened, about 10 minutes.
3. Add the tomatoes, partially cover the pan, and cook the sauce for 20 minutes, stirring occasionally.
4. Remove the garlic and season the sauce with salt and, if desired, oregano and red pepper flakes will benefit the sauce).
5. Cook until the taste has developed to your liking and the consistency is correct, 5 to 10 minutes. During this last phase, leave the pan uncovered if the sauce is too liquid, or reduce the heat and add a splash of water if it is too thick.

Ragù Classico

YIELD: 8 CUPS / **ACTIVE TIME:** 15 MINUTES / **TOTAL TIME:** 1 HOUR AND 45 MINUTES

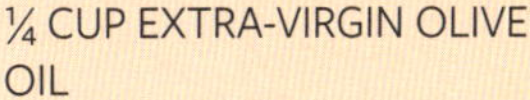

¼ CUP EXTRA-VIRGIN OLIVE OIL

1 CARROT, PEELED AND FINELY DICED

1 SMALL ONION, FINELY DICED

1 CELERY STALK, PEELED AND FINELY DICED

9 OZ. GROUND PORK

9 OZ. GROUND BEEF

⅔ CUP DRY WHITE WINE

2 LBS. WHOLE PEELED TOMATOES, CRUSHED BY HAND

SALT AND PEPPER, TO TASTE

1. Place the olive oil in a large, deep skillet and warm it over medium heat. Add the carrot, onion, and celery and cook, stirring occasionally, until they have softened, about 5 minutes.
2. Add the pork and beef and cook, breaking them up with a wooden spoon, until they are browned, about 8 minutes.
3. Add the wine and cook until it has evaporated.
4. Add the tomatoes and season with salt and pepper. Reduce the heat to low, partially cover the pan, and cook for 1 hour, stirring occasionally.
5. When the taste has developed to your liking and the ragù has the right consistency, use it as desired.

Ragù Ricco

YIELD: 8 CUPS / **ACTIVE TIME:** 15 MINUTES / **TOTAL TIME:** 2 HOURS AND 30 MINUTES

3 TABLESPOONS EXTRA-VIRGIN OLIVE OIL

1 CARROT, FINELY DICED

1 ONION, FINELY DICED

½ CELERY STALK, FINELY DICED

11 OZ. STEW BEEF, FINELY DICED

11 OZ. CHICKEN OR VEAL LIVER, FINELY DICED

1 TEASPOON FINELY CHOPPED FRESH ROSEMARY

1 BAY LEAF

½ CUP RED WINE

¾ LB. WHOLE PEELED TOMATOES, CRUSHED BY HAND

SALT AND PEPPER, TO TASTE

½ CUP BEEF STOCK (SEE PAGE 446), HOT

1. Place the olive oil in a large, deep skillet and warm it over medium heat. Add the carrot, onion, and celery and cook, stirring occasionally, until they have softened, about 5 minutes.
2. Add the beef, chicken liver, rosemary, and bay leaf and cook, stirring occasionally, until the meat is browned, about 8 minutes.
3. Add the wine and cook until it has evaporated.
4. Remove the bay leaf and discard it. Add the tomatoes, reduce the heat to low, partially cover the pan, and cook for about 2 hours, stirring occasionally and seasoning the ragù with salt and pepper halfway through. If the ragù becomes too thick, add the stock as needed.
5. When the taste has developed to your liking and the ragù has the right consistency, use it as desired.

Ragù Bianco

YIELD: 8 CUPS / **ACTIVE TIME:** 15 MINUTES / **TOTAL TIME:** 2 HOURS AND 30 MINUTES

3 TABLESPOONS EXTRA-VIRGIN OLIVE OIL

1 LARGE CARROT, PEELED AND FINELY DICED

½ WHITE ONION, FINELY DICED

1 CELERY STALK, FINELY DICED

1 GARLIC CLOVE, MINCED

2 OZ. PANCETTA, FINELY DICED

14 OZ. GROUND BEEF

14 OZ. GROUND PORK

2 BAY LEAVES

1 TEASPOON FINELY CHOPPED FRESH ROSEMARY

HANDFUL OF FRESH MARJORAM, FINELY CHOPPED

½ CUP DRY WHITE WINE

2 CUPS BEEF STOCK (SEE PAGE 446), HOT

PINCH OF GROUND CLOVES

PINCH OF CINNAMON

SALT AND PEPPER, TO TASTE

½ CUP WHOLE MILK

1. Place the olive oil in a large, deep skillet and warm it over medium heat. Add the carrot, onion, celery, and garlic and cook, stirring occasionally, until they have softened, about 5 minutes.
2. Add the pancetta and cook, stirring occasionally, until it has browned, about 4 minutes.
3. Add the beef, pork, bay leaves, rosemary, and marjoram and cook, stirring occasionally, until the meat starts to brown, about 5 minutes.
4. Add the wine and cook until it has evaporated.
5. Reduce the heat to low and add two ladles of the stock. Partially cover the pan and cook for about 2 hours, stirring occasionally and seasoning the ragù with the cloves, cinnamon, salt, and pepper halfway through. If the ragù becomes too thick, add the remaining stock as needed.
6. Stir in the milk, uncover the pan, and cook until the ragù has the right consistency. Use as desired.

Ragù di Cinghiale

YIELD: 8 CUPS / **ACTIVE TIME:** 15 MINUTES / **TOTAL TIME:** 2 HOURS AND 30 MINUTES

3 TABLESPOONS EXTRA-VIRGIN OLIVE OIL

1 CARROT, PEELED AND FINELY DICED

½ WHITE ONION, FINELY DICED

1 CELERY STALK, FINELY DICED

1 GARLIC CLOVE, MINCED

3½ OZ. PANCETTA, FINELY DICED

14 OZ. BOAR SHOULDER, FINELY DICED

1 TEASPOON FRESH THYME

5 JUNIPER BERRIES

½ CUP RED WINE

2 LBS. WHOLE PEELED TOMATOES, CRUSHED BY HAND

1 CUP WATER

SALT AND PEPPER, TO TASTE

1. Place the olive oil in a large, deep skillet and warm it over medium heat. Add the carrot, onion, celery, and garlic and cook, stirring occasionally, until they have softened, about 5 minutes.
2. Add the pancetta and cook, stirring occasionally, until it has browned, about 4 minutes.
3. Add the boar, thyme, and juniper berries and cook, stirring occasionally, until the meat starts to brown, about 5 minutes.
4. Add the wine and cook until it has evaporated. Add the tomatoes and water, season with salt and pepper, and reduce the heat to low. Partially cover the pan and cook for about 2 hours, stirring occasionally.
5. When the taste has developed to your liking and the ragù has the right consistency, use as desired.

Pizza Sauce

YIELD: 2 CUPS / **ACTIVE TIME:** 5 MINUTES / **TOTAL TIME:** 5 MINUTES

1 LB. WHOLE PEELED TOMATOES, WITH THEIR LIQUID, CRUSHED BY HAND

1½ TABLESPOONS EXTRA-VIRGIN OLIVE OIL

SALT, TO TASTE

DRIED OREGANO, TO TASTE

1. Place the tomatoes and their juices in a bowl, add the olive oil, and stir until it has been thoroughly incorporated.
2. Season the sauce with salt and oregano and stir to incorporate. If using within 2 hours, leave the sauce at room temperature. If storing in the refrigerator, where the sauce will keep for up to 3 days, return to room temperature before using.

Besciamella

YIELD: 2½ CUPS / **ACTIVE TIME:** 15 MINUTES / **TOTAL TIME:** 30 MINUTES

2 CUPS PLUS 2 TABLESPOONS WHOLE MILK

¼ CUP UNSALTED BUTTER

PINCH OF FRESHLY GRATED NUTMEG

SALT, TO TASTE

5 TABLESPOONS ALL-PURPOSE FLOUR

1. Place the milk in a small saucepan and warm it over low heat, taking care not to let it come to a boil.
2. While the milk is warming, place the butter in a separate pan and melt it over medium heat.
3. Season the milk with nutmeg and salt and remove the pan from heat.
4. Add the flour to the butter and stir continually until the mixture gives off a nutty aroma and turns golden brown, 2 to 3 minutes.
5. While whisking continually, add the milk in three increments. Reduce the heat to low and cook, stirring frequently, until the sauce thickens to the desired consistency. Use as desired.

Bagnet Vert

YIELD: 4 CUPS / **ACTIVE TIME:** 15 MINUTES / **TOTAL TIME:** 30 MINUTES

2 CUPS DAY-OLD BREAD PIECES

½ CUP WATER, PLUS MORE AS NEEDED

1 TABLESPOON RED WINE VINEGAR

2 CUPS FRESH FLAT-LEAF PARSLEY

1 CUP EXTRA-VIRGIN OLIVE OIL

1 TABLESPOON CAPERS IN BRINE, DRAINED AND RINSED

4 ANCHOVIES IN OLIVE OIL, DRAINED

½ TEASPOON FINE SEA SALT

1. Place the bread in a bowl, add the water and vinegar, and toss it to combine. Let the bread soak for 10 minutes.
2. Place the remaining ingredients in a food processor and blitz until the mixture is pureed.
3. Add the bread and blitz to incorporate. Incorporate more water if the sauce seems too thick.

Pesto alla Genovese

YIELD: 3½ CUPS / **ACTIVE TIME:** 15 MINUTES / **TOTAL TIME:** 15 MINUTES

2 (HEAPING) CUPS FRESH BASIL

2 SMALL GARLIC CLOVES

½ CUP EXTRA-VIRGIN OLIVE OIL

⅔ CUP GRATED PARMESAN CHEESE

⅓ CUP GRATED PECORINO CHEESE

2 TABLESPOONS PINE NUTS

PINCH OF FINE SEA SALT

1. Using a mortar and pestle, grind the garlic and salt into a paste.
2. Add the basil and grind until it is pulpy. Add the pine nuts and grind until they are fine.
3. Place the Parmesan and pecorino in a separate bowl and stir to combine.
4. Add one-quarter of the cheese mixture and grind until it has been incorporated. Add one-quarter of the olive oil and grind until it has been incorporated. Continue alternating the cheese mixture and olive oil until the pesto has the desired, creamy yet grainy, consistency. Use as desired.

Salsa di Noci

YIELD: 3 CUPS / **ACTIVE TIME:** 20 MINUTES / **TOTAL TIME:** 20 MINUTES

1 SLICE OF WHITE BREAD, CRUST REMOVED

7 OZ. WHOLE MILK

1 CUP WALNUTS

½ GARLIC CLOVE

HANDFUL OF FRESH MARJORAM LEAVES

1 TABLESPOON GRATED PARMESAN CHEESE

2 PINCHES OF FINE SEA SALT

5 TABLESPOONS EXTRA-VIRGIN OLIVE OIL

2 TABLESPOONS LUKEWARM WATER

1. Place the bread and milk in a bowl and soak for 10 minutes. Drain the bread and squeeze it to remove any excess liquid.
2. Place the bread in a blender, add the walnuts, garlic, marjoram, Parmesan, and salt and puree until the mixture is a paste.
3. With the blender running, add the olive oil and water and blend until the sauce is thick and creamy. When using this sauce for pasta, dilute it with pasta water until it reaches the desired level of creaminess.

Salsa al Cren

YIELD: 8 CUPS / **ACTIVE TIME:** 15 MINUTES / **TOTAL TIME:** 15 MINUTES

11 OZ. HORSERADISH, FINELY GRATED

1 CUP FRESH BREAD CRUMBS

⅓ CUP WHITE WINE VINEGAR

3 TABLESPOONS EXTRA-VIRGIN OLIVE OIL

2 PINCHES FINE SEA SALT

2½ TEASPOONS SUGAR

1. Place all of the ingredients in a food processor and blitz until the sauce is creamy and spreadable. Use as desired.

Bagnet Ross

YIELD: 10 CUPS / **ACTIVE TIME:** 15 MINUTES / **TOTAL TIME:** 3 HOURS AND 30 MINUTES

SALT AND PEPPER, TO TASTE

2 LBS. RIPE TOMATOES

2 CELERY STALKS, FINELY DICED

2 CARROTS, PEELED AND FINELY DICED

1 LARGE ONION, FINELY DICED

2 GARLIC CLOVES, MINCED

½ SMALL FRESH CHILE PEPPER, MINCED

1 LARGE RED BELL PEPPER, STEMMED, SEEDED, AND FINELY DICED

1 TABLESPOON FINELY CHOPPED FRESH PARSLEY

1 TABLESPOON FINELY CHOPPED FRESH SAGE

1 CUP EXTRA-VIRGIN OLIVE OIL

1 TABLESPOON RED WINE VINEGAR

CINNAMON, TO TASTE

MUSTARD POWDER, TO TASTE

1. Bring water to a boil in a large saucepan. Add salt and the tomatoes and cook for 30 minutes.
2. Drain the tomatoes and let them cool.
3. Peel the tomatoes and puree them in a blender or with a food mill. If using a blender, strain the puree to remove the seeds.
4. Place the tomato puree in a saucepan, add the celery, carrots, onion, garlic, chile, bell pepper, parsley, and sage, and cover the pan. Cook the sauce over low heat until the flavor has developed to your liking, about 2 hours.
5. Pass the sauce through a sieve or a food mill. If it is too thin for your liking, return it to the pan and cook it over medium heat until it has thickened.
6. Let the sauce cool and add the olive oil and vinegar. Season the sauce with salt, pepper, cinnamon, and mustard powder and use as desired.

Pasta Sfoglia

YIELD: 1 SHEET OF PUFF PASTRY / **ACTIVE TIME:** 15 MINUTES / **TOTAL TIME:** 4 HOURS

FOR THE DOUGH

2¾ CUPS BREAD FLOUR

½ CUP CAKE FLOUR, PLUS MORE AS NEEDED

1½ TEASPOONS FINE SEA SALT

2 TABLESPOONS UNSALTED BUTTER, SOFTENED

¾ CUP PLUS 2 TABLESPOONS ICE WATER

1 TABLESPOON FRESH LEMON JUICE

FOR THE BUTTER BLOCK

4 STICKS OF UNSALTED BUTTER, CHILLED AND CUT INTO 1-INCH CUBES

5 TABLESPOONS BREAD OR ALL-PURPOSE FLOUR

1. To begin preparations for the dough, place the flours, salt, and butter in the work bowl of a stand mixer fitted with the paddle attachment.
2. Combine the ice water and lemon juice and then add the mixture to the work bowl. Beat the mixture until it is combined.
3. Fit the mixer with the dough hook and work the mixture until it comes together as a smooth dough.
4. Form the dough into a ball, cover it with plastic wrap, and chill it in the refrigerator for 1 hour.
5. While the dough is in the refrigerator, begin preparations for the butter block. Place the butter on a clean work surface and sprinkle half of the flour over it.
6. Begin pounding the butter with a rolling pin until it is in one smooth, flat piece. Incorporate the remaining flour as needed to keep the butter from sticking to the rolling pin and work surface.
7. Fold the butter over itself into a rectangle. Pound it until it is pliable. Shape the butter block into a 5-inch square and chill it in the refrigerator.
8. Remove the dough from the refrigerator, place it on a flour-dusted work surface, and use a sharp knife to slash a 1-inch-deep crosswise cut into the top of the dough ball.
9. Gently pull one corner of the dough at a time until it is a square. Place the butter block in the center of the dough.
10. Take each corner of the dough and pull it up and over the butter block until the butter block is completely covered by the dough.
11. Roll the dough into a rectangle that is approximately 10 inches long and 5 inches wide.
12. Working from the short sides, fold one end of the dough to the center. Fold the other end so that it meets the opposite end in the center. Fold the dough in half so that it resembles a book. Chill the dough in the refrigerator for 20 minutes.
13. Repeat Step 12 three times. After the final fold, let the puff pastry chill in the refrigerator for 1 hour before using or storing in the refrigerator.

Pasta Frolla

YIELD: 1 SHORT-CRUST PASTRY / **ACTIVE TIME:** 15 MINUTES / **TOTAL TIME:** 1 HOUR AND 15 MINUTES

⅔ CUP SUGAR

⅔ CUP UNSALTED BUTTER, SOFTENED

1 EGG

2 EGG YOLKS

ZEST OF 1 LEMON

2⅔ CUPS ALL-PURPOSE FLOUR

PINCH OF BAKING POWDER

PINCH OF FINE SEA SALT

1. Place the sugar and butter in the work bowl of a stand mixer fitted with the paddle attachment and cream until the mixture is light and fluffy.
2. Add the egg, egg yolks, and lemon zest and beat until incorporated.
3. Sift the flour, baking powder, and salt into the work bowl and beat until the dough just comes together.
4. Form the dough into a ball, cover it with plastic wrap, and chill it in the refrigerator for 1 hour before using.

Pasta Frolla per Crostate

YIELD: 1 SWEET PIECRUST / **ACTIVE TIME:** 15 MINUTES / **TOTAL TIME:** 1 HOUR AND 15 MINUTES

1 CUP SUGAR

9 TABLESPOONS UNSALTED BUTTER OR LARD

4 SMALL EGGS

ZEST OF 1 LEMON

4 CUPS ALL-PURPOSE FLOUR

1 TEASPOON BAKING POWDER

PINCH OF FINE SEA SALT

1. Place the sugar and butter in the work bowl of a stand mixer fitted with the paddle attachment and cream until the mixture is light and fluffy.
2. Add the eggs and lemon zest and beat until incorporated.
3. Sift the flour, baking powder, and salt into the work bowl and beat until the dough just comes together.
4. Form the dough into a ball, cover it with plastic wrap, and chill it in the refrigerator for 1 hour before using.

Pasta Frolla al Lardo

YIELD: 1 PASTRY / **ACTIVE TIME:** 15 MINUTES / **TOTAL TIME:** 1 HOUR AND 15 MINUTES

1¼ CUPS SUGAR

1 CUP PLUS 2 TABLESPOONS LARD

3 SMALL EGGS

ZEST OF 1 LEMON

4⅙ CUPS ALL-PURPOSE FLOUR

½ TEASPOON BAKING POWDER OR ¼ TEASPOON BAKER'S AMMONIA

PINCH OF FINE SEA SALT

1. Place the sugar and lard in the work bowl of a stand mixer fitted with the paddle attachment and cream until the mixture is light and fluffy.
2. Add the eggs and lemon zest and beat until incorporated.
3. Sift the flour, baking powder, and salt into the work bowl and beat until the dough just comes together.
4. Form the dough into a ball, cover it with plastic wrap, and chill it in the refrigerator for 1 hour before using.

Pasta Frolla Napoletana

YIELD: 1 PASTRY / **ACTIVE TIME:** 15 MINUTES / **TOTAL TIME:** 1 HOUR AND 15 MINUTES

½ CUP SUGAR

5 TABLESPOONS LARD

5 TABLESPOONS UNSALTED BUTTER

5 TABLESPOONS WATER

1 TEASPOON PURE VANILLA EXTRACT

ZEST OF ½ LEMON

2 CUPS ALL-PURPOSE FLOUR

PINCH OF BAKER'S AMMONIA

PINCH OF FINE SEA SALT

1. Place the sugar, lard, and butter in the work bowl of a stand mixer fitted with the paddle attachment and cream until the mixture is light and fluffy.
2. Add the water, vanilla, and lemon zest and beat until incorporated.
3. Sift the flour, baker's ammonia, and salt into the work bowl and beat until the dough just comes together.
4. Form the dough into a ball, cover it with plastic wrap, and chill it in the refrigerator for 1 hour before using.

Pasta Frolla al Marsala

YIELD: 1 PASTRY / **ACTIVE TIME:** 15 MINUTES / **TOTAL TIME:** 1 HOUR AND 15 MINUTES

2⅔ CUPS ALL-PURPOSE FLOUR

7 TABLESPOONS UNSALTED BUTTER

2½ TABLESPOONS SUGAR

1 EGG YOLK

6 TABLESPOONS MARSALA

6 TABLESPOONS WHOLE MILK

PINCH OF FINE SEA SALT

1. Place all of the ingredients in the work bowl of a stand mixer fitted with the paddle attachment and beat until the mixture just comes together as a smooth dough.
2. Form the dough into a ball, cover it with plastic wrap, and chill it in the refrigerator for 1 hour before using.

Crema Pasticcera

YIELD: 3 CUPS / **ACTIVE TIME:** 15 MINUTES / **TOTAL TIME:** 1 HOUR

2¼ CUPS WHOLE MILK

PEEL OF ½ LEMON

3 EGG YOLKS

¾ CUP CONFECTIONERS' SUGAR

⅔ CUP ALL-PURPOSE FLOUR

1 TEASPOON UNSALTED BUTTER

1. Place the milk and lemon peel in a small saucepan and warm over low heat.
2. Place the egg yolks and confectioners' sugar in a mixing bowl and whisk to combine.
3. Sift the flour over the egg yolk mixture and stir until the mixture is combined.
4. When the milk is just about to simmer, remove the lemon peel and, while whisking continually, gradually add the milk to the egg yolk mixture until all of the milk has been incorporated.
5. Add the tempered egg yolk mixture to the saucepan and cook it over low heat, stirring frequently, until the custard has thickened.
6. Add the butter, stir vigorously until it has been incorporated, and remove the pan from heat.
7. Pour the custard into a bowl, place plastic wrap directly on the surface, and chill it in the refrigerator until it has cooled completely.

Pan di Spagna

YIELD: 1 SPONGE CAKE / **ACTIVE TIME:** 15 MINUTES / **TOTAL TIME:** 1 HOUR AND 30 MINUTES

5 EGGS, SEPARATED

1⅓ CUPS CONFECTIONERS' SUGAR

ZEST OF 1 LEMON

1 CUP CAKE FLOUR, PLUS MORE AS NEEDED

UNSALTED BUTTER, AS NEEDED

1. Preheat the oven to 355°F. Place the egg yolks, confectioners' sugar, and lemon zest in a mixing bowl and beat the mixture until it is foamy.
2. Place the egg whites in a separate bowl and whisk until they hold stiff peaks.
3. Add the egg whites to the egg yolk mixture and fold to incorporate them.
4. Sift the flour over the mixture and fold to incorporate.
5. Coat a round 10-inch cake pan with butter, dust it with flour, and knock out any excess. Pour the batter into the pan, place it in the oven, and bake until a toothpick inserted into the center of the cake comes out clean, about 40 minutes.
6. Remove the cake from the oven and let it cool in the pan before slicing, serving, or using in another preparation.

Pasta Frolla di Semola

YIELD: 1 PASTRY / **ACTIVE TIME:** 15 MINUTES / **TOTAL TIME:** 1 HOUR AND 15 MINUTES

1 CUP SUGAR

15 TABLESPOONS UNSALTED BUTTER

4 EGG YOLKS

6 TABLESPOONS COLD WATER

2 CUPS ALL-PURPOSE FLOUR

2 CUPS FINELY GROUND DURUM WHEAT FLOUR

PINCH OF BAKING POWDER

PINCH OF FINE SEA SALT

1. Place the sugar and butter in the work bowl of a stand mixer fitted with the paddle attachment and cream until the mixture is light and fluffy.
2. Add the egg yolks and water and beat until incorporated.
3. Sift the flours, baking powder, and salt into the work bowl and beat until the dough just comes together.
4. Form the dough into a ball, cover it with plastic wrap, and chill it in the refrigerator for 1 hour before using.

Crema Pasticcera Napoletana

YIELD: 3 CUPS / **ACTIVE TIME:** 15 MINUTES / **TOTAL TIME:** 1 HOUR

1¾ CUPS WHOLE MILK

7 TABLESPOONS HEAVY CREAM

PEEL OF 1 LEMON

6 EGG YOLKS

¾ CUP SUGAR

¼ CUP ALL-PURPOSE FLOUR

2 TABLESPOONS POTATO STARCH

1. Place the milk, cream, and lemon peel in a small saucepan and warm over low heat.
2. Place the egg yolks and sugar in a mixing bowl and whisk to combine.
3. Sift the flour over the egg yolk mixture and stir until the mixture is combined.
4. When the milk mixture is just about to simmer, remove the lemon peel and, while whisking continually, gradually add the milk mixture to the egg yolk mixture until all of the milk mixture has been incorporated.
5. Add the tempered egg yolk mixture to the saucepan, stir in the potato starch, and cook the custard over low heat, stirring frequently, until it has thickened.
6. Pour the custard into a bowl, place plastic wrap directly on the surface, and chill it in the refrigerator until it has cooled completely.

Crema Pasticcera Siciliana

YIELD: 3 CUPS / **ACTIVE TIME:** 15 MINUTES / **TOTAL TIME:** 1 HOUR

2 CUPS PLUS 3 TABLESPOONS WHOLE MILK

PEEL OF 1 LEMON

2 EGG YOLKS

¾ CUP SUGAR

¼ CUP POTATO STARCH

1. Place the milk and lemon peel in a small saucepan and warm over low heat.
2. Place the egg yolks and sugar in a mixing bowl and whisk to combine.
3. Sift the potato starch over the egg yolk mixture and stir until the mixture is combined.
4. When the milk mixture is just about to simmer, remove the lemon peel and, while whisking continually, gradually add the milk mixture to the egg yolk mixture until all of the milk mixture has been incorporated.
5. Add the tempered egg yolk mixture to the saucepan and cook the custard over low heat, stirring frequently, until it has thickened.
6. Pour the custard into a bowl, place plastic wrap directly on the surface, and chill it in the refrigerator until it has cooled completely.

Crema Pasticcera al Cioccolato

YIELD: 3 CUPS / **ACTIVE TIME:** 15 MINUTES / **TOTAL TIME:** 1 HOUR

2 CUPS PLUS 3 TABLESPOONS WHOLE MILK

PEEL OF ½ LEMON

3 EGG YOLKS

¾ CUP CONFECTIONERS' SUGAR

⅔ CUP ALL-PURPOSE FLOUR

3 OZ. BITTERSWEET CHOCOLATE, BROKEN INTO SMALL PIECES

1 TEASPOON PURE VANILLA EXTRACT

1. Place the milk and lemon peel in a small saucepan and warm over low heat.
2. Place the egg yolks and confectioners' sugar in a mixing bowl and whisk to combine.
3. Sift the flour over the egg yolk mixture and stir until the mixture is combined.
4. When the milk mixture is just about to simmer, remove the lemon peel and, while whisking continually, gradually add the milk mixture to the egg yolk mixture until all of the milk mixture has been incorporated.
5. Add the tempered egg yolk mixture to the saucepan and cook the custard over low heat, stirring frequently, until it has thickened.
6. Pour the custard into a bowl, place plastic wrap directly on the surface, and set it aside.
7. Bring a few inches of water to a boil in a medium saucepan. Place the chocolate in a heatproof bowl, place it over the simmering water, and stir until it is smooth. Remove the chocolate from heat.
8. Stir the vanilla into the melted chocolate. Stir the chocolate into the custard, place a fresh piece of plastic wrap directly on the surface, and chill it in the refrigerator until it has cooled completely.

METRIC CONVERSION CHART

Weights

1 oz. = 28 grams

2 oz. = 57 grams

4 oz. (¼ lb.) = 113 grams

8 oz. (½ lb.) = 227 grams

16 oz. (1 lb.) = 454 grams

Volume Measures

⅛ teaspoon = 0.6 ml

¼ teaspoon = 1.23 ml

½ teaspoon = 2.5 ml

1 teaspoon = 5 ml

1 tablespoon (3 teaspoons) = ½ fluid oz. = 15 ml

2 tablespoons = 1 fluid oz. = 29.5 ml

¼ cup (4 tablespoons) = 2 fluid oz. = 59 ml

⅓ cup (5⅓ tablespoons) = 2.7 fluid oz. = 80 ml

½ cup (8 tablespoons) = 4 fluid oz. = 120 ml

⅔ cup (10⅔ tablespoons) = 5.4 fluid oz. = 160 ml

¾ cup (12 tablespoons) = 6 fluid oz. = 180 ml

1 cup (16 tablespoons) = 8 fluid oz. = 240 ml

Temperature Equivalents

°F	°C	Gas Mark
225	110	¼
250	130	½
275	140	1
300	150	2
325	170	3
350	180	4
375	190	5
400	200	6
425	220	7
450	230	8
475	240	9
500	250	10

Length Measures

1/16 inch = 1.6 mm

⅛ inch = 3 mm

¼ inch = 6.35 mm

½ inch = 1.25 cm

¾ inch = 2 cm

1 inch = 2.5 cm

INDEX

A

B

D

E

Q

R

S

T

V

Z

ABOUT CIDER MILL PRESS BOOK PUBLISHERS

Cider Mill Press publishes exceptional books that combine creativity and craftsmanship. As an imprint of HarperCollins Focus, we specialize in premium cookbooks, cocktail and spirits guides, and illustrated gift books, all distinguished by compelling content, striking design, and a commitment to quality in every detail. Cider Mill Press sets the standard for books that inform, inspire, and elevate everyday moments. Learn more at cidermillpress.com.

"Where Good Books Are Ready for Press"

501 Nelson Place

Nashville, Tennessee 37214 USA